GOD, TIME AND BEING

Ghislain Lafont

translated by Leonard Maluf

SAINT BEDE'S PUBLICATIONS
PETERSHAM, MASSACHUSETTS

Originally published as *Dieu, le Temps et l'Etre,*
©1986 Les Editions du Cerf

St. Bede's Publications, Petersham, Massachusetts 01366

©1992 by St Bede's Publications
All rights reserved. Published 1992
Printed in the United States of America

98 96 95 94 93 92   5 4 3 2 1

Library of Congress Cataloguing in Publication Data

Lafont, Ghislain.
 [Dieu, le temps et l'être. English]
 God, time, and being / by Ghislain Lafont ; translated from the French by Leonard Maluf.
  p. cm.
 Translation of: Dieu, le temps et l'être.
 Includes bibliographical references and index.
 ISBN 0-932506-89-5
  1. History (Theology) 2. Time—Religious aspects—Christianity.
3. Ontology. 4. God-Knowableness. I. Title.
BR115.H5L2713   1991
231.7—dc20   91-27423
                                                         CIP

ACKNOWLEDGEMENTS

This book would not have been possible without the generosity of Father Abbot and the brothers of my community, the Abbey of Sainte-Marie de la Pierre-qui-vire, who gave me the time for it. I wish to express my gratitude to them for this, especially to the brothers who during this time performed the services usually assigned to me. I thank them too for the atmosphere of prayer and of community life which is so favorable to theological reflection and writing.

Isabelle and Philippe Essig followed my work from its initial conception to its final editing stage and generously supplied the assistance of their competency and their friendship. To them I express my deep and affectionate gratitude.

Pierre Dory and Maurice Gruau, priests of the diocese of Sens-Auxerre, helped me to complete the first part of this book, which deals with philosophy and the human sciences. Brother Sebastian Sterckx, Sister Therese of the Little Sisters, and my sister, Marie-Claire Piganeau, offered numerous and useful suggestions and criticisms for the second part, on the Paschal Mystery, and Brother William of Jerphanion kindly read through the entire manuscript. My sincere thanks to all of these people for their assistance!

This book presents the material of numerous lectures and seminars given in different monastic or university settings in France, Italy and the United States. It was the hospitality, the interest and the friendship shown by these brothers and these students that inspired me to undertake this work and to see it through to the end.

I would like to express my deep gratitude to Mr. Leonard Maluf who has translated this book into English. His theological competency together with his expert knowledge of the English and French languages have enabled him to produce a translation which I believe is excellent. His enduring friendship and his courtesy in keeping me current on the progress of his work during the long time we spent together in Rome made our common effort very enjoyable. I would like also to include in these acknowledgements St. Bede's Publications which undertook the responsibility of publishing this edition and in a special way I wish to remember Fr. Cyril Karam, O.S.B., recently deceased, who encouraged the work from the beginning.

G.L.
Abbey of Sainte-Marie de la Pierre-qui-vire
All Saints Day, 1988

CONTENTS

Foreword   vii

Part I: Time Lost and Being Undiscovered

Introduction. 3
Chapter 1: Has Evolution Run Its Course? 7
Chapter 2: Disillusionments of Revolution 20
Chapter 3: Being: Forgotten or Effaced? 47
Chapter 4: Remeberance of Things Past. 80
             Balance 95

Part II: Time in Jesus Christ

Introduction: A Principle of Narrativity. 121
Chapter 1: The Easter Narrative 134
Chapter 2: From the Garden of Eden to the Land of Hus 173
Chapter 3: Died for Our Sins. 216
Epilogue: The Paternal Invocation 242

Part III: Ancient and New Revelations of Being

Introduction. 257
Chapter 1: God Without Analogy 261
Chapter 2: God, Being and Creation. 297
Conclusion: Opening Toward Ethics and Eschatology 325

FOREWORD

This book is an attempt to establish one more guidepost, perhaps even a new guidepost, along the path travelled by today's theology toward the goal of understanding and naming God. With a perspective gained by distance, this path is seen to be inspired by two movements, which, though opposite to each other, nevertheless appear to converge at some points. On the one hand, there is the very strong sentiment that the God of Christian faith has revealed himself as "God with us," which means that knowing him is inseparable from living with him. From the dawn of salvation history, in the privileged life and destiny of Jesus, as well as today in our personal and collective struggles for humanity, God is involved, and he reveals himself through this very involvement which makes of him the God of history, the God of Jesus Christ, the God of the poor—the humble God, suffering and compassionate, vulnerable. Further, to know this God it is imperative to enter in a very real way into this divine movement of humility and of compassion: concern for the poor is not only an evangelical exigency; it is a prerequisite of theology. The other contemporary current of theological reflection is inspired by a rediscovery of transcendence, a renewed perception of the truth transmitted in the celebrated prayer attributed to Gregory Nazianzen: "O thou the absolute beyond. . . ." If God is truly God, he must be "absolved" of any relationships we may have with him, even if, through a language process due to our limited condition, we must ultimately reintroduce these relationships by attributing them to him. A clear awareness of this process will help us to avoid being taken in by its excessive simplicity and to maintain the ineffable Mystery at the heart of hermeneutics, even as we engage in the interpretation of historical Revelation. Not even the coming of Jesus Christ among us can break through this "cloud of unknowing"; on the contrary, it brings us right into that cloud and in some way compounds God's ineffability by ushering in the dark cloud of the mysteries of the Incarnation and of the Trinity. Thus, in this perspective, the divine names would function more as motivation for love's desire than as terms in any way suitable for God-talk.

I spoke of points of "convergence" between these two currents of contemporary theology. It would perhaps be more accurate to say that both inevitably lead to a stance with respect to two key notions of human existence and reflection, *death* and *Being*.[1] If God is indeed with us, faithful, suffering and vulnerable—because we too are all these things—where will he reveal himself more fully than in the death of Jesus Christ? Conversely, it could likewise be said that the death of Jesus Christ is the ultimate revelation of God and that it is this death that leads us to speak of God with attributes of poverty that we never would have predicted. The expression "God is dead" would amount in this perspective to something quite other than a stupid slogan, especially if one were to fill it out as follows: "God is dead in Jesus Christ." The statement would then conjure up the very mystery of God whose depths cannot be sounded except precisely where this mystery touches death. What we see here is a theology of God-with-us arriving at the silence of a theology of God-the-absolute-beyond and converging with it at this point. In the recognition of "God dead in Jesus Christ," there is a mortification (in the strong sense of the term) of the understanding in search of divine names which would satisfy the mind. For other reasons, taken from the idea of transcendence and not from history, the same mortification is once again found with respect to God as transcendent. Paradoxically, the consent given by the mind to this "death" of its desire to know and to speak liberates a mysterious perception of what one could call "the death *in* God": indeed, the Revelation of the Trinity can legitimately be interpreted in terms of an interplay between life and death.

This involvement of death in our reflection on God goes hand in hand, in the two currents we have been describing, with an exclusion of *Being*, though for opposite reasons. For one group (the historical theologians), Being is static and timeless and therefore stands in opposition to history, perhaps leading to a distant, immutable, impassible God, a "Greek" god, but not to a "Jewish" or a "Christian" one. For the other group (the apophatic theologians), the danger of God-talk that employs the language of Being is not that of separating him unduly from human existence; it is that of falsifying his divinity. Since "Being" is applied to every reality in this world, one seems to suggest, by attributing it to God as well, that there is between him and the world a difference only of degree and not of essence. This "god who is" would actually amount to no more than an idol.

It is my conviction, however, that these two themes of *death* and *Being* stand together at the heart of a reconciled word on God. "God at the Juncture of Death and Being" could well have been a title for this book. But it is doubtless possible to bring these two elements back in a slightly different way. It has recently been brought out again that the theme of death is not primarily a speculative one. Rather, it is linked to a history and therefore belongs to a narrative, especially in the case of the death of Jesus of Nazareth. However, since the narrative of this death is something other than the chronicle of a miscellaneous fact, since it presents this death as closely tied to a resurrection and as standing in a twofold relationship with human beings and with God, it involves elements of interpretation and of verification that I would like to show to be virtually impossible without a certain reference to *Being*. Conversely, the theme of the transcendence of God beyond all, and hence beyond death and Being alike, should not be treated in such a way that the words of Scripture as well as of its traditional interpretations are deprived of all meaning. I would like to show too that to establish a specific link between the affirmation of God in his transcendence and the salvation narrative, a certain *analogous* use of the word *Being* comes to the aid of language. But it is obvious that in both these cases we are not dealing with the same "Being" as that discarded, for opposite reasons, by the two currents mentioned.

These remarks serve as an introduction to what constitutes the core of this book (Parts II and III) which is devoted to what could be entitled "God according to narrative" and "God according to analogy," with the understanding that the narrative as such, simply in order to be told, has some need for analogy, and that, conversely, analogy is not a process closed in on itself but one which renders possible the theological mediation between God and the history of salvation. First to be treated will be the Paschal Mystery of Jesus, communicated in the founding Apostolic narrative and manifested as the origin and the end of time. Our analysis will reveal the values of *covenant* and *sonship* as governing the development of time according to a rhythm defined by the economy of the *Word of God* which addresses man on the ground of *creation* and calls forth a response. This reference to the creation, both of the world and of mankind, will lead into a reflection on a possible *wisdom* at this level, with the object of laying a foundation for a possibility, even if only a minimal one, of talking about the *divinity of God*.

These two developments, one having more to do with death and narrative, the other with Being and analogy, do not respond solely to problems internal to theology. They are also demanded by certain currents of the contemporary culture where the question of death and of time and the question of Being are beginning to reappear as of primary importance, either explicitly or more subtly. Undoubtedly, the study of these currents has been no less influential than the study of the theological problems themselves in shaping the questions raised in this book and in supplying us with useful terminology. Consequently, I have devoted a first part (Part I) to defining a certain cultural field at the diverse levels of a history of evolution, the sociologies of revolution, the critique of metaphysics and the efforts of the imaginary—novels, fiction. It is also possible that the field so defined is somewhat artificial. Let us say that I have chosen authors whose reflection seems to me to pose with some urgency the double question of time and of Being and can therefore serve as a thinking aid to anyone interested, as we are, in linking the reality and the name "God" to these two words: "time" and "Being."

It remains only to conclude by commenting on whether and how "God, time and Being," interpreted within a perspective like that which I shall have attempted to construct, can keep history open and define the paths of an ethical practice.

* * *

This book appears as the second volume of a work published fifteen years ago.[2] I give this reference first of all to point out the continuity of a research project, for there as here the question posed was that of the relationship between God and the history of salvation and of the way in which this might be expressed, at the level of God, of human beings, of Jesus Christ. In the last chapter of that book, I briefly mention some orientations which are taken up here. But I also refer here to this book because of the fact that it was written more from the perspective of the authors of the Christian tradition than from that of modern cultural research; it supplies, at this level, some material which I do not repeat here, but which illuminate what I am offering now. And, conversely, what I wrote back then can be illuminated to some degree by the present work. Finally, in order to keep the material of this volume within manageable limits, I have not taken up again in detail the questions regarding the theological naming of God: the significance of the divine names, "trinitarian" and "essential," the ways and means of theological reflection on the Incarnation. What I wrote on this subject back then can be viewed as a necessary complement at the end of the second and third parts of this book. For all of these reasons, I believe that the present volume can and should be presented as a continuation of the preceding volume.

Notes

1. Throughout this book I have usually translated the French *l'être* by *Being*, with a capital *B* to distinguish it from the French *l'étant* which I have rendered "a being," "beings," etc. The distinction derives from the analyses of Heidegger discussed especially in Chapter III of this book. The reader should beware of investing the term Being with an immediately theological connotation which was by no means intended by Heidegger in his analyses. There is, of course, ultimately a theological relevance to the distinction, and this will be developed by the author of the present book under the heading of analogy in Part III. Translator's note.

2. "Peut-on connaître Dieu en Jésus-Christ?" in *Cogitatio Fidei* n. 44 (Paris: Les Editions du Cerf, 1970). This work will subsequently be referred to by the initials *PCDJ*.

PART I

Time Lost
and
Being Undiscovered

INTRODUCTION

In this first part our task will be to sketch a cultural landscape that can serve as a background against which the present reflection on time and Being in the Christian faith can unfold coherently.

To speak of a "background" is to say that the theological procedure seeks to render an account of the Christian faith to a certain culture, which involves the double and apparently contrary movement of communication and of opposition. It involves communication, to the extent that the cultural landscape in question is that which immediately faces the theologian and within which his personal development takes place: he studies it and reinterprets it in some sense for himself, he finds himself somehow at home in this landscape and with some affinity for the elements, conceptual and symbolic, which go to make it up, to the point where all or a number of these elements can enter as instruments into the theological elaboration itself. Of opposition, to the extent that the Christian tradition of which it renders an account necessarily challenges some aspects of this landscape. First of all, even if this cultural landscape were perfectly sound and well-balanced at its own level, Revelation would offer it a transfiguration—which can take place only through the stage of questioning its limits. Moreover, to the extent that this landscape includes shadowy areas, or even real darkness, Christian reflection is conducted to point out and to surmount impasses, to reestablish forgotten perspectives, to reopen closed concepts and to erase products of the imagination which conceal reality. It is worth noting that this questioning of the culture which is inspired by the light of faith is not always, nor even most often, immediate. By the light they emit, the revealed data lead us to discover and to correct certain distortions of the culture on its own plane, so that the beauty of the landscape should itself be brought back to light, while being transformed by the illumination of faith.

These very general remarks should allow us to introduce this part with greater clarity.

1. It is not a question of sketching *the* contemporary cultural landscape: today as ever the culture is crossed by diverse and often conflicting currents. I do not claim to give a full synthesis of these nor do I propose to situate my theological reflection with respect to them. The question is rather one of sketching *a* given landscape, with the help of

a number of different investigations of well-known authors whose research has certainly penetrated profound levels of the contemporary mentality without exhausting its resources.

2. The choice of authors and the manner of presenting them, the way in which the material is ordered—all of this is not without significance and constitutes on my part an interpretation of that aspect of the culture which I have singled out as important, its construction into a graphic "figure." I take the liberty to remark here, on this matter, that it was not a *choice* involved here, if one understands by this term an act of conscious mental deliberation. Anyone who has had any experience at all in writing a book knows that among the available material and the results of research undertaken by an author, some items come almost of themselves to be included in a given project, while others, even when their importance is unquestionable, somehow manage to resist integration into the same work, and this for reasons which it is not always easy to discern. In this interpretative construction, however, in order to preserve as much as possible the objectivity of the reference, I begin with a precise exposition of the ideas of the authors discussed, and only then do I point out the questions these ideas raise and the criticisms they may invite.

3. Our selection of authors was ultimately based on the interests (in an almost juridical sense of the term) which they defend, interests which I feel should be represented in a contemporary theological undertaking. For example, the significance of biological rootedness and the consequent centrality of the *body* in every view of man, and in theological reflection as well; the corresponding necessity of taking into account the economical and the sociological foundations of human history in such a way that reflection, even abstract dogmatic reflection, opens onto an *ethic*, at the personal as well as at the social and historical levels; the strict connection between this concrete problematic and a conception of *Being*, the idea being that every history, physics, culture, necessarily calls for meta-history, metaphysics, meta-culture, and that it is important to articulate as clearly as possible where this "meta-" resides; the supreme importance of the *symbolic*, in the most general sense of the term, and the consequent necessity of finding points of contact between the human sciences, metaphysics, *ritual* and *literature*.

4. Such a cultural landscape includes principles, notions and images that it organizes according to diverse methods into a whole—one

that emerges from a discussion conducted at the epistemological level proper to these elements. I shall attempt to lay out this type of critique in broad outline. But in the ultimate evaluation one cannot silently pass over the fact that this culture is *post-* and often *anti-Christian*; it sometimes rejects elements attributed to Christianity, it takes up others, consciously or unconsciously, but in a way that subverts them, and finally it assumes positions and overall perspectives which call for other than purely philosophical confrontation. I also attempted to situate myself at this fully integrating level and it is here that I discovered what I refer to as a "gnostic attitude." I mention this point right at the start because it may help the reader to grasp the real nature of the dialogue undertaken here. The cultural data assembled and described in this part have played a real role in the interpretation of the Christian phenomenon, in terms of narrative and of analogy, which I develop in the second part of this book, but at the price of a continuous effort to reinterpret these data not in a "gnostic" atmosphere but rather in one that acknowledges the personal God who has revealed himself in Jesus Christ. Paradoxically, it is this confession of the living God which proves capable of giving place and power to the "interests" defended by the culture.*

---

*Allow me to remark that if any reader does not feel that the developments of this Part I relative to the human sciences and to philosophy, are of interest to him, or if he is put off by my style of presentation or by the difficulty of some passages, he should feel free to begin reading at Part II. This latter constitutes a theological presentation integral and coherent in its own right—one that does not necessarily require the study of the first part. This earlier material will, moreover, become more intelligible and more interesting when read or reread in the light of the theological section which follows, forming the core of this work.

CHAPTER ONE

HAS EVOLUTION RUN ITS COURSE?

The title of this chapter summarizes what emerges from a meditative reading of an important book by André Leroi-Gourhan, who beginning with reliable scientific information from the data of paleontology and prehistoric archeology, by recourse to more recent data on civilization, attempts to write a global history of humanity right up to the present day.[1] My interest in this book, which is rigorously scientific in the domains which pertain to the specific competence of the author and appropriately reserved in the presentations, hypotheses, and extrapolations necessary for the composition of the work as a whole, lies in the fact that it seems to yield enormously puzzling conclusions in giving this history a meaning and conjecturing about a future for humanity. Both the survey of the course run by evolution and the uncertainty of the conclusions to be drawn from the phenomenon are significant for our purposes and merit our close examination.

At the beginning of his book, Leroi-Gourhan notes the powerful need that drives man to turn toward his past in an effort to grasp the mystery of his origins. In the ever-recurring interest of man in the prehistoric (whether this is viewed, according to the various cultures, in "scientific" or in "mythical" terms) he discerns "a profound need for confirmation of the spacial-temporal integration of man,"[2] in other words, a need for an assurance that will allow him to live the present and to project the future. The prehistoric era can be understood only within a hermeneutical perspective:

> The analysis of the sources is perhaps more illuminating and certainly more complete if we attempt to see not only where man comes from, but also where he is now and where he is probably headed. . . . I think that, whether supported by a religious metaphysics or by a materialist dialectic, the history of origins has no other real meaning than that of situating future man within his present and rooting him in his most remote past.[3]

But does man have a future? This is precisely what the book ultimately seems not to know.

Leroi-Gourhan is in fact able to show that the industrial revolution of the nineteenth century initiated a process of social transformation in no way comparable to those which preceded it, and nevertheless in continuity with them. Today this process is headed toward a term which may not be very far away and in which, paradoxically, *homo sapiens* would be destined either to extinction, like any other zoological species that has arrived at the maximum of its potentialities, or to transforming himself into a functional cell of a totally computerized society.[4] This would mean that at the term of an evolution which was believed to be centered on man, the latter would now be reduced to a status comparable to the bee or the ant.[5] Unless this *homo sapiens* succeeds in finding a way of checking (but how?) this almost inexorable movement toward self-destruction which is the peculiar product of the exercise of a "wisdom" that was part of man's very definition.

In order to understand what evidence could justify this view, we must take into account the two methodological principles which govern the arguments in *Le Geste et la Parole*, and follow Leroi-Gourhan in his conception of the "exteriorized body" of man.

The zoological principle and the symbolic principle

The two principles in question are never explicitly so designated, but they are operative throughout the work. Actually, they amount to the same thing—they consist, on the one hand, in never losing sight of the fact of man's rootedness in his zoological history; on the other hand and simultaneously, in seeing him from the start as a being capable of symbolizing. The unity of these two principles results from a very refined analysis of the significance of evolution: a careful review of the material available through paleontology would lead us to posit that the very best interpretive model is that which, in the analysis of the evolutionary phenomenon, lays greatest emphasis not on the growth of the brain but on the mechanical conditions of development: "The pertinent forms are those which, at each moment of the process, offer the best equilibrium, from the triple point of view of nutrition, locomotion and the organs of reference, in mobility and in vitality."[6] In this regard, the general drift of evolution would be that of the progressive upraising of the living organism, beginning with the fish that is carried along by the liquid milieu in which it lives and remains entirely horizontal and ending with man who stands erect on the earth supported only by his legs, with his hands free for things other than locomotion, and with a highly mobile head, capable of looking in every direction.

Even if the development of the cranial volume (together with the simultaneous development of the brain and the nervous system) is also a decisive factor, "it remains a fact that, on the level of strict evolution, this development is itself a function of the erect posture and not, as was believed for a long time, a primordial phenomenon."[7] So it is that man "begins with his legs." This zoological principle of the true beginning[8] offers a unique advantage: it always forces us to think about man in an integral way, that is, never to neglect or bypass what is zoological or zoologically based in man at every level of his being, individual and social. There is also a disadvantage or a temptation—that of not always giving man everything that is his due, in the area of "spirituality" or of non-bodiliness. But it is here that the other principle comes in, the symbolic principle, which is strictly correlative to the preceding. The fact is that the upright position confers on man a certain distance with respect to the ground. The result is that man loses a certain immediacy with respect to the primary functions such as nutrition. The capacity to symbolize which presupposes distance and relation is intrinsically linked to the upright position. Its first manifestation will be that of the making of tools, but a more refined analysis shows that the full range of elements proper to a symbolic behavior is there right from the start. In an initial period, writes Leroi-Gourhan, "erect posture, receded jaw line, the fact that the hand is free during locomotion and the possession of detachable tools are truly the basic criteria of the human species."[9] He observes, however, that as time goes on, the phenomenon of language, some graphic skills, ethical behavior, aesthetic perceptions and religious impulses are also noted.[10]

The forms of these various sectors and the degree to which they are developed evolve, but the principle is that they are present from the start. From the very beginning man has always been man.[11] If, in a primitive and quite lengthy period, the paleanthropic symbolic behavior did remain rudimentary, like a kind of excrescence of its physiological being,[12] it was thereafter to undergo an exponential development, though never ceasing to be anchored in its zoological moorings.[13]

The "exteriorized body"

All of this provides a good basis for understanding the theme of the "exteriorized body."[14] At a primary level, the tool is "exuded"[15] by the body and appears to be no more than "an extension of the human skeleton," but the more developed the symbolic capacity becomes, the more remote becomes the relationship between tools and the human body. Man's agility and strength find in tools a means of stepping up their effectiveness with respect to matter: their dependence with respect to man who handles and employs them does not prevent them from having a kind of autonomy with respect to man himself, an autonomy which is revealed by the notion and the practice of apprenticeship. As long as the relationship between man and his tool remains relatively close, as long as his own body is actually involved in the work, we remain within the space of *homo sapiens*, and this man/tool equilibrium is but one sector of human existence among all the others. While making corresponding advances, language (the linguistic apparatus is what is meant here), writing, the aesthetic and religious forms as well as the social configuration also remain within an overall figure commensurate with what we call human.

This equilibrium man/tool/civilization is maintained for millennia, from the relative mobility of the primitive group to the sedentariness of farmers and their organization of space, the appearance of the fire arts followed by metallurgy which gives birth to urban civilization.[16] Nevertheless, throughout the course of this multi-millennial process, the distance between man's body, things and other human beings begins to become more and more pronounced, while the "exteriorized body" of tools, of technology and of behavior increases and becomes more and more autonomous. As long as there are still spaces to conquer, and on the side of man, limits beyond which he cannot go in his work, the relationship of man to his "exteriorized body" remains intact, precisely because of this margin of indetermination which persists. But what if we should succeed in filling all the available spaces and in saturating all human capacities? Now it would seem that this moment of saturation, through the sociotechnical activity of *homo sapiens* himself, is no longer totally beyond our purview. A notable turning point did in fact appear toward the end of the eighteenth and the beginning of the nineteenth century: the exponential take off of technology seems from this moment on to have broken the balance between strict indetermination and sociotechnical determination which until then had characterized *homo sapiens*, regardless of the enormous superficial differences that his figure has been able to offer throughout the long millennia of his history. The basic layout of the city hardly changes at all between antiquity and the end of the eighteenth century; it explodes in the nineteenth century.[17] The industrial revolution that takes place in this last-mentioned period is the only major transformation that would have occurred in five millennia.[18] Using a suggestive metaphor, Leroi-Gourhan writes: "an observer from another planet, incognizant of the explanations to which history and philosophy have accustomed us, would distinguish the man of the eighteenth century from that of the twentieth as we distinguish the lion from the tiger and the wolf from the dog."[19] One could even affirm a certain continuity at the technical level between the *pithecanthrope* and the carpenter of the beginning of the nineteenth century, but continuity ceases at this point.[20] What was happening at this time was the transition from one world, which had endured since the time of the first man who tilled the soil, to an entirely different world—first of all at the technical level, but then in the entire range of cultural forms.[21]

To what exactly are we referring? To the fact that man has come close to completing the construction of what we have been describing as the "exteriorized body."[22] Not only has he produced the tool that is capable of stepping up the force exerted by the hand in motion, but he has disengaged the hand entirely from any motoric function, direct or indirect, allowing machines, which have become more and more automatic and distant from him, to do the work that needs to be done.[23] At the same time, he has shown himself capable of exteriorizing even his capacity for creating symbols and has produced computers capable of performing quantities of operations which the human brain left to itself was unable to perform.[24] This twofold exteriorization of the hand and the head has foreseeable consequences of which some are already at work and others appear inevitable. We could summarize these by saying that this "exteriorized body," fruit of the wisdom of *homo sapiens*, is subordinating to itself the very one who brought it into being. First of all, it requires constant monitoring, at least at present—with the result that, just as man was beginning to believe he was master, he is becoming the slave of a highly technicized complex of which he has become no more than an organic cell, depersonalized in a sense.[25] At the same time, this exteriorized body of machines and computers is becoming progressively more potent in shaping the figure of the social body. Society is becoming more and more a global phenomenon, which means that the spacial-temporal integration of man tends to level off through a unified standard of measure, which no longer takes into account the conditions of human and physical geography, of this or that particular space-time. This means also that the importance of ethnic distinctions is beginning to disappear while a standard, unisex human archetype tends to become established everywhere.

The differences that continue to exist are gradually yielding to a single lower middle class type of human being, speaking an impoverished English everywhere in the world, engaging in the same industrial activities, watching on television the same programs which orchestrate a small number of archetypes which are as old as the hills, switching to the same favorite channels because he no longer reads and knows less and less how to write.[26] One could then seriously question whether creative freedom and the dynamic relationship between man himself and the diversified societies to which historically he has belonged will not have been but a moment in the evolutionary process which will soon disappear.[27] It is clear enough that creativity is already a quality enjoyed by a minority, and soon perhaps this minority will have to be selected and placed under special conditions in order to accomplish what will no longer be an art but merely a necessary function.[28] And finally, at the level of man's body itself, we do not know what will become of it. Leroi-Gourhan foresees as possible "a toothless humanity and one which would spend its life in bed, using what members it has left for operating a series of pushbuttons."[29]

Moreover, perhaps the individual human being will not be necessary indefinitely, and perhaps the society of tomorrow (only too proximate a tomorrow) will be but a transposition of the society of insects, extremely complex and characterized by articulated computer series, until the moment of "total victory, when the last pocket of petroleum has been drained out to cook the last handful of grass eaten with the last rat."[30]

Is there an escape?

In a word,

> freed from his tools, from his gestures, from his muscles, from the programming of his actions, from his memory, freed from his imagination by

the highly perfected broadcasting techniques, freed from the world of animals, of vegetables, from the wind, from the cold, from germs, from the unknown dangers of mountains and oceans, the homo sapiens of zoology is probably near the end of his career.[31]

If, however, he should arrive, on the global scale at which he now lives, at a realization of this imminence of his impending end, and if he should manifest the desire of remaining *sapiens*, what would he have to do? After having acknowledged that it would be "against nature" not to trust man, but that "the imagination hardly knows where to look," the last page of the book proposes a three-point plan

to thoroughly rethink the problem of the relationship of the individual to society; to examine in a concrete way the question of his[32] numeric density, of his relations with the animal and vegetal worlds: to stop imitating the behavior of a microbe culture and start viewing the management of the globe as something other than a game of chance.[33]

This program is sensible enough to be sure; one can only ask oneself why our generation or succeeding generations would adopt it. Indeed, to read Leroi-Gourhan, it does not seem that the preceding generations have ever placed such a program at the top of their priorities. What then could have led them to such a "conversion"? In fact, if we reexamine the periods which preceded that of the exponential explosion of civilization, if we consider the phenomenon of global unification that has destroyed ethnic differences and reduced individuals almost to a single colorless mould, it would appear that if man was even recently still *sapiens*, perhaps it was simply because he had not yet had the time to be otherwise and because the socioeconomic "exteriorized body" had not yet been fully achieved. The fact is that in itself the simple description of the history of civilization as the succession of various techno-socio-economic stages (such as the dawn of agriculture or that of major industry) says nothing of the motor at work in causing the transition from one stage to the next. One could conclude from various scattered observations in the work of Leroi-Gourhan that this "motor" is twofold and that its power has primarily zoological roots. Like any other animal, man possesses aggressive behaviors and seductive behaviors: war and love are the motors of human history just as they are the forces which animate the life of the animal species.[34]

Originally, aggression is linked to acquisition and acquisition to the satisfaction of the primary needs. One perception of space, for example, is that which contrasts the sanctuary, whatever that might be (the home), and the territory toward which one sets out to hunt or to chase for food—the space of the hunt and hence of death.[35] Or in an agricultural economy, the sanctuary has become the granary: arms are taken up to keep this granary from becoming the prey of animals or human beings. War against animals, for the sake of food, quickly degenerates into war among human beings, for the appropriation of food supplies, but more and more frequently, for the control of technology, or even for the enslavement of human beings who will do the work while the warriors increasingly devote their energies to offensive or defensive combat. War itself becomes a major incentive to technical progress, through the inventions it inspires for the maintenance of superiority and control.[36] In order for the program outlined above to have a chance of being realized even at a very initial level, would it not be necessary for people, if not to cease altogether from making war, at least to diminish their aggression potential?[37] But how is this really possible? It is opposed not only by the fact that man has little or no control over the exteriorized social system in which he is installed, but also by the fact that aggressivity is ultimately just another name for vital force or energy: if man were to renounce the objective of acquiring things and therefore of engaging in combat, what would he live for? Is it really possible to take away from the human animal this dynamic impulse, without killing him or driving him to extinction—in another way than by technological development, but just as surely? This diminishing of aggressiveness is also opposed by the fact (if we look now at the internal economy of a given civilization) that every technological conquest generates social forms which flow from it naturally; the very idea of "hierarchy" and hence of the relations of power is linked to a society whose roots go down as far as the relationship of man to agriculture; now this society is still ours, it will remain so as long as we continue to derive our nourishment from the products of the soil.[38] Thus, history would be no more than the development, within a society endowed with the power to symbolize, of a radically aggressive behavior, transformed to be sure by technology and language, but never really losing its roots nor its immanent logic. Leroi-Gourhan would like to do justice to the analyses conducted since

Marx to examine, in terms of dialectical materialism, the succession of the modes of production, but he shrewdly remarks that the introduction of the categories of "justice" and "injustice" does not simplify the analysis, if what we are dealing with is "a problem of strictly organic origin."[39] Indeed, when we read certain classics on the question, we are always tempted to ask whether the process of oppression linked to the modes of production is inevitable or culpable. One thing is clear: the mixture of economic and moral categories in the discussion at least calls for further clarification.

Such, is the program; such, it seems reasonable to affirm, is our powerlessness even to begin to put it into practice. Here and there, Leroi-Gourhan mentions another possible escape from the present situation, but one that will have no direct bearing at the level of the global civilization. This solution will be endowed at least with sign value and perhaps will allow us to reformulate the question in general terms. This is what he calls "cosmic disinsertion," alluding here to the behavior and to the rupture mentality which reside in a few individuals who are moved by another impulse, a mysticism, and who seek another kind of relationship with space-time and with other human beings. "To the extent that he lives in counter-time by watching and fasting, to the extent that he lives in counter-space, in the desert, in a cell or in the dust of the open squares, the ascetic lives in counter-sign with respect to the code of belonging to socially organized humanity."[40] Instead of entering into the regularization and the systematization of time in view of a techno-economical efficiency, one multiplies the ruptures or breaks with respect to rhythms, both natural (fasting, inversion of day and night) and social: "The individual who claims to be rediscovering his spiritual equilibrium can only be moving, in all civilizations and from the earliest ages, toward the cloister and, beyond this, toward the caves and the desert, ending up like Simon Stylites or the Boddhidharma with the twofold denial of time and space in contemplative immobility."[41] Moreover, this denial represents the desire and sometimes the reality of another mastery of the world and of self. But can this ascetic solution, lofty as it may be, contribute anything to humanity at a global level?

To recapitulate, in the evolution of living species, man represents a threshold, in the sense that he is the first mammal to remain perfectly erect. This upright position releases in man both technical and verbal abilities. Evolution, which seems to have reached its highest point at the level of anatomy with man standing erect, picks up momentum again at the social level: moved by the primary forces of seduction and of aggression which come to him from his profound animality, man constructs a world from which he becomes gradually and imperceptibly alienated (at least if we do not regard this construction as his destiny, in which case one could not speak of alienation). He produces the exteriorized body of a more and more independent technology, organizes himself collectively into a global body at the service of this exteriorized body. Is that then the end of *homo sapiens*? Or must he then, at some point in the process, put to death, at least in part (but according to what criteria?) the primary forces of aggression and of seduction which provided the original impulse for the course he has been on? But what would be the objective of this hypothetical "sacrifice"? Is the ascetical condition the only alternative to this process of exteriorization and to this global organization of humanity in its service? Is the ultimate meaning of the world a non-world or a beyond-the-world reserved to a small number of people who know how to die? Such are the questions with which Leroi-Gourhan leaves us. It is certainly too early to attempt to respond to them here. After all, the objective pursued in this presentation of the thought of Leroi-Gourhan, as in that of the authors next discussed, is not to inaugurate a discussion or a dialogue in the strict sense of the term, but rather to bring out certain elements of the contemporary cultural landscape and to collect suggestions to choose from for further reflection. The element to retain here is that which I have called the "zoological principle" according to which the figure of man and the outline of his history cannot be truthfully discerned without acknowledging and taking into account the fact that the human species belongs to the animal realm, with—I will not say the constraints since that is a given—but the conditions or the conditioning that this implies. Our interrogation will bear on the question of whether Leroi-Gourhan, however good his intentions, really gives full weight to the significance of the "symbolic principle" in the evaluation of this same human figure and of his history. Up to a certain point, the tool is perhaps "exuded," but what then? What is it, from the very beginning, that distinguishes human aggressiveness from that of the animal, human love from love among beasts, and what role has this distinctive element played, together with the animal element, in the progress of technology, of urbanization, but also of culture, of art, even of religion? Finally, should not the act of retreat associated with "ascetics" be read as a sign of how necessary is the presence of a dimension of "retreat," perhaps even of "death," in the lives even of those who do not flee from the world? Is there aggressiveness and love except within a perspective of death, and of the whole symbolic complex that its presence entails in individual and collective human existence? In short, if what Leroi-Gourhan intends is to show how the zoological and the symbolic are related in man, there is no doubt that what he accomplishes leaves much to be desired and calls for further reflection and research.[42]

Notes

1. *Le Geste et la Parole* (Paris, 1965), I. Technique et Langage; II. La Mémoire et les Rythmes.
2. I, 10,
3. *Ibid*.
4. "S'il s'agissait d'un mammifère quelconque, le prognostic n'aurait aucune raison de ne pas être catégoriquement pessimiste" (I, 184).
5. Cf. II, 14, 186, 201.
6. I, 41. A general discussion of the problematic according to which evolution is envisioned: I, 85-89.
7. I, 333; cf. 119.
8. I, 207.
9. I, 33; cf. 166.
10. On the paleontology of language, cf. I, 127 and II, 211; of the forms of social existence, I, 222; of the "témoins d'une intelligence non strictement technique," I, 150ff; II, 211. The principle of the strict solidarity between technology, language and aesthetics is stated, II, 88.
11. Leroi-Gourhan would agree then with Lévi-Strauss ("Introduction à l'oeuvre de Marcel Mauss," in Marcel Mauss, *Sociologie et Anthropologie* [Paris, 1950], p. XLVII) and E. Benveniste (*Problèmes de Linguistique générale*, I [Paris, 1966], p. 27) on the primitive and immediate character of the symbolizing faculty and hence of language. Cf. also Julia Kristeva, *Le Langage, cet inconnu* (Paris, 1981), p. 51ff.
12. I, 140 and 151.
13. I, 152.
14. II, 79.

15. Cf. note 12.

16. I regret summarizing in four lines the developments of history which cover a good part of the two volumes, but their detail is not important for my purposes. I note only the difference between the first stage (from the early hominid species to *homo sapiens*) and the following. The first still presents a physical aspect, especially at the level of the human face: "déverrouillage frontal" (frontal opening) (I, 182, 184-187); the following stages are situated exclusively on the level of civilization, as though the history of these were continuing that of the evolution of anatomical forms.

17. I, 253.
18. I, 255.
19. II, 50.
20. II, 60.
21. II, 255.
22. II, 79; cf. I, 207 and 237.
23. II, 48ff.
24. II, 75.
25. Cf. note 5.

26. II, p. 252-254 on the meaning of a return to the non-representational and of the appearance of concrete music; on reading and writing, 259-260; on the mass-media and the necessary ration of escape, 265-266.

27. This "tissu de relation entre l'individu et le groupe" (II, 80) with the margin of individual creation in connection with the functional modes of expression (cf. p. 91) constitutes what Leroi-Gourhan calls the "comportement esthétique," (aesthetic behavior), which generates the entire world of social symbolism.

28. On the "créateur de fictions sociales sélectionné," cf. II, 204, and the whole section "Esthétique sociale et vie figurée," 201-205.

29. I, 183.
30. I, 260.
31. II, 266.
32. "His" refers to man.
33. II, 267.
34. II, 189 and 197.
35. II, 179.
36. I, 236-237.
37. I, 258.
38. I, 243.
39. I, 238 and 257.
40. II, 194.
41. II, 147, cf. 101 and 107.

42. Leroi-Gourhan is the principal interlocutor of F. Tinland in the first three chapters of *La différence anthropologique* (Paris, 1977). If the two authors appear to be largely in agreement on what I have called the "zoological principle," Tinland brings out, with reference to the tool, that Leroi-Gourhan does not develop sufficiently his research on the factors that reveal the human character of this tool, which would amount to the "symbolic principle" in its root (cf. p. 151ff.).

CHAPTER TWO

DISILLUSIONMENTS OF REVOLUTION

1. Matriarchy and classless society

Although he gave his reasoned history of evolution an increasingly broad cultural dimension, Leroi-Gourhan remained faithful to the end to the perspective he had outlined, according to which the zoological principle seems to win out over the symbolic. Moreover, on the question of the human behaviors that become possible in virtue of this symbolic principle, his emphasis is rather on individual behaviors which give rise to or, alternatively, attack the social body, when they do not abandon it altogether. Other interpretative approaches are equally possible. I would like to look at one such approach that is especially important and which in order to study we will have to go back in time. We will be examining another presentation of the same human history that is likewise careful not to depart from the real world of biology and of work, but which offers an interpretation of these more centered on the evolution of society. I have in mind the little book by Friedrich Engels on *The Origin of the Family, of Private Property and of the State*,[1] which is important for us here not only because of the comprehensive view of human history that it offers, but also because it introduces (theoretically, but with an obviously practical aim) the theme of revolution as the ultimate meaningful articulation of time.

From the "gens" to society

At the very time when "we are . . . approaching a social revolution . . . ,"[2] Engels goes to the trouble of reconstructing the history of the beginnings of civilization in order to place in perspective—and hence to make better understood—the importance of the materialist study of history, of which he and Marx together had laid the foundations forty years earlier in the unpublished manuscripts of *German Ideology*.[3] This going back in time has a considerable amplitude and significance, since it examines the main lines of social reality—family, economics, politics—together in their diachronic and systematic relationships. Actually—and this is doubtless the great methodological contribution of this book—it is not possible to view these various moments in total isolation.[4] A careful reading of the book reveals that human history taken as a whole has seen two basic turning points in this regard that divide it into three great periods of which the first and the third correspond, and come together in a sense beyond the second. The first turning point, or better, the first frontier, forms a dividing line between a prehistoric period, guided from within by the immanent principle of *natural* selection, and an historical period whose advent and development may be traced to a *social* impulse. The prehistoric period climaxes in the "mother right *gens*" pattern which I shall describe briefly below and which is viewed by the author as one of perfect harmony.[5] The historical period originates in an economic transformation, namely, the appearance of animal husbandry, and its course is scanned by the succession of the modes and relationships of production. Its ultimate achievement, in the view of Engels, is the conflictive social pattern in which the prevailing structures are those of the male-dominated monogamous family, the capitalist economy and the State. The second (dangerous) turning point leads from this situation of conflict, which is the product of history, to the establishment of the communist society, described in this book as a transposed version of the prehistoric matriarchal society. The proletarian revolution thus takes on the meaning, if not of a return to the beginnings, at least of a fulfillment of the prehistoric figure beyond civilization: eschatology corresponds to prehistory, not to history.

1. *Prehistory* centers around the theme of the family. At any rate, this is how Engels explains it in his preface: "The lower the development of labor and the more limited the amount of its products, and consequently, the more limited also the wealth of the society, the more the social order is found to be dominated by kinship groups."[6] The prehistoric evolution of the family[7] is marked by progressive restriction in the freedom of sexual relationships: first comes a period of sexual dealings with no restrictions, where there is really no family at all, strictly speaking. All the women are polyandrous and all the men polygamous. There is no jealousy (for this is not a primitive sentiment), and even incest is not prohibited.[8] If children stay with their mothers in the earliest years, they are quick to become part of the undifferentiated community. Then comes a first restriction, which is concerned with the vertical relations and excludes marriages between generations; this is the so-called "consanguine" family. Then, within each generation,

another restriction is first established between brothers and sisters and soon extended to relatives of various degrees. This is the so-called "punaluan" family which is defined thus: "the mutually common possession of husbands and wives within a definite family circle, from which, however, the brothers of the wives—first one's own and later also collateral—and conversely also the sisters of the husbands, were excluded."[9] This formation is often called by Engels "group marriage," a group being defined as an ensemble of persons among whom the sexual relationship is prohibited but who are open to any exogamous relationship. Such a group, thus precisely and strongly defined, gradually began to take what one might call a "political" turn: it is the *gens* that is here described, "a firm circle of blood relations in the female line between whom marriage was prohibited, and by other common institutions of a social and religious character, it henceforth increasingly consolidated and differentiated itself from the other *gentes* of the same tribe."[10] Obviously, since it is maternal filiation that is decisive (because the father is not always identifiable), the *gens* is defined and governed by a "mother right," particularly in what pertains to the relationships of inheritance.[11] Nor does one leave the matriarchal *gens* when it is observed that as the bonds of relationship based on the prohibition of incest begin to develop and to become more complex, the number of monogamous couples also tends to increase: the fact is that the number of men and women who can marry each other diminishes as the prohibitions increase. Moreover, this monogamy, which is the fruit of necessity more than of mutual love, is not absolute; if it is respected so long as the marriage endures, other unions are fully possible after its dissolution. This marriage, called "syndiasmic" or "pairing," does not then exclude successive polygyny or polyandry. In this matriarchal *gens*, made up of more or less stable syndiasmic families, the economy has a clearly accentuated collective character. This is what Engels calls the "communistic household" consisting of the totality of the resources gathered in the hamlets. Their management is the woman's business, while the men bring in the produce from the outside, from the harvest or the chase.[12]

Engels has a lofty idea of this *gens* pattern and he enumerates its social advantages: quarrels and conflicts settled by the community; a domestic economy common to a set of families; decisions made in common, when age-old custom has not already settled matters; the equality of all, care of the sick and education of children taken charge of by the community; no extreme poverty; private property limited to small family gardens and to the tools for work owned by individuals (*spontaneous* division of labor).[13] But it is very obvious that such a regime is possible only when the population of a region is not very dense and production is rudimentary. It will have to be replaced by something different when the situation has progressed beyond these elementary conditions.

This prehistory takes humanity from a stage of sexual intercourse without restrictions to a division into matriarchal *gentes* that see the evolution of paired (syndiasmic) but unstable monogamous couples governed solely by *natural selection*;[14] incestuous unions between parents and children, and then between brothers and sisters, gradually disappeared as the unions of a more marked exogamic type yielded stronger and more resistant offspring. It was only very gradually and unconsciously that consanguineous unions were avoided, without clear advance knowledge of the result.[15] The prohibitions, if they came to be at all, simply made explicit the way of life that was gradually taking hold. In this sense there is no discontinuity between the starting point and the point of arrival of this prehistory: the period is one of the progressive implementation of a social form that is somehow inscribed in the genetic capital of humanity. No hiatus exists at this level between nature and society. Monogamy of the syndiasmic type is like a two-atom molecule evolving within the fiber of the matriarchal *gens*: natural selection can go no further.[16]

2. If the impetus that is to provide a new forward movement is in some sense based on what has gone before, it is nevertheless no longer a natural but rather a *social* one; its point of departure is no longer the dynamic of blood but rather that of *economics*. The appearance of animal husbandry fundamentally alters the relationship of man to his source of subsistence, and by doing so transforms the entire social structure. In fact, everything takes place according to an internal logic ingeniously reconstructed and described by Engels:[17] the stable source of food becomes decentralized with respect to the "communistic household"; the herds and flocks graze outside of the hamlets and are dependent on the activity of the male member of the family, who therefore acquires more and more importance. But above all, the way is opened to *private property*: as the male of the syndiasmic couple, the man traditionally has ownership of the tools that serve him in his daily search for sustenance; he spontaneously takes possession of the

animals and even of the pastures through which this sustenance is henceforth assured. A capital is created which is the possession of the male. From the point of view of *inheritance*, private property thus generated is to transform family statute and law. If the father really wants *his* children to inherit, the inheritance must fall to the children of the father alone rather than to the *gens* to which the mother belongs. This entails the redefinition of the *gens* as *father right*, and in order for this right to be put into practice without fail, it is also necessary to have a *strict and indissoluble monogamous marriage*. Paternal sonship will thus be assured. It is clear then that the introduction of animal husbandry as a fundamental economic modification has a number of consequences: private property, the reversal of the relationship between man and woman to the advantage of the former—the woman being henceforth relegated to the private sphere of the administration of an individual home and of the upbringing of the father's children only— and finally, the establishing of the monogamous family.[18]

We cannot take time to follow here in detail the development that led from this first social revolution (or rather from this first intervention of the social in a human species which up until this time has evolved by natural selection) to the situation that Engels and Marx find in the nineteenth century. The modes of production, which each time define new relationships of production, mark out its various stages and create the social divisions of labor (ranchers/plowmen; farmers/artisans; producers/merchants) as well as antagonistic social divisions (men/women; masters/slaves; rich/poor). The *State*, as a political superstructure, rapidly replaces the *gens*, so as to insure the perpetuity of the system thus engendered and the maintenance of its divisions and antagonisms. To the extent that his historical knowledge allows, Engels painstakingly studies the origins of this transition from the "mother right *gens*" to an historical structure of capitalist, male, monogamous, state type. Employing as a benchmark the case of the Iroquois (who remain a point of reference precisely because they never were compelled to go beyond the *gens* type of social existence), he successively treats the Greeks, the Romans, the Celts and the Germans. He then summarizes the data thus assembled by distinguishing and contrasting the *gens* (up to the lower stage of barbarism) and "civilization" (from the higher stage of barbarism and on up), the pejorative accent being placed on the second and not on the first of these two terms. In every area, the gentile structure ("barbarism") crumbled under the impulse of economic development: the division of labor, the break-up of the family and of society into antagonistic classes, the formation of a merchant class and the development of metallic currency, the formation of a state—such are the characteristics of "civilization," whose most notable trait, finally, is the oppression of a poor and slave class, more numerous than the other. The societal division into proletariat and bourgeoisie has now emerged.

3. Thus, the introduction of a *social* organizational principle, in the wake of *natural* selection, was not to yield the anticipated results. The proletarian revolution must then put an end to the fundamental antagonisms of bourgeois society, and it will do so, within the framework of a numerous and technically developed humanity, by restoring the "communistic" social forms of the primitive *gens*. Engels does not supply in detail the elements of the process nor does he set a date for its implementation. He seems to think that once the basic structures have been reinstituted, the rest will follow by itself.[19] If the evil began through the appropriation of the goods of production (animal husbandry), the suppression of the private ownership of these same goods will restore the entire economy to the level of a social industry and of a public affair and will reinstate the strict equality of the members of the human community in relation to labor. The disappearance of the inheritance system will restore to woman her dignity and will make her equal to man, whether she works in industry or whether her work at home regains its character as a public service to the community; monogamous marriage, having lost the economic foundation for its strictness, will see so much the more the blossoming of its affective foundation which was formerly limited mostly to furtive and passing unions; firmly supported by the bond of love and freed from male domination, marriage will not seek to outlive love (why should it?), resulting in the possibility of successive unions for each man and each woman.[20] As for the education of children, it too will retrieve its public character.

Necessary development or culpability?

Looking closely at the rigorous correspondence established by Engels between the fundamental principles of the primitive *gens* and those of the society which is to come about as a result of the imminent proletarian revolution,[21] one can only be struck by the enormity of the wager: it is simply taken for granted that from the effective reinstating of these principles a just society will be reborn—spontaneously.

The audacity of such a wager could be justified if one could place the entire history of civilization (which begins, let us remember, with the emergence of the social dimension itself) under the sign of *moral evil*. By simply suppressing the corrupt forms that multiply as they emerge from their matrix, the private appropriation of the means of production, and by restoring the good ones, that is, the institutions of the *gens* transposed into our industrial society, success would obviously be insured. Engels, however, does not make such a unilateral evaluation. It must be acknowledged that the shape of the history of civilization depends also on the constraints of development. So it is that in the texts in which he analyzes history, we find elements to evaluate that are the inevitable result of these constraints, and numerous others that are the result of moral evil. Unfortunately, the synthesis is not made—a fact that dangerously compromises the reasonableness of the wager. Let us briefly sort out the three different and uncoordinated insights that govern the movement of his thought.

1. At the end of the chapter in which he expounds with evident satisfaction the model form of Iroquois society, Engels nevertheless remarks: "However impressive the people of this epoch appear to us, they are completely undifferentiated from one another; as Marx says, they are still attached to the umbilical cord of the primitive community. The power of this primitive community had to be broken, and it was broken."[22] The matriarchal *gens* brings to its term, as we see above, the natural evolution that began its course in the undifferentiated population of the beginning. To go beyond this, to break the *umbilical cord* of *undifferentiatedness*, an intervention of another nature is therefore required. Only at this price, as Engels himself observes, was it possible for civilization to accomplish things that were far beyond the capacity of the old gentile society. One could question what sense there is in returning to social forms that prevailed prior to this rupture of an excessively undifferentiated community.

2. When Engels describes the first stages of this rupture, or the intervention of the "social," which amounts to the same thing, it appears that civilization follows a coherent logic. The intervention of animal husbandry, followed by that of agriculture (with metalworking

in particular, which made possible the ploughshare) inevitably entail certain social modifications, namely, the division of labor, the reorganization of the family, etc. None of this should be surprising. This whole complex of *distinctions* and therefore of *exchanges* had to be imposed on the primitive community in order that it might continue to develop.[23]

3. What we have here is a necessary break from the primitive community, structures of distinction and of reciprocity. How can Engels place all of this under the sign of evil? Regarding the power of the primitive community that "had to be broken," he writes:

> it was broken by influences which from the very start appear as a degradation, a fall from the simple moral greatness of the old gentile society. The lowest interests . . . inaugurate the new, civilized, class society. It is by the vilest means . . . that the old classless gentile society is undermined and overthrown.[24]

I would like to point out the use of the "theological" term *fall*. The transition from the matriarchal community, still natural and come to maturity through a harmonious evolution of the entirely undifferentiated initial population, to the socially organized society, is in some sense the original sin, which will continue to grow throughout the history of civilization. Elsewhere we read,

> Civilization achieved things of which gentile society was not even remotely capable. But it achieved them by setting in motion the lowest instincts and passions in man and developing them at the expense of all his other abilities. *From its first day* to this, sheer greed was the driving spirit of civilization.[25]

Here again, evil is at work from the very beginning.

Ultimately, it is only the third of these insights that Engels retains in describing the establishment of the new society. The intrinsic necessity of a break with the primitive community in order to enable it to continue with renewed vigor, the internal logic of the economical processes without which no progress would have been possible—all these things are swallowed up by the moral evil which is supposed to have manifested itself from the very first day. Engels makes no attempt to distinguish, in the history of civilization, between the transformation due to its forward movement itself and those which legitimately could be attributed to greed. The latter carry the day completely, and so it only remains to extol a return to precivilized social forms. *Culpability* having from the very beginning devoured and dissolved *necessity*, the only solution is to go backward beyond this culpability. Engels leaves us with the task of thinking out how this return to gentile forms, albeit transposed, will not entail the establishment once again of an undifferentiated society, of a vast cell of maternal type where the umbilical cord would become binding and where the desire of groups or of individuals for distinct identity would be regarded as culpable because it would be immediately likened to the original greed. He also leaves it to us to deal with the question of how a "communistic" society (in the matriarchal sense that he gives to this term) could actually be possible in the highly specialized world in which we live.

The myth of revolution

One could ask why it is that Engels prefers to adopt a point of view that could well be called "theological" with respect to the notion of civilization which he views as intrinsically marked by a "fall," an original sin, instead of taking the trouble, to the extent that this is possible, to do some sorting out between the positive values and the culpable deviations in the history of civilization. The response could come from the fact that the lofty idea that Engels has of the primitive *gens* is also, if not "theological," at least "speculative" or ideological. Indeed, when we look more closely at the description of prehistory proposed here, we see that it is entirely dominated by *the myth of the primitive state of undifferentiation*: the Iroquois tribes are what observation reveals them to be, but their organization owes its appeal only to the fact that it can be linked, by way of *natural* selection (and hence without the divisive intervention that comes from man) to the population in which sexual exchange was without restrictions: a population where everyone belonged to everyone and vice versa, which amounts to saying that no one belonged to anyone and that people lived in a state of *total undifferentiation*, the "natural" in its pure state. Engels acknowledges that we have no direct access to this type of population, any more than we have to the "consanguine" form that is its first "natural" development. He attempts to show that one can, nevertheless, deduce its existence from the ethnological data that is available to us.[26] In any case, the image he portrays is that of a kind of *internal* evolution of the earliest society and, whatever restrictions natural selection may bring to sexuality, the latter has no *discriminating* aspect, just as work and food do not create any difference: the earth belongs to everyone and its resources to the "communistic household" which, in the image of Mother Earth, is administered by women.

We might almost conclude from these observations that society is good only to the extent that it is not yet *born*; when it arrives at the limit of its "natural" internal evolution, it can go no further without serious rupture. The trauma of its birth is already "original sin." The question can then be raised whether the proletarian revolution would not be an immense effort, on a global scale, to regress back beyond the era of social existence, an enormous psychodrama seeking to return to the original times and to erase the suffering caused by the ruptures that civilized life necessarily entails as much as possible. By placing all of civilization under the sign of "the fall," Engels attempts to enclose in brackets the entire dialectic of history, for the benefit of a primitive harmony to which eschatology will eventually correspond.

If this is so, whatever accuracy there might be in a number of his analyses on the evolution of civilization, on the close connection that exists between the sociology of the family and economic development, between the division of labor and the origin of social divisions and antagonisms, the *overall view* of Engels (and doubtless that of Marx as well, to whom he constantly refers) does not rehabilitate time in its truth nor does it offer a creative solution to human history at the point where we have inherited it today. This view belongs in the category of what I will describe below as the problematic of the image and its double.[27] And if this is so, can the revolutions that spring from this problematic yield anything but tragic illusions?[28]

The failure of Engels leaves us, however, with a valuable positive pointer: a correct evaluation of human time and of the reality of history must necessarily include a process of careful discrimination between what pertains to the development of a humanity inextricably involved in duration and what pertains to evil, to egoism, to sin. Only in this way can we avoid crediting the one with what really belongs to the other and building on a confused foundation a society which can only be oppressive. *But how will we arrive at this discernment?*

2. The immediate revolution

In the preceding section, I focused my criticism of Engels on one precise point. Whatever partial and fragmentary validity his analyses of sexuality, of the family, of labor and of society may have, their significance is ultimately lost because they are synthesized into a mythology of a return to the undifferentiated, whose concrete application can only engender tragic disillusionment, as numerous experiments in the course of the past century have demonstrated.

However, as classical Marxism continues its course today, other interpretations of Marx-Engels have also surfaced, especially in the last generation. One can expect that these will produce (and perhaps they have already produced) other revolutionary and post-revolutionary practices. But I would like to focus here on a line of thought, that of Jean Baudrillard, which, though certainly post-Marxian,[29] nevertheless introduces novel elements which are decisive. From his thinking I would like to retain three essential elements: economic criticism ought to focus on the processes of *consumption* as much as and more than on those of production; revolutionary practice can and should be *immediate* instead of being preceded by a long period of preparation, which often means that it is simply deferred; this immediate revolutionary practice should be a reestablishment of the authentic social form, defined as "symbolic exchange."

Consumption as a system

The intuition of Baudrillard, verified by a great number of concrete analyses, is that *consumption* is a phenomenon just as abstract, complex and codified as is production, such as Marx analyzes it. Far from being governed by the simple relation of a need to a use in view of a satisfaction, which could be described as natural or normal, consumption is tightly framed and denatured in a system of signs and codes that is dehumanizing—one could even say *hors humanité* (totally outside of the human).[30] To consume is simply to perform an act that fills an empty slot at a given moment within a coded system, thus permitting the latter to function—the entire process being totally unrelated to any human need or to the intrinsic value of the commodity in question. Antique objects in a neo-bourgeois interior, the technical object in the hands of a "primitive" aborigine[31] the work of art, signed by the artist and auctioned off at a very high price, in the drawing room of the nouveau riche,[32] but also the purely "functional" furniture in the "model" apartment or office are there neither for their intrinsic value, nor for their aesthetic character, nor for their performance coefficient:[33] they are there in order to conform a given space to an ephemeral and discriminatory system of signs. The interior done with period furniture signifies the *relationship* to a mythical time (the diachronic aspect) and gives its owners a *status* equal to their competitors, who are marked by the same status symbols, while *separating* them from others (the synchronic aspect). It constitutes a code element which generates class opposition just as effectively as do the modes and relationships of production. The advertising industry,[34] at whatever level, (from this point of view the politics of art galleries and the televised advertisement of laundry detergents belong to an identical process) is continuously supplying new code elements, but not the "system" principle that governs consumption. If I were being honest with myself, I would not hang this particular "Picasso" in my parlor, but the fact is that neither Picasso nor I are at issue here; "this" Picasso hangs *itself* spontaneously on my wall, linking me thus to the class of "Picasso" owners and differentiating me from other classes. But one could say as much for the mass-produced television stand, which, in conjunction with other gadgets of its kind, defines a social stratum for a time. In these two cases, as in all others without exception, it is the systemic organization which governs the consumption, both because every "object" has meaning only within a system ("Picasso" calls for "parlor" and "parlor" for "Picasso") and because every system has meaning only in its opposition to another or to other systems (the "period furniture" system has meaning only in its opposition to the "mass-produced furniture" system).

System of consumption, semiotic revolution and immediate revolution

This organization of consumption into a system is not limited to the objects which I have mentioned, following Baudrillard. It is universal and just as pointedly concerns the body, sexuality and death, the media and power, aesthetics.[35] Analyze the situation with precision and attention and you will find that everything in these areas is nothing but a game of codes. In other words, our civilization today is marked by the "semiotic revolution" which follows the industrial revolution and perhaps abolishes it as well. The term *semiotic* used here comes from the science of linguistics, and more particularly from the distinction, established by F. de Saussure, between signifying and signified—a distinction which becomes drastic separation in the analyses of authors like Lévi-Strauss, Lacan, Derrida.[36] Meaning, if there is any meaning at all, can only be the result of the ordering of signifiers that have meaning only in their reciprocal relationship. Once the signified has been ignored, there remains only the code system of signifiers. Taking all this to the extreme (but data processing as currently practiced strongly suggests this extreme), both meaning and reality itself would be nothing but variables to infinity of the primordial opposition: 0/1—senseless reduction of the real to binary representation.[37]

This semiotic revolution goes hand in hand with the dislocation of linear time, the idea of which (past, present, future) was still implicit in the industrial revolution and in the *expectations* of the proletarian revolution. This dislocation belongs to the cultural field, not only of semiotics itself, but also more generally of philosophy to the extent that it presents itself as post-metaphysical. The concept is supplied by Heidegger and developed by Derrida.[38] At the time of the industrial revolution, on the contrary, there was still a certain perspective of linear time: the modes of production succeeded one another in history according to a certain order, which Marx attempted to explain by means of dialectical materialism; and the fruit of his analysis was that, in the course of history and by way of the various stages of the proletarian revolution, we would arrive at that eschatological "after" where a generously shared well-being could be enjoyed by all. This vision was not entirely without foundation, based as it was on the processes of production and their inner dynamism, which were the source of the social signs and their evolution. In this sense, those who are struggling today within the perspectives opened by the industrial revolution of the nineteenth century think they are preparing for and certainly await a social revolution for tomorrow. But neither Marx (who could not have) nor the Marxists (who perhaps did not want to) took into account the *semiotic* revolution, the fact that the strict enslavement of human beings does not come, or no longer comes, from the injustice of the relationships of production. It comes from the anonymous tyranny of signifying codes that could be indefinitely modifiable themselves, but are incapable of yielding any social change at all. Tomorrow will not and *cannot* bring anything more than historically insignificant variants to the necessarily discriminatory complex of systems. One set of codes is worth as much as another, and not one of them is "worth" anything at all. One could say, without danger of over-simplification, that the criticism leveled by Baudrillard against classical Marxism is that of always *awaiting* the full revolution for *tomorrow*, and so of being caught up in a linear conception of time and thus, paradoxically, *never* really making this revolution because of a *future* which is always on the horizon, leaving it a perfectly illusory time.

Thus, if a social revolution is necessary, it must be made not tomorrow, but *immediately*,[39] not for reasons of particular urgency, but for a *structural* reason: at the level of the semiotic revolution and of the coded systems, we are no longer in the dimension of linear time and tomorrow will bring nothing that is not already in existence today. If one wishes to surmount the social discriminations and the class oppositions, it must be done *now*; there is no particularly auspicious moment for *shattering the semiotic system*. The industrial revolution made the proletarian revolution appear on the horizon; the semiotic revolution should trigger an *immediate* and universal revolution.

Toward "symbolic exchange" . . .

But what actions does this revolution involve and what does it aim to establish? We shall first look for a response to this second question. It cannot be a matter of resolving the contradictions of production and of consumption by returning to a pre-dialectic and pre-semiotic stage, to social forms governed by "intrinsic value" and "need," just sharing, etc. It is a matter of going beyond the *signs* which have become constitutive of the industrial society and the semiotic society, to establish a *symbolic* social form, a society that would amount to "symbolic exchange."[40]

It is not easy to *say* or *define* symbol, such as Baudrillard understands it: indeed, it is radically impossible to do so. What we can attempt to do is to show how "symbol" contrasts with "sign." The sign, which establishes a social relationship between those who "make the sign," is always a *sign of* something: a present *of great value* will signify the esteem I have for you; a word *of great significance* will tend to establish a certain order of relationships (we are reminded of the subtle interpretations provoked by certain statements of our government officials). It is not important that "value" and "significance" come from an objective content or from a systemic position, or that come under the categories of "reference" or of "code." The crucial point is that there is *mediation* in the establishment and in the maintenance of the social relationship, that something, if only an ephemeral set of signifiers, intervenes between the social partners and *defines* the mode of their relationship. As long as this mediation subsists, we are in the *sign*; if and when it disappears, we reach the level of *symbol*.

Symbolic exchange is that which, beyond or without any intervening value, comes to be *in pure relationship*. It is difficult to describe, precisely because we have *lost* this mode of exchange and no longer have concrete experience of it. Baudrillard explains as follows: "The symbolic, in its power as meaning subversive of sign, can be named only by allusion, by refraction, because signification, which names everything on the basis of value can only express value, and the symbolic is not value." Or again: "We can say nothing of that which is outside of sign, i.e., other than sign, except that it is of *ambivalence*, which means here the impossibility of distinguishing respective, distinct terms, and of giving them positive value as such."[41] We have a word for the symbolic, nevertheless, and a negative definition: in the model social figure, the terms do not exist outside of *relationship* and what circulates between them is entirely transitive, has no existence outside of this transit itself.[42] Baudrillard employs the term *reciprocity*[43] or even *reversibility*,[44] in the sense of "personal correlation of one individual to the other in the act of exchange." The exchanged item itself, whether this be an object or a message (a gift, e.g., in the economic sphere, or a word in the linguistic sphere) has no value in itself; its content is, literally, in-significant: it continuously annihilates itself in the very process of exchange. Its mediation is transitive. If it takes on any consistency whatever, whether real or significative, outside of the exchange, this would ruin the exchange as symbolic because it would lead immediately to the substantiation not only of the object or message but also of the terms between whom the exchange is being made. The same damage would be done if one of the two terms were to have a one-sided initiative: a gift without counter-gift, a word which does not offer the immediate possibility of a response. Ambivalence, reciprocity, reversibility cannot be reduced: this is the very operating procedure of the symbolic, the original social form which, however repressed it might be, remains at work within the *simulacra* which have tried and are trying to stifle it, and which must therefore be immediately restored. Immediately, because "afterwards" or "later," we will be at exactly the same point in this respect.

According to the descriptions of Baudrillard, symbolic exchange is spontaneously at play at the social level; every gift *immediately* calls forth a counter-gift, every word, a response. It is essential to authority that it be ambivalent: thus, in the ancient civilizations, the king is the one obeyed and at the same time the one sacrificed and the subject is the one who obeys and the one who puts to death. The relationship is thus perfectly ambivalent, which would not be the case in a unilateral relationship power/submission: the strong term must be exterminated and the weak term, the exterminator. Symbolic exchange is at play at more subtle levels as well. With respect to the *body*, for example, reciprocity is not only and not even primarily in the polarity male/female, but in the reciprocity of the body and its other: the "body and its shadow," "the body under the body," as if man existed only in the subtle exchange where it is not known who is the self and who is the other, for here too, and perhaps here primarily, ambivalence is constitutive.[45] Reciprocity in *language* between the terms themselves or rather between the term and an "other" which inhabits it, as if each word or each syllable were also an ambivalent sign of a presence and of an absence, as the reflection of Saussure on *Anagrams* seems to suggest.[46] Finally, symbolic exchange functions as challenge, excess, overbid: Baudrillard is doubtless thinking of certain forms of potlatch,[47] but more precisely of the most profound meaning with which such a practice can be invested: a *sacrifice*, of one's possessions or of oneself, but one which immediately requires and provokes a paroxystic reciprocity: the flame brought to red-heat and the return of the flame, a ritual through which the symbolic exchange reaches an insufferable level and annihilates itself to be born again in another way.

. . . . *and toward Death*

We could summarize all of the above in a single sentence; "Life brought to death, this is the very way the symbolic functions."[48] We spontaneously think of life as accumulation, value increase, meaning, coding.[49] The fact is that "life" in this sense gives rise to segregation, class strategies, oppression. We dream too of "immortality," but is this anything more than a projected version of accumulation?[50] If we wish then to arrive at life, we must bring it to "death," a term given to symbolic exchange where nothing comes to a stop, nothing stands still on the way, nothing hardens into something substantive, nothing allows itself to be reduced to a code. "Death should never be understood as a real event of a subject or of a body, but rather as a *form*—that of a social relationship, perhaps—where the determination of the subject and of value is lost." Thus, in the context of the language we speak, where we spontaneously express ourselves in determinate terms, designating subjects and values, to affirm "death" is to abolish these determinations, this intransitive material, for the benefit of a constant circulation.[51] It is to acknowledge and affirm that reality at its deepest level consists in this perennial process of coming and going, of blossoming and decay; it is above all to see to it that it be just that. If the ecstatic moment of destruction and of loss is neglected or impaired, we are no longer living in the true *form* of the real. Now this moment of destruction of every mediation and of every term can truly be called "death," if *death* signifies, by antonomasia, a negativity. But this would amount then to a death which is constitutive of reality. In a commentary on Bataille, Baudrillard dares to express himself in statements which closely resemble those of the Gospel (and this unlikely proximity is not without significance): "Death (excess, ambivalence, gift, sacrifice, expenditure and paroxysm) and hence true life is absent from the reality that we live. We refuse to die and we accumulate instead of losing ourselves."[52]

In other words, death, in this sense, is the general principle of reversibility; it can come into play, as the text cited above expresses it, at the level of social exchange with the living, but it comes into play also in the social exchange with the dead. Ours is the only culture which has ever regarded the dead as having ceased to exist and which ignores the basic phenomenon of initiation, which is precisely the way in which man is introduced into this living fellowship between the dead and the living, and through which the death which affects a particular individual loses its importance, since this vital exchange is still going on.[53] But death as *form* is at play also at those more subtle levels of which I spoke above when I was describing symbolic exchange. Death is everywhere the form and the force of exchange.

With these observations in mind, the other sense of death becomes intelligible—the pejorative sense which is pertinent to our civilizations: "Death is no more than this; to be cut off from the cycle of symbolic exchanges."[54] Death in this sense is the diametric opposite of symbolic death: it is there wherever there is accumulation; it is there whenever language stops at what it says instead of cancelling it out in the exchange of the saying itself, and it is there whenever we take time into consideration. Indeed, the fact that time spreads out in linear fashion would entail as a consequence that there are residues, before or after, and that these are not taken up into the exchange. Life, moreover, in the sense in which it is generally understood, is nothing but this accumulation of residues.

Historical perspective (Diachronic aspect)

It is interesting to note that the theme of symbolic exchange has a regressive side to it. The immediate revolution is supposed to restore a lost truth. Indeed, Baudrillard credits "archaic" societies with living according to symbolic exchange; and the same goes, it would seem, for the feudal arrangement.[55] From the point of view of signs, without which no social order could be established, one could say that, in these societies, the signs are immediately reciprocal; they have no reference value except in reference to the exchanges between casts, clans or individuals: they are *obligatory* signs, to the extent that, outside of their continuous exchange, the symbolic social form would not be sustained.

The diachronic or historical process through which symbolic exchange was lost can be characterized as a progressive emancipation of the sign with respect to its primitive essence of symbolic reciprocity. In a first period (that corresponds to an era that goes from the Renaissance to the Industrial Revolution), the universe of signs, instead of conveying living relationships within which the sign destroys itself, undertakes the task of referring to a universe of reality, of which it is the double or the counterfeit. Whether we are dealing with the production of objects, with language or with art, or with social organization, the signs appear as the "reflection of a total order," of a Nature, of a referent that is universal and obliged to do all and to say all. Something has entered in between man and man; from immediate symbolic expression, we have passed to a universe of signification *measured* by Nature. Objects, words, works of art, in the correlation of their forms and the density of their substance are a double of reality. But the industrial revolution demolishes this theme of Nature. By its power to transform, to produce and to reproduce without any formal relationship with the great universal Referent which modeled the forms of the preceding universe, it gives rise to a new order of relationships based on labor, manipulation, distribution, bringing in the market economy on a grand scale. Taking over from the majestic paradigm of Nature, to which that of Man as imitator and participant could be linked, is the Law of equivalence, which becomes the rule of the circulation of merchandise, and in this way, the source of specific social signs. One last stage is reached when the products break loose from the processes of production and begin to organize themselves into a network of signs, which could be characterized as "floating," in the sense that they are no longer related either to Nature or to production.[56] They are then "free" to be distinguished, separated, reorganized according to schemes and models that will be reflected in new social stratifications. Baudrillard excels in describing the totally abstract character of the "system of objects," but also of the models pertaining to sexuality, information, aesthetics—everything which was previously "value" and, at an even earlier stage, "nature" now becomes a set of codes. Most characteristic of this new civilization is the fact that it is civilization *without responsibility*. Advertising, communications, political power, systematized outside of any exchange with their intended beneficiaries (today, with cybernetics, even through a reduced participation of the very people who developed the systems) are addressed to the other without the slightest possibility of a response. Let us look at a few statements of the author:

> The widespread order of consumption is none other than one in which it is no longer permitted to give, to give back or to exchange, but only to take and to use.
> Power belongs to the one who can give and *to whom it cannot be given in return*. To give, and to do so in such a way that no one can return the gift is to break the process of exchange to one's own profit and to establish a monopoly.
> The same is true for the sphere of the media, which supplies a flow of words, *and does so in such a way that a response can come from nowhere.*[57]

It will be noted that it is not at all (or not only and in any case not primarily) a matter of bad will on the part of those who happen to have control over consumption, power or the media; it is the very structure of these things as signifiers, organized without any real foundation and outside of any symbolic exchange, which is believed to remove them from all possibility of receiving a "response."

We are then no longer in the era of the industrial civilization, but in that of the *semiotic* civilization, one most totally removed from the reality of exchange, most geared to life as accumulation, most foreign to the presence of "death." Its product is in fact that generic, anonymous man, himself as it were mass produced according to a model resulting from the conjunction of codes imposed on him from the outside—that man described, from another angle, by Leroi-Gourhan; totally exteriorized man.

Demolish the codes—immediately

The preceding pages have attempted to respond to the question: what does the immediate revolution aim to establish? It remains to be asked what actions this revolution involves. How does one go about immediately establishing symbolic exchange?

If we thumb through the pages of *L'Echange symbolique et la Mort* looking for examples of this immediate revolution, the only possible one, we find:

- unauthorized strikes,[58] without apparent motivation, without regularity, avoiding the control (which one could call semiotic) of the unions. The absence of any symbolic or real referent can only have the effect of disorganizing, radically subverting industry, for these are actions "*hors-code*," totally outside the code complex.
- the taking of hostages,[59] acts of terrorism, suicides—all selectively targeted actions, of apparently insignificant scope, but which (above all, for example, if they are accompanied by claims or demands that are exorbitant, and intentionally so) are in reality a provocation to a response, a way of putting the system to death by an out-of-code action which demands the same type of action in return.
- obviously, the great student uprisings of Paris in May 1968,[60] before the organizations and unions took them over.
- on a very different plane, the New York graffiti in 1972:[61] that invasion of the subway, of the buses, of the pedestals of statues,

of blank spaces in general by graphics of no ascribable origin or identifiable signification; words, nicknames, signs—subversive writing making demands that can in no way be reduced to familiar categories, an out-of-code cry of appeal for a response from society.

By their subversive character, such practices effectively indicate the totally *other* nature of what a symbolic exchange would be, as compared with the social structures which derive from production or consumption. But this indication remains a negative one, for nothing concrete is said or even suggested to us as to what could serve as a *response* to such actions. If it is of the very nature of exchange that the terms cancel each other out, one should, in the subversive act itself, *immediately* discern and render a response. This however is obviously not the case. No effective social form is brought into being by these "provocations" which are not "invocations." And if these subversive actions remain unilateral, without immediate response, then, according to Baudrillard himself, they become substantified and do not bring about any true symbolic exchange. Another way of saying the same thing would be to observe that such "out-of-code" actions *call for* a response. Do they not depart, by this very fact, from the blueprint drawn up by Baudrillard? Indeed, an *appeal* implies an interval of linear time between it and the response, which presupposes at least a summary investigation of meaning or signification in order to "elaborate" this response; and we would thus be making our reentry into "code" instead of entering into genuine "symbolic exchange"!

The impossibility of symbolic exchange does not then appear to me to be an accident of present circumstances; such a relationship is rather impossible of its very nature. As conceived by Baudrillard, symbolic exchange seems just as *mythical* as the society which the proletarian revolution would like to create through the destruction of the social and a return to the natural. Here, the myth is not one of a return to an ultimately biological origin; it lies rather in the projection of a *pure*, immediate, unconditioned *reciprocity*.[62] The extremes meet, however, and here too, blood is the price paid for mythology.[63]

In his very extremism, Baudrillard leaves us with something worthwhile when it comes to collecting the elements necessary for a meeting of time and of being in the sphere of the divine. I do not know if any author, among those in recent years who have followed Mauss in dealing with the subject of *exchange*, has gone as far as he in the perception of reciprocity and in the determination to reintroduce it into the realities of social existence. Above, I cited a text from his writings which is remarkably close to the "Whoever loses his life . . . will save it" of the Gospels. This similarity is perhaps not without significance. In the same order of ideas, the constant effort of Baudrillard to reintroduce *death* into the heart of the very structure of social relationship (with his distinction of death as driving force behind exchange—the positive sense—and death as the loss of exchange—the negative sense), analyzing it as the necessary reverse side of life and as "sacrifice," finds a fascinating (and at the same time a terrifying) place as my own thinking develops through this book. Baudrillard has some harsh things to say about "God,"[64] whom he holds responsible for maintaining as separate what should be involved in exchange and whom he sees as lending strong support to power that is totalitarian and without response. Perhaps he is not altogether wrong and a critical review of our own ideas about God is a process that should always remain alive, even from within the most theologal faith. But would it not be legitimate to inquire whether the Trinitarian God is not the only divine model that could truly respond to the description he proposes of "symbolic exchange"?

This only too brief incursion into what one could call the ideologies of revolution shows us at least that, if one endeavors to *think through* the history of humanity and to go beyond the apparently foreclosed meaning on which Leroi-Gourhan leaves us, one is lead to assertions that go beyond a history of evolution and link up to the *extremes* of time, even if, in the cases studied, this occurs in a "mythical" or "barbarous" way. In any case, one is lead beyond the circumstances of the present moment. It is for this reason that it is not outside of our purpose nor out of line with the preceding chapters, to listen to directly philosophical voices on the same theme, to find out if and how the question of the time of man is linked to the question of Being.

Notes

1. Friedrich Engels, *The Origin of the Family, of Private Property and of the State*. The original English translation of the book is the work of Alec West (1942), but the citations that follow will be taken from a later edition

with introduction and notes by Eleanor Burke Leacock, (New York: International Publishers Co., Inc., 1972).

2. *Ibid.*, p. 138. This revolution is described as imminent later in the same paragraph.

3. Preface to the First Edition (1884), *Ibid.*, p. 71. In this book, Engels essentially relies on the book of Lewis H. Morgan, pioneer of ethnographical studies in the United States in the second half of the nineteenth century. The book is entitled: *Ancient Society, or Researches in the Lines of Human Progress from Savagery through Barbarism to Civilization* (1877). Engels also utilizes some notes made by Marx in the margins of this work and in reference to it. I will make no attempt here to determine what ideas are taken from each of these two authors. I take the book as a whole. Powerfully constructed and very clearly written, it has its own inherent intelligibility.

4. The book of Leroi-Gourhan, which we studied in the preceding chapter, has, as I mentioned, some methodological similarity with this book. But Leroi-Gourhan leaves aside the history of the family, doubtless because, since the time when Engels wrote, it has proven to be infinitely more complex than the latter thought it was.

5. Engels borrows this definition from Bachofen, and he explains: " . . . he uses the term 'mother right,' which for the sake of brevity I retain. The term is, however, ill-chosen, since at this stage of society there cannot yet be any talk of 'right' in the legal sense" (p. 106). This statement should be noted: the social form which goes through the whole book of Engels as a leitmotif is one which is prior to relationships of right. In the second Preface (1891), Engels describes the contribution of Lewis H. Morgan to his research and points very clearly to the inspiration for his own book: "This rediscovery of the primitive matriarchal gens as the earlier stage of the patriarchal gens of civilized peoples has the same importance for anthropology as Darwin's theory of evolution has for biology and Marx's theory of surplus value for political economy" (p. 83).

6. *Op cit.*, p. 72.

7. Here I am following Chapter II, "The Family."

8. *Op cit.*, p. 100.

9. *Op cit.*, p. 104.

10. See p. 107.

11. Speaking of the "exclusive recognition of descent through the mother," Engels refers to the "relations of inheritance which in time resulted from it" (p. 106), but he never explains how.

12. "In the old communistic household, which comprised many couples and their children, the task entrusted to the women of managing the household was as much a public, a socially necessary industry as the procuring of food by the men" (p. 137; p. 117ff., p. 227ff.).

13. Page 159: "And a wonderful constitution it is, this gentile constitution, in all its childlike simplicity!" Cf. also p. 229, and *passim* in the book, where the gentile organization (of mother right) is a constant reference point for the author's reflection.

14. Pp. 103 and 117 (where he cites Morgan); p. 107, with reference to the *gens*: it derives "not only necessarily, but also perfectly naturally from the punaluan family."

15. P. 109.

16. P. 117.

17. Pp. 117-135; cf. 218-219.

18. The transition from "mother right" to "father right" is described by Engels as "one of the most decisive ever experienced by humanity" (p. 120). Indeed, in the logic of the book's presentation, it is the first revolution, the first "turning point" of which I spoke above. The second will be the proletarian revolution, destined to reverse the tragic movement initiated by the first. On the monogamous family, which is the "cellular form of civilized society" (p. 129), just as the syndiasmic family was the ultimate "molecular unit" of the gentile fabric, cf. among many other passages: "The Greeks themselves put the matter quite frankly: the sole exclusive aims of monogamous marriage were to make the man supreme in the family and to propagate, as the future heirs to his wealth, children indisputably his own" (p. 128).

19. Pp. 144-145.

20. Pp. 145. We thus go back to the syndiasmic couple of the original *gens*, which was monogamous but unstable.

21. The following is a table of some of the correspondences established by Engels:

GENS	CIVILIZATION	CLASSLESS SOCIETY
Monogamous, unstable syndiastic marriage.	Indissoluble, monogamous marriage.	Monogamous love marriage. Successive unions possible.
Spontaneous division of labor between man and woman. Equality of the spouses.	Class conflict between man and woman. Enslavement of the woman.	Juridical equality of the rights of man and woman. Re-entry of woman into the scene of public labor.

| Communistic household (collective, ruled by matriarch). | Private property (individual, male) | Common property. |
| Children common to the *gens*. | Children within the family. | Education of children, public affair. |

Can we say that this process is dialectical (position-scission-restoration)? Not really, because Engels (like many others) distinguishes between what one could call a good scission, one which results from finitude and gives way to exchange, and a bad scission, one which derives from the unruly passions of man. The restoration (*Aufhebung*) is both suppression (of the previous moment) and return to the original. Ultimately, it is more the latter than the former.

22. Pp. 160-161.

23. Cf. note 17. The entire Chapter IX describes this process, and contains a strange mixture of analyses of the changes required by technical progress and negative descriptions of moral decadence.

24. P. 161.

25. P. 235.

26. Pp. 87-88, 99-100, 109. Regarding the basic revolution which transforms the reckoning of descent in the female line and mother right into its reckoning in the male line and father right, Engels writes: "As to how and when this revolution took place among civilized peoples, we have no knowledge" (p. 120).

27. Cf. infra, Chapter IV, note 77.

28. It is possible that, coming at the term of the long career of Engels-Marx, the work analyzed here hardens to some extent a figure of history which some manuscripts of Marx would have presented in a more nuanced way (cf. M. Abelès, "Anthropologie et marxisme," in *Encyclopedia Universalis*, Suppl. II, "Les enjeux," [Paris, 1985], p. 428). It is likewise possible that the Marxists of today are also capable of greater nuance. But two facts remain which justify the choice of this book here. On the one hand, the strict regressive tendency which underlies what presents itself as an idea of progress. This tendency was there already with Marx: "More than the nature of primitive communities it is the history of their decadence which fires the passion of Marx" (Abelès *op cit.*, p. 427). And do we not find this same passion with his interpreters? On the other hand, whatever nuances may be brought to the subject in university circles, it would seem that it is always the "Marxist vulgate" (*ibid.*, p. 432) which is effectively at work in revolutionary procedures and seems ultimately to deprive them of their efficacy when it comes to constructing states worthy of the name in the aftermath of the revolution.

29. Baudrillard is constantly comparing his ideas with those of Marx, cf., *Le Miroir de la production* (Paris, 1973), which is a systematized collection of ideas which were already to be found in the *Critique de l'économie politique du signe*, (Paris, 1972), e.g. p. 154ff., 201-203, etc. (cited subsequently as *CE*).

30. This thesis of Baudrillard is expounded in *Le Système des objets*, (Paris, 1968), cited *SO*. See the general conclusion and in *CE*, *passim*.

31. *SO* pp. 103-119.

32. *CE*, pp. 127-143.

33. *SO*: the entire work is built on the distinction functional/non-functional, which are both object of codage.

34. On advertising, cf. *SO*, p. 229-270.

35. For body/sexuality/death, cf. *L'Echange symbolique et la Mort* (Paris, 1976), chap. IV and V (cited *ES*); for information and the media, *CE*, p. 200-228 ("Requiem pour les media"); for aesthetics (with reference to *design*) *CE*, p. 229-255.

36. I speak below of this distinction signifying/signified, in the context of an exposition of Derrida; chap. III, no. 2 (cf. note 81 which is devoted to the relationship between Derrida and Baudrillard).

37. *ES*, p. 90.

38. Cf. *infra*. chap. III, no. 2, the section "Collapse of time."

39. *ES*, p. 282.

40. *ES*, p. 8; in this introductory page, Baudrillard indicates in a suggestive way his basic sources of inspiration: the theme of exchange, as developed by Marcel Mauss; the anagram idea in Saussure; the death instinct in Freud.

41. *CE*, p. 196.

42. *CE*, p. 62.

43. *CE*, p. 208.

44. In *CE*, "reversibility" is a pejorative term, tributary of the semiotic civilization, while "reciprocity" is characteristic of symbolic exchange (cf. p. 8 and *passim*). The violent writing of Baudrillard is not aimed at absolute coherence; it is up to the reader to pay attention.

45. *ES*, p. 189. I would like to underline here that the symbolic polarity of the body is not, or not primarily, in Baudrillard, the polarity male/female (cf. CE, p. 110), but that of the individual body with its "other," which is prior to or deeper than the one which enters into economic and semiurgic exchanges, cf. the parable of the Student of Prague, at the end of *La Société de consommation* (Paris, 1970) (and *ES*, p. 201 and 217). I will return at the end of this book to this polarity, which is both enigmatic and suggestive, of the body with itself.

46. *ES*, p. 285-287.

47. *CE*, p. 9 and ES. p. 7.
48. *ES*, p. 201.
49. *ES*, p. 224.
50. *ES*, p. 197-200.
51. *ES*, p. 12 (with the important notes).
52. *ES*, p. 237.
53. *ES*, p. 203.
54. *ES*, p. 207.
55. *ES*, p. 79.
56. These three times of the diachrony are those which, in *ES*, pp. 77-88, Baudrillard calls the "simulacra" of symbolic exchange. But, from the time he wrote *SO*, he was already distinguishing carefully between these three periods, the first still having the right, for what it produced, to the term "symbolic"; the great rupture is that which occurs in two stages—the industrial revolution and the semiotic revolution.
57. *CE*, pp. 209-210.
58. *ES*, p. 47.
59. *ES*, pp. 64-66, 252, 267, 273.
60. *ES*, p. 214, n.1; cf. *CE*. pp. 214 and 218.
61. *ES*, pp. 119ff.
62. One might ask whether Baudrillard is not here implicated in what appears to be the weak point in the thinking of Lévi-Strauss. We are familiar with the view of the latter that the rule, concretely the prohibition of incest, is the act of birth of *culture*, precisely because this rule makes possible *exchange*. But it would seem that Lévi-Strauss, little by little, blunts the relationship of exchange to the rule, and tends to view exchange as the "nature" of the "human spirit." The foundation of the real is then brought back in the direction of a pure, spontaneous reciprocity, unconnected with any regulative *word*. Thus sociality would ultimately be based on a "natural" reciprocity, while for Engels, it is based on a biological given brought to its point of perfection through "natural" selection. In both cases, the originality of the cultural order is effaced. On this complex process of the "resorption of culture in nature," cf. F. Tinland, *La Différence anthropologique* (Paris, 1977), chap. IV, "De la Règle," devoted to a careful discussion of Lévi-Strauss. Cf. also Y. Simonis, *Claude Lévi-Strauss ou "la passion de l'inceste,"* (Paris, 1968), p. 335-337.
63. This presentation of Baudrillard was already completely written when I gained access to his most recent work *Les Stratégies fatales* (Paris, 1983). The least that could be said of this book is that it scarcely softens the violence of the author's earlier writings. On this subject, cf. P. Valadier, "Le terrorism, défi à la démocratie," in *Etudes*, 360 (1964), especially p. 588ff.
64. *ES*, p. 210, n.1.

CHAPTER THREE

BEING: FORGOTTEN OR EFFACED?

1. The technological era, end of metaphysics and dawn of thinking

The thinking of Heidegger is most often approached by way of his penetrating study of *Being*. This study, however, is not unconnected with an interpretation of history and of civilization which fits in easily with the positions which I have just summarized. According to Heidegger, our *technological* era can be understood only as the tragic end of a long and catastrophic history of "metaphysics." Thus, the "question of Being" would be central to the evaluation of "time." Let us attempt to follow Heidegger along this path of reasoning.

Portrait of the technological world

A world in the state of collapse. A devastated terrain. A humanity reduced to its animal component, humankind become beast of burden.[1] Such, according to Heidegger, is the figure we see emerging at this point in the technological era.

Let us spell out the characteristics of this figure in greater detail. At the center, perhaps, the production type: he is dominating and violent; he exacts of nature, striving constantly to get it to unveil its secrets; he imposes on nature, he makes it yield.[2] Instead of allowing its potentialities to appear or to blossom on their own, he makes it render, produce. And by the same token, he ravishes nature. From the moment a power plant is installed on the Rhine to extort energy from it, a change has taken place in the meaning of things: the river is walled into the plant, it is a function of the plant. And in places where the plant is not visible, it will be exploited in another way; the river of the landscape, commemorated in song by Hölderlin, becomes an object for which one puts in an order at a travel agency. There is no Rhine any more; only an energy source and a piece of merchandise.[3]

But it is clear that nature is not alone in suffering this violent treatment; everything is under requisition, first of all man, "the most important of raw materials".[4] Man is consigned to production, becomes a slave of the machine, a functionary of technology. This task becomes his most accurate definition; human "reserves," for example, are concentrated or diffused according to the exigencies of technology. Diversities among human beings, cultural, national, ethnic or other have become obsolete: humankind has been reduced to strict uniformity through its service to technology.[5] The superman would be the one who, by instinct or by training, would have a clear and confident perception of how to pursue this process and how to employ things and people in its service. This instinct may set him off from the subman, but the two are alike in being defined by reference to the production process.[6]

In the universe of technology, language as a way of speaking and even of knowing gives way to information, i.e., the ensemble of news that must be known in order to enable the production processes to develop to infinity, but also the ensemble of news that must be disseminated to insure that public opinion enters into these processes. Information *forms* as much as it informs, and, naturally, to the extent that it does so it deforms or distorts. In this age of cybernetics and of its highly multiplied possibilities of information, not only of that transmitted among human beings but also of that now stored in machines, what will be left of man?[7]

The most troubling aspect of this technological world resides perhaps at the level of communication; the market is organized into an immense process of exchange, according to a universally acknowledged system of reckoning, but for whom and for what? Consumption is a process of usury rather than of usage; we use what we have extorted from nature or from man and, on an ever more vast scale, we continue to organize this meaningless process of usury. If a product is lacking, it is simply replaced (*ersatz!*), not so much to respond to a need as to avoid leaving an empty slot in a space which one can always fill, even if one does not know why.[8]

The world of technology is a world of listless wandering where man can no longer find his bearings. The world wars which raged in this world have no more meaning than the peace which follows them. What are we to do with peace after all, and what was the point of going to war in the first place?[9]

The essence of technology

This deplorable portrait, the description of which could be extended indefinitely, should not give rise to lamentations of a moral character, as if the problem lay in the fact that we neglected to do all in our power to keep technology within appropriate limits, or in the fact that we were unable to foster the values or to supply the "soul supplement" that would have been necessary to counterbalance the development of the machine.[10] Heidegger's aim—and this is his great merit—is to undertake a far more penetrating analysis of the situation and he attempts to uncover its profound meaning which goes far beyond an ethical judgment. The ethical judgment, if one is called for, will depend on an investigation which directly links the deplorable concrete aspects we have just seen to more radical dimensions of man—those which have to do with his relationship to Being and to time, and with the history of this relationship. This is what Heidegger is after when he undertakes to go back from technology as instrumentality and manipulation (and he has nothing to say against it at this level) to what he calls the *essence* of technology. And what is this essence? It has to do with the fact that technology is the end of what Heidegger calls "metaphysics";[11] it is the fruit of its long history; it is the point where philosophy "gathers its extreme possibilities,"[12] the end-station of a journey of which Plato marks the starting point and for which he supplies the constant inspiration. If one is not aware of this fact that technology is situated at the terminal point on the long road travelled by metaphysics, it is absolutely impossible for him to understand it and he remains unarmed against its totalitarian penetration.[13] So then, in order to go to the bottom of the problem posed by the expansion of a technology which has become terrifying, we must change the subject slightly or at least link it up to an investigation on metaphysics.[14]

The fate of Western philosophy

To elucidate this connection that exists between technology and metaphysics, I would like to trace in reverse the long historical process which Heidegger calls the "fate of Western philosophy," and thus rediscover the chain of events, at once necessary and fatal, which has brought us to where we are today.

Heidegger employs a strictly untranslatable term *Gestell*[15] to designate the fatal stage to which we have arrived today. This word collects[16] and suggests all the variants of its root, which incarnates (not only in the sense of *expressing*, but also in the sense of *taking flesh in a concrete way*) the process of manipulation, of artificiality, of destructive abstraction which must be conveyed; "stellen": to put down, to place, whether in front or behind, violently or gently; to produce, to extract, to dispose of, to displace, etc.[17] Now all these terms have to do with a certain attitude of the *will*, which has made itself its own end and is constantly referring everything to itself,[18] in a process which paradoxically combines excessiveness (because there is no other rule than pure self will, self interest) and exactness (because, for this aggressive action, it will employ the most coldly calculating reason to its very limit: whence the inflation of the sciences and the lack of restraint in their technological application).[19]

This attitude of the will, turned in on itself and its will to live, goes back to Nietzsche. It was he who tried to show that the basis of reality is a life force, perceptible and vital immediacy, which constructs value fields liberated from all enslavement to rationality and to law. Now this re-centering of reality as a dynamism of a will to live centered on self, a "will to will," a "capacity to return to self, without any conditioning, as to the will to live,"[20] is indeed a *reversal*, an overturning: Nietzsche inherits a world which for ages has been characterized by the rational as an all-powerful force supposed capable of assimilating anything imaginable and any kind of history, be it of the idealist brand of Hegel (the dialectical movement of absolute Spirit) or the materialist variety associated with Marx (the historical process of production), and he reverses this primacy of the rational into a primacy of the will.

From Nietzsche, then, we are sent back to Hegel, whose transcendental idealism appears in its turn as the radical form of a process which began with Descartes; at the dawn of modern times, the awareness that our consciousness has of itself becomes the basis of all certitude.[21] On this basis is built the distinction between subject and object, the real being viewed as both objectified and sustained by consciousness, which thus becomes the ultimate criterion of truth. The reflection of the *Cogito* on itself has for a corollary the primacy of representation, all Being taking the form of the presentation of the object that man supplies for himself on the basis of the certitude of self. Here would be the place to trace the vicissitudes of this construction of reality on the basis of the self-positing of the subject—from Descartes, where the process begins, to Hegel where it is consummated, two important stages, according to Heidegger, being Leibniz, with his principle of sufficient reason and Kant. We will limit ourselves here to the observation that with Hegel the foundation is totally and definitively located in the subject—this at the term of a course of thought which resumes and articulates the unity of Being, thought and history.[22] It is the absolute character of the course followed as well as its subjective rationality that Nietzsche wished to overturn.

However, the current of modernity, set in motion with Descartes, is also, if not the overturning, at least the displacement of a long process that preceded it. Descartes shifted onto the certitude of the *Cogito* what the inspiration of Greek philosophy, still dominant in the Middle Ages, had placed on the manifestation of particular being (*to on*). It is not easy to define the exact meaning of the term "being" in this context. We could say that what is meant is the reality as *revealed, uncovered, placed in the limelight,* made evident and, consequently, made available, "at hand."[23] This manifestation is made possible by the interplay of causes which make beings present, in the diversity of their ideas and of their essences, under the light of a transcendent Good[24] or in accordance with the combined influence of the four causes.[25] Perhaps the analysis supplied by Heidegger of the notions of *world*[26] or of *subject*[27] in Greek thought would clarify this stage of Western philosophy. There is in these terms an aspect of *stance,* of position which gathers and supports: a kind of solidity of the being which reveals itself and appears as a whole guaranteed by the strong bonds of causality. But there is also a dynamic aspect, in the sense that that which collects or supports offers itself to the various beings to ground their becoming. Finally, this presentation of a being become manifest serves here as a foundation for *truth*: the unveiling of a being is the measure of its truth. Looked at from the side of man, truth will then be expressed in terms of the conformity between the thing and the intellect.

It is with Plato that philosophy, according to Heidegger, began to focus on the being thus conceived, in the evidence of its self-manifestation, the clarity of its concept, the offer of its availability.

From this appearing of the being thus conceived with Plato to the absolute spirit of Hegel, the line is continuous; some shifts of emphasis occur in the process, but we ultimately arrive at the total self-manifestation of the being, without remainder and without mystery. The Nietzschean reversal, because it does not fundamentally alter the perspective, reveals the tragic and fatal side of this way of viewing reality which ends with the oppression of man by the *Gestell* and by the social forms which it engenders.

What happened then at the beginning? Answer: philosophy *forgot* the ontological difference, that is to say the fact that the being which stands before us and which we were too quick to seize with the mind and with the hand actually proceeds from *Being*. From the beginning we should have thought through this relationship between a being and Being, this "fold," as Heidegger calls it, which is rendered neither by the concept nor by the representation nor by the self-positing of the self as consciousness, mind or will. This brings us to what is probably the fundamental intuition of Heidegger's work; if there is, in whatever way one might express it, an ontological difference, a non-identity, in the particular being which constantly presents itself to us, between this being itself and Being, this difference should not immediately give way to a mental exercise which would explain it and then instantly explain it away in favor of the being, by means of another and more subtle way of thinking the identity. This is however exactly what took place and it was this that led to the appearance of "metaphysics" and, more generally, of Western philosophy and culture. What happened (and perhaps it had to happen?) is what one could call a faulty shifting, or shunting, a kind of uncoupling or buckling in the manifestation of the being, or—which amounts to the same thing—in the correct evaluation of the ontological difference between Being and the being.[28] While the vital articulation between Being and the being, the fold that binds them together even while keeping them distinct should have remained in the forefront of thought and thus preserved for Being its inventive, originating power, it is instead, with Plato, the being as that which is, as a being, which has come to the fore. No doubt it is seen in the light of Being, and it is this Being itself which still brings the being to presence, but Being as differing from the being in the difference itself, is no longer thought: the forgetting of Being.

Metaphysics could thus be called a logic of the being; it attempts to reflect on the latter at the level of what grounds it, in the most universal way, that is the Being of the being; in this sense it is ontology. But, in an ultimate search for totality, it also strives to rationally establish the foundation itself, which leads it to posit a Supreme Being (Étant) *causa sui*; in this sense it is theology. Now this onto-theological constitution of metaphysics, linked to the initial displacement of which I spoke at the beginning, carried in itself in seed the entire development of the history of Western culture. There is a profoundly coherent line (should we speak here of "fatality"? Heidegger speaks of *fate*) which leads from the ideal appearance of the being in Greek thought since Socrates to the meaningless assault on the resources of nature which characterizes the terminal epoch.[29] It is the analysis of this continuity which allows us to situate the "essence" of technology at the level of "metaphysics": from the moment that the being, that which is, was revealed as it were for its own sake, outside of its vital articulation with Being, it was laying itself open to be grasped (*Begriff*); and it is not long before the apparent gentility of the mental act of conceiving drops its mask and appears as aggression (*Angriff*).[30]

The peril and the salvation

Thus, since the first Platonic forgetting (of Being) the shape of Western philosophy begins to emerge: from the "ontic" stage to the "transcendental" stage and then to the "volontary" stage, this last assuming concrete form in the development of the *Gestell*. This, in a nutshell, is the logic according to which Heidegger views technology as an end or climactic point and it is the reason why he describes it as the terminal mode of the being as it wanders away from Being. This essence of technology thus appears as extremely dangerous. "The *Gestell* deploys its essence as *the* peril."[31] Given this long genealogy and this philosophical consistency, the peril of the *Gestell* is by no means amenable to ethical prescriptions or precautionary measures. I noted above the warnings of Heidegger in this regard.[32] It is not even a matter, if this were but possible, of steering clear of technology; there is no ecological attitude in Heidegger.[33] What then?

We find ourselves confronting here what one could call the "question of the after." It is clear enough that the technological era in which we live cannot have an after, at least not in the same way in which each of the preceding epochs, since Plato, has had its specific after. If there is now to be an *after*, it is not an "after the technological era," but an "after Western civilization." Are we allowed to hope for this and can we venture to imagine what shape this "after" might assume?

Obviously, one cannot expect from Heidegger a "clear and distinct" response! It would seem, however, that a number of constants emerge from the passages where he raises this question, which is truly *the* question of our times.

1. Several times, and with great insistency, Heidegger cites a passage from Hölderlin:

> But where the peril is, there grows
> also that which saves,[34]

and his commentaries on the verse tend to corroborate that it is not a question here of a juxtaposition: to the extent that the peril grows, there would grow likewise, but elsewhere, a saving force which, at the appropriate moment, would triumph over the peril. On the contrary, it is the peril itself or, what amounts to the same thing, the *Gestell* at the limit of the peril it poses, which *may* turn around and reveal itself as that which saves.[35] The most insightful explanation of this possibility is found in the conference appropriately entitled *The Turning* (*Die Kehre*): with the limit of the peril corresponding to the limit character of the *Gestell*, we reach the limit of the concealing of Being, which has been at work since Plato. To the era of peril/*Gestell* corresponds forgetting as forgetting; so, if by a kind of instantaneous turnabout we were able to catch sight of where we are, that is in a state of absolute forgetfulness, then the very thing that has been forgotten would manifest itself: the apocalypse of Being in a lightning flash. One would have to have gone to the extreme limit of the distress, of the peril—to a situation where there would no longer be a mixture which could deceive—to *make it possible* for forgetfulness to be revealed as forgetfulness, which amounts to saying that it is this process itself which opens up the epiphany of Being.[36]

2. I have stressed the words *may*, *possible*. Indeed, the second constant in the reflection of Heidegger is the realization that it does not belong to us to activate this turnabout. Only Being itself can suddenly recommence to shine at the moment of ultimate distress. We should take time here to comment on the different statements of Heidegger that express this initiative which is not our own. In the *Question of Technology*, "that which reconciles" grows at the same time as that

which provokes and that which exploits; the *Gewährt* is more ancient than the *Gestell* and the *Gefahr*, and we can observe, we can see up to the point where. . . . [37] Heidegger's *Overtaking of Metaphysics* ends with a kind of presentiment of the Ereignis "which conducts certain mortals along the pathway of the ponderous and poetic abode."[38] In the *Why Poets?* it is the infinitely vast circle of the Open which has "touched" those who, more than others, have entered into the abyssal depth of distress.[39] In *The Turning*, it is Being which suddenly shines forth, and then looks towards us, and it is into its gaze that we gaze.[40] One is reminded of Psalm 35 (36): "in your light, we see light. . . . " Thus, if salvation is to come, its advent will take place through the "grace" of Being at the ultimate moment of the peril of the being.

3. This growing salvation, if it bears fruit at all, affects "some mortals." The two terms merit comment. *Some*, that is, not all—but then who? Those "who were first to reach the abyss of indigence and of distress,"[41] who have gone farthest into the peril? No doubt, but also those—the same people, to be sure—who have a presentiment of the paths that lead nowhere, the only ones that Being follows: the people who think reflectively, who reason like Paschal,[42] the poets, the men of expectation. Without excluding themselves from the peril, which they experience perhaps more acutely than anyone else, they allow something to arise, at the very heart of the peril—something which, perhaps, will reveal itself. *Mortals*: the term defines exactly the people we have just been talking about: "What is important is not the fact that we live by the presence of atoms, but rather that we be able to be the mortals that we are, that is people who remain under the call of Being. Only this kind of living being is capable of dying, that is to say, of taking on death as death."[43] Why is it that "remaining under the call of Being" means being "mortal"? What is the meaning of "death as death"? Rilke replies: "Death is the *side of life* which is turned away from us, which is not elucidated, explained by us."[44] The widest circle of Being, the Parmedian sphere, the Open (these terms are equivalent) has its hidden side. Hidden from whom? From those of calculating reason, from life in the state of perpetual aggression toward nature and toward man. Perceived by whom? By those who meditate and wait, knowing that what is hidden will reveal itself so that the unity of the two faces may be made manifest. The "mortal" is not then the one who will necessarily pass away one day from life to death; he is

one who today stands under the hidden side or face, under the call of Being, under the touch of death thus understood. In this sense, the "mortal" is also the one who consents, as opposed to the one who wills. He is, equivalently, the man of *Gelassenheit*.[45]

One is thus allowed a presentiment of salvation: a kind of reversal which one may rightly expect, if one analyzes the basis of forgetfulness, but one whose coming does not in any way depend on man. The latter can at the most allow himself to assume the posture of awaiting. But we do not know any more; the categories of "transition"[46] which Heidegger employs to suggest the figure of the "world" and of the "thing" under the illumination of Being do not amount to prophetic descriptions or advance notices, and they remain in any case outside of any religious field. We are still in the technological era; some among us are able to keep ourselves under the call of Being, but what is to happen next?

If, in spite of its summary character, this presentation is not too inaccurate, it should enable us to draw the following conclusions: the agony of an *imminent* after, for which no figure can be discerned, is related by Heidegger to a basic metaphysical attitude, which remains the same even if it has become more and more decadent in the course of a history which is just as much that of human culture and human activity as it is that of thought. We have *lost time* because we have *forgotten Being*.

At the point to which we have arrived today, there is, however, a hope, that of a truly total turnabout of the situation, at the very moment when this has reached a paroxysm of absurdity—a turnabout which, from the side of man, requires a waiting for that which is to be *given* but which one can in no way prepare oneself to grasp, because grasping or comprehending would still belong to the metaphysical attitude. We know then neither what will happen nor how we ourselves will be involved in it; we know only that the stakes are immense, for the subject of this total turnabout, is none other than the global space of Western civilization. It is perhaps not even possible to formulate any kind of a rational foundation for our hope, because the terms employed in this process would again belong to the era of metaphysics and of technology. Once again, all we can do is to remain under the call of *Being*, in silent awaiting for that which can only be *donation* and in which the true figure of *time* will also be received. At this point, it seems that we would rediscover *death*, for is not this attitude of awaiting, this remaining in a place and for an object neither of which are clearly defined—is not this very awaiting the consent to a fundamental mortality, to the death of the autonomy of every *being* satisfied with its pure presence to self?

I will come back to Heidegger at the end of this chapter and at the end of this part, and also at the beginning of the third part of this book. A single question will be posed here, in anticipation of further critical observations: if the technological era does not know an *after*, does the *gift* of time and of Being which we await have a *before*, or are we to conceive of salvation as a *pure beginning*, forever unconnected with anything that might have preceded it?

2. "The unnameable recurrence which is to come. . . ."

So the resolution to the alarming question of the after is linked, in Heidegger, to a reading at once historical and philosophical of the Western cultural tradition, on the one hand, and on the other, to a hope, strong in its determination but weak as to its object—a hope for the new figure, desired and at the same time unforeseeable, of time and of Being.

Even this hope, tenuous as it is, may appear still too presumptuous, and the philosophical analysis which authorizes it too quickly closed. A still more radical path has been caught sight of by some, and we must follow its course here, not for the pleasure of having made as complete a turn as possible in the contemporary cultural landscape, but because of the human and moral repercussions that it entails.

In the perspective which concerns us here, one could synthesize the reflection of Heidegger by saying that our era is sick from too much "presence": its present is as it were cancerous and devours all the spacing of time and all the mystery of Being; nevertheless, a new era will intervene—perhaps. A contemporary writer like Jacques Derrida would go further, would undertake a far more radical critique of presence. It is not even a question here of a critique, properly speaking, for this word itself expresses a certain judgment and suggests a possible reform; consequently, it implies that there is a place from which one could utter a decisive word on time or at least wait for such a word. What we will find then in Derrida is what has conveniently been called a "deconstruction." The shattering of presence will here be such that it will simultaneously sweep away every conceivable reference point and will bring about the total shipwreck both of the past and of the future: it is the totality of time which will be irreparably lost.

In another way than Heidegger[47]

Derrida discerns in Heidegger and adopts, at least at an initial stage and in a kind of provisional way, the primacy of the intuition of Being: at a radical level, beyond all ontology or metaphysics, where this intuition informs all language in an absolute way, where Being, which is in no way a predicate, is that without which no sentence can be constructed: an indispensable verb, but beyond any determinate rational content or logos, the "supplement of copula" without which no one could say anything, but about which no one can say anything, even though one would love in a sense to know everything and to be able to say everything. This is because Being never happens for its own sake; it never happens except as individual being and as present: at the very moment when it produces a being and when the being so to speak takes shelter in it, it disappears, it fades away, it is forgotten. It is there only in the form of a faded trace. Should one say that it reveals itself as presence of the present, and that the ontological difference offers itself to be thought in this way, as the difference between the present and its presence? No, because when we employ this terminology we are still in the semantic field of the being (*l'étant*), not in that which is proper to Being (*l'être*): presence as presence of the present is but the inscription, in ontological terms, of that which is not of the ontological order but which only comes out in the vocabulary of the ontological difference. The idea of presence is not the idea of Being; it is the trace of faded Being. One could say that it is the pure indicative of that which cannot be indicated, of that which remains at the horizon of all linguistic expression without itself being the object of any such expression.

Now, with this as the starting point, two ways can perhaps open up: the first is that of Heidegger; this way appears to remain on the inside of the ontological difference: it would be that of persevering, enduring in the thinking of Being, awaiting or perhaps risking a language where Being might be disclosed and where that which speaks in every linguistic expression might be able to say itself as well: the waiting for Being as the proper name (but it is possible that the proper name in question is not Being at all, if it is true that Being always vanishes when it comes to be as a being). The second way would consist in going beyond the ontological difference, in attempting to think beyond the presence, to reach, by way of and in all the individual differences, a *différance*, more "originating" even than the ontological difference between Being and the being, one of which the ontological difference would be no more than a manifestation, a gesture (*un geste*), a style—that of our western culture.[48] This *différance* would not be difference between terms, it would be on this side of presence (and hence also of absence). How are we to speak of it?

It is this second way, in any case, that Derrida would like, if not to employ, because it did not exist before him, at least to help to describe. In doing so, he situates himself explicitly at the extreme limit of that contemporary cultural talk which, in varying degrees and from perspectives which can vary, radically questions what one could call a constellation of the presence whose elements all form part of an ordered system; what we have here, in the wake of Heidegger but going further than he went, is a shattering of an ontology which, "in its most interior course, has defined the sense of Being as presence and the sense of language as full continuity of the word," but it is also a question, with Lévinas, of acceding to the primacy and to the solicitation of the other, as absolute otherness, which also amounts to a critique of classical ontology; one must concur with and even go beyond Nietzsche and Freud in the effective suspicion they launched against the idea of the pure awareness of self, an approach which runs parallel to another which would be a rigorous critique of the *Cogito*, from Husserl back to Descartes. . . . [49] At the end of the whole process, one would have to counter a mentality of presence, of awareness and of Being with a mentality of the trace, of the difference and of the totally other. In this perspective, it is clear that there could be no question of even the most tentative eschatological or protological discourse; one would find oneself, so to speak, always already "aboard" without knowing what boat one was on, with stops along the way perhaps, but with no home port nor destination. All the stars which make up this constellation of presence are extinguished together: the privilege of the voice, which is the form par excellence of presence, disappears, and with it, step by step, the entire system of signification and hence the very idea of a meaning; the word which the voice pronounces par excellence, the word *Being*, falls apart to the extent that it is nothing but the pure affirmation of presence; the fall of ontology entails that of all theology, God talk being closely linked with the economy of signification; but even history can no longer be put into words, if it is true that temporalization has no meaning except with reference to the present, which is radically denied any primacy here. As for the awareness of self, its claim has long since been shown to be illusory.[50]

As Derrida remarks in his essay on *La Différance*,[51] it is difficult to know where to begin in introducing a mentality of deconstruction, for the sketch can only be "strategic and adventurous": since there is no fixed point of reference, enjoying any kind of transcendence, the writing can only be strategic, a strategem aimed at approaching that which can only escape any attempt at being grasped; it can only be adventurous, because the very idea of an end which would be pursued and would thus direct the enterprise is part of what needs to be "deconstructed." The procedure depends on a *game*, I would like to say on a "navigation by sight" which, contrary to what its name suggests, is the art of steering a boat when the visibility is zero. A second difficulty, likewise emphasized at a theoretical level and which the very practice of deconstruction constantly comes up against, is the fact that if it is necessary to speak or to write in order to "deconstruct," then one is as it were constrained to remain within the very system one is trying to abandon, for the whole system of words and of concepts imposes itself as the only tool of expression. This fact gives rise to the frequent practice of the "erasure," which is a graphic way of expressing what is wrong with the procedure from the start: always having to say what one would prefer not to say: finding "the words to say it" and immediately emphasizing that they are constitutionally improper.[52]

Under these conditions, every order of exposition is as good as another, and together they are perhaps worth nothing at all. I will speak first of all of the deconstruction of meaning, then of the collapse of time and finally of the definitive shattering of ontotheology.

The deconstruction of meaning

In spite of what was said above, it is perhaps through reflection on speech (voice, concept, word . . .) that one can best approach this "deconstruction" of philosophy and of culture.[53] The logos is in fact precisely the ally of onto*logy* (and vice versa), as it is also of the awareness of self, located in the *I* which speaks, and of time measured on the basis of the *present* word. If language discloses its radical frailty, it is the entire complex of human thought that is thus shattered.

It is at the very root of language, or speech, that the process of deconstruction begins to appear, at that mysterious point where the human voice and the idea, the phonetic and the conceptual, reveal themselves together and at the same time, without our being able to know exactly how to distinguish or relate them. The basic reference here is to the linguistic theories of Saussure,[54] who is the source for two central elements of the analysis of the sign—the arbitrary and the "differential"[55]—on the basis of which the dislocation of signification can be brought to light. Let us review this analysis very briefly. There is no "natural" necessity that links a given sound to a given meaning, a given complex of phonemes to a given conceptual content, a given acoustical image to a given idea, or, to finally use the accepted terms, a given "signifying" to a given "signified." In itself, this assertion has nothing revolutionary or deconstructive about it. With more or less important differences, it runs through the analysis of language since Aristotle—at least if one takes it in the sense that there is no natural link between the word and the thing which it represents through the mediation of the concept. In a sense, Benveniste takes up this assertion in the most classical manner when he clarifies and corrects the theory of Saussure and says that it applies to the relation of the sign to the thing rather than to that of the oral signifying to its mental correspondent, the latter pair being as inseparable as the two sides of a sheet of paper.[56]

Deconstruction appears (at least in principle) at the moment when one focuses on this arbitrary character of the sign, as a kind of separation between the signifying and the signified, a liberation of the signifying with respect to any conceptual content to which it would have been more or less necessarily linked, or again, as a rupture between the field of signification and the world of reference; one could say again, as a floating of the signifying element with respect to the signified and hence as a certain autonomy of the former. Indeed, it is evident enough that, if the signifying element has a certain autonomy, it is going to be necessary on the one hand to take it seriously and on the other (but this is perhaps another way of saying the same thing) to review the whole theory of signification which since time immemorial has been based on the continuity of the signifying with the signified and of the sign thus constituted with the thing.

It is here that the other aspect of the analysis of Saussure comes in: the differential character of the sign. "In language," says Derrida following Saussure, "there are only differences without positive terms," such that, if a signification emerges, it does so solely through the game of articulation and spacing of differences; however far one pushes the analysis, one finds only this movement, which assembles and takes apart, without anything being able to display a value in itself, independently of the arrangement game. As in micro- or astral-physics (and the fact that these particular examples are used is not without significance), meaning is found only in the more or less random constellation of elements which come together and drift apart, without fixed point or value.

The following consequences, in what pertains to the process of signification in general, may be drawn from this autonomy of the signifying:

1. If the signifying is arbitrary, there is no reason to privilege one type of signifying over another. In particular, the privilege which is accorded to the spoken language, to the voice as present, is shown to be without foundation.[57] The word has no more intrinsic dignity than writing, nor does phonetic writing have it over the ideogram or writing in general over any other kind of plastic signification. If we had to look for a kind of fundamental principle governing signification, we would have to look beyond any particular sign, in what one could call, if one wished, the "*gram*," while knowing that this *gram* itself can never strictly speaking be grasped; it is (if the word *is* has any meaning in this context)[58] that which is at work in every process of signification, and which condemns to failure every effort to absolutize any possible action of this process.

2. If the signifying is differential, if there is no stable unity of sound and of meaning, no indivisible correspondence between expression and content, but if instead the signifying elements just keep coming together in an unstable manner, then it is no longer possible to assign the origin of meaning to any signified nor to any signifying. Signs send meanings back and forth in a game without beginning and without end, without there being any "absolute simplicity" at the beginning and without there being any particular *telos* toward which one is moving. This renunciation at the beginning and this always-already-there (which is also just as much a never-yet-there) of the signifying game is expressed by Derrida by means of a variety of terms. That to

which the signifying game ultimately refers is an "archi-synthesis,"[59] the prefix *archi-* referring, to be sure, to an idea of beginning, but the term *synthesis* saying, precisely, that this beginning or principle is merely the dynamic in perpetual motion of all the signifying systems. The term "archi-trace"[60] is also employed in this connection implying an "unmotivated becoming of signs"; here again the prefix *archi-* is meant to indicate that, in suppressing the imaginary theme of a beginning, one does not however wish to suggest anarchy and non-sense, but the word *trace* (is it really a word?) opposes its unmotivated and elusive becoming to the unfaulted fullness of what was formerly viewed as an originating presence. In other words, since, as I have already pointed out, we have at our disposal, for speaking and writing, only a language culturally constructed on the basis of logical and metaphysical presuppositions, it is difficult for us to avoid the question of the origin; and we cannot content ourselves either, once the question has been posed, with answering it in the negative, because a pure and simple negation would remain in the domain defined by the opposite affirmation: a solution will consist then in juxtaposing two irreconcilables: *archi-trace*. The prefix *archi-* maintains for the *trace* thus proposed an originating character, but of an origin which can in no way be said and which, for this very reason, one "erases." The erasure is the expedient (of which one cannot yet know if it is only provisional) to allude to that which is to be signified, as we exit from the cultural field which however supplies us with its problems and its terms. Derrida also refers to this impossible beginning as "différance,"[61] a term which is "neither a word, nor a concept,"[62] whose specificity with respect to "difference" cannot be heard and which itself challenges the privilege of the voice and of speech; he describes it as

> the movement of play that "produces' "—by means of something that is not simply an activity—these differences, these effects of difference. . . . *Différance* is the non-full, non-simple, non-structured and differentiating "origin" of differences. Thus, the name "origin" no longer suits it. . . . The movement according to which language, or any code, any system of referral in general, is constituted "historically" as a weave of differences.[63]

A reference to the Freudian distinction between the principle of pleasure and the principle of reality, and to the "economic detour" which one must make through the second in order to rediscover the first enables Derrida to clarify his thought. In the *différance*, there is indeed *detour*, but not *in order to*, not as a *ruse*; it is detour as it were in the pure state, "*différance* as the relation to an impossible presence, as expenditure without reserve, as the irreparable loss of presence, the irreversible usage of energy, that is, as death instinct, and as the entirely other relationship that apparently interrupts every economy."[64] There is no origin of signification.[65]

3. The *I* of "I think" thus finds itself effaced; not more than anything else, for the subject has neither special position nor privilege; it is built into the *différance* of which it is merely a moment. The *Cogito* which poses as an ultimate and founding reference of presence and of Being is in reality a word of death.[66] In reality, the speaking subject is always already built into the moving system of signifying differences, that of the word and others, and from what outside vantage point could one discern a founding subject, before the event of word or signification?[67] The "I think" indicates first of all its own participation in the "originating and non-simple" thought game; in other words, as *I*, it signifies its death, its ephemeral character, its disappearance—already there because very near. The *I*, even in the moment in which it is uttered, is no more than the temporary emergence of the *differance*. There is no pure presence to self.

4. In these perspectives, it is the very idea of signification which is subverted, deconstructed, to the extent that this idea classically implies a subject in the act of signifying, through the mediation of a "sign of," of a representation, a situated referent. The sign, on the contrary, from the point of view of its arbitrary and differential aspects, has as it were a life of its own which refers to nothing at all, except perhaps to the movement which keeps endlessly producing it.

Collapse of time

One is perhaps bound to say the same things if one attempts to specify with what *time* we are dealing within the perspective opened by the deconstruction of signification. One is at the heart of the matter, because the question is one of reducing the inflation of the present in the culture. From the point of view, already, of a phenomenology of time, Derrida had shown, against Husserl, the illusion of a pure awareness of the present, and had pointed out that in every perception of the present, we find also the past and the future, which are there by "retention and protention"; now, far from considering these elements as disturbing as it were the purity of the present, one should view them as "originating" and should as it were overturn the claim for the present by a confession of pure repetition, that is to say of the *différance*:

> Repetition, trace in the most universal sense, is a possibility which should not only inhabit the pure event of the now, but should constitute it by the very movement of the *différance* which it introduces into it.[68]

This overturning is of considerable consequence: it aims at nothing less than the undermining of a linear view of time, which Heidegger calls "the popular conception of time,"[69] dominated by the consciousness of the present. As Derrida understands it, "temporization," which overturns the primacy of the present, is not "a simple dialectical complication of the living present as an originating and unceasing synthesis—a synthesis constantly directed back on itself, gathered in on itself and gathering—of retentional traces and protentional openings";[70] if it were only this, it would be no more than a modality of that cancerous present of which I spoke above. Should we give primary attention to the future and the past, viewing presence only in the footprints of which it is not the origin and for which it does not even constitute a landmark? This is perhaps what we should do, but we have no word to express the total overturning; in fact, time both as a concept and as a term disappears if, as Derrida says at the end of a long historical analysis devoted to the question of time, "time is that which is thought on the basis of Being as presence and if something—which bears a relation to time, but is not time—is to be thought beyond the determination of Being as presence, it cannot be a question of something that still could be called time,"[71] so that "perhaps there is no 'popular concept of time.' The concept of time, in all its aspects, belongs to metaphysics and it names the domination of presence."[72] This brings us back to the Freudian theme of the "delayed action," but of a delay which never goes away and in which we remain. Thus, instead of being referred to Being, we are referred to death. Perhaps the primary thing intended by the erasing of the popular concept of time is in fact this reference to death as a concrete structure of the living present. The present is an ephemeral emergence of a movement which is "essentially testamentary."[73] The correlative, in fact, of linear time is eternity, a total fullness, the truth attained and identity finally liberated from any exterior, any outside. The correlative of temporization, in the volatile and unmotivated world of signs, is death, as paradoxical horizon of all production of meaning.

It follows from these brief remarks on the deconstruction of presence, after that of meaning and in conjunction with it, that the concept of *history* no longer retains any more truth and substance than does that of *episteme*—precisely to the extent that history strives to thematize duration in the perspective of a return of presence.[74] History, even within a perspective which one could qualify here as hermeneutical, always consists, if you take into account the variables that occur, in the "reconstituting, according to another configuration, of the same system."[75] What is really needed is to return, beyond this repetition of the "same," to the pure otherness which characterizes the trace, to that " 'past' that has never been present"[76] of which Lévinas speaks and, one could say, to that future which will never come to pass or at least which cannot in any way be anticipated.

The shaking of ontology

The deconstruction of meaning and the collapse of time are also the shaking of ontology, and of the theology which is linked to this ontology. And vice-versa. We must understand *shaking* in the strong sense: "It is the domination of beings that *différance* everywhere comes to solicit, in the sense that *sollicitare*, in Latin, means to shake as a whole, to make tremble in entirety." An earthquake is what we are talking about. And this can hardly surprise us if we assume a mutual interplay between the terms sign, time and being.

The arbitrary character of the signifying marks the abolition of the metaphysical and of the theological. If, indeed, this arbitrary character extends to all the fields of signification which show up against the horizon of an unmotivated trace, then the privilege of the word disappears and, with it, the primacy of the Logos, which founds all metaphysics and all theology. However considerable may be the divergences between the schools and the authors, every word which expresses in the here and now a concept signified implies a reference to an infinite *Logos* which is the source at once of the existing reality and of the signification, and of the existing reality before the signification; between the referent of the sign, the *res*, and the divine *Logos*, there is a relation which is anterior to the recognition and to the signification of this referent by a human signifying. The signifying which corresponds to the signified and the latter to the *res* find their ultimate ground in the divine *Logos*. To isolate the signifying from the signified and to view the language game, the game of the signifying elements, as having no other origin than that of the *archi-trace* and of the movement of the *différance* is obviously to shake a metaphysics and a theology of full presence to their foundations: "That the signified should be *trace* originally and essentially (and not only for a finite and created mind), that it should be always already in signifying position, this is the apparently innocent proposition in which the metaphysics of *logos*, of presence and of consciousness, should reflect the writing as its death and its resource."[77]

Another way of saying the same thing consists in deconstructing the concept of *Positive Infinity*[78] as a description of God in the classical theologies. If indeed one thinks one has found in the *gram* the "originating principle" (which is neither principle nor originating) from which there continuously springs up the game of all the significative and expressive differences, whether they be phonetic, graphic or plastic, then otherness remains irreducible; there is always a possible "supplement" at every level of signification. Whatever it might "be," the infinite can only allow itself to be thought from the side of this "supplement"; it can only be other, totally other, or better, always other. One cannot gather it into a pure and total Presence to self; it is on the side of the unthinkable-unutterable-impossible. In this sense, the statement of Lévinas which consists in envisaging a Positive Infinity as opposed to the Totality has something contradictory about it. If one wishes to speak of infinity, one must proceed from the side of pure otherness; one is then outside of presence and outside of discourse; this would be a more consistent attitude than that which would wish to ground language on the in-finite, which, as the word suggests, is and can only remain a negative attribute. To bring things out in a more striking way, one could say that the infinite is mortal or that there is nothing of the immortal in it, because it is a game without beginning or end of *différance* continuously giving rise to differences. The name God is perhaps no more than a concealment of death through the effacement of differences. And this is why, when confronted with reality, it offers no meaning. As for the infinite, one can just as well call it *originating finitude*, and this equation is just one more example of the deconstruction of language; neither *infinite* nor *finite* has any real relevance.

Sketchy and elementary as they may be, the above summaries of deconstruction theory suffice to suggest how broad is the terrain that it covers, as is corroborated by a synthetic passage such as the one which follows:

> Such a *différance* would at once, again, give us to think a writing without presence and without absence, without history, without cause, without *archia*, without *telos*, a writing that absolutely upsets all dialectics, all theology, all teleology, all ontology. A writing exceeding everything that the history of metaphysics has comprehended in the form of the Aristotelian *gramme*, in its point, in its line, in its circle, in its time and in its space.[79]

If this is so, the theme of the *différance* reveals itself as *tragic*[80] or, more exactly, reveals to us the time and space in which we firmly believe we live as always already cracked by an abyssal break which even the most supposedly purified conception of Being (like that of Heidegger), can in no way fill in. If we retain our old way of thinking, things will follow their fatal course, but if we consent to the *différance*, will we have the courage not to turn away our eyes before the unnameable recurrence which announces itself, and yet can do so, as necessarily happens every time that a birth gets under way, only under the species of the non-species, under the mute, silent (*infante*), terrifying and formless form of the monstrosity?[81]

Conclusion

I have cited Heidegger and Derrida. Other authors might have been cited—contemporaries like Lévinas or Lévi-Strauss, earlier writers like Nietzsche and Freud. We have seen moreover that Derrida wanted to go to the root of the criticism leveled by his predecessors at "metaphysics" and at the era it dominated. A philosophical *koine* exists, whose common denominator would be the rejection of a "compact thinking," the kind of thinking defined by the people of the metaphysical era—a kind of ideology which accompanied and justified the excess of their triumphalistic endeavor. Let us take time here to briefly review its general characteristics.

Philosophy without death, or the compact order of the totality

The intuition which governs this "philosophy without death" could be described in a general way as that of *full presence*: a perception of a gathering, in the now, as much as possible, of everything that can be an object of Being, of thought and of action, so that the other dimensions of time take on meaning by way of reference to this overarching presence and so that there never lacks a reasoned explanation for absence; a gathering, on the other hand, as globally inclusive as possible, such as would be signified by a term like *cosmos*, in the sense of an ordered and positively unlimited totality (or one limited only by itself). Thus, just as there is no period of time which cannot be reduced to presence, neither can there be any chink in space which cannot be reduced to the full occupation of a place without remainder. According to the various standpoints one may assume, this cast of mind yields, in very schematic form: in *metaphysics*, an overall view of substance as an absolutely primary datum of Being and, correlatively, the definition of its situation and the tabulating of its alterations by way of the all-embracing, necessary and sufficient grid of the four causes, which explain everything without remainder. At the level of *knowledge*, we enter the world of the Logos, namely, that of the entirely thinkable character of substance. Through the mediation of the concept, substance can be said by the word, so that neither in content nor in presence is there any discrepancy or distance between that which is and that which is said—the process of truth, *adaequatio intellectus et rei*, which removes all gaps, fills in all distance. If, in parallel fashion, we were to talk about *action*, its whole meaning comes from an effort of reduction between the remoteness or absence of the object and the need that one feels of it; the whole practical order works at this reduction, whether at the lower levels of production and of consumption or at the higher, which, without specifying further, one could call the levels of culture. If the modes of action are diverse, the diversity comes from the specific objects and desires, but the intention to achieve presence is ever the same. If it is a question of *certitude*, that is to say of incontestable possession of one's knowledge as well as of one's action, the function of the *Cogito*, which could be described as paroxystic affirmation of presence, is precisely to guarantee both presence to oneself and the validity of that which re-presents itself, thus supporting the claims of truth and of substance. Even *history* can be taken as totality, all the more surely if one perceives it as the dialectical movement leading to absolute spirit which reconciles substance and subject, but even if one sees it as the historical process of production which unceasingly, be it at the price of successive revolutions, reabsorbs social differences and tends toward the abolition of contradiction. And finally, in whatever way one approaches "God," whether he be viewed as origin, end or guarantee, it is as final ratio and ultimate ground of this totality of presence that he is posited and rendered knowable, his eternity grounding and insuring moreover the immortality of man—the final protestation of philosophy against death. The major problem faced by this thinking of full presence is, to be sure, that of *evil*, but is it not possible to "fit this also into the universal order"? Does not hell itself, whether that of Plato or that of St. Augustine, find its ultimate justification in a total *order* of justice, where the real and concrete suffering of the damned is cancelled for the just in the contemplation of an abstract justice?

The above paragraph could serve as a profile, in broad outline, of what today, following the terminology of Heidegger, has come to be called *onto-theo-logy*. A few remarks are in order before going on. This profile certainly follows an inner logic, such that it seems at first sight difficult to take what you want of it and leave the rest; but this logic is built up as it were *negatively*: the very description of ontotheology is offered us by people who have left it completely! Whatever foundation there may be for its allegations, the description comes in as a background for something else, that is to say, for the promotion of ideas which have a different orientation and which presumably intend to take into account what ontotheology conceals. In this sense, supposing for the moment that it is in fact legitimate to say that from Plato to Hegel, to Nietzsche, indeed even to Heidegger (for the closure of metaphysics seems to recede as the generations go by and it seems that there is always a young upstart to reproach his immediate predecessor with still being in the grips of ontotheology), philosophy belongs to ontotheology, one must, in each case, strive to see how. It could possibly happen that, in concrete cases, the logic of the profile would have to yield somewhat to the reality of a particular philosophical journey.

Critique: restore "death"

This methodological remark was necessary to "qualify" as it were the description of a philosophy of full presence. It does not however call into question the general drift of the description. It also enables us to understand something the reasons for which we have seen by entering into more precise analyses, namely that the thinkers who denounce this thrust of presence are not seeking to come to terms with it, to rectify, by supplying neglected or forgotten elements, the systems it has managed to produce. Their intention is rather to abandon it and to set out on other paths. Paths not illuminated by presence nor by fullness: in time, to let night come into play, where one knows not what time it is and where waiting, deprived of any landmarks, does not know what dawn will arrive and will know this perhaps only after it happens, beyond despair; in space, to give a greater role to the empty spaces, to the blanks, to the marking of time, the unpredictable of journeys where the revelation is in the movement itself rather than in what the eye takes in; in word, to hear the music and the silences, the game of words rather than any definite signification attached to them; in action, to respect the unmotivated, the endeavor, the temporary, the tentative; as for certitudes—that of the self and that of what it represents to itself or what it imagines—to simply renounce them in favor of a waiting—for a gift to be returned as soon as it is received. Of history, what can be said but that it is traced or it traces itself, deriving from the future as well as from the past—but who knows its paths? Nowhere in its course is it to efface the deficits, the blunders, the surprises and the things which are completely incomprehensible. As for substance, to consistently treat it as less important than relation, than intersubjective dealings and differences. On every level, in sum, to allow that which had been concealed or forgotten to return: that which, precisely, one could designate by a single term: *death*, that negative image or mould which is always there and to which alone, paradoxically, presence could be applied; by respecting this death, could not one develop an art of living and of thinking, more modest, more realistic—the only style of life which could ultimately stamp out the other death, that which is constantly and very really occasioned and produced by our determination to fill in all the gaps as if we were immortal?

It is not necessary to dwell at length on the importance of this inquiry, nor on the authenticity of its inspiration. The entire aim of the present book is to listen to these questions, to verify whether the Catholic tradition has lost sight of them or not, to strive to find out how to answer them in a way that would not amount to an evacuating of their basic intention. I will return then at length to these points in the pages that follow. For the moment, however, we have only to observe that the *koine* here described calls everything so strongly into question that it hardly provides people *of this time* with a *concrete* modus vivendi. The unqualified "no" directed at the entire destiny of western philosophy, the "erasure" imposed on an entire culture does not favor the construction of an *ethics*, personal and collective, in view of tomorrow and for today. The authors we have questioned remain ultimately mute if we put to them in turn the three questions formulated by Kant: the first (what can one know?) appears immediately irrelevant; if the general principle of reciprocity and of exchange can in principle supply a foundation for the second (what should I do?), it threatens to remain entirely inoperative: at the level of generality at which it is formulated, the principle of exchange can just as well support the second commandment of the Gospel as the immediate revolution of Baudrillard— and so, which of the two should one choose and why? One can hardly say either that we find in these authors a response to the third question: for what are we allowed to hope? First of all, the *what* remains entirely indeterminate and nothing allows us to specify it even the tiniest little bit; then too, is it really *allowed* to hope: where would the permission come from in the view of our authors? And finally, *who* is in a position to hope? Some mortals, says Heidegger—but as for the rest of us?

Notes

1. "Überwindung der Metaphysik," in *Vorträge und Aufsätze* (Tübingen 1954) 2nd ed. 1954, pp. 71-99, (cited *VA*), p. 72.
2. "Die Frage nach der Technik," in *VA*, 13-44, here p. 22.
3. *VA*, p. 23ff.
4. *VA*, p. 25 and 92. Cf also "Wozu Dichter?" in *Holzwege* sixth edition, (Frankfurt am Main, 1980), p. 285.
5. *VA*, 96-97.
6. *VA*, 94.
7. *VA*, p. 25-26; *Holzwege*, p. 285. Cf. also *Der Satz vom Grund*, (Pfüllingen, 1986), pp. 230ff (cited *SG*).
8. *VA*, p. 92; *Holzwege*, p. 288.
9. "Die Erde erscheint als die Unwelt der Irrnis," *VA*, p. 97; war and peace, *VA*, p. 92f.
10. A part of the conference, in *SG* is devoted to a discussion of the significance of an expression like: faced with technology, "everything depends

on us," that is, as to whether or not it remains human (*SG*, pp. 198ff.). Cf. Also *VA*, 14-15; *Holzwege*, p. 286.

11. This is said in all the texts which treat formally the question of technology. To the texts referred to above, one could add, for example, "Das Ende der Philosophie und die Aufgabe des Denkens" in *Zur Sache des Denkens*, (cited *ZS*) Pfüllingen, 2nd ed. 1976, 61-80, cf. p. 64.

12. *Ibid.*, *ZS*, p. 63ff.

13. For the entire following section, cf. Michel Haar, "Heidegger et l'essence de la technique," in *Études germaniques*, 32 (1977), 299-316, especially sections 3 and 4. For this whole study I found very useful the analysis by Reiner Schürmann of the "retrospective categories" employed by Heidegger, in the *Le Principe d'anarchie* (Paris, 1982), pp. 222-244.

14. Heidegger frequently portrayed this fate of Western philosophy such as he envisioned it: for example, in "Überwindung der Metaphysik," sections IV-VII and XIV-XVIII, *VA*, 73-77 and 84-87; in the conference "Le nihilisme européen," II, see p. 105-119. A very suggestive visual outline of the interpretation that Heidegger gives of the history of Being may be found in the fragment entitled "L'être," published in the *Projets pour l'histoire de l'être en tant que métaphysique* in *Nietzsche*, v. II (cited *N II*), p. 379-380.

15. Haar, *art. cit.*, p. 305, note 17, discusses the translations attempted by various authors and holds to that of André Préau: "arraisonnement." The translators of the famous conference "Die Kehre," in French, "Le Tournant" in *Questions IV* (Paris, 1976), pp. 142-157 prefer instead to leave the word untranslated and they justify this decision on p. 155, note 1.

16. Heidegger himself points out the signification of this gathering in *VA*, p. 27, comparing *Gebirg*, *Gemüt*, and *Gestell*.

17. On purpose, in very short spaces of text, Heidegger accumulates all the derivatives of *stellen*. For example, Die Kohre (Pfüllingen, 1962), pp. 37ff. *Holzwege*, p. 284; this is obviously difficult to reproduce in translation.

18. *VA*, pp. 88-89.

19. *SG*, pp. 197-202. Exactness corresponds at the final stage of metaphysics to the *certitude* of the preceding epoch. Calculating thought "assures" the will to will in its undertakings. One could say, therefore, (but I have not found a text in which Heidegger himself says so explicitly) that, while initially a matter of correspondence, or *adequation*, truth later becomes *certitude*, and finally manifests itself as *calculation*.

20. *VA*, p. 76.

21. *VA*, p. 84-85.

22. Cf. *Identität und Differenz* (Tübingen, 1957), p. 49f. But cf. the note of Michel Haar on the "complex relationship" of Heidegger to Hegel, *art. cit.*, p. 300, n. 7.

23. "At hand": *vorhanden*. Cf. below, Part III, chap. I, note 7.

24. Cf. "Platons Lehre von der Wahrheit," *Wegmarken*, Gesamtausgabe, Band 9 (Frankfurt, 1976), p. 203f.

25. *VA*, pp. 14-19.

26. Cf. *Ce qui fait l'être-essentiel d'un fondement ou "raison"* (a periphrasis of Henry Corbin to translate *Vom Wesen des Grundes*, in *Questions I*, p. 112-113).

27. *Nietzsche*, v. II, *op. cit.*, pp. 429-436.

28. *Ibid.*, p. 209.

29. *VA*, 77-78.

30. This presentation, "going backwards" from the fate of Western philosophy should make it possible for us to better understand, "going forwards," one of the essays of Heidegger ("Das Ende der Philosophie und die Aufgabe des Denkens," in *ZS*, p. 61f. I have reworked the translation and placed in brackets the names of the authors who illustrate the periods of the history of the "ground"). If one calls "ground or foundation that from which the being as such, in its becoming, its passing and its permanence, is that which it is and as it is, as capable of being known, handled, manipulated," then the history of this ground can be summarized as follows: "The ground has, each time according to the style of presence, the character of grounding

- as the process of ontic causation of the real [Plato, Aristotle],
- as that which makes transcendentally possible the objectivity of the object [Descartes, Kant],
- as that which dialectically mediates the movement of Absolute Spirit [Hegel], or the historical process of production [Marx],
- as will to power constructive of values [Nietzsche]."

31. "Le Tournant," *Questions IV*, p. 142 (the emphasis is my own).

32. Cf. *supra*, note 10.

33. Cf. Reiner Schürmann, "Que faire à la fin de la Métaphysique?" in *Martin Heidegger*, L'Herne (Paris, 1983), p. 363.

34. "Le Tournant," p. 147; *VA*, p. 36; *Holzwege*, p. 292.

35. *VA*, p. 36f.; "Le Tournant," p. 148f.

36. This may perhaps be explained as follows: at a completely psychological level, throughout the time in which one forgets something, one is unaware that one is forgetting it; or, if one does have a kind of presentiment of it, for example through a certain feeling of uneasiness, one does not know what one has forgotten, one is unable to identify it. It is only when one has ceased to forget that one becomes aware both of the fact that one has been in the state of forgetting and also of what it was that one was forgetting: an illumination takes place and one "rediscovers." In the case here in question, the forgetting has to do with Being: the forgotten is in some sense absolute and there is nothing that one can fall back on: an extremity of distress, but one

in which paradoxically that which had been forgotten can reveal itself in a flash. This is "forgetting" in the absolute which may turn around, as it were, and become an epiphany of Being.

37. *VA*, 40.
38. *VA*, 99.
39. *Holzwege*, p. 300.
40. "Le Tournant," p. 154f.
41. *Holzwege*, p. 292.
42. *Holzwege*, p. 302.
43. *PR*, p. 268.
44. Cited in *Holzwege*, p. 298.
45. Cf. Jean Greisch, "La contrée de la sérénité et l'horizon de l'espérance," in *Heidegger et la question de Dieu* (Paris, 1980), p. 183f.
46. Cf. Schürmann, *Le Principe d'anarchie, op. cit.*, p. 245-267. See in particular p. 250: "Heidegger is not portraying any utopia, but the *formal* characteristics which apply to every turn, whether it leads to something better or something worse. Even if 'the relationship of Being to man' were one day to be unveiled, we have no guarantee that life would be more livable. The saving essence of technology does not hold any salvation for man. It defines a modification of the unveiling, its transformation into 'event'."
47. I refer here to the long passage where Derrida, apparently with conviction, defends certain basic positions of Heidegger against the attacks of Emmanuel Lévinas: cf. the whole section entitled "Of Ontological Violence," in the study "Violence and Metaphysics," published in *Writing and Difference* (Chicago, 1978), p. 134f. Then, for the two possible "ways," cf. two commentaries on the same extract of "Der Spruch des Anaximander," "Différance" and "*Ousia* and *Gramme*: Note on a Note from Being and Time," studies published in *Margins of Philosophy*, trans. Alan Bass (Chicago, 1982), cf. pp. 23-27 and 64-67.
48. I cite here an important text to which I shall return: "It would be a question of thinking a *Wesen*, or of making thought tremble by means of a *Wesen* that would not yet even be *Anwesen*" (*Margins*, p. 65).
49. Lévinas, Heidegger, Nietzsche and Freud are referred to in a general way in *Of Grammatology*, trans. Gayatri Chakravorty Spivak (London, 1974), p. 70, and the study on "Différance" (in *Margins*, p. 1-27) is developed in dialogue with these various authors. It is in *La Voix et le Phénomène* (Paris 1967) that the discussion with Husserl is developed. (On the question of the *Cogito*, see also, among other places, *Margins*, p. 294-5).
50. The inner coherence of all the figures of the constellation is repeatedly underlined by Derrida: it is a question ultimately of Western civilization taken as a whole, a civilization whose closure is announced. See the

particularly brilliant exposition of this point of view at the beginning of *Of Grammatology* (*op. cit.*, p. 10-14).

51. *Margins*, p. 6.

52. Hence the frequency of the formulas where he writes that, "in the classical terminology" of phenomenology, of metaphysics, of linguistics, or other, "one would say" this or that to describe what he is talking about, but that it is precisely this formulation that needs to be deconstructed—while maintaining moreover that there exist no proper means to express what he is trying to say. Derrida denies that he is doing "negative theology" ("Différance," *Margins*, p. 6), but in fact nothing is more similar, from the formal point of view, to deconstruction than the critique of theological language—found even in the most "affirmative" theologians, like St. Thomas Aquinas, for example.

53. It is from this angle, in any case, that Derrida raises the question, perhaps simply because, since all speech involves signification, one here finds oneself immediately engaged in deconstruction. Cf. "Différance," in *Margins*, p. 9: "Let us start, since we are already there, from the problematic of the sign and of writing"; p. 10: "But first let us remain within the semiological problematic." This is also the course followed in *Of Grammatology* in its first part.

54. *Cours de linguistique générale* (édition critique) (Paris, 1976), p. 100-102 and 163-166.

55. *Margins*, p. 10.

56. "The Nature of the Linguistic Sign" in *Problems in General Linguistics*, trans. Mary Elizabeth Meek (Miami, 1971), p. 43-48.

57. On the "gramme," cf. *Of Grammatology*, p. 8-9. For a penetrating critique of the privilege of the *phone*, particularly, but not exclusively in Saussure, *ibid.*, p. 30ff.

58. "*The trace itself does not exist* (To exist is to be an entity, a being-present, *to on*)," *Of Grammatology*, p. 167. "Trace" and "gramme" are equivalent non-words. Cf. also *Margins*, p. 23.

59. *Of Grammatology*, p. 60.

60. *Ibid.*, p. 61.

61. Almost everywhere in the work of Derrida, already in *La Voix et le Phénomène*, (Paris, 1967), p. 75. Cf. the article especially devoted to it in *Margins* (cf. *supra* note 1). The three expressions which I retain here (over and above *gramme*) are not the only ones. One would likewise have to analyze the *supplément* theme which runs through the whole second part of *Of Grammatology*, devoted to Rousseau, and which we meet again in the text "The Supplement of Copula: Philosophy before Linguistics" (*Margins*, p. 175-205), devoted to the astonishing article of Benveniste, "Categories of Thought and Language," in *Problems*, p. 55-64. The "supplement" is pre-

cisely that, whatever it might be, which does not allow itself to be reduced to the system presence/sign/time/Being. For other terms, see *Positions*, trans. Alan Bass (Chicago, 1981), 40 and 43.

62. *Margins*, 7 and 11. Concept and word in fact both imply the adequate presence of thought—both of the unity of thought and of the phoneme.

63. *Margins*, p. 11f. There are other definitions of "*différance*," in function of other cultural references (Nietzsche, Freud, etc.) but they can be reduced to these. These "definitions" are explicitly given under the reservation of erasure: "We ought to show why *production* concepts, such as those of constitution and history, remain in complicity with what is at issue here . . . and I utilize such concepts, like many others, only for their strategic convenience and in order to undertake their deconstruction at the currently most decisive point," *Margins*, p. 12 (translation slightly altered). Earlier in the same text Derrida had noted that the "voice" which is most suitable for what is here in question is the *middle* voice—a kind of neuter in contrast to the active and passive voices.

64. *Ibid.*, 19. Cf. the references to *Nachträglichkeit* (= a deferring) *passim*, and especially in "Freud and the Scene of Writing," in *Writing and Difference*, 196-231. On the importance of psychoanalysis for the task of deconstruction, cf. *Of Grammatology*, p.21.

65. Cf. *Of Grammatology*, p. 324, note 9; *Margins*, p. 11.

66. *La Voix et le Phénomène*, 60 and 108.

67. *Margins*, 16.

68. *La Voix et le Phénomène*, p. 75, cf. p. 72ff.

69. *Of Grammatology*, p. 72. "*Ousia* and *Gramme*: A Note on a note from Being and Time," in *Margins*, p. 29-67.

70. "Temporization" denotes the movement of the difference as detour, and could perhaps be distinguished from "temporalization" which would designate the original constitution of the "popular" conception of time, which is described in the passage here cited. Cf. *Margins*, p. 21.

71. *Margins*, p. 60.

72. *Ibid.* p. 63.

73. *Of Grammatology*, p. 69.

74. *Ibid.* p. 10. In a completely different context, that of a critical study of Lévinas: "*The economy of which we are speaking does not any longer accommodate the concept of history such as it has always functioned, and which it is difficult, if not impossible to lift from its teleological or eschatological horizon*": "Violence and Metaphysics," in *Writing and Difference*, p. 148 (emphasis is Derrida's). See also *Positions*, p. 56-60.

75. *Margins*, p. 60.

76. *Ibid.*, p. 21. Same reference for the following citation.

77. *Of Grammatology*, p. 73, cf. 12-13 and 72-73.

78. *Ibid.*, p. 78. For what follows, I am drawing on the discussion with Lévinas, in *Writing and Difference*, p. 109f.
79. *Margins*, p. 67.
80. *Writing and Difference*, p. 250.
81. *Ibid.* p. 293. This last citation, and in a general way, this discussion of Derrida provides the opportunity to look back briefly at Baudrillard, whom I was only able to touch on above by way of describing his intellectual milieu. If one compares it to the theoretical ideas of deconstruction, it would seem that the "critique of the political economy of the sign" to which Baudrillard devotes himself goes still further. We saw above that the theme of the arbitrariness of the signifying is at the origin of a grammatological program (or perhaps only of a presentiment), of an erased thought which would take seriously this generalized arbitrariness of signification and of the language and "gramme" games of which it consists, and which would endeavor to envisage from afar an art of thinking that depends on the unmotivated trace, in acceptance of death, and, at the very least, of an excentrated self-awareness, since the proper name itself is subject to a limitless critique. Baudrillard goes still further, in the sense that, for him, the arbitrariness of signification is still part of the process which has brought us to where we are; one will have to go still further. Doubtless, Baudrillard agrees with Derrida on the non-pertinence of the construct Signifying→Signified→Referent, whose theological and technological mischief he acknowledges; he attacks Benveniste on this point and admits the autonomy of the Signifying, placing a major dividing line between the Signifying on the one hand and the Signified→Referent on the other. Nevertheless—and this is his originality—he brings the criticism to bear on the systemic organization of the Signifying elements. We have seen that if the Signifying no longer signifies by designating a Signified, it produces meaning effects through differences, references and articulations with other Signifying elements. Now, viewing things at the economical level, this system or these systems obey a logic of equivalence and a class strategy which gives its true figure to our world. The dehumanization of man, as we saw above in our brief presentation of his view on the meaning of the process which began with the industrial revolution, takes place through the "semiotic revolution," that is to say, the process which, by freeing the Signifying of all reference to the Signified, leads to their being organized according to a law of form and of meaning which is far from being innocent.

It is evident that if, on the one hand, one rejects the classical, "metaphysical" sequence of Signifying→Signified→Referent in itself or in its most recent formulations as the distinction (vigorously opposed by Baudrillard) of denotation and connotation (there are only in fact connotations: no Signified is privileged; no Signifying can be elevated above the system in which it signifies)—and if, on the other hand, one takes into consideration the semiotic revolution based on the liberation of the Signified as still caught up in a destructive and oppressive system, it is necessary to find another path of salvation, whose course will doubtless be very difficult to point out. This salvation does, however, exist, according to Baudrillard. And it is what he calls *symbolic exchange*; the revolution consists in passing from semiotic exchange to this symbolic exchange.

CHAPTER FOUR

REMEMBRANCE OF THINGS PAST

History, sociology and philosophy are not the only cultural areas where a conflict comes into play between the mentality of the compact and one of spacing, between the ideal of pure presence and an openness to the unexpected. There are also, and perhaps above all, the languages of the imaginary, of fantasy. Baudrillard worked out a critique of the work of art in terms of its having become a specific piece in the semiotic process of consumption,[1] but it is the work of art in itself that really should be the topic of discussion—the work of art viewed within an historical development which doubtless parallels that of the other components of the culture.[2] Do the epochs defined by Heidegger as representing the successive stages of an ever more profound forgetting of Being correspond also to epochs of the history of art and of literature? What narratives, what rites has each of these employed by way of taking refuge in its own way in a full and pure presence which cannot be found in the real world or, alternatively, by way of hinting at what the future should bring? The language of the imaginary is privileged because of its ambivalence: it can express the exodus out of time and Being, but, in another sense, it transgresses the limits of the present, anticipates eschatology, gives voice to the presentiments of desire and, in this way, makes possible a birth.

Research in this area would be endless, and I am not equipped to conduct it in any depth. I will limit myself therefore to two suggestive topics: first, the extraordinary stage effort of Antonin Artaud appears as an at once genial and abortive attempt (and both of these qualifications are important) to restore, almost in liturgically, a sacred space and an ideal time through which to escape from the highly technicized world of today: a modern attempt at rituality. Second, in a less tragic, more everyday manner, a literary genre, the novel, whose chronological limits seem to follow closely those of the modern era, could be viewed perhaps as witnessing to an individual search for alterity. Would the *"nouveau roman"* put an end to a literary adventure at the dawn of which we find *La Princesse de Clèves*, and if so, what kind of literature is being announced?

1. The Theatre of Cruelty: the sacred and myth in modernity[3]

Few contemporary authors have so identified themselves with their work as did Antonin Artaud—a work which he wanted to be effective even before being literary and which it would not be incorrect to view as an evocation or a desperate incantation of lost origins, as a superhuman and ultimately futile effort to establish a sacred space which would prevail over the disfigured space which is that of today's world. In the study of the theater undertaken by Artaud, he seems to me to see the rite and the myth *as in their nascent state*. We know practically nothing of the secret origins of the practices and of the words with which the ethnologists concern themselves: both are immemorial; now one can read Artaud as if one were watching a creative genius at work, fashioning a sacred space and time. But this is not entirely correct, because the writings of Artaud are but the prolegomena to his creative effort or the commentaries on its failures: they are then already, before as well as after, rationalizations. But to the extent that they are associated with an effective endeavor, with a unique lifestyle and with a personal history without parallel, they do, I believe, restore the sacred in action.

Stage action, according to Artaud, deploys effectively a poetic space;[4] it begins with the setting up of the place, which is not a theater but a sacred place, which draws on the architecture of certain ancient churches or temples of Upper Tibet,[5] a space which would first of all be ritual, magical[6] and would suggest the primitive organization of the cosmos. Moreover, all who enter into this religious, metaphysical space are active participants in the poetic moment which will there be played out; the major distinction between actors who alone perform and spectators who are mere onlookers immediately collapses.[7] Stage action is not a spectacle, it is a rite[8] from which one cannot withdraw once one has stepped into the space where it is performed.

This spacial poetry unfolds through an "intense liberation of signs"[9] which reveal and organize the basic forces of life at work from the beginning.[10] Stage gestures cause the human anatomy to dance[11] at a primal depth which is very close to the primitive forces of life; but the latter are also evoked by unexpected things, by unusual and subtle lighting effects, by sounds, even by almost magical musical effects; by the human voice too, but at a level at which it is music, not articulated meaning.[12] Stage space is thus organized dynamically by symbolic means more primitive than the Word.[13] This anteriority of the theatrical to the word might give the impression that stage poetry according to Artaud is disordered, arbitrary, chaotic; it is none of these. This theater which is close to primitive life follows the rigor of creation, the necessity of primordial conflicts.[14] If, measured against the formal regulations which emanate from the human word and from man's limited intelligence, they appear violent and disordered, the fact is that they obey a rigid and ineluctable order. They constitute a spiritual architecture,[15] they proceed from a highly reflective mathematics,[16] they are meticulously, scrupulously[17] staged, that is to say, put in place, put in rite. Only at this price can they evoke a cosmic liturgy.

Devoid of all improvisation, by reason of the seriousness of its religious nature, stage action requires a magical director,[18] a unique creator,[19] capable in a given situation of recapturing vital forces and of perceiving symbolic correspondences which express them and render them present. The stage manager is this director: he is in a true sense the demiurge[20] who creates symbolic space and sets it to work; his judgment is absolute and his power total,[21] not that they proceed from an insolent and superficial whim but because they come from his perception, or better still, from his clairvoyance. In this theater prior to the word, where intelligible themes are insignificant variants of the essential Theme of the primordial conflicts, the author, whose role is preponderant in the spoken theater and whose creation is purely logical, plays second fiddle to the stage director who is the true creator of the symbolic space and of its essential dynamic.[22]

So conducted, stage action deploys a powerful psychic efficacy[23] whose place and mode must be clarified, despite the difficulty in doing so. Since it is a question of an organic space where significations prior to the word are being articulated, this efficacy is not that of the theater which could be called "logical": it does not concern the multiform levels of human psychology, that is to say the conflicts of human beings with one another or even with fate;[24] the catharsis idea which, from Aeschylus to Racine, tends to produce tragedy, is not its concern; still less, to be sure, are the petty conflicts which are staged in contemporary theater.[25] But neither is stage action a propedeutic to social and revolutionary action;[26] if it is involved, it is not at this level (which would necessarily be bound to certain political theories and hence to logos); in itself, it has nothing to effect on the outside. It is a question of a "true action, but without practical consequence";[27] its aim is to incite "a kind of virtual revolt, which moreover can have its full effect only if it remains virtual,"[28] in order to "reach the profound regions of the individual."[29] It is a question of a "soul therapy,"[30] which Artaud compares to psychoanalysis.[31] We must however understand this analogy correctly: for Artaud, the aim of theater is hardly a strictly individual cure aimed at restoring a compromised psychic equilibrium,[32] it is actually a question of "reaching back to the essential";[33] what takes place on stage would make us go back beyond human life as we know it, would call forth "the whole rush of cosmic forces," would wrestle with "problems which go beyond eating, drinking or sexual endowment."[34] It is beyond these characteristics, basic as they are, of our corporeity, that we should be transported by the power of theater. If theater is propedeutic, it is to a life that precedes individuality that we know it wishes to restore us. It is only really operative when it effects an "internal dissociation,"[35] when it makes it impossible for us to avoid risk and danger on entering into this theater. A synthetic text will enable us to summarize these observations:

> The theater must make itself the equal of life—not an individual life, that individual aspect of life in which *characters* triumph, but the sort of liberated life which sweeps away human individuality and in which man is only a reflection. The true purpose of the theater is to create Myths, to express life in its immense, universal aspect, and from that life to extract images in which we find pleasure in discovering ourselves.
> And by so doing to arrive at a kind of general resemblance, so powerful that it produces its effect instantaneously.
> May it free us, in a Myth in which we have sacrificed our little human individuality, like Personages out of the Past, with powers rediscovered in the Past.[36]

A text like this enables us to understand the profoundly ritual character of theater, that is to say its essentially visible and non-verbal aspect and its unique capacity to renew the human organism. Artaud opposes the "petty sensuality" of the period in which we live to the "physical means" whose precise function is to attack this petty sensuality and to enable us to return "to the subtlest notions."[37] Through theater man is internally brought back to the primeval conflicts and opened up to an essential liberation;[38] he is brought back not by the mind alone[39] but by the totality of the theatrical experience to that primordial past which the great myths evoke. More precisely still, he is brought back to a key moment, that which separates the simple and harmonious act of the very first creation and the thickness, the heaviness that immediately followed that simple act.[40] Theatrical action renders man present to that tragic line of division between the Simple and the Double.[41]

It is this essential place which accounts for the ambiguity of the theater, for its cruelty and for its hope (I employ a term here which is perhaps not fully faithful to Artaud). The theater is a theater of cruelty because it reinserts man into the inescapable pain of the primitive conflicts linked to the primordial separation, to the heaviness of matter, to the obstinacy of evil. Theatrical action should lead to paroxisms of interior struggle where these primitive cosmic polarities are relived; its effect is devastating, and this is why it can be compared to the action of the plague. But this ineluctable, cruel, destructive work, precisely because it causes the primitive break to be symbolically relived, can lead beyond this break and help us finally to reach that beauty for which Plato yearned, that inextricable fusion of everything we know only as divided: beyond every conflict between matter and mind, idea and form, concrete and abstract, we arrive at the place where all appearances are dissolved "into one unique expression which must have been the equivalent of spiritualized gold."[42]

If this is really what theater is and if its stake is really this high, one cannot escape its necessity; theater is not an art, a decorative adjunct, a picturesque spectacle. It is the sole space of salvation, because it is the sole symbolic action which can bring us back to the origin. Either one enters into this space and subjects oneself to its cruelty, or one is ripe for "disorder, famine, blood, war, and epidemics."[43] If we are not willing to live symbolically the primordial conflicts and to be brought back in this way to the primitive harmony, we will fall into a disintegration beyond remedy. The dramatic breakdowns of the contemporary world are an indication of the urgency of theatrical symbolism: it is this or nothing.

The writings of the last period of the life of Artaud, let us say beginning with the *Nouvelles Révélations de l'être* ("The New Revelations of Being"), are often hermetic and almost impossible to decipher in detail. But constant features keep returning which are consistent with the author's writings on the theater and help to bring out their full meaning. One could say the same for the two last "theatrical" manifestations of Artaud, the conference of Vieux-Colombier and the radio broadcast *Pour en finir avec le jugement de Dieu* ("To Be Done with the Judgement of God"), which are also consistent with the solitary and theatrical behavior of Artaud during his whole life.[44] The life and work of Artaud appear then as a unique and insistent effort to revive and to perform the sacred rite which exorcizes[45] the cosmic failure of present existence, of *Being*; this rite should enable us, with a maximum of "action, of intensity, of density"[46] to relive the fundamental and primordial crisis, for a resurrection. Artaud incarnates the demiurge of this recreative rite which aims at restoring a language *before* meaning (hence glossalalia and sound effects), a body and a world *before* the separation: the "body without organs," and in particular without sexuality and without excrements, that is to say a body without dissemination, without multiplicity, without dependencies.[47] With this as a background, one can understand the violent, conflictual, obscene, blasphemous dimension of the language of Artaud. At the time of the writings on the theater, anathema is leveled against the forms of contemporary theater considered decadent; but let us make no mistake: this anathema extends to everything one will be able to read later: "All the preoccupations enumerated above stink unbelievably of man, provisional, material man, I shall even say *carrion man*."[48] For Artaud, it was always a question of eliminating this "provisional, material man" for another materiality, another body, another man, if contemporary theater is preventing this elimination, it is this theater that ought to be eliminated, but also (and here we return to the last writings of Artaud) the forces, the wizardries, the perverse demiurges which produce and sustain this provisional man, "robbing true man of his birth": Christianity, its god, its priests, its sacraments (which present themselves precisely as a spectacle at which the faithful assist, while they really amount to a demiurgy of the man to be eliminated), but also (and at the same level) the "frightful corporal rites" which from the Caucasus to the Apennines, from the Carpathians to the Himalayas assure the perpetuance of this pestiferous world. By a careful study of the last writings of Artaud it would perhaps be possible, if not easy, to reconstruct the "mythical narrative" corresponding to the enormous ritual effort of "theater"[49] whose fundamental moment would be the scission between "the organic life of pure embryo" where the human anatomy can dance according to its truth, and "the passionate life and integral concreteness of the human body" dominated by the primordial impurities of ingestion and of sexuality.[50]

Theatrical rituality and religious rituality

Artaud wanted to set in motion an immense Rite, true and efficacious, capable of recapturing the world at its origins and of reorientating it at the price of an inexorable and cruel procedure. But this Rite could not be sacred, if, in the term "sacred" one sees a reference to "gods" situated between earth and heaven, to "revelations" which would indicate their will, etc.[51] Rite can no longer be personalized. This is no doubt the essential difference between the rituality Artaud wished to create and that which religious ethnology is able to discover and analyze. Judeo-Christian civilization, within the framework of which Artaud writes, even if he rejects it, has progressively engaged in an immense demythization enterprise, to the extent that faith in one God acting in history, and then in the Incarnation of the Son of God, established an immediate relationship between the one God and human beings and rejected the mediation of intermediary beings at the periphery. In the world of the religions, on the contrary, these intermediary beings are necessary and they occupy the position to the point where they no longer refer to anything other than themselves; whether they be personalizations of cosmic forces or of primary elements, whether they be distinguished on the basis of their relative height in the heavens (the stars) or depth in the abyss (the monsters), or whether they form the object of a tribal memory (ancestors), they are themselves the beings we have to reckon with. So it is that the ritual gestures and the narratives which supply their foundation or their justification have the significance of conciliation, of propitiation, of expiation or of offering which correspond to the reality which is attributed to them. This means that the myths and the rites have an undeniable social significance, which theatrical rituality lacks. According to M. Eliade, for example, the myth

> tells a sacred story, that is to say, a trans-human revelation which is located at the dawn of the Great Time, in the sacred time of the beginnings (*in illo tempore*). Being real and sacred, the myth becomes exemplary and consequently repeatable, for it serves as model and at the same time as justification for all human actions.[52]

Tradition consists essentially of reference to the origin and of interpretation of the will of the gods or of the ancestors; actions tend to be repetitive, initiatives rash, society organically constituted and stable.

In the Western cultural sphere, Christianity has depopulated interstellar space and marine depths; on the other hand, it has offered an original rituality, to which we shall of course return, which in principle, but also little by little in practice, has opened the way to social forms directed toward the future. If one objects to this *Christian* rituality, that of the New Covenant in the Paschal Mystery of Christ sacramentally celebrated, and if one can no longer promote a *pagan* rituality centered on the world of spirits and of gods, no other way remains open but that of a *secular* rituality, which will have more or less of an impact on the forms of cultural and social life. The Theater of Cruelty which Artaud wanted, with its cosmic references, is a form of this rituality. Now, the point to be brought out here is that, pagan (sacred) or profane (secular), rituality shows the same basic characteristics. Although these are well known, I would like briefly to enumerate them.

1. Myths and rites are *immemorial* and *anonymous*. They were revealed, said Eliade, back "at the dawn of the Great Time" but it is not really known who revealed them, how the narrative was constructed, how the rites came to be formed; one simply finds oneself within a tradition and, paradoxically, the beginning toward which this tradition is totally geared appears inaccessible in its actuality. One might point out in this regard that, if Artaud was striving to establish a theatrical rituality more or less sustained by the myth of Heliogabalus which he himself recounted, he felt, at a certain moment, a need of anonymity and insisted that his works which were about to appear not bear the name of the author: the individual cannot, should not count in the tradition of the Rite.[53] Rituality is *without author*.

2. The significance of this anonymity comes to light, paradoxically as I have said, if one takes into account that toward which ritual tradition tends, the origins, and how it tends in this direction. What we have here is truly a fascination, with the double aspect of seduction and repulsion. There exist side by side an absolute need to relate to one's origins and a rejection of what they were. In a work to which I will return,[54] Marthe Robert speaks of the "old common foundations of the myths and legends where archaic humanity *deposited its horror of being born*"; the story which the myths tell would thus be that of the passage between the (happy) time before birth and the (unhappy) time of the after: the tragic line of division. Others would say, but this probably amounts to the same thing, that the myth recounts the passage

from nature to culture, from an undifferentiated state to a differentiated state, through a process at once necessary and, to some degree, culpable. Thus it is that the narratives oscillate between the nostalgia of the before, which gives rise to repetitive behaviors of a fusional type aimed at a return to the primitive lack of differentiation, and the fatality of the after, which provokes the reiteration of sacriligious behavior, the deicide or homicide through which the primordial hero founded every difference.[55] In this sense, if myth is supposed to found society and culture through the primordial narrative of their advent, it does so only in self defense; the repetitive behaviors which it arouses, in the sacred area of the cult, are either attempting to go back beyond what they recount, into the element anterior to differentiation, or they are repeating symbolic behaviors which are actually destructive and not really creative of history. Here again, we see the proximity which exists between pagan rituality and the secular rituality of which Artaud has supplied us with a model.[56]

3. One could make the same point by suggesting that the world of rituality fuses two realities which are really diverse: *finitude* and *culpability*. Birth is only horrible if it is culpable; one seems unable to view birth as only difference and limit; evil is attached to it—an evil which should not have been (and this is quick to be localized in matter or in the body); the mythical hero is responsible for the two aspects, indistinctly, so that rite which is supposed to exorcise the one (evil) rejects or attempts to bypass the other (birth). One seems unable to go back further and to rediscover the distinction established from the beginning of Genesis between creation (good finitude) and the offer of covenant (on the basis of which *another* notion of culpability can be understood). In mythology, the question of origin and that of evil are inextricably intertwined.

4. It follows that rituality knows neither history nor eschatology. Salvation is behind us, in a return to "Paradise lost," that is to say to the other side of the dividing line between the first and second moments of the "creation"; it would be more accurate to say: to beyond the dividing line between the tragic appearance of distinct beings and the original state of fusion of which the symbol, in Artaud, is the "body without organs," unconnected with any distinction, relation, function. Memory is in any case not a memory of the future; its language expresses the hope for the past before the fall, the desire to retrace the course of evil back beyond the initial drama, how-

ever one conceives this. This going back is moreover possible only in the closed and sacred space of the cult; time and space no longer have any meaning.

The effort of Antonin Artaud is a failure in the end. Not only what one might call a professional failure, at the level of theatrical activity, but above all a failure in supplying a real meeting point between the excessive effort of evoking and making present the origin and the actual life of human beings: the scission remained total. Now, in the individualized and rationalized world in which we live, Artaud was unable to find the support of a society in tune with a primitive and traditionally initiated narrative to be lived in scission without destroying itself or abandoning its members to internal dispersion; the madness of Artaud stems perhaps from the excessive gap between the intensity of his mythical and ritual effort and the commercial and technological world in which he lived. And yet we cannot rid ourselves of Artaud, not only because he continues to be read[57] and various cultural movements claim to draw their inspiration from him,[58] but above all because his unreconciled life manifests the search for a reconciliation. If rite and narrative are still alive among us, where and how are we to find those who will offer us the origin, but in such a way that we can live in this world, and not be driven out of it by madness or death, as if in punishment for having conjured up something which transcends our being?

2. The Novel and its Double

The undertaking of Antonin Artaud is exceptional in its intensity—the more so because the choice of theater as a way of rediscovering the immense original conflict involved an active participation, a body and soul engagement in the power of symbols. But, at a more modest and more ordinary level where we merely find works that are first written and then read—works which I would not, however, call innocuous—we encounter the literary genre of the novel, whose production is ultimately motivated by the same desire as that which inspires the theater. Artaud traced the advent of modern, individualistic and psychological theater to the Renaissance; this is the very era in which, according to Baudrillard, the sense and the practice of symbolic exchange had been lost. However, this "decadence," or, if you prefer, this turning point did not abolish the need for a narrative of evocation. In an age when civilization is losing something of its cosmic and liturgical amplitude to construct itself little by little upon other supports—the primacy of the individual, the scientific approach to reality, a bourgeois and commercialized society, democratic ideals—at this moment we witness the development of the novel, which, if it was not totally unknown before, experiences a tentacular success which we must endeavor to explain. Attempts have been made to do just this:[59] I am more struck by those which, on the diachronic level or through the analysis of structures and motifs, have underscored the continuity between the novel and its predecessor, myth.[60] Even if there has been a change of method and a shift of accent, the constants at work in rite and in myth now seem able to find expression in the new space created by the novel genre.

Contemporary man is a reader of novel, a lover of fiction, if indeed he is not himself an author of fiction. Gradually, from the dawn of modern time to our own day, literature has been taking on the form of the novel in a one-sided, almost exclusive way. Nevertheless, by a very significant paradox, the inflation of this literary genre has not made it possible, at the level of criticism, to come up with a widely accepted definition of novel; no one seems to be able to pin down and to correctly synthesize what would be the fundamental characteristics of the genre. It is as though literature has found here its ever present but forever indefinable horizon.[61] It is here, it seems to me, that we see the full value of Marthe Robert's suggestion that the inflation of the novel genre and its boundless variety should lead us to inquire not so much into what the novel *is* as into what it *wants*.[62] Thus, we would call novel any literary production which would give voice to a specific *desire*: the novel would be a privileged language of desire. As for the prevailing desire, concealed as well as revealed by plot, it would be that of giving oneself (and offering the reader under the form of veiled confidence) another origin than one's own. Negatively expressed, the novel would be the laying aside of a real identity and of the burdensome history it has entailed; positively, it would be the imagining of, indeed perhaps the attempt to acquire another identity and another history.[63] And when one reads a novel, what one is seeking is perhaps to escape from one's history and one's origin so as to be someone else for the duration of a reading session.[64]

The novel is then first of all a denial,[65] its author and, to a lesser extent perhaps its reader, a renegade.[66] Robinson Crusoe denies his family, Don Quixote his past, Julien Sorel gives himself a well "born" father, Lucien de Rubempré abandons his original name to make a new future for himself. Birth is always viewed, although in different ways, as having been a misfortune. The novel, born of the repudiation of this birth, inevitably carries the mark of scission:[67] it is the self-begetting of a *double*;[68] it is the struggle, on behalf of this double and against reality which one cannot even call prosaic, because the novel itself is in prose: the prose of the novel would wish to substitute itself for any other prose, and the tragedy for the novelist, and even for his reader, will perhaps be the ultimate impossibility of this substitution. Before going on however to consider this tragic issue, let us note that this theme of the rejection of one's birth provides the first hint of an explanation of the phenomenon of *mimesis* which René Girard observed, but seems to view as primary, although in fact it is but secondary, derived. It is because the hero of the novel (and behind him his "maker") does not know what he wants to be that he strives to imitate the other, with all or some of the consequences analyzed by Girard. But, if he does not know what he wants to be, he knows very well what he does not want to be, namely himself, in the image he has of himself and hence of his filiation.[69] We will moreover have to examine ourselves below and ask why it is that this attitude of self-rejection, indeed of self-hatred, is so common—where it comes from and what it reveals. Whatever the case may be, denial, scission, projection of a double conformed to desire—these common notes are distinguished according to the two figures which the child thus renegade successively forms of himself: the found Child and the noble Bastard.[70] Perhaps we have here, in the individualized experience of the modern family and the "familial novel" to which it can give rise, the equivalent of the distinction to which I alluded above, following Marc Augé, between the mythical hero and the tragic hero which are situated on both sides of the basic dividing line which is at once creation of the world, birth of culture and advent of evil.[71] In fact, to imagine himself the Found Child is to erase his real birth and, in a variety of ways, to return to the other side, "to expose himself" in fantasy, for example, to being received by other parents, always and everywhere attentive; it is to live other adventures at the end of which the true identity, that of the Double, will be revealed at the proper moment. It is always a question of leading a life which takes place in "another" world, "on the other side" of this world. Then, to consider oneself a Bastard is to exclude the real father in order to imagine another possible one, far away and unknown, but above all in order to come to this present world of sexuality, of ambition and of work from another beginning, from another basis more promising of success. In the first case, it is a question of a basic horror of birth in general, linked to the disappointment of this birth;[72] the path of the hero is that of the return into an elsewhere which is also a before: a return to the undifferentiated, to the zero point of civilization, in the rejection of the economical and the sexual spheres.[73] It is the world of fairy tales, be they popular or romantic—to a greater or lesser extent, that of Robinson and of Don Quixote. It will be noted moreover that this return to the other side of the beginning is lacking neither in prophetism (the heroes oppose their truth to perdition and to the lie of other men) nor in the will to power: the tales frequently end with the victory of the prince: Robinson reigns supreme on his island and Don Quixote dreams of kingdoms, where Sancho Panza hopes to live a happy life or to rule as king.[74] In the second case, the misfortune of birth, more effectively linked to the figure of the rejected father, does not give rise to a flight, but instead, and according to ever new modalities to the taste of novelistic creativity, to an aggressive attitude, which is or is not rewarded, through which desire hopes to appropriate that toward which its real destiny would presumably not be leading it: the summit of pleasure, of social success and of money.

This is not the place to dwell at any length on these two figures, on the nuances which they involve and the way in which they relate to each other (after all, no novel belongs exclusively to only one of these figures, if it is true that every author, and ultimately every human being more or less knows the aspiration to Paradise lost and the rage to make a name for himself). The important point for our purposes is this linking of the novel with human desire, "the secret desire which man nurtures not to have been born of anyone, to have begotten himself and to be the child of his own works"—whether the result of this wish proves naively happy or definitively tragic. The novel genre is the writing of this desire in which author and reader meet and are accessory, haunted as they both are, in different degrees, by this fateful propensity to put away the founding narrative, its realism and its pain, in favor of a story of origins and of fulfillments that are imaginary, but more reassuring or more exalting, even if their unfolding and their outcome were marked by the tragic.

Finally, deprived in effect of his fictitious identity and having for a long time been deprived of his real identity, the hero of the novel (and perhaps also the person who created him) can only disappear. This is what happens in the folk tales where the hero, having emerged victorious from his tribulations and having married the far-away princess, has no more story that is worth being told.[75] Things are more tragic in the novel where the protagonist ends up dying, if he does not become mad after having set out definitively into the Realm of fantasy. Novel writing is thus perhaps a conjuration, by its author, of the misfortune of having been born and of having been born thus, without having been able to effectively correct this initial disgrace—a conjuring which takes place either by a return to the other side of the origin, or by an ascension to the summit of power. Through this death, the hero and its author would be able, according to René Girard, to arrive at the "romantic truth," that is to say, at the *renouncement of desire*. The impossibility of transgressing the fiction would ultimately shine forth: the death of the hero, which is also the end of the novel as novel would signify the vanity of the boundless quest for the Double—whether this revelation engenders despair, resignation or, in come cases, as with Dostoyevski, hope.[76]

Is the death of the hero which coincides with that of desire the only solution to the romantic attitude? Would the human being then—every human being, if it is true that today everyone is, if not author, at least reader of novel—have to wait to die in order to renounce this penchant for substitution? What then is the meaning of man's effort, ceaselessly resumed, as long as he lives, to combine in himself the real identity, which as we shall see below is linked to the faith accorded to the stories told by those who witnessed our birth, and the fictitious identities which he dreams of for himself and which he recounts to himself and to others? Between the stories we hear and the stories we produce, why does the preference always go to the latter?

It is not yet the moment here to propose a line of research which would enable us to comprehend this strange attitude. It would be necessary to find out, upstream, why it is that every individual is disappointed with his or her origin to the point of wanting to trade it in for another, and, downstream, if there are recurrent models which would allow him or her a comparison and fan his or her desire. Would it then be possible to suggest a trajectory of human existence where the *hearing* of the narrative would not necessarily be disappointing and where there would be sufficient *promise* to enable us to survive without being obliged to imagine worlds which do not exist? If the imagination is one of the most creative resources of human existence, why is it that we most often put it to work behind us to recreate a memory instead of harnessing its energies to the real objectives which require it? Conversely, if it is in fact possible to find an attitude which would reduce this ultimately fatal denial of origins, at what level is this attitude rooted and how are we to describe it?[77]

BALANCE

The authors discussed have been but a select few and the investigations fragmentary; it would seem, however, that as an ensemble they present a sufficiently coherent figure to make it possible now to draw up a balance of the whole. I would like to register first of all the positive aspects of this figure and to acknowledge the witness it gives to a human quest toward which it is impossible to remain indifferent—especially if one knows, as a believer, that every human quest is also ultimately a quest for God: "Tell me what is your man and I will tell you who is your God." We will next have to recapitulate the inadequacies or the limitations which have been brought out in the course of our exposition, and attempt to discern the overall attitude (which I will qualify as "gnostic") which explains them; in so doing, we will already be well on the way toward recapturing in another manner the positive aspects of the figure. Finally at the juncture of this credit/deficit operation, I would like to risk a few tentative statements about God, in view of the fact that the authors studied have all written in a world marked by Christianity (whether the period in question is to be considered Christian or post-Christian).

Toward a principle of "heteronomy"

In their diversity, perhaps even in their mutual opposition, the currents studied are demonstrating, either explicitly or by contrast, in support of what one could call "a principle of heteronomy"; one might even say that they profess a sort of "passion" for heteronomy: salvation, whatever this may be, cannot come from the present social or individual figure of this world. It must therefore come from some other place, whatever be the nature of this "other."

Does not the catastrophic aspect which our civilization presents at this point in its development come in fact from the rejection of such a "principle of heteronomy"? Is it not a result of the inability to stand back with respect to any form of the "immediate" trilogy of possession/knowledge/power, from the inability to endure any measure, theoretical or practical, individual or collective, which would put a break to an exponential growth in these domains? To employ once again the expression of Baudrillard, people are unable or unwilling to reintroduce into life the "form of death" which is precisely what would enable it to be saved. In biblical terms, one would say perhaps that, in ways which are their own and without reference to the Christian faith, the authors mentioned are actually returning, for their own purposes, to a conviction expressed in the ancient narrative of Genesis, namely, that this cumulative and unreserved knowledge, which the narrative calls "the knowledge of good and evil," is not always or necessarily beneficial and that we would perhaps be well advised to keep a safe distance from it.

On the manner in which this distance should be kept and the reasons for doing so there would be nothing like general agreement, as we shall see; the stand for heteronomy can be a radical one, but it can also be tentative—a method, perhaps, whose ultimate aim would be to recover a lost autonomy or to await a final flowering, rather than a fundamental structure, albeit impossible to ponder, of man's very humanity. Nevertheless, without entering yet into the discernment of the true heteronomy, I would like to attempt to enumerate here the positive insights which every principle of heteronomy seems to me somehow to embrace.

1. It is true that man cannot understand himself except within the framework of a journey which transcends his own limits, within which he finds himself and over which he can gain a certain measure of control only by consenting to it. However one speaks of *history* or of *historicity*, man is not its ultimate principle. He is born into the world and he lives there in a density, a materiality, a set of differences and of relationships of which he is not himself the key. In this respect, the breadth of a zoological rootedness, the impact of the constraints linked to social and economic forms, the subconscious at play in those forms of which the linguistic principle of the opposition of phenomena is an elementary illustration—all of this leads very far away indeed from an analysis of history based on awareness as pure presence to oneself, to time and to the world. The terms employed by Derrida (trace, gram) are symbols which point in the direction of this non-belonging of man to himself: at this level, these terms are unexceptionable.

2. In this perspective, there begin to appear, in negative image, the prerequisites for elaborating a *metaphysics*, if such a thing is even possible. What our authors resolutely reject is a kind of "compacted thinking" which would forcibly bring together "Being, time and consciousness" under the controlling notion of "presence"; if one wishes

to rediscover these notions and what they might possibly designate, it is certainly necessary to deconstruct this presence; the whole question is, however, to know how! Indeed, to consider Being as presence is at the same time to link it to time—Being as a kind of upsurge of time—and to link time to it: time as pure dimension of Being. Time and Being tend then to become confounded in the pure perception of the present of consciousness. Time is not recognized in its temporality, nor Being in its beingness (*étantité*) (whatever one might understand by these terms). A way of stating the problem will then have to be found such that each of these notions, Being, time and consciousness, may recover its proper intelligibility as well as its intricate relationship to the other two. Paradoxically, this can only happen if man consents to a certain non-presence to himself, to an anteriority which he does not found, even if he can situate himself with respect to it, to a flux and to a space which he cannot leave, even if he can locate himself within it.

3. The first principle of an *ethics* would in some sense be the act of consent to this native excentration, and thus "death" to any temptation to autonomy and to absolute self-affirmation. This consent could generate a kind of behavior defined as "symbolic exchange." How this exchange is conceived will have to be clarified so that it may give rise to something other than the "immediate revolution" whose ethical ineffectiveness we have seen. In other terms, this exchange should enable us to define an authentic framework of social justice, particularly in the two key and related domains of sexuality and of work. This discernment of "symbolic exchange" in its true meaning should moreover take place in such a way that one can clearly distinguish between the finitude and the growth which make the exchange possible, on the one hand, and the whole domain of the fall and the concrete mark it has left which prevents it, on the other.

4. The theme of symbolic exchange has implications in the area of the *word*, which should be communication before being information. When this hierarchy is preserved, we again have exchange and the way has been opened to a whole idea of invocation, which restores to the word its truth: the "saying" envelops the "said" and not vice versa. But within this communicative exchange, priority must be given to *hearing* over *expression*, which, in this domain of the word, is the way of indicating an anteriority in which man finds himself and which he does not himself found. We find here again the invitation that came out of our investigation on the "remembrance of things past": one cannot

supply oneself, and still less can one supply the human race, with a *founding narrative*. The question of knowing from whom and where this narrative is to be heard remains open. In any case, only this hearing, or if you prefer, this waiting can open existence to an authentic human life-plan.

The dualistic handicap

The demands which I have just enumerated are important; they define a *mentality* in which alone it is possible, it would seem, to receive, to reflect on and to live the salvation of time and of Being. Unfortunately, they are treated here in a perspective which, on a first analysis, could be said to be *dualistic*. By "dualism" I do not intend to allude to a type of thinking which would apprehend *duality* in the real: the real to which we have access is, in fact, dual and every apprehension of it is naturally marked by this duality. "Dualism" in the sense intended here is what we have when the data thus discovered remain contradictory or irreconcilable. Now this is precisely the case when it is said that we are under the regime of the concealed, of the forgotten, of the deflected: these terms can in fact only be employed in reference to something manifest, to something recalled, to something on course; but this something, according to these authors, cannot be said; there is no clear knowledge of it: looking toward the past, one cannot assign its memory to a real time or place; looking toward the future, one does not know what shape it will take. This original something, this primordially and ultimately elusive something, will not be said: it will be signified by "erasure, expectation, revolution, imaginary substitution. . . . " It is as though the real were divided into two layers: one to which we have access, which is marked by crippling constraints, and another which is at once necessary and impossible.

The descriptions carried out in the course of this part suffice to justify this impression of "dualism"; I would like to make here a rapid synthesis of the relevant material, before going on to suggest another way of looking at things.

Is history impossible?

In introducing this investigation, I observed that only those authors had been retained who, for the most part, concerned themselves with the *historical dimension* of civilization. The diversity of the points of view favored by the individual authors was to lead to a complex, diverse, but for this reason "complete" concept of history: zoological rootedness (Leroi-Gourhan), work dimension (the relationship man/nature: Engels-Marx), structures of social reciprocity (the relationship man/man: Baudrillard), the more directly cultural elements (the relationship man/spirit: Heidegger). It is already beneficial, to be sure, to have been able to establish these components of historical reality by analyzing the points of view of these authors: every concept of history, and consequently every effective historical praxis will have to incorporate these elements, and perhaps others as well.

We must however acknowledge that each of the authors considered concludes in his own domain to a certain *failure of history* and sends it back, in some way or other, to square one: Leroi-Gourhan is very hesitant when it comes to pronouncing on the survival of the human species; Engels, Baudrillard and Heidegger, each in his own way and in his own domain, denounce a kind of original evil, a massive thrust fault, at the very beginning of the historical process, as though it were only through this "fall" that history, in the final analysis, was born: the history of the family, of private property and of the state, to the extent that it differs from a strictly "natural" evolution, is under the evil sign of the appropriation of the means of production (Engels); social history is born, about the time of the Renaissance, from the loss of the social structure, at once fundamental and non-historical of symbolic exchange (Baudrillard); cultural history is born of the fall, at once necessary and tragic, of Being into forgetfulness—a drama in which none other than the prestigious Plato is involved, if indeed he is not its cause (Heidegger).

This being the case, while the scientific literary genre of his study allows Leroi-Gourhan to maintain a certain vagueness of expression, the other authors cited look forward to an *immediate or imminent future*, whose proximity is, in a sense, assured by the crisis character of the contemporary situation: this future has, in each case, a *cathartic* aspect as well as a *generative* aspect: whether it is a question of the revolution of the proletariat, of the symbolic revolution or of the overthrow of the *Gestell*, the failed past disappears, violently in the first two cases, while Heidegger, for his part, makes no concrete conjecture and calls only for perseverance in waiting. And then something entirely new is to be born: a society without classes, quite individualistic

(Marx), or on the contrary, entirely taken up in exchange (Baudrillard), or an entirely new and unpredictable economy of the *Ereignis*, of time and of Being (Heidegger). This new thing has something of the protological, the spontaneous about it, because the past is abolished without remainder, and something of the eschatological, because there is nothing that suggests the possibility of any type of further process once the new has been established. Thus time, *our* time, is strictly lost.

Under these circumstances, one is justified in asking whether our authors, while being sociologists and philosophers, do not actually come closer than it might seem to a vision of a mythical type, like that of Artaud, and whether their world is not therefore more that of the novel than that of reality. Is it not, after all, from our reality, embodied and impure, that an Antonin Artaud wishes to free himself through the ritual device of the Theater of Cruelty, and does not the novel have a similar aim, namely, to liberate us from our inglorious filiations and from our humdrum histories?

Thus history is in every way impossible: upstream, it is cursed; downstream, it has no place. But, as for the point where these two non-existences meet, the tragedy is that if in the case of the rite or the novel it remains imaginary, or if in the case of the overthrow of the *Gestell* it is imponderable, this meeting point is nothing less than bloody destruction and oppressive innovation, if revolution is adopted as a solution. Is it not then safe to conclude that there has been some error of judgment in the analysis of historical processes, since its *real* products are either illusory or tragically disappointing?

A gnostic attitude?

The attention of the authors studied is centered on what one could call the "processes of accumulation": whether at the level of the "management of the globe," of the accumulation of the goods of production or of consumption, of intellectual and practical manipulation of beings in all the different ways in which they can be kept "at hand," the challenged or rejected history is under the sign of a multifaceted effort of appropriation without controls. It is this negative aspect which entirely occupies the field of reflection, an aspect for which the remedy can be nothing other than a strictly *radical* change.

Is not this concentration on the negative perhaps a kind of prejudice, which would conceal other, quite possibly beneficial, aspects of the historical process? Before seeing if there is an answer to this question, it could be noted here that, according to the point of view they adopt, the authors are not in agreement on the chronological moment of the "fall" into accumulation: the appearance of animal husbandry and the fundamental sociological transformations which this entails (Engels); the loss of Being to the benefit of particular being at the time of Plato (Heidegger); the appearance of the order of Nature at the Renaissance (Baudrillard). If the diagnosis is always bleak, it is not so always with reference to the same moment nor for the same reasons; this can at the very least lead one to question the *universally valid* character of this diagnosis. But one will also observe that, in each of the hypotheses considered, we are not told who are *responsible* for the "fall" and for this entrance into the accursed process of accumulation. As I have noted, Engels ends up putting the blame on a normal process in the development of the acquisition by human beings of their capacity to invent and to diversify the means of producing their subsistence, but he does not say how or why the transition from "cultural progress" to "moral fault" came about; likewise, when he traces back to Plato the process of the concealment of Being in beings, Heidegger does not make an issue, as such, of the responsibility of the man Plato: the name Plato is an indicative of time and of place, as well as of an author in whose writings the new process is revealed; but the process itself displays a character which is at once harmful and inevitable, if not necessary. Baudrillard, finally, does not say from where and how this "order of Nature," which is supposed to have supplanted symbolic exchange, arose at the time of the Renaissance.

We are faced, then, with a diversity in the determination of what one could call the "crucial moment," and thus in the evaluation of the "ideal reality" (that which preceded this crucial moment) whose manifestation one hopes or one wishes to provoke; but the basic attitude is the same—one which recognizes an inexplicable "fall" and invests this with the twofold and quasi contradictory character of *necessity* and *culpability*, each seeming to undo the other.

Derrida, it is true, takes a strong stand against the "temporal" aspect of this problematic of the fall and, consequently, of a certain restoration, once the culpable necessity has been overcome.[78] He does not, however, himself escape from this inexplicable dualism, which he views as an immediate given, in a structural way, and which is supposed to be at play between the always already concealed "trace" and the metaphysics of presence.[79] But where does this concealment come from, and how can we remedy it? These are questions to which he has not really responded, although we find some references to the (temporal?) waiting for this "unnameable recurrence which is about to appear." Consequently, to return to the terms employed by our authors, one could say that Oblivion, Delusion, the *Différance*, the Appropriation of the means of production, *Déhiscence*,[80] Original Finitude, etc., are so many mentally constructed entities whose object is to account for the deplorable situation in which we find ourselves, while *not* implicating human liberty (because the situation is necessary) and implicating it *too much* (because it is culpable). These entities are not "principles," because a "principle" can in some way be recognized or heard; but, while not being "archic," they are also not "anarchic," because it is thanks to them that we are able to get our bearing at all. However this may be, we find ourselves, in all these cases and with all these figures, before a situation, inexplicable but founding, of necessity and of fall. Now has this not always been the fundamental characteristic of gnosticism?[81]

For a reevaluation

If it is "gnostic," the cultural landscape portrayed by means of the studies conducted above has something in it of the *imaginary*, the contrived; it blackens the surfaces that show, of which any possible positive truth is in principle concealed, and it converts this darkened zone into its opposite, deemed light and luminous, but which either has not yet come, or is incapable of piercing through the darkness, at once inevitable and culpable, of reality as one believes it to be. Now, if there is something contrived about this double entry stage, would it not be possible to go see what is *really* there behind stage?

Obviously, there can be no question of denying the deficiencies and the "densities" of the socio-cultural complex in which we live, but rather of seeking perhaps to situate somewhat differently their nature and possibly their origin. Now this cannot be done except, if this is possible, by a *positive appreciation* of history, *as it actually is*, taking place around us and viewed then as something other than a mere succession of deficits accumulating in geometric progression and, correlatively, by the rediscovery of a perspective on available *beings* which instead of concealing Being, would rather bring it to light. One would have to inquire whether what "gnosis" treats by way of succession does not actually exist simultaneously.

This amounts to raising the question as to whether what our authors refer to as "death," "distance," "exchange," whose manifestation they reserve for later on, has not already been there, giving to production/consumption its ordered appearance and actually respecting the mystery (Being) present as beings are grasped or come under human control. If this has in fact been the case, one would situate differently the incontrovertible presence of *evil*, viewing it as deflection or concealment, and one would have to explain the growth of this evil, which runs parallel to a "just management" of the economy and of philosophy, and at their expense.

This could be done in a number of ways:

1. One could attempt to offer *another version* of history, that of society and economy as well as that of philosophy and of culture; indeed, a unilateral narrative focused on decadence, forgetfulness and loss is in some sense too facile. Real events simply do not happen that way. To be true, a history must be attentive to the positive aspects which are there to be discerned: a progress in the use of tools does not in itself generate evil; on the contrary, it *qualifies* in a new way the relationship of man to nature; appropriation, at whatever level it may take place, can enrich the individual or the group in a way which is not necessarily closed, etc. Once again one must analyze the meaning of the ruptures and of the reforms which have so often attempted to compensate, in every order of reality, for the perceived deviations and excesses; such procedures presuppose a certain perception of the *truth* to be acknowledged and pursued in the domain in question. It is likewise possible to note the order of values—the liberation, for example, which certain technological advances have been able to bring to certain forms of slavery and the modifications of the social order to which this has given rise. When one reads the histories of science, of society, of technology, of thought, supplied by people who are competent in these various matters, one gets the impression of figures whose complexity is enormous and not always respected in the surveys of "universal history" like those reviewed above. Nevertheless, it must be acknowledged that a respect for the infinite complexity of history in

the narrative which one makes of it presupposes a certain *universal perspective* in which one could make the effort, *without fear*, to follow a thread where good and evil are intermingled, because one is *assured of a certain salvation* applicable not only to a privileged part, but to the whole of reality, with the exception of evil. But *who* would supply us with this perspective and *from where* would it come to us?

2. One could take up again from the beginning the question of *nature vs. culture*. The difficulty, often insurmountable, seems to be that of keeping alive the *hinge* between the two. Lévi-Strauss made this consist precisely in the *rule*, initially the famous prohibition of incest, which produced *exchange*. And Baudrillard very powerfully brought out what he called the "form of death" inherent in exchange, to the extent that the "regulation" which this exchange implies does not come about without a renunciation of a savage and ever threatening process of accumulation. The temptation, however, is either to repudiate the rule and to allow all the possibilities of development to grow in anarchic fashion, the "law" of the strongest being the best, or conversely to turn exchange itself into a kind of "nature" whose functioning must be regained or forced. This temptation arises when one forgets the *origin* of the rule, that is, the *word*. If it is true that, in every order, the "natural" processes *call for* exchange, they do not produce it, while the mutual word that generates exchange *requires* concrete and living spaces which it orders but does not create.

The point of weakness, of "fallibility," to use the term of Paul Ricoeur, resides perhaps in this vital articulation, whose place can change, but which remains always "in the nascent stage," between all the "natural" forces (not only in the zoological or economical orders, but just as much in that of knowledge and desire) and the regulation by the "cultural" word which orders them for exchange. The word in fact can either not be said or be badly said, it can be not received or be badly received and responded to, with the result that *disorder* becomes inscribed, often in an indelible manner, both in nature and in culture: here begins the history of "evil."

Thus, in order to avoid all forms of gnosis, we must undertake once again the *theoretical* study of this relationship between *nature* (everything which demands to be "born") and *culture* (the whole order of the word which desires and establishes exchange), but also, inasmuch as this is possible, the *historical* investigation of the avatars of this relationship. Now this is scarcely possible unless one raises at different levels the question: *who* speaks? *To whom?* *Who* responds and *how?* In other words, the relationship between nature and culture should be able to be expressed in terms of the relationship between what is given and responsibility, both on the synchronic plane and on the diachronic plane.

3. The avoidance of all gnosis requires, finally, a reassessment of the *question of Being*. The history of Being traced by Heidegger is built on a rigorous opposition between available being, in the successive forms which it has taken and which have fashioned our civilization, and Being still unthought, whose unpredictable manifestation we await. The "gnostic" aspect of this opposition must be overcome, and this hardly seems possible except by going back over the notions at issue, their inner relationships, the history of their variations, the reasons for their distortion.

This new look at the question of Being is in every way correlative to a review of the question of history and to a reevaluation of the relationship nature/culture: indeed, as soon as one endeavors to recover the possible *value*[82] of historical developments, to reevaluate the presence and the responsibility of the word in the management of nature, one is necessarily lead to a nuanced appreciation of beings: they can no longer be viewed as being nothing more than that which conceals Being; they can just as well be that which manifests, reveals it, while conversely, Being may well never come about if one posits *a priori* its absolute separation from beings. In writing this, I think I am being perfectly faithful to one of the intuitions of Heidegger, namely, that *the being* is not separable from the totality of the process of civilization: to every conception of physics, of culture, of technology there corresponds respectively a metaphysics, a meta-culture, a meta-technology. These "meta-" disciplines cannot remain the same if the evaluation of the meaning and of the range of the disciplines themselves changes. By the very fact that I have, in a general way, denounced a gnostic attitude, I am obligated to review in particular the question of Being.

Heteronomy, narrativity and analogy

If the above observations are correct, it would be necessary and it should therefore be possible, to *rewrite*, at the level of the human sciences and of philosophy, more nuanced histories than the radical but oversimplified presentations which have been proposed to us. But in order to do so, to be able to discern and to apportion the elements of progress and of decline, of discovery and of error, it is doubtless necessary to establish *ultimate references* which are themselves founding and open. How shall we arrive at a view of time which, at the same time, respects the density of matter, the dissuasive power of the word, the possibility of a future as well as the wounds which culture has inflicted on itself? How shall we reach a reality of *Being* which does not get lost in particular being, but which does not lose the being either, and what language can we find which would not be reductive like that of onto-theology, nor intangible, like that of a totally aimless awaiting?

It is here, I think, that we can recover, while striving to give it its full force, the *principle of heteronomy*, which, as I noted above, has to some extent inspired the culture which I have described. I would like to propose here to understand it as a *founding* principle of heteronomy and to attribute two "valences" to it: that of *narrativity* and that of *analogy*.

To posit a principle of *heteronomy* is to situate the whole reflective enterprise within the perspective of *distance* revealed in various ways in the preceding investigations. But to speak of *founding* heteronomy means that this principle must be thought in such a way that it *also* founds for man and for the world an authentic identity, a measured knowledge, a responsible liberty. And it is here that the two valences mentioned come in.

To view the principle of heteronomy as a principle of *narrativity*, and hence to lay strong emphasis on the category of *narrative*, is to take up again the *real* time of man under the fundamental category of *hearing*: indeed, a narrative comes forward to be heard; then it yields itself to interpretation and is repeated. It points to a voice of which one can anticipate neither the saying nor the said, which is in a true sense originating because it is original, but one whose inaccessible character should found the temporality of man and of the world in a positive way and revise the way in which we perceive them. What one seeks in making oneself attentive to the heteronomy of the narrative is to restore to time its true figure, by rooting it in an origin which one can *hear*, that is to say which can come to expression, to the word, but in such a way that the latter cannot reduce it or dominate it; by opening it to an eschatology which can be—not described—but *evoked*, in such a way that the present can receive a direction; by defining the conditions of an authentic present, which can be *lived* (that is to say, carried into *saying* and *doing*), but without being in any way its own sole raison d'être. The principle of narrativity also foresees the possibility of hearing somewhere, not a myth of origins, but a *true founding narrative*, that is to say, one which allows us to discern the actual processes of human, personal and social existence, to be able to properly appreciate sexuality and work, as well as the history to which they give rise, to situate correctly the origin and the influence of evil.

One could say the same thing of the principle of *analogy*, the other valence of the founding heteronomy. I do not hesitate to employ this term "analogy," even though it may be a bit worn through the treatment it has been subjected to in the course of the ages, and by reason of the sad conflicts of which it has been the object. Indeed, everything we have been saying so far would allow us, before entering into the technique of its usage, to understand this term *analogy* on the basis of its prefix, *ana-*, which would appear to hint at everything that is at issue here; this prefix in fact rightly situates the dispute over the sufficiency of the *logos*, such as we are able to employ it. It is a question neither of transposing our *logos* into an empyrean heaven where it would have its true stature, nor conversely of substituting for it the illogic or the alogic of a pure and simple erasure, but rather of striving to link up the whole order of the *logos* to that which overarches it without annihilating it: the *ana*-logical, that is to say, that which cannot be said except in a limited and ultimate way, at the highest frontier of discourse, *but which can nevertheless be said*, for, at the heart of any discourse whatever there is something which indicates (in a way that it pertains precisely to philosophy, if not to define, at least to illuminate) an openness to this frontier and a desire to reach it. Far from reducing the unsayable to that which can be said, the principle of analogy links up all discourse to the analogue which founds it. However, if it very strongly challenges human autonomy and implies, at the level of the word as well as at that of liberty, a renouncing of self-sufficiency and an openness to that which does not come from the self, it does not have a destructive effect, and the "form of death" which it implies does not, as we shall see, have anything ambiguous about it. On the contrary, and this is precisely what we need, it enables us to think *Being*, in such a way that the nuances of *reality* and of *mystery*, through which it can be *thought* but not *dominated*, may be safeguarded.

Of God who comes to language

The principle of heteronomy, developed in these two distinct but correlative and articulated valences, of *narrativity* and *analogy*, is the theoretical principle which underlies the further developments of this book, whose aim is to interpret the figures of reality in a way which would be neither "compact," nor "gnostic." Now this principle should make it possible in fact (and this is indeed the true goal of this book) to rediscover a language suitable for talking about the living God. The authors studied so far reject God, when they do not ignore him altogether. But in their very rejection, some *prolegomena* to all discourse on God are taking shape: after all, if one must speak of God at all, it cannot be of a God who would be no more than the raison d'etre of the world, one who would be viewed only as the ultimate source of our own capacity, part of a "system" of which he would serve merely as the keystone. Of such a God, one would be able to speak in the same way in which one speaks of anything at all, but also (and this other side of the coin is too seldom stressed) one would be able to speak of anything at all as of God. For God in this hypothesis is no more than an attempt at the extrapolation to infinity of available being, of pure presence to self, of the will. In this regard, one might ask if Heidegger is right when he says that "man can neither pray nor sacrifice to this god. Before the *causa sui*, man can neither fall to his knees in awe, nor can he play music and dance before this god."[83] Both the history of religions and secular philosophical reflection on worship make it necessary to qualify this position considerably: the fact is that in the religions, the God whose uniqueness is stressed is not the object of cult; one worships rather the intermediary and active gods who have much in common with human beings and the world, and it is on this common basis that a cultic exchange, on the basic model of *do ut des*, becomes possible and develops. In actual fact, the difference is not between a cultic indifference with respect to a god *causa sui* and an authentic cult rendered to one who would truly be God; it is between a cult which one could call *circular* (god and the real making a vicious circle) and a *linear* cult rendered to a God who is other, different.

God who is different: this cannot mean a God *totally* unknowable and unutterable (how could one pronounce a name *absolutely* lacking in surety?), but rather a God susceptible of a *proper nomination*, and one to whom, for this very reason, one can refer time and space, Being and the founding word in a *non-systematic* way: a God who is founding *because* he is without—"absolved of"—foundation. The whole "problem of God" is perhaps right here: how to name a truly different, "absolved" God, if we can do so only *on the basis of* what is founded, which is all we have around us? The question is all the more urgent for the reason that if such a God could be named, it would become clear that the univocal language with which we speak of everything and of anything would be totally suspended from the nomination of this God! If one no longer speaks of God as of just anything, then there is no longer a "just anything," but rather, realities of Being and of knowledge whose own univocal nomination is suspended from the mysterious, proper nomination of God: would *Being* and *time* then finally have arrived at their truth?

Notes

1. "L'enchère et l'oeuvre d'art", in *CE, op. cit.*, p. 127-143.

2. Baudrillard speaks of this, in negative terms, a propos of *Bauhaus*: "Design et environnement ou l'esaclade de l'économie politique", in *CE*, pp. 229-256.

3. In choosing to speak of Antonin Artaud, on the question of rite and of myth, I am attempting to return, with an author whose influence on contemporary culture is considerable, in spite of the fact that his name is not known by all and that he is rarely cited in the theological world, to a path which was being charted in my theological youth by authors like Eliade and Van der Leeuw, Ricoeur with his classical *Symbolique de Mal* (Paris, 1960), Jacques Dournes in his marvelous *Dieu aime les païens* (Paris, 1963), etc. The special interest of the study of Artaud is the fact, as I put it, that we see the mythical attitude in its "living" state, in someone who is a contemporary of ours. I have consulted in particular the following works: Alain and Odette Virmaux, *Artaud, un bilan critique* (Paris, 1979); Jacques Derrida, "La Parole soufflée" and "The Theater of Cruelty and the Closure of Representation," two studies published in *Writing and Difference*, trans. Alan Bass (Chicago 1978); Henri Gouhier, *Antonin Artaud et l'essence du théâtre* (Paris, 1974); Gérard Durozoi, *Artaud, l'aliénation et la folie* (Paris, 1972). I was unable to consult the important work of S. Sontag, *A la rencontre d'Antonin Artaud* (Paris, 1976), until after having written these pages. (The texts of Artaud will be cited according to the *Œuvres complètes* [cited *OC*] except for *The Theater and its Double* and other cases where I was able to find an English translation. Translator's note.)

4. "A poetry of space", *The Theater and its Double*, trans. Mary Caroline Richards (New York, 1958), cited *TD*, p. 38f.

5. *TD*, p. 96; *OC*, V 35, p. 100.

6. The use of the words *magic, religion, rite, metaphysics* is almost constant when Artaud is speaking of theatre. See *TD*, pp. 9, 11, 12, 31, 32, 61, 63, 78, 80, 90, 91, 103, 111, 115-116, etc. These words are moreover very close in meaning, a meaning which may be approached with the help of the term *sacred*, such as it is employed in "On the Balinese Theater", which is initially characterized as "purely popular and not sacred" (*TD*, p. 56), although two pages later, Artaud compares it to a "sacred rite" (p. 58) and although, in reference to a detail of costume (women's headcoverings), he speaks of an "impression of inhumanity, of the divine, of miraculous revelation." This apparent contradiction is resolved as soon as one understands that it is a question of a natural sacred, that of the forces of nature in conflict and in the resolution of conflict, and not of the sacred of a particular religion or of a specific revelation.

7. *TD*, pp. 81, 85-86, 96: "A direct communication will be reestablished between the spectator and the spectacle, between the actor and the spectator, from the fact that the spectator, placed in the middle of the action, is engulfed and physically affected by it."

8. Cf. *OC*, V, p. 100: "I conceive of theater as something religious and metaphysical, but in the sense of an absolutely effective magical action." V, p. 38: "I conceive of theater as a magical performance or ceremony, and I am bent on restoring to it its primitive ritual character."

9. *TD*, p. 61. This expression is again taken from *On the Balinese Theater*, a text whose intense and enchanting poetry best suggests what Artaud had in mind in his study of theater. These liberated signs are: "music, dance, plastic art, pantomime, mimicry, gesticulation, intonation, architecture, lighting and scenery" (*TD*, p. 39), but this list is not exhaustive.

10. *TD*, 83: "A theater which, abandoning psychology, recounts the extraordinary, stages natural conflicts, natural and subtle forces . . . "; *TD*, 90: "These ideas which touch on Creation, Becoming, and Chaos, are all of a cosmic order." Cf. *OC*, V, 52.

11. *OC*, XIII, 109. We will see below the full meaning of this expression taken from "The Theatre of Cruelty", written in November 1947, but which is fully consistent, it seems to me, with what he had written in *The Theater and its Double*.

12. Cf. *The Theater and its Double*, pp. 93-100 and *passim*. The idea that the theater, such as Artaud sees it, gives no preponderance to, indeed reduces to unimportance the spoken text, but only utilizes the voice for its incantatory value, is constantly reaffirmed. An amusing example of this intentional depreciation of literary meaning and beauty may be found in his letter to Jean

Paul Paulhan, of November 27, 1932, in which Artaud speaks of an Elizabethan piece translated by André Gide which he could have staged: " . . . were it not for the rich and perfect language in which André Gide cast it, a richness and a perfection which are above all grammatical *and which will be almost totally invisible at the time of the performance* . . . " *Antonin Artaud: Selected Writings*, edited and with an introduction by Susan Sontag, (Susan Sontag trans.), (New York, 1976), p. 304. The emphasis is ours.

13. *TD*, p. 60 (with reference to the Balinese theater): " . . . in a secret psychic impulse which is Speech before words"; p. 62: "One senses in the Balinese theater a state prior to language and which can choose its own. . . . "

14. This is the whole sense of the term *cruelty*, which refers to the rigor of the primordial conflicts and to the Danger which they contain and which their true theatrical evocation involves: "a kind of cosmic cruely, closely related to the destruction without which nothing comes into being" (*OC*, V, 139). Artaud frequently undertakes to correct misunderstandings due to his use of this term. Cf. *TD*, 113-114; *OC*, V, 155; etc.

15. *TD*, 55.

16. *TD*, 58; *OC*, V, 58: " . . . precision, like that of the mechanism of a clock . . . rigor, the mathematical exits and entries of actors passing each other by while constructing a veritable geometry in the air of the stage," etc.

17. *OC*, V, 96.

18. *TD*, p. 60: "a kind of manager of magic, a master of sacred ceremonies."

19. *TD*, 94.

20. *TD*, 114.

21. *TD*, 53-4, 119: " . . . to create in complete autonomy." This would help to explain the terms of the letter to Jean-Louis Barrault of June 14, 1935: "If I am staging a play, I DO NOT WANT so much as the blinking of an eye which does not belong to me. . . . I am the kind of person who cannot stand having anyone with me in any work, whatever it may be. . . . " This is not a matter of unfathomable pride nor of enormous vanity; it is the demiurge of the sacred rite who here makes himself heard (V, 262).

22. On the "old duality between author and director" and the primacy of the latter, cf. *TD*, p. 94 and *passim*. On the concrete way in which author and director could work together, cf. the letter to André Gide, of August 7, 1932, *OC*, V, 118-122, of which the impertinent remarks to Jean Paulhan cited above do not convey the whole substance.

23. Efficacy: *TD*, 36; intellectual efficacy: *TD*, 71; internal psychic efficacy: *OC*, V, 208, etc. "We want a theater that functions actively, but on a level still to be defined": *TD*, 115.

24. "Its object is not to resolve social or psychological conflicts, to serve as a battlefield for moral passions, but to express objectively certain secret truths, to bring into the light of day by means of active gestures certain aspects of truth that have been buried under forms in their encounters with Becoming." (*TD*, 70; cf. 78-79, 123, etc.). The word *forms* is important here. In the prologue written for the publication of *The Theater and its Double*, under the title *The Theater and Culture*, Artaud insists on the necessity of going beyond the forms, of treating them brutally, of destroying them (which is precisely what makes the stage language he praises), but all in order to reach *life* at another level (*TD*, 12-13).

25. "The relationship of Artaud to the Greek tragedies is very complex" (A. and O. Virmaux, *op. cit.*, p. 226). One could say as much regarding his relationship with the Elizabethan theater, because, although he has some harsh things to say about Shakespeare, *TD*, 76-77, in #1 of his program in the *Premier Manifeste* of the Theater of Cruelty he proposed an adaptation of a work of the Shakespeare era (*Arden of Feversham*), translated by André Gide; cf. *supra* notes 12 and 22). In any case, a specific turning point takes place at the Renaissance period: "We have been accustomed for four hundred years, that is since the Renaissance, to a purely descriptive and narrative theater-story-telling psychology" (*TD*, 76). Racine is also held responsible (*TD*, 84).

26. *OC*, V, 101.

27. *TD*, 115.

28. *TD*, 28.

29. *OC*, V, 106.

30. *TD*, 85; *OC*, VIII, 350-351.

31. *TD*, 80-81.

32. A comparison between the theater of Artaud and psychoanalysis is conducted by J. Derrida in "The Theater of Cruelty and the Closure of Representation," in *Writing and Difference*, p. 241-243.

33. *OC*, V, 95.

34. *OC*, V, 195. Cf. what we will say below on the question of the body in Artaud.

35. *Ibid.*

36. *TD*, p. 116. One could note that it is toward the *Past* that stage action ultimately leads us.

37. *TD*, 81.

38. *TD*, 30: "Like the plague, the theater is a formidable call to the forces that impel the mind by example to the source of its conflicts."

39. *TD*, 87: ". . . the active role given to obscure poetic emotion."

40. *TD*, 51 and 114. I cannot cite at length these two very strong passages which reveal, here more than elsewhere, the consonance between Artaud and the mythical attitude, and, as I will bring out below, the Gnostic attitude.

Stage incantation should cause us to be reborn into another world, one inextricably interwoven with good and evil, evil being lodged in matter such as we know it. Cf. also the passage on the "hidden god" who, "when he creates, obeys the cruel necessity of creation" (*OC*, V, 155).

41. Cf. *TD*, 31 where we are told of the great dark myths and the "magnificent Fables" which "recount to the multitudes the first sexual division and the first carnage of essences that appeared in creation."

42. *TD*, 52. This phrase is the conclusion of an article which is in fact entitled "The Alchemical Theater," alchemy being another modality of return to the primordial by transmutation and fusion of present essences. Cf. also *OC*, V, 41.

43. *TD*, 80.

44. On these two events, cf. A. and O. Virmaux, *op. cit.*, p. 54-59.

45. A propos of the Balinese theater: "All of which seems to be an exorcism—to make our demons FLOW," *TD*, 60.

46. *OC*, V, 208.

47. It is striking that it is in *The Theater of Cruelty*, written for, but not used in *Pour en finir avec le jugement de Dieu*, that we find the most pointed statements on the "body without organs," the body with organs being the fruit of the initial deviation. It is not so much a question of "theater" in this text, but what is here written gives the ultimate meaning of theater according to Artaud (*OC*, XIII, 107-118). On the "body without organs" in the interpretation of Artaud by Deleuze and Guattari, cf. A. and O. Virmaux, *op. cit.*, p. 322-323.

48. *TD*, 42.

49. Artaud did in fact actually write this mythical narrative: it is *Héliogabale ou l'anarchiste couronné* (*OC*, VII, p.15-141), which is at once narrative and interpretation of narrative. Héliogabale is the living incarnation of the contradiction and of the war of Principles, of the primordial conflict and the forms that this engenders, but he is also the very figure of Anarchy (in the etymological sense of the term: of non-principle in which everything is resolved); he is the "mythomaniac in the literal and concrete sense of the term" (*OC*, VII, p.117), at the dividing line between the "archies" and anarchy, who places his power at the service of the "true myths" which he applies "for the first and perhaps the only time in history." One could take, element by element, the characteristics of the stage according to Artaud and the analysis of the life and the behavior of Héliogabale. Moreover: "The life of Héliogabale is theatrical. But his theatrical manner of conceiving existence aims at creating a true magic of the real, etc." (*OC*, VIII, 350).

50. *OC*, XIII, 108.

51. Cf. *supra*, note 6.

52. *Mythes, rêves et mystères* (Paris, 1957), p. 17.

53. On this point, see G. Durozoi, *Artaud, l'aliénation et la folie*, (Paris, 1972), p. 173-176.

54. *Roman des origines et origines du roman* (Paris, 1972).

55. Cf. M. Augé, *Génie du paganisme*, (Paris, 1982), p. 149. According to Derrida ("La parole soufflée," *Writing and Difference*, p. 180) the essence of the mythical itself is the dream of a life without difference.

56. "Restored to its absolute and terrifying proximity, the stage of cruelty will thus return me to the autarchic immediacy of my birth, my body and my speech. Where has Artaud better defined the stage of cruelty than in *Here Lies*, outside every apparent reference to the theater: 'I, Antonin Artaud, am my son/my father, my mother/and myself' " (J. Derrida, *Writing and Difference*, p. 190).

57. The publication and diffusion of the *Œuvres Complètes* sufficiently attest to the cultural importance of Artaud in the contemporary world.

58. Cf. on this point A. and O. Virmaux, *op. cit.*

59. Cf. an overall view in the articles devoted to the novel (under *roman*) in the *Encyclopedia Universalis*, t. 14 (1972), p. 315-337.

60. Cf. M. Augé, *op. cit.*, p. 147-148; C. Lévi-Strauss, *L'Homme nu*, (Paris 1971), p. 585.

61. Marthe Robert, *op. cit.*, Part I: "Le genre indéfini."

62. *Ibid.*, p. 39.

63. *Ibid.*, p. 30-38 and *passim*.

64. There is agreement, on this point, between Marthe Robert and René Girard in his works of literary criticism, *Mensonge romantique et Vérité romanesque* (Paris, 1961) and *Critiques dans un souterrain* (Lausanne, 1976). I will cite according to the more recent paperback editions. Girard calls the desire that underlies the writing of the novel "metaphysical" or "ontological," as opposed to the "physical" desire: the latter refers to an object which the narrator desires; the former is directed at the double, the otherness, through imitation of the desire of the other (cf. among other places, *Mensonge romantique . . .* , p. 103).

65. Marthe Robert, *op. cit.*, p. 133 ff., 191, 246, 275.

66. *Ibid.* p. 238.

67. *Ibid.* p. 188.

68. *Ibid.* p. 260, 299.

69. It seems, because of his discussion with Freud and psychoanalysis in general (on which I do not wish to take sides here), that Girard does not give sufficient importance in his theory of the novel to this question of the rejected identity and hence of the conflict with the image of the father. In spite of an acceptance in principle (*Critiques*, p. 33) and the recognition of the capital importance of the problem of the father and of patricide in Dostoyevski (*ibid.*, p. 107-113), the analysis of this rejection and the inquiry into its causes is not

pushed very far—a fact which will have important consequences when Girard moves on from the novel to myth and to Christian thinking.

70. Marthe Robert, *op. cit.*, 41-62.
71. Cf. *supra*, note 55.
72. Marthe Robert, *op. cit.*, p. 135 f, 143, 191, etc.
73. *Ibid.*, p. 136, 140, 181, 203 f.
74. Artaud, such as we understand him, situates himself rather on the side of the found Child and of his horror of birth, than on the side of the Bastard. This is why his work bears so strongly the mark of the rite and of myth.
75. Marthe Robert, *op. cit.*, 95 f.
76. *Mensonge romantique*, chap. XII; *Critiques*, p. 133-135.
77. If my comments are well-founded, they may help the reader to better understand what I was trying to say above (Chapt. II, 1, note 27) when I remarked that the problematic of Engels belonged to the mythical theme of the Image and its double. Marthe Robert, *op. cit.* p. 199-203, retraces the figure of a line, that of the found Child, which was carried forward by Hesiod in antiquity and Don Quixote in modern times. Engels could have a place here as well: in his book, here and there as it were, the nostalgia of origins is at work, the rejection of finitude viewed as culpable, and the desire to push back the frontier of birth. Unfortunately, we are no longer here at the level of poetry, of the novel, or even of the Theater of Cruelty. Because it presents itself as being scientific (and because it actually contains a number of pertinent remarks when it analyzes civilization), the myth of Engels pretends to be in contact with historical reality, and the "rite of return" can here only take the form of an actual bloody revolution, because it is a matter of returning beyond civilization. The tragedy is that, beyond the revolutionary rite, one finds not Paradise, but, as in the case of the myth and the novel, death and madness.

Like the so-called primitive societies, like the theater of Antonin Artaud, like the author and the reader of the modern novel, Engels rejects en bloc the complex and mixed human identity which the present state of civilization offers him and substitutes for him, in an imaginary future, the prenatal identity of the natural society, whose characteristics are mainly the negation of what we see around us today. I would add that, if one could find a synthetic book on the history of civilization written from the point of view of unlimited economical liberalism, one would doubtless recognize here some of the traits of the Bastard figure! Who will give us a figure at once more complex and more realistic—that of the courageous Child who combines an accepted filiation with a continuous effort to correct the present and to confront the future?

78. Cf. "Ousia and Gramme," in *Margins*, p. 73f. and *Positions*, p. 54, and see p. 102, note 25.
79. For example: "The trace must be thought before the entity. But the movement of the trace is *necessarily occulted* . . . when the other announces

itself as such, it presents itself in the *dissimulation of itself.*" (*Of Grammatology*, p. 47. The emphasis is my own).

80. "Déhiscence": I am alluding here to an observation of Jacques Lacan, which I did not have occasion to take into account in the text of this first part. I refer to an important point in the study of the famous "mirror stage." I briefly recall the problematic: the bearing of the identification a child gives himself when he sees himself in a mirror for the first time is decisive for the rest of his life. This glance in the mirror communicates to him a kind of total experience of his form, a first image of the me, on the basis of which he will be able to structure his relationships with the external world: a formation which is highly beneficial, because it will enable the child to establish himself with respect to himself, to supply a center for the multiplicity of his movements, to escape a piecemeal perception of his body parts, which themselves, up until this point, have not been clearly differentiated from the objects of his environment. What we have then is a process of identification which conquers fragmentation or dispersion and should enable the child, with his newly acquired self-identity, to open himself to the encounter with others and to enter freely into language. Now this is not what takes place, or it does so only with difficulty: the image of the "I" becomes as it were a place of refuge, a field of retrenchment, whose word will be one of defense and of repetition. Lacan attributes this hardening to the fact that the image thus formed would be premature—and we must understand this last word in a rather strongly organic manner: the image intervenes at a moment of "anatomic incompletion" (= before the *fontanelles*, or soft spots, have closed), and they harden up as it were with the organism itself during the first months of life. The image produced at the "mirror stage" would hence be not only the beneficial form of a desirable identification, but the permanent stigma of the primordial Discord between completed nature and the premature subject who enters into it too quickly. It is Lacan who writes "primordial Discord" with a capital "D," and he speaks of a "déhiscence of the natural harmony, which Hegel wanted to make the fruitful malady, the happy fault of life, where man, distinguishing himself form his essence, discovers his existence." An Hegelian *felix culpa* is here interpreting the analytical data. Happy? It is in any case at the root of narcissism, of the death instinct, of the suicide tendency. According to traditional Gnosticism too, if we can rely in this matter on the judgment of Lacarriere, "we are all premature individuals. . . . That original Error which has sown imperfect seeds, premature entities into an immature world is the source of that sentiment of solitude, of perdition, that world discomfort which are the lot of man." (Cf. J. Lacan, *Écrits*, [Paris, 1966], p. 94-97, 186, 345; J. Lacarrière, *op. cit.*, note 4, p.40 and 80). With all of this, I do not wish to question the clinical truth of the "mirror stage"; but does its ultimate interpretation require this secularized gnosticism?

81. I refer here to the little book of Jacques Lacarrière, *Les Gnostiques*, (Paris, 1973). The interest of this book derives from the fact that it shows in a striking way what one could call the *stakes* and the *urgency* of the gnostic decision. The world presents itself as it is, with its ruptures and breaks of every sort: how are we to interpret it and be prepared to face it in interpreting it? The historical gnosticisms have given their responses and promoted their practices, but the principle of gnosticism, that is to say, the principle of the primordial break, and the essence of the practice—a turning back, a revolution, or simply what Derrida calls the awaiting of the "unnamable"—seem to have remained unchanged.

82. We may recall that Heidegger proceeds to a deconstruction of the notion of "value," in connection with his critique of onto-theology, which is as strong at its own level as is that of Baudrillard in sociology. Cf. H. Mongis, *Heidegger et la critique de la notion de valeur*, (La Haye, 1976). But if the very idea of value is contested, how can we recognize anything at all as being "of value"?

83. *Identity and Difference*, English trans. (New York: Harper & Row, 1967), p. 72, to be compared with M. Eliade, *Traité d'histoire des religions*, (Paris 1949), p. 54-55; J. Dournes, *Dieu aime les païens*, (Paris, 1963), pp. 51-54. Is not the entire drift of Augustine's argument in the ten first chapters of the *City of God* aimed at convincing his readers that only the one God (and therefore neither angels nor demons nor spirits of any kind) has a right to be worshipped?

PART II

Time in Jesus Christ

INTRODUCTION

A PRINCIPLE OF NARRATIVITY

A conversion to hearing

In the preceding part, I have interpreted a number of investigations as so many attempts to reach a *lost founding narrative* which would establish man's temporality, exorcise his evils, anticipate his transformation. In other words, the theme of the primordial break would reveal the secret desire for a founding heteronomy on the plane of time and of history. Nevertheless, if the works studied have a touch of narrativity, the latter is the work of man himself, who is attempting to reconstruct a genealogy on the basis of the situation in which he finds himself—whether this regards the history of thought, the history of civilization as a whole, or merely that of an individual. Likewise, the liturgical or mystical attitudes regarding the present or the future or the conjectures regarding the future of history, are *produced* by man himself as he confronts his problems. Nevertheless, it is evident that, if the object is to rediscover a heteronomy on the temporal plane, the latter can only reveal itself to a *hearing*: man cannot supply himself with his own origins, nor can he create his end; nor is he capable of responding by himself to the question posed to him continuously by the overlapping of finitude and culpability: there are things that must be *learned* (*apprendre*) before they can be *taken up again* (*reprendre*) to be employed in a creative way. The whole question regarding the founding narrative of temporality, resides then in this dilemma: *production* or *hearing*?[1]

The primacy of witness

For witnesses must come forward: the lost narrative cannot be "immemorial," "archaic," "anonymous":[2] it is a question of *hearing*, not of reading or of imagining, even if the witnesses speak of realities or of circumstances that transcend the logical level of human words. What one wishes to learn is something that one cannot give to oneself: his birth, his call, evil and its forgiveness, request and promise.

Given this limiting character of the object of testimony, the witness can only give account of what he has himself received. On the one hand, he has himself been founded, and on the other hand he has received information regarding this foundation that makes it possible for him to bear witness. It is the very founding which he himself has experienced and acknowledged that enables him to render testimony to the Author of this founding, recognized at once as origin (point of departure from which a founding narrative becomes possible) and beyond origin (because he is not defined by his relationship to that which is founded). Testimony then takes on a peculiar language, because it expresses at one and the same time the Origin beyond origin, the witness' own experience and the universal foundation, as well as his destiny.

The epistemological status of original testimony will then have to be established with care, as will its criteria of veracity. We could suggest here that the ultimate verification is intimately bound up with the power of liberation released by the founding narrative: if, after having heard the witnesses' story, one finds oneself endowed with a marvelous capacity of courageously echoing this word and of pioneering the paths of a future instead of coming up desperately against the imminence of an end of civilization, it is probably because this narrative was and remains true.

"Even if it communicates nothing, speech represents the existence of communication; even if it denies the evidence, it affirms that the word establishes truth; even if it aims to deceive, it banks on faith in witness."[3] This statement of Jacques Lacan is extremely suggestive to the extent that, in the very ambiance of psychoanalysis, which is that of the word at its most infirm, or perhaps in a crisis of inflation, one discerns by negative image the authentic aim of the word: communication, truth, witness. There are good grounds to believe that in the process of restoring these lost components, the progressive restitution of hearing is a decisive factor. One is always capable of producing speech that falls short of, or remains outside of communication and therefore of reality, but if one wishes to speak truly, it is necessary to learn to listen again in order to know how to respond. Now there is in a way an organic link between speech without hearing, the horror of birth, the wish never to have been born of anyone, in short, the self-constitution into a solipsistic *Cogito*, the rejection of the whole idea of having received *name* and *body* from another and a hardened attitude before the witness that attests this origin. What we are saying is that the search for the lost narrative presupposes a conversion of heart to hearing, a readiness to listen to witnesses who might come forth, a desire for reconciliation with one's own body and with the world, an attitude of acceptance, however tenuous, toward reopening a history with human beings. This attitude, which could also be called *faith*, incarnates in man a true passion for heteronomy and prepares one to acknowledge witnesses if they come forth.

In an effort to better clarify the nature of this original testimony, I would like to compare it, on the one hand to the *scientific narrative of origins*, such as paleontology can supply, with respect to man, or astrophysics, which extends to the universe as a whole, and on the other hand, to the *narrative of birth* which every human being normally receives from those who brought him or her into the world. In the first case, it is actually a question of the ultimate origins which we are looking for (and this is probably why everyone is so fond of well-done popular presentations in these matters), but at the level of the language of *science*. In the second case, we are dealing with a particular origin and with an individual identity (regarding which everyone is also basically curious), but at the level of the language of *testimony*.

Scientific history of origins[4]

First of all, I will attempt to show the contributions of this multiform discipline before pointing out its limits from the point of view that concerns us here.

On the positive side, such a discipline witnesses to the importance of *body* or, in general, of *materiality* for human existence—which should allow, correlatively, for a renewed evaluation of *time*. From this point of view, it contributes to removing any basis for a mythical or a gnostic attitude. Paleontology, for example, works on body data; it studies fossils, when possible in the environment in which it finds them. We could say that its object, in the ultimate analysis, is the progressive formation of the human bodily figure, according to a process whose beginnings are lost in the night of time, but whose stages one attempts to recover as it moves toward the appearance of that upright being endowed with free hands and the inchoative faculty of symbolizing described by Leroi-Gourhan. The techniques are quite different in the case of astrophysics, but the intention is the same: to retrace, if possible, a history of the world all the way back to the original explosion, and to sketch the subsequent history, first of the solar system and then of the entire universe. We are dealing here with a history of body and of bodies, and also with a certain delimitation of the available temporal framework. We are in a field where myths and gnoses have no place.

A second benefit of the scientific investigation of origins is that it effects, in principle, the dissociation impossible until then between birth and fall, matter and evil, finitude and culpability. Whatever its term, *this history of body is not a history of evil*; it traces a natural development, ethically neutral and entirely lacking in tragic connotations. It has the effect at its own level of inquiry of exorcising the archaic "horror of birth" and constitutes for this reason a corrective pedagogy for man in search of his origin.

This dissociation between finitude and fault appears perhaps even more vividly in the light of the latest researches on the total history of the universe. We have now a *finite* image of time, at least of our own time; we have learned to understand it within the context of the history of the solar system and we are able to predict when the conditions for human survival will have disappeared from the earth, before the latter has faded into non-existence. Even if it is not for tomorrow, this gives us at least a specific awareness of finitude, which will by no means be unfavorable to the hearing of a *founding* narrative.

Nevertheless, however interesting the research it promotes might be and however probable some of its conclusions, the scientific history of origins cannot yield the *narrative* we are looking for. Indeed, this narrative should tell us *where we come from* and it should be made for us in such a way that we can bring faith to the one who speaks to us and to what he tells us. In contrast, what scientific history shows us is rather the fact that evolution has been following a course which—at least for the moment—ends with man. Striving to conjecture how man appeared in a delicate network of phyletic series, it must finally acknowledge that the reality which has thus appeared presents unique morphological characteristics, in virtue of which it surpasses every other living being. Whatever his preferences may be for one or another of the overall theories of evolution, the man who looks at himself from the perspective opened by paleontology can scarcely avoid the conclusion that everything has ultimately been drifting toward himself and that this evolution has not produced anything else that even approaches him. The narrative of his origins and the evocation of his end cannot come to him from this avenue: he is looking for a "beyond" to which or rather to whom he can relate. Instead, he is shown that he is himself the "beyond" of everything that lives and moves on the earth. This is not really his problem.

One could say the same thing in other terms. The scientific history of origins is not a narrative; its literary genre is not immediately narrative. It is a reconstruction conducted on the basis of unwritten documents, according to methods which are continuously being revised and refined, by man himself. This is not a narrative which man hears; it is a tentative text which he produces. I believe that it is radically impossible for anyone engaged in this type of discipline to ever arrive at saying precisely where and when man appeared (whether this "where" and this "when" is envisaged in the singular or in the plural is a question of no importance here), what *name* he bore and who gave it to him, and what was his first occupation. Science reconstructs the event of man's appearance as though no one had been there to give him a name; this is why it is not concerned (and cannot be concerned) to promote a kind of "birthday celebration" of humanity, although the learned paleontologist will joyously celebrate his child's birthday. This distance between the necessary warmth of a family celebration and the collective silence with respect to the concrete origins of humanity is sufficient to demonstrate the inadequacy of a scientific explanation of the anthropocentric type. This explanation is certainly not useless nor is it completely without interest; but in order for it to really signify something, it must be inscribed within a vaster ensemble, defined by a true *narrative*. If it says something useful and true regarding the appearance of man on earth, it can say nothing about the birth of humanity properly so called, nor certainly about his eschatalogical fulfillment. Here it can only yield to narrative and to celebration—but how would it be possible to *celebrate human origins* at a level of thinking and of discourse where there is no one to whom "Our Father" might be addressed? If, on the other hand, there were to exist a feast at which all human beings could hear again the words "You are my son" and respond to this by saying "Our Father," would it not be in this feast that humanity would finally rediscover its roots? In this respect, we could ask ourselves if the ancients who *celebrated* in a single and complex celebration, the origins of the world, the enthronement of the king and the return of the new year, did not have an attitude which *it would be absolutely necessary to recover* in order to insure that our quest for origins and for destiny receive the response that it is capable of receiving.[5]

Narrative of birth and personal identity[6]

In order better to grasp the nature of this desire for a lost founding narrative, we could hazard here a few considerations on the identity of the human individual and his dependence with respect to the birth narrative. As we saw above, the reaction of man to his birth is ambiguous. On the one hand, he more or less rejects it, forgets, effaces or simply ignores the narrative or story he is told about it, in his desire for another identity which one could call "romantic"; on the other hand, he remains passionately attached to his birth, to the point that if he lacks this narrative altogether, as in the case of the children of "unknown parents," he will do anything in the world to discover his origins, or if the narrative was erroneous, he will be seriously disturbed when he finds this out.[7]

A moving passage of the book of Ezekiel[8] sets forth the remote origins of pagan Jerusalem by means of an allegory of a child who was not accepted at birth by her foreign parents. Her body was not acknowledged; it was not carefully separated from that of its mother, but rather pulled away forcibly; she was not washed or clothed, and there was no one there to give her a name. She would still be there, abandoned, without real identity, if God had not come to address a word to her and thus create the first living relationship on the basis of which the child was able to grow.

This allegory indicates the extent to which man's identity is constituted by his body being *acknowledged* and by the word of the other being *heard*. What comes into the world at a birth is not only a "creative variation in the progress of time," the advent of a new signification, the irruption of a not yet edited program. Or rather, it is all of this, through the event of a conception (this too consisting of body and of word), of an intra-uterine development, of a bodily exit from the womb, of the arrival of a flesh and blood Being. But in order for this arrival to be truly a birth and to confer its identity on the child, this history of its body must be acknowledged by those who are responsible for it: the care given to it, the closing of its umbilical opening that makes it a separate being, the word that gives it a name—all of this serves both to endorse the story of the conception and birth and to introduce the child into a society where he will be able to be addressed and where, in turn, he will be able to invoke. So the confidence of an identity and the freedom and security of a human life depend at a very profound level on the actions and on the word of someone other than the self—from the very beginning.

This initial relationship, however, is extended and reinforced by *narrative* and by *feast*. What the child lived through as he came into existence, the memory of which is profoundly inscribed in his being, reaches his explicit awareness through the narratives or stories he hears as he begins to ask more and more questions. The *testimony* rendered to him by very concrete individuals, his parents, brings to word what already exists in his lived experience. Nothing can replace this word which bears on events, in part outside even of his implicit experience, because the child had not been born and perhaps not even conceived when they took place, and in part in his experience—but which he is incapable of verbalizing in any way. This witness, borne and received, is essential to enable the "I," which will henceforth never cease to express itself, to take root in its time and in its space. The news which thus arrives "late on the scene" and which corresponds to "prior" events structures the identity; it enriches the memory with things not explicitly recalled but none the less founding. In other words, the story of his origins comes to man as testimony to the fact that his identity is first of all something given to him, a gift. This identity is prior to self-mastery and to responsibility: these latter, far from establishing his original identity, emerge and develop in accordance with his acceptance of this story, to which the one who hears it spontaneously brings *faith*. It is this witness-faith ensemble, and not a primary and solipsistic evidence of self, which ultimately grounds the conscious identity.

The *name* summarizes and signifies this story of the birth: it is first of all a name given by the parents, which the child hears. Once accepted and assumed, the name becomes the medium of exchange and of covenant, the symbol through which the never-ending game of demand and of gift, of hearing and of responsibility is played out. Man does not have power over his name, since it is something that he has received, any more than he has power over the story of his birth. Subsequently it will be up to him to make of his name what he wills: to open himself to the appeals that this name receives or to close himself in on a name become sterile.

The story, or narrative is also "necessary" if man is to truly recognize himself as *body* and not merely as consciousness. The narrative in fact brings to word, not only that which has reference to one or more personalities, to the quality and to the vicissitudes of a love, to the advent of a consciousness, etc., but also and inseparably concerns a history of bodies and of the body in which everything has become incarnated and which symbolizes everything. On the contrary, a *Cogito*, independent of narrative and based only on the evidence of thought, can only be the result of a previous cleavage, unconscious perhaps, and can only bring on another. Because the *Cogito* estranges from the founding narrative, it is already in rupture from a global identity and, to the extent that it aims at founding a conscious identity, it sanctions the divorce between the Me and the body.

When the narrative is received, on the contrary, it inspires *celebration*, for example, of the birthday. Celebration arises spontaneously from the truth of time, of narrative and of the body. It would be artificial if it served only to scan the succession of the years: why celebrate moments in which, according to a purely astronomical recurrence, a year is simply being added to others, thus bringing one closer to death? And the feast would be no less artificial if its aim were to put all temporality in parentheses for a moment, or if it merely wished to create a space of play (or of cult) outside of time and space, where pure presence would be glorified. But celebration is true when it expresses the *superimposition of times*. It is symbolic behavior or action capable of saying that the time of this individual, of his body, of his heart, is not exhausted in the pure present; he *is* also the time of his origin and of his destiny, that of his parents and of his posterity, and also, as we shall later see, that of God with him. This time comes forward, thanks to symbol and narrative, without confusion or separation, in celebration. Celebration is a repetition of birth, an evocation of life, an anticipation of glory: it is rooted in a story or in a number of stories and it sets the stage for others; it takes place through an original display of symbols and of bodies. It resumes and prolongs the grace of the beginning and, quite literally, re-news life.

Everything we have just said obviously presupposes the *truth* of the narrative. In this respect, one could first of all say, inverting the proposition, that truth is here always presupposed, because it is of the very essence of narrative, as it is of every addressed word, to be not totally verifiable. Every word relationship is rooted in a mutual consent to faith: in a dialogue procedure, verification is part, not of the bringing to evidence of what is said, but rather of the *intellectus fidei* (I take the expression here outside of its theological connotation). This is more true when it is a question of a narrative of origin told to a child; in this case, faith too, is more spontaneous than in any other, because hearing a word about his birth belongs to the most profound level of a man's being. One could, if necessary, establish a sufficient probability for certain elements of the narrative, through procedures that pertain to historical criticism. However, here more than anywhere else in the domain of history, the evidence is fragmentary; when one has obtained it, the truth can once again be obtained only by way of a renewed faith in those who told the story, whose authority and testimony is acknowledged. Once again, it is impossible to have an identity and hence to live except by accepting to *hear* a narrative which brings to word that which one has *received* but not produced: his body and his name.

The problem of the truth of the birth narrative comes from elsewhere: from the fact that neither those who tell the story nor the one who hears it are capable of fully reaching the truth.[9] Consciously or not, the narrative conceals elements, anecdotic or psychic, which were present to the original history of the child, even before his conception, and which are therefore inscribed in his own body or in his psyche without having been brought to verbal expression. The acceptance of the narrative is marked by these elements, and we have here perhaps one of the reasons which leads or will lead the child to modify, even to falsify, his identity, once the need of assuring himself of one by faith in testimony has been satisfied. In a sense, the entire history of the world, of its evil, of its salvation, of its forward thrusts and of its relapses, is present in every individual history, for there exists a solidarity of fact, *bodily inscribed*, between all the ages of humanity as well as between two immediate generations. And perhaps the effort of each individual human being consists throughout his whole life in, on the one hand, taking his turn as the bearer of a creative word, and on the other, in recovering from his original and historical evil. Thus, in a twofold way, he reestablishes himself in the truth.

These observations on the necessity of a birth narrative, with its inevitable ambiguities, and on the faith, likewise mixed, which is given it, can help us to form a rough outline in negative image of the characteristics of the more comprehensive founding narrative of which we have need, if there is a possible solution other than assorted gnostic variants of myth. This narrative must bear on the origins, not so much to describe the facts in anecdotal detail (we will see that this is not possible) as to compel us to acknowledge the One who originates; it must also define an orientation, without which time cannot take on its value and outside of which one is condemned to the nostalgia of a "before" (an idealized prior historical situation), whatever it might be, of the present condition; finally, it must also account for evil, which is not possible unless we adopt the perspective not only of pardon (evil is no longer imputed) but of salvation (a positive condition is restored). With all these characteristics, the narrative at once situates the world and man in a perspective where they are not primary, and it validates their being and their destiny; a history is possible, one that reaches into corporality and time, whose issue lies before us and not behind us.

From the preceding investigations, I would like to retain a number of points that are important for our purposes:

1. The identity of a human being, both from the personal point of view of his individual birth and from the universal point of view of his belonging to humanity, is *founded* on a *narrative* which the human being accepts to hear.

2. This narrative owes its existence to *witnesses*, more or less directly encountered, but in any case real and personal, to whom one accords one's faith.

3. This narrative has to do with the whole of man, and therefore in a very real way with his *body*, that is to say with a spacial-temporal insertion and history.

4. The ambiance of this narrative is very naturally *feast*, or *celebration*, not as an escape from time and space for ritual benefits which would pertain to an *in illo tempore*, but as a high point which invests time with a certain rhythm and confers on it its true figure.

5. Man has a tendency, however, to *keep clouding over the narrative*, to replace it with narratives which are *produced* rather than heard, or with *constructed* descriptions and speculations, or, under the guise of legitimate scientific research, he contents himself with the reconstruction of the evolutionary process which *sets the stage for* the

arrival of man, but does not give him birth. But the real issue is precisely birth.

These two examples, the scientific history of origins and the narrative of individual birth, can help us to understand in some small way the place and the modality of a *founding narrative*. The scientific history of origins tells us something of these to be sure, but according to how it has been able to *reconstruct* them; as for the future, it leaves us, as far as man is concerned, with a rather bleak prospect, and as far as the cosmos is concerned, with an ineluctable future of darkness and glacial cold. Nevertheless, the need to hear a comprehensive narrative remains, and thus also the question: *who* can *tell* us what time is all about?

Conversely, the narrative of individual birth is indeed a narrative *heard* and not produced, through which a person can establish himself in time and envisage life. But the genealogical capacities of the memory are weak and the testimony here involved necessarily limited. This *individual* narrative does not dispense with the need for a *universal founding narrative*; and again: *who* will be able to testify at this level?[10]

It is to these questions that I would now like to outline a response.

Notes

1. The level of investigation at which I attempt to place myself is neither that of literary genre, nor that of narrative technique. It seems to me that the new emphasis on narrative in theology in recent research is worked out at two levels: on the one hand, the necessity of resorting to an alternative literary genre, given the bankruptcy of onto-theological discourse in the cultural perspective dominated by the theme of the "death of God"; the names of J. B. Metz (among other articles: "A Short Apology of Narrative" in *Concilium*, May 1973, 84–96) and E. Jüngel (cf. *God as the Mystery of the World: on the Foundations of the Theology of the Crucified One in the Dispute between Theism and Atheism*, trans. Darrel L. Guder [Grand Rapids, Mich.: Eerdmans, 1983], 299–314, cf. the bibliography on p. 304, n. 14) should be mentioned here. The other level of investigation is more that of the formation of narrative, whether from the hermeneutical (cf. Paul Ricoeur, *Temps et Récit*, vol.I, Paris, 1982), or structural point of view (for the problematic and a bibliography, see e.g., Claude Chabrol and Louis Marin, *Le Récit évangélique*, Paris, 1974). Without ignoring these two aspects, to which I will have more

than one occasion to refer, I shall attempt to situate myself at a level that is in some sense anterior to these: the narrative as witness and locus of human non-autonomy, an event of discourse where an absolute primacy of hearing is manifested, or again, the place of a discourse which, in the most fundamental sense, is not produced.

In this perspective, one can perceive the affinity of the two valences of the principle of heteronomy: if the narrative is heard, it will be, in its very texture, a compound of narrative and meta-narrative (on this expression, cf. C. Chabrol, op. cit., 58–63). And the latter will not, in my opinion, be able to dispense with a reflection on Being. As we will see later, when we speak of Genesis 2–3 and the Book of Job, the two aspects of the principle of heteronomy, analogy and narrativity, function together.

2. It matters little whether the production be recent, as for example the *Theatre of Cruelty*, or immemorial and anonymous as in the myths assembled by Lévi-Strauss. Conversely, it is very important that a *heard founding narrative* be referable to clearly identified authors who are its authors *because they were eye witnesses*: this is, I believe, the *theological* significance of old problems like that of the Mosaic authorship of the Pentateuch; in a sense, this question comes out unscathed from all the clarifications brought to bear by historical-critical exegesis: if Moses cannot be appealed to as guarantor of the Law, then there is no Law.

3. *Écrits* (Paris, 1966), p. 251.

4. I am not thinking here of any particular narrative, that of Leroi-Gourhan or any other more recent account, but of *narrative* as a necessary mode of a presentation of origins; for astrophysics, cf. H. Reeves, *Patience dans l'azur. L'évolution cosmique* (Paris, 1981).

5. Cf. J. van Goudoever, *Biblical Calendars*, 2nd revised ed. (Leiden, 1961), pp. 36–44 and R. Martin-Achard, *Essai biblique sur les fêtes d'Israel* (Geneva, 1974), pp. 93–104.

6. For what follows, I am much indebted to the work of Denis Vasse on which I have often reflected, and in particular *L'Ombilic et la Voix* (Paris, 1974), chapters II and V. I thank some dear friends, in particular B. and M.-O. Lafont, J.-M. and A.-M. Lévêques, C. and C. Ramphft who were kind enough to share with me the fruit of their experience in this domain.

7. Cf. Jacques Lacan, *Écrits*, op. cit., p. 277.

8. Ez. 16:3–14.

9. "Parents always tell the truth, but they do not tell the whole truth, and it is in this divergency that deception comes in. And I ask myself if, intuitively, the creation and the resurrection might not be precisely events in which there is no divergency between what is said and the experience of the event" (B. Lafont).

10. The testimonies that I received often noted how difficult it is for children to reflect on or even to admit a "before" with respect to their birth. That there could have been a time when they were "not yet born" sometimes strikes them as unacceptable (is this already a mark of "sin" in them?). In any case, this provides a good opportunity for parents to impart an elementary catechesis on God and his creative love.

CHAPTER ONE

THE EASTER NARRATIVE

Fragmentary as they may be, the points I have made on the principle of narrativity and the examples supplied can tentatively suffice to indicate what seems to me to be the general interpretative norm of any reasoning and any text which would claim to bring out the ultimate meaning of human existence and to respond to the need of salvation which is inherent in it. This norm is that of a *primacy of hearing*, which is structurally and chronologically prior to any *production of meaning* and remains continuously present to the latter to direct and inspire its efforts.

It is in the light of this principle that I would like now to look at the narrative which the Christian faith views as founding, not only of its particular existence and of the communities which it brings together, but of human history in general: I refer to the narrative of the resurrection of Jesus of Nazareth, who was crucified at the end of a short life marked by an intense prophetic activity in the midst of the Jewish people. The form of this narrative and the conditions of its transmission will first be considered so as to clarify its epistemological import and to verify its founding value.

I.
A FOUNDING NARRATIVE

The problematic proposed entails the choice of a viewpoint from which to present the narration of the Paschal Mystery of Jesus: the story will be told by going from the Resurrection to the Resurrection passing through the cross. The reason for this is clear enough: alone of all the prophets and the suffering just of history (and this latter category includes many whose example and teaching remain important and necessary), Jesus of Nazareth was proclaimed risen, that is to say, mysteriously conducted beyond a death in which his witness as a suffering just man was perfected and fulfilled. It is on the basis of a confession of Jesus living "beyond" death that the Christian community came into existence and that it continues to witness and to live. Now such a proclamation and such a confession belong, and they alone belong, to this *founding narrative* which must first of all be *heard*, precisely because, from a certain point of view at least, they transcend the regime of time and of space and point toward a fulfillment which is also a new "creation." Taken by itself, the death of Jesus does not exhibit this founding characteristic, and the danger is that it would receive this only through productions of meaning, through interpretations which one could suspect of being mythical or belonging to the ideal order: projections onto a miscellaneous event, as well attested as any other of Roman history, of ideological constructions supplied by a humanity at a loss for salvation. Precisely in virtue of that which it tells and of that to which it witnesses, the narrative of the Resurrection belongs to another epistemological level, one which necessarily presupposes the recognition of a founding heteronomy. This is why the Easter narration must be received on the basis of the Resurrection.

In doing this, we are in no way downplaying the value of the cross! The resurrection is that of the crucified: then too, the founding density of the Resurrection brings to light the *founding significance of the cross*, while the *realism* of the crucifixion of Jesus of Nazareth qualifies in turn his resurrection. Ultimately, there is but one narrative, that of the Resurrection of the crucified and of its overall significance, which founds a history and a world. After a first hearing of the narrative of the Resurrection, we will take a long look too at that of the cross, for its own sake and in the Old Testament figures which brought out its meaning in advance. Then we will return to the Resurrection. In this way we hope to make possible a total hearing of the founding Paschal narrative.[1]

A community of witnesses

If it is a question of hearing a narrative, we should expect that the first thing one will want to know is *who* can make this narrative, *where* can it be heard and responded to, what *community* can stand between those who witnessed and those who hear the story today. The decisive question is one of *testimony*: since it is a question of a *dated* testimony, we must also reflect on the signification of the written documents to which this testimony is consigned.

To one whose heart is open, nothing is more important than that he encounter witnesses worthy of faith, that is to say, witnesses from whom he can hear with joy the story that reveals to him his true origin and his transfigured destiny. Access to the founding narrative passes through a *present* community of witnesses, which itself adds faith to that which it transmits. Its testimony is not "immemorial" but goes back step by step to *primary* witnesses, these too clearly identified—primary witnesses, in the sense that they were the first to be founded by that to which they bear witness and to form its narrative.

In fact, the narrative of the Resurrection is not without author, nor is the apostolic witness anonymous. At the very beginning, when the testimony was forming, and subsequently in the process of its transmission, it has always been a question of a *responsible* narrative, corresponding to a *mission* of witness and opening into a *festive experience*. The reality of the Resurrection and its fruit as new creation can reach man only through the mediation of the believing community that guards and transmits the apostolic testimony which it repeats and celebrates in the Eucharistic feast. It is not possible to confess the Resurrection and, in this confession, to experience its liberating force which neither myth nor gnosis can give, outside of the church of the apostles, for it is from this church, in a very concrete way, that *one hears the narrative*, not one time only, but always; it is in the church that one professes faith in this narrative and that one celebrates its joy.

This point is very important: at this founding level, it is a question of *hearing* and of *commitment*, and not one of *reading* and *commentary*. In this sense, we must simply concede to Derrida that, when God is involved, the primacy goes to the *phone* (the voice), and not to the written word: the written word, in fact, when preached and proclaimed, becomes spoken word in this very act. When one stands before the *text* alone, one is *immediately geared to reinterpretation*, that is to say, to a certain *production* of meaning. When, on the other hand, one *hears* witnesses, one is bound to *that which is being commemorated and which one could never have produced*. The interpretation will come *afterwards* as *intellectus fidei* ultimately governed by that which will first have been heard.

This is not without consequences regarding the object of the narrative itself: if it is possible to be sensitive to the wisdom and to the ethical grandeur of the Sermon on the Mount, to the posthumous aura of a man named Jesus, and still remain detached from an ecclesial community, it is no longer possible to do so when it is a question of believing in the risen Christ. In the first case, one receives a new inspiration toward the *production* of what one considers authentic behavior; in the second, *one receives the revelation* of one's origins and end in an interpersonal and community exchange, and also in the insertion into the bosom of a narrating tradition where one accepts to be at home and to take one's place.[2]

A situated testimony

If there is continuity in the tradition of the witnesses, the testimony itself is also precisely situated: the witnesses do not refer to a "once upon a time" lost in the night of time or in the desert of the ages. We have here a very illuminating paradox: the *founding narrative* offered by Christianity is situated neither at the beginning nor at the end of time, but at least part "in the middle of time." We are dealing with a narrative about a concrete person, Jesus of Nazareth, with whom those who first spoke of him lived and whose teaching and prophecy they heard: we have here a firm anchor in time. But it is of this same Jesus, whom all his contemporaries saw living and dying, that they say that he is risen; to a language of time and of history has thus been juxtaposed a language of origin and of fulfillment, for which no proper words exist, but only images or prepositions and prefixes which transpose the word at the very moment it is uttered. We have then a *situated* testimony, because clearly identified individuals, the apostles, spoke of a Jesus whom they knew, but this testimony is *founding* because their narrative regarding this Jesus transcends the limits of historical language to make of it a language of origin.

An inspired testimony

This testimony is inspired because, although primary, the witnesses to whom the Christian community owes the Easter narration are not its founders. Having lived on the borders of the event to which they bear witness, they are themselves founded by it. Their narrative bears the mark of that dimension "prior" to them, that "other" dimension, without which it would not have a founding character. And the apostles do not present their testimony as purely human (although it has, as I have said, a strong anchor in time and one cannot detach it from the men who bore it): they claim to speak under the impulse of the *Spirit* and in virtue of the *mission* they have received from the Risen One. In this sense, they render their testimony as coming from elsewhere and view themselves as no more than messengers or servants of a word which itself is founding. As for the narrative in which they render their testimony, it includes the inseparable elements of the *fact* itself which was announced to them (and of which they were not eyewitnesses) and the *inspired interpretation* they received of it. The fact *and* the meaning form part of the founding event to which they bear witness.

This last point is important: too often in the recent or the remote past, the Resurrection has been dissociated from the apostolic witness which makes it known, and hence from the experience by which the apostles were themselves founded. Then the Resurrection is either reduced to a pure fact (but what is a "pure fact"?) which, although extraordinary and a bit bizarre, is nevertheless well attested and can serve therefore as an *external proof* for the veracity of a doctrine known from elsewhere. Or, maintaining a prudent reserve regarding the reality of the fact, one focuses almost exclusively on the interpretations which the apostles and their disciples are supposed to have produced, which became more and more sophisticated with time. Actually, the notion of witness implies that the apostles *received* and *heard* the announcement of a Resurrection at once factual and meaningful. In all respects, they are *included* in their testimony; they do not control it in any way and they are the first to be founded by the founding narrative for which they hold the responsibility for all men.

One could attempt to say the same thing by underlining the *sacramental* aspect of the experience of the Resurrection—an aspect that will govern the narrative is based on it. There is in fact an equilibrium between the *visible* and the *invisible* that is worthy of note. It has often been pointed out that the apostles did not present themselves as eyewitnesses of the Resurrection: they *witness* to it as they do likewise to the exaltation, the glorification of Jesus, the forgiveness of sins and the outpouring of the Spirit. Nothing of this belongs to the order of the visible. But we are not dealing either with a pure invisible, because the apostles testify to having "eaten and drunk" with the risen Jesus and to having received from him the order to witness to these actions which they did not see but of which the living Jesus, whom they both saw and heard, is himself the guarantor. The structure of their witness is then complex. It rests on what they have seen and heard: the living Jesus and the mission to witness received from him; moreover, the works of power performed in his Name have also rendered a visible testimony. But on the other hand, this witness goes back to God, their *revealer* and his action on Jesus and the meaning of this latter for Jesus and for the whole of the divine plan of salvation. Taking all of this into account, we have here a specific *epistemological level* of discourse which I call "sacramental," while also describing it as "inspired."[3]

It is likewise essential that the community which guards and transmits the apostolic witness be a "sacramental" and "inspired" community. It is through the Spirit sent by the Risen One that the apostles announce the Resurrection and it is the Spirit who, by his internal working, confirms this message. The testimonies which were left to us and which we find in the New Testament under the forms of confessions of faith, hymns, organic narratives, etc.—all of this is transmitted to us as coming from Christ through the Spirit. There is an inseparable reciprocity between the exteriority of the witness and the interiority of the Spirit: the latter is, moreover, the Spirit of Christ and sends us back to the "God of the Fathers." If we need the Spirit in order to confess that "Jesus is Lord," a complementary truth must also be affirmed, namely, that we can make this confession only on the basis of the apostolic preaching and within the Christian community.

The Eucharistic celebration

If the realism of the Resurrection is linked to the reality of the Church which witnesses and of the Spirit who attests, it is easy to see that the *place* where the witness is borne in a vital and effective way is the Eucharistic celebration. Its very raison d'etre is *to make heard this founding language in a founding manner*, and in such a way *that it be immediately responded to*. The hearing is brought to perfection only through and in the moment of the *response*, consisting of faith and of commitment, through which those who hear and receive authenticate for themselves and for others the message that they hear. A study of the Eucharistic celebration has a place here. For the moment I will limit myself to the task of bringing out a few elements of the complexity of the Eucharistic *language*, and of qualifying the *time* of the celebration:

1. If we remain first of all at the level of language properly so called, prescinding from its plastic environment, we find here a whole gamut of forms, each of which actualizes a true orientation of human desire. I mention first of all the basic invocative form, accompanied by doxology; then, in counterpoint to this, the form of the confession of sins and the request for forgiveness, that is, for the restitution of an

authentic capacity of doxological invocation. Another pair comes in, that of thanksgiving and intercession, thanks to which two specific relations are established which are based on the double recognition of the superabundance received and of the poverty which opens itself in prayer; and here, the moment of the narrative is founding, because it is the presentation in story form of the favors bestowed by God which underlies the thanksgiving (which is itself, in a sense, thanksgiving) and grounds hope, which is the only solid basis for intercession. Finally, there is the form of the offering, through which the community consents to the communion sacrifice and transcends itself in the acceptance of its origin and of its destiny. Invocation, praise, confession, thanksgiving, narrative, offering—such are the literary genres which constitute the Eucharistic word in its integrity and, in the final analysis, restore to human language its truth.

2. In such a language, however, one cannot isolate the linguistic symbols of which it is made up from the entire complex of plastic symbols to which they are intimately linked. The bond between the articulate sounds of the mouth and the movements of the body is not left aside but rather affirmed: there are prayer gestures which correspond to prayer formulas; they embody them, and, in turn, render them more authentic. The exigency of a decor (in the sense that Gadamer speaks of the decorative element in art) is likewise born, as it were naturally, of the type and of the rhythm of the words which are exchanged in the Eucharist. The language of the latter emerges within a spacial framework and a division of this framework without which the words would not be able to reach the fullness of their meaning: the light, the vestments, the props are not external to the significance of the language: they create its milieu, whether of superabundance, or of what one could call super-austerity. But above all, one of the moments of this language is related to a symbolic behavior which brings into play the most spontaneous of human gestures: eating and drinking; the interplay of the forms of nourishment says in its own way what the words narrate, and it is precisely this intimate connection of narrative and gesture that gives to Eucharistic language the fullness of its human meaning and of its real capacity to signify what is beyond man.

3. Finally, Eucharistic language is endowed with the specific characteristic, which should be taken into consideration, that it organizes into a certain order a series of speakers, who take turns listening and speaking, one or more of them, however, exercising a representative

function, which also is an essential part of the concrete economy of all language: if it happens that one speaks for oneself, at least one always speaks to others, which relates personal language to social reality, and one speaks often, even if only implicitly, in the name of a group of others. It is this community order or structure that makes possible the vital articulation of witness and response.

Although somewhat sketchy, these few reflections on Eucharistic language reveal that the founding effected by the festive hearing is not merely a matter of internal memory and of the heart: it takes on an actuality which is linked to the specific economy of the time and of the space which celebration reveals, without being separated from the economy of "ordinary" time to which the community which hears and responds belongs.

It is very important to underline here that the time of hearing which is that of the Eucharistic celebration is characterized by this *superimposition of times* of which I speak above, and which seems to me to respond to the demand of Derrida for a certain transcending of the "vulgar conception of time" (or, more accurately, which renders possible this transcending which Derrida called for while judging it impossible). Actually, it is not a question here of a mythical time/space (or of an outside-of-time/outside-of-space) nor of a strictly cosmic or human temporality with no other prospect than an eternal return or a meaningless duration. Rather, we find here, together, (1) the present time, which is at once that of the celebration, but also of the human life of exchange and of work, of growth and of liberation, (2) the time of the Paschal Mystery of Jesus, which gives to this present its ultimate coordinates of eschatological future and of founding past, and (3) the specific but not unreal "outside-of-time" of the Word and of the Spirit of God. The famous category of *memorial* reaches here its highest speculative density as symbol and language act which reveals and founds the figure of time.

Scripture and the reinterpretations

I have laid great emphasis on hearing and on its festive place, which seems to me essential to the notion of *foundation*. Nevertheless, if the founding narrative is essentially something heard and celebrated, it has also been and it remains something constantly *re-said* and *written*. We have here a process with profound anthropological roots, made up of the dialectic between the moments of proclamation/faith, hearing/response and writing/reinterpretation, all three essential to the overall process of communication, so that the *founding narrative* makes itself heard also in the ever new *reinterpretations* which continue to be made of it. The moment of writing/reinterpretation is physically marked by the work of the hand, intellectually, by the work of *composition*, linked to the proper resources of spaciality. In the founding case which concerns us here, I speak of "reinterpretation" because, as I have said, an interpretation is included as such in the founding narrative and contains the categories of meaning which the apostles themselves *received* and which are no more than the actualization of the message of Jesus regarding his Father, the Kingdom and the gift of the Spirit, himself and the Church; this actualization is intrinsically linked to the fact of the resurrection from the dead and manifested together with it. This whole complex of elements goes to make up the founding narrative which is "at work" within every authentic reinterpretation.

But this founding apostolic narrative, *the hearing of which is alive* at any moment of the Christian economy, is accepted only because it responds to certain fundamental questions of humanity, which we could conveniently assemble (as I did above with reference to Heidegger) under the three great questions of Kant. Now, if the apostolic testimony gives us a basic landmark for discerning what we are allowed to hope for, what we can know and what we ought to do, it allows us also to *reformulate* these questions and to *reconstruct* the responses by reference to this landmark. The figure of the time to come, the knowledge of Jesus Christ and of his total Mystery and the concrete ethical orientation of life are thus continuously subjected to *reinterpretation*: one could say that we have to do here with "mediate" actualization of the message of Jesus (in contrast to the "immediate" actualization which constitutes the apostolic testimony). At this level, but only at this level which rests *unceasingly* on the apostolic testimony, there is continuously also *production of meaning*.

We arrive on the scene today, the last (although others will come after us) in the venerable history of these reinterpretations. Before us, in various cultural and political contexts, with the means and methods at their disposal, but also in function of the past heritage of Christian reinterpretation, others have *produced Christian meaning for the Church*. It is our task to follow up their effort and to express today our hope, which is founded on the Mystery of Christ and determines our concrete personal and collective engagements. For this task of discernment and of renewal, we benefit from the assistance of the Spirit (I said above that the community which *hears* the founding narrative is to some degree "inspired"). We also benefit from the perennial criterion which is the Eucharistic celebration of the Church with its all-embracing language, and from the example and method of the early Christian community, whose reinterpretations have the proper characteristic of being, at their own level, *founding*, and, in a proper sense, *inspired*. Without intending to make an exhaustive enumeration, one could say that three elements came principally into play in the reinterpretative work of the first communities: the conviction that the resurrection of Jesus fulfilled the Scriptures, of which it supplied the proper interpretative key; the conviction that the resurrection of Jesus discloses the meaning of his life and of his teaching, such as these could be recalled and such as they were to form the object of an ever more intense study and research; finally, the pressures, both religious and political, which forced the communities to organize themselves, to understand themselves in contradistinction to other religious tendencies, Jewish or Greek, and to interpret the delay of the Parousia as well as the fall of Jerusalem. The fruit of these founding reinterpretations, both as for method and as for content, in which also the founding narrative makes itself heard, remains normative for us, that is to say that they are also, in a certain sense, an object of *hearing*, although such a hearing does not exclude our own processes of reinterpretation, governed by the same demands as those of the apostolic era.

Reinterpretation and truth

The truth of a reinterpretation is determined from the way in which the *founding narrative* makes itself heard in it and yields, through the engendered productions of meaning, the same effects of conversion to God and of human liberation as did the narrative itself. This truth, therefore, which will never be either apodictic or exclusive of other interpretations, will depend, it seems to me, on three factors:

1. Its correspondence to the festive anamnesis in which the community hears and receives its foundation: truth and liturgy (in the theoanthopological sense of the term).

2. The justice and the charity of the behaviors which it inspires, both within the hearing community and outside of it: truth and ethics.

3. The quality of the method according to which the available texts are read: truth and critical judgement.

If these three elements are present, that is to say, if they constantly overlap and intertwine, mutually correcting and reinforcing one another, one can hope that the meaning produced in an interpretation is in line with the founding narrative.

With reference to the third element, truth and critical judgment, I would like to indicate here the hypothesis according to which it seems to me most correct to work, and which will consequently serve as my point of reference in what follows, as I undertake a reading of certain texts. According to this hypothesis, one considers the writings of the New Testament (but also the Old Testament and, to the extent that they are employed, the more recent documents of the Christian tradition) as belonging to what is called *literature*; it is at this literary level that they must be taken up. Every literary production finds its unity in the composition and articulation of its parts—whatever might be the formal principles (symbolic, logical, representational, sonorous . . .) according to which the composition is realized and unity achieved; on the other hand, every element derives its signification not only from its own content but from its position within the whole. As Émile Poulat pointed out, Tacitus or Thucydides are as much "works" as they are "sources," and we could rightly add that they are "sources" only to the extent that their secret as "works" has been penetrated.[4]

This *primacy of the literary* as original written production of meaning appears to me to be fundamental; it is the only approach that will prevent us from viewing texts as highly impure ores containing teachings to which only a ruthless exercise of critical activity will allow us to arrive, while the rest is discarded like superfluous and useless dross, or, conversely, from seeing them as no more than impersonal chronicles whose degree of truth is proportional to their chronological proximity to the events they describe. Is it not precisely by being faithful to the very nature of a *text* that one will best be able to receive its message? Having said this, it is clear that I leave untouched the problem of the nature of the literary critique or critiques which would be capable of favoring a faithful and therefore a fruitful reading of the texts. The fact remains that, if people agree on the principle of the literary nature of a text, suitable methods of reading will more easily be found than if they subject the text from the start to a process of historicization or dogmatic inquiry, without having first paid attention to the words, the symbols, the images, the literary patterns, etc., present in them. To be sure, we stand on solid ground when we practice what one could call "spectral analyses" which enable us to discern the relative age and the origin of various elements of the text, but only on condition that we do not forget that these elements take on meaning only within the literary organization without which they *literally and literarily do not exist*. The same could be said for "comparative analyses," for example between the various gospels, which enable us to understand better the significance of the differences observed and to speculate as to the relative antiquity of this or that passage or interpretation.[5]

If what was said above regarding the liturgical, ethical and critical criteria of reinterpretation is true, and if these criteria are correctly applied, then it is legitimate to assume that it will be possible to discern in the texts, such as they present themselves literarily, the *recurrence of the founding narrative*. The latter is not in fact present in the literary texts in the same way as it was in the oral preaching of the apostles at the beginning, precisely because it is an organic production of meaning. It is not even possible, in some cases, perhaps even in any case, to retrieve the *initial literary form* of the founding narrative. But it is always possible to discern its *figure*, the *profile* of the Christ it proclaims; just as it governed the literary production, this figure or profile likewise governs our own reinterpretation. If the literary works of the New Testament are born of a *founding hearing*, the latter resounds, each time in a new way, in every reinterpretation. And the truth criterion of our own reinterpretations resides in the harmony which we are able, in our turn, to construct between the figure of Christ risen in the Spirit and the expression of our demands as human beings bound to a culture and engaged in a struggle.[6]

It is clear that the preceding pages do not pretend to offer a definitive solution to all the complex problems of fundamental theology which they raise. Let us say that they define an articulated complex of *hypotheses*, in the strong sense of the term, within the framework of which the present work will be conducted: their aim would be to validate its procedures, while the latter should contribute, in turn, to verify these hypotheses.

1. At the beginning (chronologically) and at the origin (structurally) is found the moment of *hearing*, through which the figure of time is revealed and founded.

2. The *founding narrative* founds the very persons who are the first auditors and reveals to them the meaning of what they have lived and experienced.

3. The *testimony* of those who have lived, heard and transmitted is situated in time, in duration; it comes from real, concrete human beings and is transmitted in the same way from generation to generation.

4. Bearing on the *overall figure of time*, this testimony has its essential place in the Eucharistic celebration, where the *narrative*, proclaimed and responded to, *founds* the present and the future figure of time.

5. Heard and responded to, the *founding narrative* is subject, from the earliest times and till the end of time, to *reinterpretation*, but its basic shape or figure may be discerned in the reinterpretations if these are conducted according to the appropriate criteria of liturgical fidelity, ethical truth and critical authenticity.

These hypotheses, relative to the formation, the transmission, the celebration and the reinterpretation of the Easter narrative indicate already, though in a still very formal way, the figure of the reunion with time. Indeed, if the time of "pure and full presence," which recent thinkers rightly declare irreparably lost, is truly eliminated by the very fact of the *founding narrative*, this does not mean that all temporality is lost. The opposite is in fact the case, because it is into this very time that the narrative comes, and it commemorates not a mythical hero, but Jesus of Nazareth, while also witnessing to a beginning which man would not be capable of giving to himself and establishing the possibility of a future and of a present.

An examination—even a rapid and partial one—of the *content* of this founding narrative will doubtless confirm us in the rediscovery of time in its truth and of that which founds it.

II
FROM THE SIDE OF LIFE

This examination of content will in fact be brief; there can be no question here of undertaking a complete examination of the New Testament texts relative to the resurrection of Jesus. I shall limit myself to two examples taken from among numerous other possibilities and considered here as having sample value. The first will be the kerygmatic formula which is reported to us a number of times in the first part of the Acts of the Apostles; the second, one of the gospel narratives of the Resurrection, that of Saint Matthew. We have here two literary genres which are sufficiently diverse to enable us, by studying and comparing them, to respond with some plausibility to the twofold question: to whom and of what do the Apostles render testimony?

1. "This Jesus whom you have killed, God has raised up"

Our task is to comment briefly on the literary motif which is found eight times in the early discourses of Acts, placed by St. Luke on the lips of Peter, and then, for the last of these discourses, in the mouth of Paul.[7] In these similarly structured texts, the phrase "we are witnesses of these things" is found four times: it is clear then that we have to do here with the object of a testimony. Of what do the Apostles come forward as guarantors? To understand this, it is necessary to point out the antithetical character of the formula: in every case it is constructed on an opposition *you/God*, and the action involved, in each case, has *Jesus* for an object. "You" refers to Peter's auditors who together bear a common responsibility for the death of Jesus: "This Jesus . . . you crucified and killed by the hands of lawless men" (Acts 2:23). With respect to this Jesus, a man well known by the auditors, the "you" action ends in death. In contrast, God "raised him up, having loosed the pangs of death" (2:24). In six out of the eight texts, the action of God is expressed in terms of resurrection; in another we read (still in the same perspective of opposition between "you" and "God"): "God has made him Lord and Christ" and in another: "God has glorified him." In three of the cases where the formula "God raised him" is found, the phrase is amplified by a complete description of the action of God with respect to Jesus: exaltation to his right hand, dignity as head and Lord, the gift of the Spirit made to Christ so that he might spread it abroad and accomplish the remission of sins. It is clear then that an opposition is being established between the action of death imputed to a "you" and an action, *for the same Jesus*, through which God gives life in abundance, not only to Jesus, but to "you" and to all.

This act of God is then *total*. Indeed, even if the accent is on the resurrection, brought out by the antithesis between "you" (who killed him) and "God" (who restored him to life), the apostles witness to a more encompassing totality. If they affirm the Resurrection, they do not do so by separating it from the rest. What they "narrate" is the totality of the irruption of a new world, which simultaneously concerns "this Jesus whom you have put to death," but also Israel and ultimately all men. For Jesus, it is the sequence resurrection, exaltation by and to the right hand of God, establishment as head, savior and Christ; for human beings, through the mediation of Jesus thus glorified, it is the remission of sins and the sanctifying and mission inspiring effusion of the Spirit: "it is of these things that we are witnesses," says Peter. All of this forms an indivisible whole, whose origin is the act of God and which humanity is being invited to accept as founding narrative.

In the perspective which concerns us here, a number of important points can be highlighted:

1. The reciprocity of which I spoke above between resurrection and cross is brought out here by the opposition *you/God*: the realism of the Resurrection is suggested by the realism of the death while the unfathomable effect of resurrection invites us to interpret the death in a very much more profound way: both death and resurrection will constitute the founding narrative.

2. The economy of time receives a twofold characterization: on the one hand, the event attested to is *remission of sins*, for the past, and gift of the *Spirit of promise* for the future. The *culpability* factor, of which I have several times observed that it becomes inextricably intermingled, in the "gnostic attitude," with the factor of *finitude*, receives at the same time reality and annulment: culpability pertains to "sin," a notion whose place and role in the reality of time will have to be evaluated; but, as a result of the fact that sins have been "remitted," another economy of time, marked by the Spirit, is opening up.

3. The *name* of God is defined by reference to his action, which is opposed to that of the "you": "he who raised Jesus from the dead." The narrative renders testimony to God as the one who is the transcendent Worker of the economy inaugurated in and through the resurrection of Jesus. One cannot receive the apostolic witness without adhering to the name of God which it implies. Two remarks will help to situate this name: on the one hand, because we are dealing here with a concrete narrative and with an unconditioned divine initiative, this name is free of any necessary, systematic link with the human reality,

and it will thus be able to elude any onto-theological interpretation; on the other hand, however, as it is a question of a name defined by an action of which the man Jesus is the object, it is not immediately evident if and to what extent one should or one could "absolve" God of this relation.

2. The women, the guards and the disciples (Mt 27:57—28:20)[8]

To better understand the meaning of the message of the Resurrection according to St. Matthew, it is doubtless preferable to view as a literary unity the whole ensemble formed by the burial narrative, the apparition of the Angel of God to the women and the various movements which follow and culminate in the meeting with Jesus in Galilee. This whole is marked by antitheses and correspondences of which I shall here propose a profile without claiming that it is the only possible one.

It seems that the text is organized according to two successive movements, the first of which is devoted to the *Resurrection* (27:57—28:6), established through *the testimony rendered by God to the prophetic word of Jesus*: this testimony is rendered to *the women of faith*, not to the weak, the disciples, or to the people of bad faith, the high priests and the Pharisees, both of which groups of men have remained at the stage of the burying of the body of Jesus. The second movement is devoted to *teaching* (28:7-20): that of Jesus spread throughout the whole world through the apostolic preaching and initiation; that of the high priests and of the Pharisees, a petty lie confined to a little Jerusalem circle. Let us endeavor to look at this in a little more detail.

The buried body and the true word

The reality of the burial of Jesus is attested by two absolutely parallel procedures, although of opposite intent, of which the women seem to be the unconscious witnesses: I read in parallel Mt 27:58–61 and 27:62—28:1.

Once Jesus is dead, a disciple, Joseph, concerns himself with the burial and goes to ask the body of Pilate; having acquired it, he provides all the necessities in grand style (clean linen shroud, new tomb), then he rolls the stone to the door of the tomb and departs. Pious as his actions may be, they seem to see no opening beyond death, and the *disciple* no longer seems to have any great faith in him who was once his master. Some women however, once Joseph has left, persevere—we are not told why—and remain seated there.

The following day (it is the day of the Sabbath, which Matthew designates by a circumlocution) the high priests and the Pharisees take the same road to Pilate. More on the alert than Joseph ("hatred makes lucid," said Emmanuel Mounier), they have retained a mysterious word of Jesus regarding his resurrection; they do not believe it, but they are not about to let the disciples abuse it (the example of Joseph shows however that there is really no such danger) and they too concern themselves with the sepulchre which holds the buried body: they seal the entrance of the tomb and set a guard. The very next morning, the women (who, for their part, have respected the Sabbath) return to the tomb, and we are still not told why. We have seen then the *disciple* who buried his Master with no questions raised, the *high priests* who do raise questions and who reinforce the burial as it were, and the *women*, persevering and silent.

There then takes place an apocalyptic event heralded by the great earthquake. But it seems that this new scene commences with a humorous touch, with reference to Joseph the *disciple*. Indeed, the narrative has said of him (27:60): "having rolled a great stone (*proskulisas*) to the door of the tomb, he departed"; and now of the Angel of God it says (28:2): "[he,] descending from heaven, came and rolled back the stone [*apekulisen*] and sat on it." The verbal correspondence here is striking and, on the other hand, because nothing is said of the seals placed by the high priests and the Pharisees, one cannot avoid the impression that the Angel of God, not wishing to condemn Joseph, responds with a riposte and points out to us that there *is* going to be a future to all of this in what concerns the disciples.

However this may be, we next hear a description of the white and luminous garb of the Angel of God (in terms which recall the garb of the Ancient of Days in Dan 7:9) and it is then that the moment of judgment comes: it is rendered between the *guards*, who symbolize the fears of the Pharisees before the word of Jesus, and the *women*. Of the guards we are told that the fear with which they are struck by the presence of the Angel of God renders them "as it were dead": the very ones who were guarding the dead body are symbolically put to death.

To the women, on the contrary, the Angel of God says: "Do not *fear!*" which, in this context of antithesis to the guards, means also "live!" and implies that to the word which Joseph had never even thought of, and which the Pharisees dreaded, the women had added faith; they had stayed behind the first evening, and had returned after the Sabbath, because they had believed in the word of Jesus. At the moment of judgment, they receive a confirmation of their faith, both through the *testimony rendered by the Angel of God*, and through the *sign* of the open and empty tomb. In this respect, the fact of seeing Jesus would perhaps add nothing to the eschatological certitude and joy in which the Angel of God has established them.

It seems to me that the theme that unifies this entire first literary unit in our narrative is that of the *prophetic word of Jesus*: the *disciple* did not remember it, the *high priests* and the *Pharisees* dreaded it (and at the end we find them symbolically dead), the *women* believed in it. And *God* has rendered testimony to it.

The lie and the mission

The remainder of the text is directed toward mission: the women's going to the disciples prepares for the encounter of the latter with Jesus; it takes place against the contrasting background of the guards' going to their agents and of the lie that this provokes.

As soon as they have been affirmed in their faith, the women are sent to evangelize the disciples. The latter have been absent since the arrest of Jesus (26:56) and they have been seen to return again, in the person of the disciple Joseph, only for the burial of Jesus; they need to be reinserted into the Mystery of Christ, and it is quite natural that those women who have believed should be their evangelizers. The meeting with Jesus, which takes place while the women are on their way to the disciples, seems in reality to be directed toward the latter: Jesus says nothing original with respect to what the Angel of God had said, except for the fact that he calls the disciples "my brothers," and what we have here is perhaps a word of redemption and of creation: redemption, in the sense that Jesus pardons the lack of understanding and the flight of the disciples; creation, in the sense that he renders them capable of showing themselves thereafter to be his brothers, that is to say, people who listen to him and put his teachings into practice.

While the women are on the way to transmit their message to the disciples and to set them in turn on their way toward Galilee where Jesus will meet them, the guards go into town to tell their story of the event: they who had "dropped dead" and did not have the key to unlock what they had gone through, report the event with a total lack of meaningful interpretation. After deliberation on the part of the chief priests, they receive the commission to spread abroad a "teaching" (*os edidachthesan*) and are amply compensated for their efforts. Now this "teaching" consists in the admission that precisely that has taken place which they had been posted to prevent (cf. 28:13 and 27:64). And this is exactly what they do, thus perpetuating a "word" in Jerusalem.

On the other side, the disciples finally encounter the risen Jesus. We are not surprised, given the profile of the disciple of weak faith which the first gospel has set before us a number of times, that some of them react with doubt to the very vision of Jesus—for we know that it is not enough to see, or, more exactly, that in order to see one must believe. Anyhow, the word of Jesus directs them toward the infinite of space and of time: they receive a mission of witness, of initiation and of teaching (*didaskontes*) regarding everything that Jesus had said: the resurrection of Jesus takes on meaning with and in the initiating and doctrinal mission which is entrusted to them. At the very moment when the high priests and Pharisees were endeavoring to undermine the brute *fact* of the Resurrection in the closed milieu of Jerusalem, Jesus in a sense is testifying to the *truth* of the Resurrection by the amplitude of the mission he entrusts to the disciples of broadcasting to the whole world the words he had spoken.

If this commentary is correct, it brings to light with peculiar force the *primacy of hearing*, which I have posited as the first principle of an attitude centered on a founding narrative. The women have, in fact, heard the word of Jesus before his death, that is to say a "narrative," reduced to bare essentials and doubtless presented in enigmatic form, of what was to follow his death; it is this firm hearing which shapes their attitude of silent awaiting and enables them to receive a confirmation which they never doubted would eventually come.

There is also in this text an opposition, different from that described by the Acts of the Apostles, between "you" and "God," but one whose inner meaning is the same; one could formulate it in this way: "this Jesus whose body you have carefully buried has risen, he is alive." As in Acts, we have here an event which concerns Jesus and which is expressed by way of opposing an attitude turned towards death (here, not death inflicted, but death recognized and affirmed) and the irruption of life. But this event does not stop at Jesus: it opens onto a new temporality, spread over a universal space, one defined by the initiation into the narrated founding Mystery, the point of departure of a way of life defined by the gospel of Jesus. This temporality is not autonomous: it depends entirely on the presence of the risen Jesus; one could say that the new figure of time is that of an "accompanied" time: not the extension of a pure presence to self, but the unfolding of a presence-with.

The presence of God (because the "Angel of God" is here God himself, as the parallel with Dan 7 shows), appears here as *witness of the word of Jesus*: attested in a transcendent manner, not only can this word be received as true and its fulfillment regarded as assured, but it is suggested (and we will have to come back to this point) that this word itself belongs to the very space from which the attestation comes to it: the resurrection of Jesus, prophesied by a true word, belongs to the world of God who confirms its truth.

To whom and of what do the apostles render testimony? On the basis of the two "specimens" which we have just analyzed, one could say that they render testimony *to* God, of what he has done and of what he has himself testified in Jesus of Nazareth, the crucified one. They render testimony *of* that which has been accomplished in Jesus and which is well expressed by the words of Saint Paul: "declared to be the powerful Son of God, according to the Spirit of holiness, by the resurrection from the dead," which implies the promise of a new life for all and the end of the reign of sin and death; moreover, the resurrection of Jesus confirms the validity of his teaching and defines the orientations of this new life which has been offered to all.

As for the language with which this testimony is rendered, it corresponds to what we have seen when speaking of this above in a more formal way. It is a question of *recitative* language, but one the narrativity of which is situated at the extreme limits of verbal possibilities. In one sense, it is a question of a recitative language which is homogeneous to the spatial-temporal dimensions of the human word; it tells what has happened to Jesus of Nazareth, both before his death and after his resurrection, and this narrative claims to give meaning and orientation to the lives of the concrete and embodied human beings to which it is addressed; in this sense, it is in no way a mythical narrative or a gnostic speculation; the points of anchorage in concrete reality are evident. But in another sense, this language is heterogeneous to these normal dimensions of human existence: it evokes an eschatological destiny, of which the Resurrection itself shows that it is not within the power of man; it aims at describing a primary origin, which by definition escapes all before and after patterns. So, in order to express these extremes, one must immediately name God, who is its author, and express the dimensions of Jesus which escape a univocal kind of narrativity. The language of images, of symbolic expressions, of "extraordinary" events such as those of apparitions which escape the spacial-temporal rules of play, is here inevitable, but by the same token the language is founding *for it is what is said at the limit-level which makes possible a more homogeneous language and it is that which the limit-language evokes which makes possible a meaningful human temporality.*

In reality, if one admits the thesis I attempted to develop above regarding the heteronomy of founding language, the specific notes of the language of the Resurrection will not surprise us in the least. Indeed, whatever it may be, founding language cannot be produced; it escapes then, by definition, both the prose of our daily discourse and the poetry of a ritual, imaginary or gnostic projection of our desires, in a fictitious world which we prefer to acknowledge as true, in preference to the other. To be sure, it is a question of a narrative which transcends the homogeneous narrativity of a natural or social history. But it does not do so in the manner of a "once upon a time" unconnected with our reality; it transcends by founding and by endowing history with direction and value. As for the homogeneous elements, those consequently which can supply a continuous narration, they are so organized that the reference to what I have called the transcendent Operator and to "the extraordinary event" which he brings to reality can intervene in the course of the same discourse. And without this transcendent element, the latter would lose all meaning.

The testimony rendered to the Resurrection opposes, in various ways, what one could call a "side of death" (the putting to death of Jesus, his burial, but also and perhaps above all, the human beings involved in this process and the closed circle in which they move) and what one could call a "side of life," of which God is both author and witness, and which regards first of all Jesus of Nazareth, but also all those in space and in time who accept the witness borne to him, are released of blame and promised life.

Today, as in the early days of the Church, we cannot leave the matter here, and we must certainly attempt to reflect on the question of why the *founding narrative* concerns this particular human being, in the middle of time, Jesus of Nazareth. How are we to conceive of a founding time which superimposes itself on an already real chronology? And, on the other hand, what are we to understand by the experience we frequently encounter of the "remission of sins"? What was the past role of culpability in the unfolding of time? And is this role as effectively annihilated as a proclamation of the remission of sins would have us believe?

If one wishes to raise these types of questions in a more immediately theological manner, one will ask: why is Jesus the only one of all the suffering just and of all the persecuted holy ones whose resurrection should have been proclaimed? Or to express the matter in terms of divine names, how do we understand the fact that a fundamental name of God should be: "He who raised Jesus from the dead"? How does it happen that the Name is invoked by way of reference to a particular, determinate individual? And if one should reply, anticipating somewhat the results of theological reflection, because Jesus was his Messiah and his Son—the question then becomes: if Jesus is truly all of this, why was he allowed to die? What is this "set purpose and foreknowledge of God" according to which Jesus was "handed over"? How are we to relate, with reference to God whom we confess as the transcendent Operator, or Agent of the Resurrection, the Name of life which this act allows us to give him and other, more negative names, as for example: "He who abandoned Jesus to death"? And the question comes back with reference to the "remission of sins": what link is to be established between the resurrection and death of Jesus, on the one hand, and the cancellation of all sin, on the other?

This leads us to enter into a reflection on what could be called the *time of Jesus*: what interpretation should be given to his death and to his life, in the light of the founding proclamation of his resurrection? This question brings into play not only Jesus' identity or our own, but also that of God. We shall endeavor to proceed without confusion, reading the accounts of the death of Jesus, then exploring the figures which confirm the meaning of these accounts.

III
THE CROSS, SPACE OF SONSHIP

As far as one can make out through the Gospel presentations, Jesus made himself known as the Prophet of the imminent Kingdom of God; his every effort was aimed at gathering together the People of Israel so as to prepare for the awaited irruption of that which from the very beginning had been his hope; doubtless it was also his desire to associate this people with his prophetic mission so that, through Israel, purified and gathered together, the Kingdom might be extended to all the nations and the New Covenant established over the whole earth. This preaching of the Kingdom, in the view of Jesus, involved essentially the fulfillment of the Revelation of God, through the unveiling of his Name—the name of Father—which, if not unknown to Israel, had been little used by her in her faith and her invocation. Jesus did not reveal this face of God in an abstract and theoretical manner, but simply by giving this name to God, by speaking of him as the Father and, more precisely, as his Father.[9]

Then Jesus died. His death has something particularly disconcerting about it, precisely to the extent that he was presenting himself as the last of the prophets, as one sent in the service of the fulfillment of God's designs, as the revealer of the Father. Many prophets had died before him, but how could the last of these have run aground? How could the one who proclaimed the imminence of the Kingdom disappear without God's intervening, even at the last moment, to declare with power that his prophet was right and to acknowledge his Son with a Father's tender love? Why should this ultimate innocent, with the fidelity not only of a just man, but also (at least in his view) of an envoy and of a son, have suffered the terrible fate of those who came before him? This question, relative to the fate of Jesus, implicates God above all, as any story of an innocent subjected to suffering almost automatically does. How, in the case of Jesus, can the name of God still be "he who abandons"?

We should note here that the resurrection of Jesus, properly speaking, does not give any real response to this question. Even if it is true that the Resurrection causes other names of God to appear, beginning with the initial one "He who has raised Jesus from the dead," these positive and glorious names do not effectively erase the others. The Resurrection does not justify the Cross; even supposing (but this would be a very superficial understanding of this Mystery) that it did in fact compensate the Crucified for his sufferings, it does not explain why the innocent had to pass through such a trial nor does it absolve God of having abandoned him. The question about God posed by the ultimate trial of the cross does not receive a response from the Resurrection, or at least does not receive its full response; one must first look elsewhere.

I propose that this elsewhere may be found in two synoptic narratives of the death of Jesus, that of Mark and that of Luke. We shall undertake a reading of these which will be somewhat analogous in method to that which we offered above for the narrative of the Resurrection, and we shall attempt to draw conclusions from this reading capable of illuminating the perspective opened in the following chapter by the figures of Adam and of Job. It will then be time to return to the Resurrection.

1. Mark 15:24–39[10]

The times

In the Gospel of Mark, the crucifixion and the death of Jesus take place within the course of six hours: from the third hour when he is crucified, to the ninth or a little later, when he expires. The three first hours are full of noise and of words; everyone speaks to Christ in a frightened tone of irony: the passersby, the high priests and the scribes, even the robbers crucified with him. Then comes a time—again three hours—of darkness and complete silence; darkness covers the earth, although it is still the middle of the day, and in a sense cuts short the peoples' words; Jesus, for his part, says nothing. A third, very brief period at the ninth hour contains a word, only one word, of Jesus, the active response of someone standing by (the narrative does not tell us to what group of persons he belongs), followed by a last cry of Jesus and death.

But there is the time after the death. It is marked by two episodes: one which concerns the Temple, down in the city; the other is a reaction of the Roman centurion, in front of Jesus.

The words: will he come down from the Cross?

These time segments, carefully distinguished by the evangelist, are characterized by words. There is in fact no more action: Jesus, crucified, immobile, has become in his body the clear expression of the failure of his mission. As a prophet, he is reduced to silence, as a wonder-worker, to impotence. Nevertheless, he will be invited three times to do one last performance which could repair all the damage at the last minute: *let him come down from the cross*. Let us listen to each of these appeals in order.

The passersby have heard rumor of the claim of Jesus reported at his trial: "I will destroy this temple that is made with hands, and in three days I will build another, not made with hands." They comprehend well the apparently blasphemous meaning of this. To destroy the Temple was to destroy the religion of Israel, whose center had for so long been the Temple. The Temple was the place where God manifested his Glory, the place of his encounter with his people, since the tent constructed by Moses in the desert, brought up by David to Jerusalem while awaiting the construction of the Temple of Solomon—and then its reconstruction after the exile and recent restoration under Herod. To claim to destroy the Temple was one of the most serious blasphemies that could be imagined: to destroy the religion of Israel and to replace it with another which could only be idolatrous! Now the blasphemer is crucified, immobile. His passion is the evident sign of the futility of his pretension; it testifies in favor of the religion of the Temple. For Jesus to accomplish what he foretold, he will first have to come down from the cross! This is the challenge that is now made to him.

During the trial of Jesus itself, the scribes and the high priests have posed the decisive question to Jesus: "Are you the Messiah, the Son of the Blessed One?" and they have heard a positive response from Jesus, who then went on to announce a mysterious enthronement at the right hand of God. It is for this very reason that they have handed him over. Now it seems to them that the cross on which Jesus hangs is in itself the annulment of his filial and messianic claim. If, however, this claim *did* have some foundation, let Jesus come down from the cross! What a Messiah this would make! Then it would be possible to believe—this is the challenge shouted at him from below. But Jesus says nothing in reply; he remains immobile, and darkness covers the whole earth.

At the ninth hour, Jesus finally breaks his silence, but only to pronounce the mysterious phrase; "Eloi, Eloi, lema sabachthani?" The exact meaning of this word on the lips of Jesus at this moment and the spiritual experience which it expresses have been much discussed. Before seeking a response to this question, it should be noted that this phrase occurs here first of all because of the way in which it was understood by the people who heard it: "He is calling Elijah." Elijah, in fact, was supposed to be the precursor of the Messiah; such was the commonly accepted conviction, based on an oracle of the prophet Malachi, to which the narrative of the Transfiguration, earlier in the Gospel, had already alluded. Hearing the cry of Jesus, the bystanders understand that in his abandonment, the crucified is desperately calling on the one who was to precede the Messiah, to introduce him to the people and protect him from his enemies. So Jesus is given something to drink, the idea being to give him a respite which would allow Elijah to come to fulfill his mission by taking him down from the cross!

It would seem then that from the third to the ninth hour, in the presentation that St. Mark gives us of the death of Jesus, the question pending is: "Will he come down from the cross?" and this is why we are justified in seeing a nuance of fear in the irony of those who address Jesus—what if he should actually come down? In any case, the confession of the filial and messianic identity of Jesus depends on this challenge.

The death of Jesus

But Jesus does not come down. Once again he lets out a great cry, and expires. In other words, with respect to all those who stand about him, he loses the case; he has not given the final sign which could have redressed the situation; his claims therefore are finished and his identity is insignificant. Jesus is unable to justify what he has said of himself at his trial and on previous occasions. He claimed that he would destroy and rebuild the Temple: it is he himself who is destroyed; he tried to pass himself off as the Messiah, the Son of the blessed One, he announced his enthronement at the right hand of God; in reality, he is dead. His inability to come down from the cross marks the triumph of his opponents: not only a triumph, ultimately rather sordid, of people who might be jealous of another human being who excels them, but above all, at least in appearance, the triumph of the true religion over imposture. In the eyes of the bystanders, it is also an abandonment by God: he has remained invisible and inactive throughout this whole scene; he has not brought the least help to the one on the cross. If God has done nothing at this moment, one can say that he has never been with Jesus. Abandonment at the decisive moment signifies that Jesus was never really sent by God, nor was he accompanied by him at any moment. He was not commissioned to announce the nearness of the Kingdom, and still less was he mandated to present a view of God which would, to some degree, break with the tradition of the ancients or to bring to light a name of God, the name of Father, which up to that time had only been used very sparingly.

Toward a new Temple?

However, the evangelist does not end his account with the last sigh of Jesus. He mentions an episode relative to the Temple (harking back to the claim Jesus had made regarding the Temple and to the insults of the "passersby") and he describes the reaction of the Roman centurion on duty at the foot of the cross (harking back to the messianic and filial claim of Jesus and to the insults of the "high priests and the scribes"). The veil of the Temple, as is well known, separated the two sacred rooms of the Sanctuary and the Holy of Holies and prevented people from either seeing or entering into the Holy of Holies. Before the destruction of the first Temple, the Holy of Holies contained the sacred objects which were the sign of the Presence of God, the place of the manifestation of the Glory, the means of encounter with the Most High. Destroyed or lost at the time of the exile, these objects had not been replaced, and the Holy of Holies was thus empty—whether one interprets this void as a still more eloquent sign of the Presence or, on the contrary, as the carefully concealed expression of the non-Presence. Whatever the case may be, the narrative of Mark tells us that at the moment of Jesus' death, the veil of the Temple was rent in two from top to bottom. That which had been hidden was now evident to all; the suppression of this hidden and mysterious character of the Holy of Holies, henceforth open to the eyes of all, is a first profanation of the Temple. But there is more. When the veil is rent, the emptiness appears: the void of the Holy of Holies—the signs of the Covenant and of the Presence have deserted it! The signs are no longer there, neither is the secret guarded by the veil: there is nothing there anymore, the Temple is desacralized, profaned, deconsecrated. It reveals its own emptiness: the rending of the veil at the moment when Jesus dies is indeed that destruction which Jesus had foretold.

But then the reader of the Gospel is lead to raise the question of the rebuilding: if the death of Jesus has effected the destruction of the man-made Temple, how will Jesus go about rebuilding the new Temple, not made by man? The paradox which no one, believer or adversary, could have expected is that Jesus would destroy the Temple by means of his own death, as though there were some mystical identification between the monument of stone and its spiritual signification and the body of Jesus, such that the death of the one was the destruction of the other. But this paradox calls for its own continuation: the restoration of the Temple passes through the restoration of the body of Jesus. Mark does not say anything on this question, but the play of symbols and their absolutely simultaneous character leaves us with an expectation which is far from being totally blind. We begin to realize what is happening—Jesus, by destroying the Temple with his death, is showing that he is, like the Temple, the Place of the Presence of God. "In three days" it will be revealed that Jesus is the Holy of Holies.

Confessing the Son

What is merely suggested by the rending of the Temple veil is said clearly by the word of the centurion. First of all, it is a centurion who speaks: neither a passerby, nor a high priest, nor a scribe, nor even that "one of those standing by" who had given Jesus a drink, but a Roman soldier, of whom the text has thus far not yet spoken. Even if he is qualified by a direct article ("the centurion") he has not yet been introduced, which means perhaps that this article might here signify a kind of universality. The centurion speaks for all the pagans, for all those who have not been involved in the story of Jesus because they had nothing to do with "Judea and Jerusalem"—as though the New Temple is to be for the nations.

Now the centurion is right in front of the cross and sees Jesus expire. What was in this last sigh we do not know. But perhaps there was a highly expressive tonality because, seeing him expire "in this way," the centurion receives an internal illumination—the silent, mysterious way in which this man has died is evidence for him of a transcendence: "Surely this man was the Son of God." It is not because Jesus has come down from the cross that the centurion confesses this divine filiation, but because he has died! We know that all through the Gospel of St. Mark, Jesus forbids anyone to proclaim him Son of God. At the moment of his death, and thus independently of any prophetic teaching or of any thaumaturgic accomplishment, Jesus is recognized as Son of God by a pagan, and no one can take exception to this assertion which refers back to the first verse of the Gospel, where Jesus was likewise presented (but outside of his concrete history) as Son of God. Just as the rending of the veil of the Temple contrasted with the insults of the passersby, so the confession of the centurion is in triumphant contrast to the jeers of the "high priests and the scribes." The latter wanted Jesus to come down from the cross in order that they might acknowledge his messianic character, but the centurion is able to look at the cross of Christ, at the dead Christ, and read his divine filiation. We have here a striking contrast and an astounding revelation: it is not the fact of his ability to come down from the cross that turns out to be the proof, the manifestation, the epiphany of Jesus as Son of God, Messiah and savior. Rather, it is his death. It is in his death and not in his life, it is in his failure and not in his success or in a last minute escape that Jesus is revealed in his condition of transcendence.

It is clear that the presentation made by St. Mark of the death of Jesus is a studied and sophisticated composition. The two themes of the Temple and the divine filiation echo each other in a succession that goes from the trial of Jesus to the decisive events of the time after his death, passing through the ironical and apprehensive words of the passersby and of the priests. The death of Jesus thus takes on a twofold depth: the moment of failure is real, a fact which is underlined by the impotence of the Crucified to come down from the cross, but this failure is in reality an act of rebuilding and a manifestation. As is the destruction of the old Temple, the death of Jesus is the prelude to the building up of the new religion founded on his body—a religion whose ultimate principle is the very identity of Jesus who reveals himself in his death: the identity of Son.

2. Luke 23:44–45[11]

Luke's account has more the appearance of a chronicle. Jesus is on his way up to the place of crucifixion surrounded by a crowd that is apprehensive and menaced by the specter of impending punishment, and to this crowd he addresses a word of lamentation. We are then told what takes place during the time when Jesus, now crucified, is still

THE EASTER NARRATIVE   163

alive: from the side of the bystanders, leaders, soldiers and one of the
malefactors, jeering insults, but the people who have come up with
Jesus look on, silent and ashamed. Jesus extends his mercy to all: in
the form of a prayer for those who have done or are doing him harm,
in the form of pardon for the one who requests it. Then comes the third
period, that of the actual death of Jesus. After a reaction by the centurion (the tenor of which is less dense than it is in the narrative of
Mark: there is an acknowledgement of the "death of the Just," as opposed to a confession of the Son of God), the crowd goes down again
with the same sadness exhibited when they were on the way up and
during the time of the crucifixion.

In this perspective, the third time segment of the chronicle, which
could also have been told in an objective, matter-of-fact manner, takes
on a more striking relief. It describes in fact, briefly but clearly, the
end of a world, then it relates the last moment of Jesus.

The end of a world

At the threshold of this third time of the chronicle, the attention of
the reader is in fact captured by a chronological indication: it is the
only one found in the narrative. It is about noon, we are told, when the
sun is at its zenith. Now the sun disappears and, for this reason, darkness extends over the earth (it is Luke who brings out this relationship
of cause and effect). The day comes to an end just at the point when it
should have been most radiant. Then, before the death of Jesus (and
not afterward, as in Mark), the veil of the Temple is torn, as if to say
that the religion lived in the Temple and symbolized by it was collapsing, and with it the people who were defined by this religion. A twofold eschatological symbol: the world gives way, the Temple falls. In a
sense, nothing remains but Jesus on his cross; but Jesus is to die, in
solidarity with this world and with this Temple.

The voice of the Son

It is then that the voice of Jesus makes itself heard. It is no longer
addressed either to the world, or to human beings, not even to those
belonging to his people. Jesus has finished talking to men and the latter

are, by their own choice, under the eschatological judgment whose symbols have been revealed or under the mercy which Jesus has requested for them and offered to them. Now the voice of Jesus turns toward the Father, and it concerns Jesus alone: "Father, into your hands I commend my spirit." In the midst of the universal destruction in which his crucifixion and his imminent death involve him, to which they even in a sense identify him, Jesus keeps on his lips the invocation of God and gives himself over totally to him whom he does not cease to call Father.

This perseverance of Jesus in invocation at the final moment of death tells us two things. First of all, that invocation, if man consents to utter it, is indestructible, beyond the grasp of death. It manifests all its intensity in the event of death: it is as though the last moment on the cross was precisely the moment par excellence for saying "Father," not only from the lips, but from the depths of the spirit and of the whole reality of the body which is breathing its last in this invocation. The filial abandonment is all the more manifest in that everything which could have sustained it is disappearing; perhaps, in this totally stripped and pure invocation, we begin to discern what the Son really is.

On the other hand, this invocation, because it arrives after the signs of the end—the alteration of the world and the destruction of the Temple—points to the dawn of a new world and of a new religion of which it will serve as the foundation. When everything has disappeared, the voice of the Son still remains, and the word which it utters is founding a filial world, which cannot yet be seen because it is still in the darkness, but which can be heard because Jesus says "Father."

By the arrangement of his narrative, by the way in which he isolates in the chronicle of mercy the eschatological moment of death and of invocation, Luke suggests that the invocation in which Jesus gives himself back totally to his Father *opens the time of sonship*; it enables us to catch a glimpse of a renewed world and of a different time frame, marked in the most complete way by a relationship of Son to Father and of Father to Son: this relationship was the goal of the entire climb of the preceding history, with its trials, its losses and, we must add, its sins. Fulfilled for the first time in the final prayer of Jesus as he dies, this relation will put its mark on everything that will follow. Here too, as in Mark, but in a different way, the filial death of Jesus points to a resurrection.

3. Death and Sonship

This reading of the texts which come from the Synoptic Gospels (I have not spoken of Matthew who, in these passages, is close to Mark) seems to reveal how the *death* of Jesus and his divine *sonship* are closely linked. The contexts are different, but they complement each other so as to point in the same direction. Mark is the more tragic of the two; his composition brings out more strongly the impotence of Christ: separated from his disciples, apparently stripped of his mission and of his power, tortured in his body, immobile on the cross in spite of the repeated invitations to come down from it, Jesus lets out a word of agony which nothing prevents us from taking quite literally, echoing an aspect of his distress. He enters into death with a great cry. But the evangelist invites all those who have clear-sighted vision to follow the gaze of the centurion and *to find in this tragic moment itself* the ultimate (and even the only) confession of the Son of God, the dawn of the new religion in the new Temple whose marvelous appearance this death enables us to glimpse.

Luke underlines this relationship between the death and sonship in a different way. He makes us assist at the end of a world (whose lot can be viewed with hope because it has been enveloped with words of mercy) and at the hinge that joins this world with another that is to come, he places the filial invocation of Jesus. Cut off from every human being and from the whole world by the darkness that extends over the earth and by the religious destruction of his people symbolized by the unveiling of the sanctuary, Jesus keeps on his lips the invocation of Father. It is, at this precise moment when the old world is on its way out (and Jesus, in his body, is going with it) and before the other has as yet broken in, invocation was all that was left, as though the Son would appear in the purity of his relationship to the Father only in this moment of history when nothing else is holding up. A peaceful purity, but one which would be opposed to the tragic experience of abandonment only by one who had no knowledge whatever of the traditions of the spiritual and mystical life. Paradoxically, these two aspects are in fact compatible and it is *sonship* which constitutes their unity.

Jesus is assimilated to the cosmos: his death is preceded by apocalyptic signs which destroy the harmonious succession of day and night. He is assimilated to the people of Israel, with respect to what this people has that is most priceless and most pure, the Temple, the place where God makes his abode among men. What dies together with him is not then only a world of sin, gone so far toward the abyss that it could never again be restored—it is not only an impure people or a Temple which has more or less deviated from its purposes. But it is also, and perhaps above all, the world as creation and the Temple as Holy of Holies. *Sonship is something beyond.*

Jesus is not only assimilated to the cosmos and to the Temple. In his person, he has come as the final prophet of the Kingdom, as Messiah, as Son. It is thus that he has revealed himself, and demanded that people believe in him, through a preaching centered on the plan of God. Now by his death, his prophecy collapses and his messiahship is annuled: everything which in his person and in his message had been directed toward this world of creation and this people in whose midst God dwelt is brought to mortal destruction, without any assistance seeming to come to him from the creator God, Lord of his people, who sends the prophets and raises up his Messiah. The Gospels are discreet when it comes to describing the soul of the Christ, but the little they tell us can help us to discern from afar how profound was his trial before the silence of God. The painful destruction of his body, strong as creation, the dereliction of his heart, pure as the Temple, the shattering of hopes, divine as the One who had raised them—who could have comprehended these things? No one: and the one who was undergoing them less than any other, at the time when he was bent under their weight. But the question was not to understand; it was to allow oneself to be led and to persevere in the confession of the Living God. A rejected prophet, a frustrated Messiah, Jesus *remained Son*, and he was so all the more, in a sense, in that all the rest, however holy it may have been, was taken away from him. And Jesus did not refuse to remain son. According to Mark, the very manner—motionless, silent—in which he died witnessed to the fact that he was the Son. According to Luke, who expresses the spoken form of this filial attitude, it was perseverance in the invocation of the Name of Father which bore this witness, as if Jesus was finally seen in the plenitude of his filial condition at the very moment when all the rest had been totally removed from him.

The time of Jesus

The time of Jesus is that of sonship. It is the duration of a total process of stripping aimed at enabling that sonship to appear in its truth; a relationship which is beyond all, which is not founded by anything but which founds all. For Jesus it is all as if, in order to reach this fuller level of sonship, he had to be led beyond all the rest, which was itself a fruit of paternal love: not to deny the Temple (the place of God's Glory), nor the world and the body (gifts of God's creation) nor the messianic mission (the fruit of God's sending), but to experience, by way of their apparent destruction (and the appearance here is one that takes on all the vivid aspects of reality)—to experience sonship as pure relationship, the Name of Father as a Name which one continues to pronounce because the invocation of Father in the heart of the Son is more intimate and more radical than any other possible benefit given by the Father to the Son, including the charges entrusted to him. The time of Jesus is directed toward a pure invocation whose symbol is death to absolutely any other reality.

Regarding this time of Jesus, scanned by the adventure of sonship, we must see that it is marked by the "form of death" and "symbolic exchange," and we must progress in the understanding of the fact that, by way of the Resurrection whose witness the Christian community keeps alive, it is the *founding time*.[12]

Form of death and symbolic exchange

The authors studied in the first part of this book called our attention to a dramatic concealment of death in our civilization and they were inviting us to riddle with holes a way of thinking and of behavior described as "compact," so that time might be rediscovered thanks to the chinks thus created in a world of auto-possession without wrinkles or crevices. In this way, to use again the terms of Baudrillard, a beneficial "form of death" would be able once again to regulate a social life fully characterized by symbolic exchange. The story of Jesus directs us to the specific focal point of this form of death: that human beings are involved in the concrete form which it takes is not to be contested, but in its pure essence this form is the path of a relationship *with God*. The deplored concealment is the fruit of a random, negative relationship with God, the opposite of a filial existence. Consequently, a deconcealment would be able to come about only through a positive acceptance of the Word or of the behavior of God, even if this should take on the form of abandonment, and then a positive and constructive relationship with human beings and with the world would once again become possible. We have here a fundamental conception or figure of time which it will take us some time to analyze.

The founding time

Because the resurrection of Jesus is unique among the histories of faithful human beings, it also reveals the *uniqueness* of this filial relationship of Jesus to his Father: the Resurrection witnesses to the fact that the space of filiation traversed in the mystery of the Cross is without analogue: it invites us to reflect further on the meaning of this filial time of Jesus which seems to be at once the matrix and the model of the whole of human time. We find it surprising that a founding narrative could refer to the "middle" of time, but if it is in this "middle" that pure sonship and its stakes were revealed, then a certain light begins to break on the real economy of time.

Conversely, reflection on the cross as the space of filiation points us towards the meaning of the Resurrection. Whatever we might say about this, it is out of the question that the Risen One can live henceforth other than for the Father whom he invoked on the cross; it is impossible that he could take back for himself, or that he could be simply given back what he had freely left behind before his death. The invocation on the cross is not a tentative cry because it expresses the ultimate profundity of Jesus. This invocation cannot itself die in the sense of a "second death." One cannot imagine the risen one in a static condition, as though returned to a calm after a storm of struggle which has ceased with death; one cannot conceive of him as having been put in possession, by way of recompense, of the Power of the Name above every other name, and of a Body finally glorified—all things which would indeed henceforth be his. If there is resurrection, if there really is the gift of Power, of the Name and of the Body, this can only be within the imperishable dynamic of an invocation of Father into which the Risen One passes totally and forever: "symbolic exchange" in which, as we shall see, the Father does not remain behind.

Thus, we begin to see why it is that the narrative of the Paschal Mystery is *the* founding narrative: it renders testimony to the economy of time, which is that of a progressive approach to the mutual perfection of the relationship between man and God.

The twofold Name of God

The last part of this chapter has enabled us to glimpse the positive sense of the disconcerting name "God who abandons," abandonment being revealed as the mysterious face of Fatherhood. But this name does not annul the other: God is also "he who has raised Jesus from the dead," who had given him body and mission and gives them back to him transformed by resurrection. We must distinguish between the *gift* by which Jesus is constituted and sent, and the *abandonment* through which he is lead to the perfection of the filial relationship. One of the tasks we still have before us will in fact consist in exploring and, if possible, expressing the harmony that exists between these two divine names.

CONCLUSION

From this inquiry bearing on the Christian narration of the resurrection and the death of Jesus of Nazareth, we can draw a few tentative conclusions. In search of a founding narrative worthy of being heard, we have encountered that of the Christian community, told as a memorial and celebrated in rite. God is the One who raised his son, Jesus of Nazareth, making him the principle of the new life, beyond the remission of sins, giving authority to the teaching and to the example of this Jesus through the gift of the Spirit. A trajectory of life is thus possible, founded on this gift which is also a promise. But the resurrection of Jesus, which founds a world of justice and of love, is the *response* on the part of God to the perfect, integral way in which Jesus entered into the trial which was set before him. In the course of this trial, God withdrew and offered no assistance, so that Jesus was led, through his perseverance, to reveal the ultimate and primary character, the originality and the dynamism with respect to God of his condition as Son. God, with respect to Jesus, withdrew beyond the range of the Commandment, of the Law, of Wisdom, of the Promise, but also of the final sending of the Messiah. And through all of this is revealed that which, as we shall see in greater detail, was from the beginning: God as Father, and man, beyond all essence and all law, as son.

So the figure of time is revealed, on the side of God, as an extremely delicate game of gift and of abandonment, and for man as an interplay or dialectic, also difficult to properly conduct, of joy and of trial. And all of this takes on meaning and can be realized in reference to and in function of the *primordial time* recounted in the *founding narrative* and celebrated in the *Eucharistic celebration*; that of Jesus of Nazareth dead and risen.

Notes

1. Cf. J. Moingt, "La révélation du salut dans la mort du Christ. Esquisse d'une théologie systématique de la rédemption," in *Mort pour nos péchés* (Brussells, 1976), pp. 117–172. On the relationship resurrection/cross, see pp. 118ff.

2. What I am saying here recaptures, in another cultural context, the intuition of Irenaeus regarding the apostolic tradition (*Adv. Haer. III*, 1–5). The difference is that today the "gnostic" attitude is entirely secularized and is not based on the interpretation of any scripture; likewise, it is here the absolute necessity of *hearing* that leads us to insist on the Church of the Apostles, as the *concrete* community where it is possible to hear *real* witnesses. As at the time of Irenaeus, the alternative seems impossible to escape: either a recourse to an inexplicable "fundamental break," which one simply accepts or beyond which one desires to return, or the hearing from authorized witnesses of a foundation which orientates our future and our present.

3. In order to clarify the difference which I am trying to establish between *interpretation* and *reinterpretation*, I would like to make a comment with regard to the opposition established by Fr. Moingt, *op. cit.*, p. 139, between "sudden illumination" or "instructions given by Christ to his disciples between Easter and the Ascension" on the one hand, and "intellectual activity, reflection, rereading" on the other. It seems to me that, in order to profitably conduct this reflection and this *relecture* in the various concrete circumstances of the mission, the apostles were not only assisted by the Spirit as necessities arose, but they also received from this same Spirit an *initial* inspiration attesting to the truth of the resurrection and supplying the ultimate hermeneutical principle of the scriptures, namely, that the Paschal Mystery of Christ is its fulfillment. Now I believe that this has something of the "sudden" about it, just as the fundamental "illumination" of Paul on the road to Damascus was sudden, making him see in a flash the real nature of what he was zealously engaged in uprooting as blasphemy. It is this initial inspiration which I call here "interpretation," while for the rereadings (even when, in the case of canonical Scripture, they are inspired), I reserve the term "reinterpretation."

4. É. Poulat, "Critique et théologie dans la crise moderniste," in *Recherches de Sciences religieuses* (1970), p. 549.

5. In the interpretation of the Gospel or Old Testament narratives which I will have occasion to present here, I will be using a method which I learned in the school of the late Norman Perrin whose courses I followed at the Universersity of Chicago during the academic year 1971-1972. One will find this method employed in "Toward an interpretation of the Gospel of Mark," in *Christology and a Modern Pilgrimage*, edited by H. D. Betz (Claremont, 1971). This method was intrinsically open to certain developments made possible by structuralism while at the same time strongly linked to *Form-und Redaktionsgeschichte*. But its originality and its greatest merit lay, in my opinion, in the emphasis it placed on the literary dimension of the text.

6. In these pages, which merely outline the discussion (it would require a whole book to expound this question of the *founding narrative* and its *reinterpretations*), I have attempted to present briefly for their own sakes the ideas set forth in my discussion with Pierre Gisel on "La pertinence théologique de l'histoire," in *RSPT* 63 (1979), 161-202, notably on the primacy of hearing, the permanence of a fundamental "figure" at the core of the reinterpretations, the pluralism of the latter and their "probable" degree of truth, the primary importance of the Church (here presented as Eucharistic community). By situating these observations in the framework of a kind of phenomenology of the original narrative (cf. the Introduction), I hope in part to have met the demands of Pierre Gisel in "L'assomption du réel au travers du nom," *ibid.*, pp. 580-592.

7. Acts 2:23-24, 32, 36; 3:15; 4:10; 5:30; 10:39-40; 13:28-31. Regarding these texts there is general agreement today in saying that they are, on the one hand, fully in line with the literary structure of the discourses, which, as such, are the work of Luke, and, on the other, that they offer a faithful reinterpretation of the primitive kerygma. Cf. e.g. E. Haenchen, *Die Apostelgeschichte* (Göttingen, 1959), p. 5, as well as in his commentary on various individual passages. C. H. Dodd, *The Apostolic Preaching and its Developments* (London, 1936), pp. 7-35; G. Schneider, *Die Apostelgeschichte* (Freiburg, 1980), I, p. 271; J. Schmitt, "Résurrection de Jésus" in *DBS* X (1980), col. 491, etc.

8. X. Léon-Dufour, *Resurrection and the Message of Easter*, trans. R. N. Wilson (1974), pp. 106-116; R. H. Fuller, *The Formation of the Resurrection Narratives* (London, 1972), pp. 71-93; S. Van Tilborg, *The Jewish Leaders in Matthew* (Leiden, 1972), pp. 106-108; C. H. Giblin, "Structural and Thematic Correlations in the Matthean Burial-Resurrection Narratives," in *NTS* 21 (1975), pp. 406-420; P. Jullien de Pomerol, *Quand un évangile nous est conté. Analyse morphologique du récit de Matthieu* (Brussels, 1980), pp. 194-200.

9. These few lines attempt to summarize the consensus which appears to have been established among theologians on the basis of three types of

investigation: the first on eschatology in the consciousness and teaching of Jesus (with reference, in particular, to *logia* such as Mk 9:1 and 13:30; Mt 10:23); the second, on the attitude of Jesus in the face of his probable, and then imminent death; the third, on the prayer of Jesus and the name Father. The literature on these subjects is so vast that any bibliographical notice borders on the ridiculous. I give a few references here: W. G. Kümmel, "Die Naherwartung in der Verkündigung Jesu" in *Zeit und Geschichte* (Tübingen, 1964), pp. 31–46; Vögtle, "Réflections exégétiques sur la psychologie de Jésus", in *Le Message de Jésus et l'interprétation moderne* (Paris, 1969), pp. 41–113; H. Schürmann, *Jesu ureigener Tod; exegetische Besinnungen und Ausblick* (Freiburg, 1975); M. Hengel, *La Crucifixion*, French translation, (Paris, 1981, Part II, chapter 2); J. Jeremias, *Abba: Studien zur neutestamentlichen Theologie und Zeitgeschichte*, (Göttingen, 1966).

10. T. A. Burkill, "St. Mark's Philosophy of the Passion" in *Novum Testamentum* 2 (1957), 245–271, and "The Trial of Jesus", in *Vigiliae Christianae* 12 (1958), 1–18; D. Juel, *Messiah and Temple*, (Missoula, Montana, 1977).

11. F. Bovon, *Luc le Théologien* (Neuchâtel-Paris, 1978), pp. 175–181 and 208 (bibliography); R. Meynet, *Quelle est donc cette Parole* (Paris, 1979), pp.186–188.

12. It is difficult, perhaps even impossible, when one speaks or writes on the *human* adventure of Jesus, to totally avoid the use of words and expressions that could be taken in an *adoptionist* sense. Everything I say, here and below, a propos of the "adventure of sonship" should be understood of the whole *human* odyssey in the course of which Jesus lived up to the Name which had always been his in God—that of Son.

CHAPTER TWO

FROM THE GARDEN OF EDEN TO THE LAND OF HUS

If the founding narrative refers to the *time of Jesus*, situated "in the middle of time," it does not follow that everything that preceded this time of Jesus had nothing to do with the founding. This would be the place for a theology of the times before the Time, not only in their actual unfolding, but in the way in which they have been interpreted and have thus *prepared* for the interpretation and the understanding of the *time of Jesus*. In other words, this would be the place for a theology of the Old Testament as a progressive adjustment of the *figures* on which the Face of Christ was inscribed by anticipation. As I remarked when speaking of the "inspired and sacramental witness" of the apostles, the reference to these figures was from the beginning a part of the revealed manifestation of the meaning of the Resurrection, and the developments that followed, whether of the apostolic era or of the post-apostolic tradition, continued to apply this fundamental principle of interpretation. The place where this relationship of figures to reality is revealed in its fullness and where an experience of *founding* can truly be lived is the liturgy of the Easter Vigil where the Mystery of Christ is recounted with the whole plenitude of meaning that springs from the figures, while, conversely, the intensity of the liturgical memorial brings to reality these figures that scanned the course of time waiting for their meaning to be unveiled.

The object of these remarks is to introduce a partial meditation on the figures that can help the understanding of faith in Jesus, in his mystery of sonship. I would like to reflect first of all on two figures who fall into the category of *innocents put to the test*—Adam in the garden of Eden and Job in the land of Hus: this is the object of this chapter. We will then concern ourselves with the problem, already mentioned, of the *remission of sins*, because this relationship to sin seems to characterize the time before Christ, while the time after Christ would seem (although this is not so evident) to be one of liberation from sin.

The figures of Job and of Adam can help us to comprehend the Cross of Christ, to the extent that in both cases we have an irruption, in the midst of a situation of reputed innocence, of a *trial*, or test; man comes out of this victorious only to the extent that he finally accepts the *distance* of God, revealed by this trial, and bends his wisdom to make it come under the rule of this mystery at once hidden and revealed by this trial itself. The trial in fact seems calculated to bring out the unlikeness of God, the object being, once this has been humbly accepted, that man might be graciously elevated to a *true* likeness. The transfiguration to "the image and likeness" does not take place—and we will have to try to see why this is so—without a certain disfiguration, a too-rough image one might have, either of God or of man himself. The trial would seem to be a key moment in the process of coming to understand God and the nature of the relationship we have with him.

It is not impossible that the two figures in question, Job and Adam, were related to each other by the biblical author himself.[1] Indeed, it is striking that the framework and the unraveling of the action strongly resemble each other in the two cases, so much so that one might ask whether the author might not have been consciously trying to give us a kind of parable of the true Adam in the prose narrative that begins and ends the Book of Job. In both cases we find the same protagonists: God, man and woman, and an adversary; this latter and the woman contribute through temptation to the trial of the man. Adam succumbs, but Job resists. There is a rather strict parallel in the narration itself: from a situation that is happy and without history we pass to a situation of trial that is caused by the fact that God reserves or withdraws what he had previously given. Finally, according to whether the man does or does not emerge victorious from the trial, there begins the time of mercy or that of transfiguration.

At the time when the Book of Job was written,[2] Israel, through the reflection of human wisdom and above all through the study of the Word of God contained in the Law and the Prophets, has acquired a vision of God, of things and of men according to which the people is striving hard to live. We are at a moment when the notion of creation has reached a profound level of refinement: man has here been able to recognize the work of a Wisdom, harmonious and friendly to men (cf. Prov 8), and Job views creation as a gift of God marked by attention and loving concern (cf. Job 3). The laws of the universe are grounded also in this creative wisdom and witness in their turn to the solicitude of God. Finally, God, who has entered into a covenant relationship with humankind, has given his Law—and it is generally understood that to observe this law is to live. At the time of Job, an osmosis is tending to take place between the Law and Wisdom, the one more social in nature and bound to the history of a people, the other more individual and linked to reflection on human existence, but both coming together to supply, *on the part of God*, this "knowledge of good and evil" that man at the beginning was not, as we know, supposed to appropriate by himself. Thus, at the level of the Law and of Wisdom as well as at that of creation, mankind is under the multiform gift of God.

The gift of God is confirmed and multiplied when it assures a just retribution to whoever does good as well as to whoever does evil. Among a great number of other texts, Ps 18 (vv. 25-26) can supply us here with an expression of retribution:

With the loyal you show yourself loyal;
with the blameless you show yourself blameless;
with the pure you show yourself pure;
and with the crooked you show yourself perverse.

Now Job is introduced to us as "blameless and upright, one who feared God and turned away from evil" (1:1 and 8:2, 3). Even if the narrative presents him as living in a pagan land, it makes of him the very model of a man sensitive and faithful to this universe of creation, Law and Wisdom that are the gift of God. His obedience and his righteousness are impressive. He himself, at the time of his misfortune and when he is on trial before God, makes a thorough inventory of these things in a marvelous text that Philippe Nemo gives the magnificent title of "Job's litanies of blamelessnesses" (cf. Job 21 and 31). Job does not make perfection reside in the legalistic observance of primarily cultic precepts, but gives evidence of a constant concern, not only not to wrong other people, but to serve them: he goes thus to the heart of the precepts of the Law. His "fidelity to the decrees of the Most High" concerns most especially the poor, the widow, the orphan, the blind, the powerless, the indigent, the persecuted, but this does not exclude a fidelity to God himself in prayer. Job is the paragon of man attentive to the most refined, the most human and at the same time the most divine demands of the Law of God, to the most central directives of Wisdom. Thus it is that, both through his experience as a happy man, blessed in his family and in his goods (cf. Ps 128) and as a faithful man whose righteousness is without wrinkle, Job is able to perceive with his whole being the harmony that his fidelity to God establishes in his whole life. What is written in the book under the form of admonition, threat or promise, is realized concretely for him; his happiness and well-being is not linked to a succession of haphazard circumstances, it is the realization, in the life of a human existence, of that balanced, just harmony of beings and things before God. Nothing—at least according to the teaching of that book—can break this harmony, except injustice and sin. And since Job carefully avoids perversity of any kind, he rightly thinks that he can lose nothing of this exact equilibrium in which he lives and that has a name: happiness.

In the perspective established by the Book of Job, the gift of God, that in some sense has materially to do with the goods of human life—family, riches, health—is in reality rooted much more profoundly in the reality of a *covenant* in which God takes the initiative and in which these good things are in a sense the enduring symbol. And they acquire their most radiant value from this symbolic value, that is acknowledged and confirmed by human fidelity.

So when the Book of Job is written, there already stands behind it a long history of the experience of Israel, a lengthy meditation on Wisdom and the Law: a "word of God" is profoundly inscribed in the mentalities and judgments of the people, and the drama that is precisely that which will constitute the essence of the trial will stem from the fact that things will begin to occur that will appear to contradict, even to subvert this word. The redaction of the narrative of origins in the oldest document of the Pentateuch, the Yahwist narrative, responds to other demands.[3] The author is probably writing some time during the reign of Solomon, perhaps at a time when the situation of royalty in Israel is weakening and when the threat of a break among the tribes, that David had united with difficulty into a single kingdom, are becoming real—perhaps only because the conduct of Solomon, particularly in religious matters, is provoking fears. Whatever the exact circumstances may have been, the Yahwist, inspired by a theological hope, wishes to give reasons for this hope by reflecting on history as it has come down to him in the oral traditions of his people and by interpreting it with the help of a theological *credo* of which the life and the trials of King David have been a splendid illustration. Election, blessing and sin, curse and mercy stand at the center of this *credo*, and the various traditions make it possible to illustrate their relevance and their truth; history becomes a pledge of hope for the future. The author has undertaken, in the reiteration and theological presentation of his people's traditions, to go all the way back to the origins of man and to his primitive history. Thus it was possible for him to grasp in their nascent state, in their very first appearance, the elements that would forever constitute the plot of human history, until the time when, through the mediation of the final descendant of David, salvation would be spread over the whole earth: the gift of God, election and happiness, then the interruption that puts to the test by calling this happiness into question, the weakness of man and the essential breaks or ruptures that this entails—with respect to God, to other human beings, to the earth—mercy and the hopes that it inspires. The story of Adam and Eve thus takes on the significance of a paradigm of universal history as well as of a fundamental reflection on the essential coordinates of human existence. Not only is it the starting point beyond which it would be impossible to go back, but it also supplies a perspective on whose the basis a painful but reconciled future could be envisaged. Of Adam the Yahwist could have said, as did St. Paul many years later, that he was "a figure of what was to come," a figure carried forward through the patriarchal figures, on through that of Moses, but above all illuminated by that of David.

Now this primitive and primordial history superimposes two narratives on each other, that of the creation and that of the commandment, through which panoramic, multi-dimensional portraits of God and of man emerge. I shall endeavor to do a careful reading of these interwoven narratives that should bring to light their various levels of perspective and the points of intersection.[4]

1. Eden, place of drama

The spaces

When history begins, we are in indefinite space. The land is desert-like—no grass, no shrubs, almost a lunar landscape. There is nothing there.

There is nothing because water has not yet come down from heaven. The earth is separated from what is above; heaven is neuter, for it has not yet revealed itself to earth in its power to fertilize with rain. There is nothing there because there is no man to make this uncultivated wasteland yield some or all of the potentialities it harbors.

Nevertheless, this landscape, stretching like a desert as far as the eye can see, is *not* lunar, for even if there is no water coming from heaven to fertilize it, nor any human being on the earth to cultivate it, at least there is a fine spring coming out of the earth, a source of moisture, that signifies the expectation, the hope of a flowering.

We will find this limitless space again at the end of the narrative (cf. Gen 3:23) but in a very different context: there it will be a question of man sent back by God to this wasteland, this "soil" from which he had been taken. But at this moment, man will be able to cultivate the land. It is almost as if everything that happens between the first mention of the soil (2:5) and the last (3:23) were actually opening the whole earth to the agricultural genius of man.

The narrative, however, puts space a little more in focus: "God planted a garden in Eden, in the East" (2:8): at the place where the earth receives the morning sun for the first time, a space emerges, set off by its very luxuriance. Bathed in light, it is traversed by water in four directions. This garden stands out in striking contrast to the desert earth. It is like a clearly defined center where one's gaze can settle, a place where something could happen and allow itself to be framed.

The text narrows the focus still more: it speaks of "the middle of the garden," a place marked by the presence of two trees with famous names. Since the beginning of the narrative it is vegetation that has defined the spaces. The first look opened onto the indefinite horizons of uncultivated soil; the second discovered a marvelous garden, planted with trees about which we are told that they were beautiful to look at and bore fruit good to eat; the third conducts us to the center of the garden that is again marked by two trees. These trees, with their mysterious and profound designations (of knowledge and of life) are the poles of the garden: if something is to happen, will it not happen here? And if some dramatic issue is to emerge, will it not be with reference to these two trees to which the narrator's art has led our gaze?

The characters

The first character, the "first to come on stage" one might say, is God, the Lord God. He is designated immediately by his proper name. No effort is made at this point either to justify his existence or to define him. There is no preamble to explain him: the God question is not posed, because his Name is immediately pronounced. God is simply there, unexplained, and the narrative shows no uneasiness in saying his Name without prior introduction. But strange things are affirmed of this God, and first of all it is said that he made heaven and earth. In these spaces into which the narrative confidently leads us, only to conduct us further to the center of a garden, God is not present as anyone might be. He made them—not only the spaces but all the rest as well. God plants (the trees), forms (man, the animals), and fashions (woman). Yet, different as is the manner of his presence, God is truly there. We are even told that he takes a walk in the garden in the cool of the day! Could anyone be more naturally at home in the garden and with all that is in it?

Above all, God speaks. To himself (2:18 and 3:22), and to each of the other characters: to man (2:16 and 3:9, 17), to woman (3:13 and 16), to the serpent (3:14–15). It will be interesting then to hear what he has to say.

Finally, God acts: he places man and woman in the garden, then, at the end of the story, he displaces them and sends them out into the boundless wasteland.

After God, there is man; he is made from the soil, he is as old as the boundless wasteland. He is the first being to tread upon this barren land and, for a moment, he remains alone.

Then come the animals. They too are formed by God, but under significant circumstances. God has observed, he has said to himself, perhaps in the form of a off-stage protest, that it is not good for man to be alone (2:18). Solitude is harmful for him and God wishes to remedy this, by making him "a helper as his partner." And the narrative shows us that God is not immediately successful with his plan: he leaves the garden, returns to the wasteland and forms a number of living beings that he brings to the man. The man names them, and by this very act takes possession of them, but he does not acknowledge them as this "helper, his partner." In a sense, the animal population of the earth represents the ensemble of "artistic failures" in God's effort to provide man with a partner; it consists in the mass of living beings in which man does not succeed in recognizing himself. He can of course give them names, but not his own name.

It is then that God creates woman. He fashions her in the garden and not outside of it. However, he does not fashion her from the "soil" as he had in the case of man and the animals; he does not even use the rich soil of this garden planted with trees. He draws her from the flesh of the man. He does violence in a way—in spite of the fact that he takes anaesthetic precautions—to the integrity of the man from whom he takes something only to give it back to him, transfigured in the form, at long last, of this "helper, his partner." Woman, the masterpiece of God's works, is formed like no other creature through the environment in which she was made and the substance from which she was drawn—woman, the perfect partner of man who cannot really know himself except by giving his own name to the one who is brought to him. They come together because they are one name, one flesh.

The fourth character to come onstage is the serpent. God probably formed him from the soil, like all the beasts of the fields that he had made. Cunning and crafty, he forms part of those beings in which man did not recognize himself, to which he did not join himself, to which he gave, not *his* name, but *a* name. Designated as a "beast of the field" he is first situated beneath the man and the woman. But observe that he comes into the picture just at the time when one of the two trees in the middle of the garden is about to come into focus: man, made from the soil and brought into the garden, woman made from man in the garden and brought to the man, the serpent made from the soil, standing upright on his tail near the tree—the order of entry onstage brings us back once again to the middle of the garden, to the center. If something is to happen, it will surely be here.

The preliminaries of the drama

That the man, who was formed by God and received from him the breath of life, should be a tiller of the soil, a farmer, is almost taken for granted by the narrator. God places man in the garden to till it and to keep it—the garden that he himself had planted. If he shuts man out of the garden at the end of the narrative, it will only be to send him away to till the soil from which he had been taken (cf. 2:5, 15; 3:23). This task of tiller of the soil is self-evident. At least—and this is the point we wish to bring out here—it is not introduced by any word of God. It is as though man, placed and settled in the garden, was immediately able to discover the techniques necessary to cultivate it.

However, if man does not hear any word with reference to agriculture, he does hear one relative to the consumption of the fruits of the garden. Indeed, this is the first word that is reported to us as coming from God. Until this point everything has been done in silence—

or, at least the narrative did not consider it useful to transmit what was said. But now we hear the voice of this God who, we have been told, made man and settled him in the garden.

These first words of God to man are first of all a word of gift: "You are free to eat from any tree in the garden," a gift in keeping with the creation of man and with the planting of the garden of Eden. Within the contours of this gift, however, there is a restriction, pertaining to one of the two trees in the middle of the garden. Regarding the tree of the knowledge of good and evil it is said: "You must not eat from it"; regarding the other tree nothing is said, which doubtless implies that the tree of life belongs to the whole group of trees that have been given to man to eat from. Man will not be separated, so as to die, from the tree of life—unless he transgresses the interdict pertaining to the tree of the knowledge of good and evil.

This word of God thus opens the space for a drama! By setting off a sector in the garden, little though it be, and placing it under interdict while allowing free access to all other sectors, it sets the conditions for a response. The stakes of this verbal exchange between God and man are immense: life or death. Everything that man has been able to do as a farmer settled in the garden to cultivate it and to keep it, he has done in a kind of spontaneous way, by innate ability. Everything that man has uttered up to this point has been in terms of naming the animals as he takes possession of them, or in the context of the mutual and spontaneous recognition of his like, in naming the woman with his own name. But a word space is now opened that seems to pertain to another order: a space of responsibility that, by way of the interdict, establishes between God and man, between the One who made and the one who was made, the possibility of a mutual word, a verbal interchange.

Such are the preliminaries of the drama. This drama will be played out between God and man, with life and death at stake and on the basis of a word in which God has taken the initiative, creating the tension proper to tragedy by an exclusion established within the contours of the gift. What will happen now?

The silence of man

The narrative does not mention any word of man, neither of response in thanksgiving to the benefits of his own creation, that of the garden, of the animals or of woman, nor by way of taking a position with respect to the twofold word of gift and reservation that God addresses to him. Man speaks to the animals that God has brought to him, to the woman whom he has received from God, but he does not speak to God. Are we to assume that, in the mind of the author, this silence is one of acquiescence? Man silently acknowledges the gifts of God and puts them to use. Even the interdict does not provoke any reaction on the part of man. Perhaps by placing a limit on man's field of activity, God is showing him that a transgression is possible: an interdict would have no meaning except with reference to a real power that could be exercised. The interdict thus arouses in man a first awareness of his connivance with the tree shown to him and the fruit that is denied him—a first awareness that will soon serve as a support to temptation. However, for the moment, man does not say anything. This revelation of his power and the possible openness of his desire stand within the hearing of the word of God. It is God himself who presents the action as dangerous and positively forbids it. The gravity of this word, pronounced by the benevolent God from whom man has received everything, would then easily enough, if necessary, appease the urge, that only the interdict has signaled. Therefore man naturally submits himself, his power and his desire, to the divine injunction; the latter is understood as a "rule of play," as a "set of directions" that calls for no other response than its faithful execution.

The temptation

The drama is born when another word makes itself heard: no longer the word of God, with its nuance of mysterious exclusion, nor the human word of mutual recognition between man and woman, nor the word of the lord of the animals, but the word of the serpent, of which the author tells us that he is a "beast of the fields." This designation underlines the subhuman identity of the serpent and classifies his word: man should immediately refuse any hearing and any response to this being who is inferior to him, and perhaps the beginning of sin consists precisely in the fact that he gives him a hearing. In any case, what does the serpent say? More crafty than any of the wild animals, he suggests, in the form of a question, the exact opposite of what God has said, that will then induce the woman to reconfirm God's word in its exact tenor and hence to focus precisely on the interdict pertaining to the tree that is in the middle of the garden. The serpent then comes to the attack and contests the veracity of the word of God: he dissociates the interdict from the punishment attached to transgression and supplies another explanation: God is jealous of his privilege as God and does not wish to share it. Now this privilege is in fact communicable: "you will be like gods." This affirmation arouses the desire of the woman whose view of the forbidden fruit is now transformed: it could raise the couple to equality with God. The temptation is a form of hedging where the two possible outcomes are mutually supportive; it scrambles the image of the good God that Adam and Eve have by suggesting the image of a jealous God; it strives to arouse a desire to be "like gods." God is jealous of what man can acquire; God in reality is nothing but that which man can become and his tentative superiority comes only from the interdict itself. Let man transgress this, and in a sense there will no longer be either men or God, but only "like gods."

The stakes of the temptation

The word of the serpent would not have had any meaning or appeal for man if it had been false. But as we have seen, the divine warning had entailed a first dawning of awareness on the part of man of his capacity to do what he had been forbidden to do. The temptation, coming back to the same point, develops this awareness of self and man sees himself more and more as capable of doing what he has been forbidden to do and of reaping some benefit from the very thing that God is preventing him from doing. The new image of God as jealous corresponds to the new image of man as powerful. Therefore, the question can have a hold on the mind of man, who inevitably loses an initial simplicity and childhood, both in his invocation of God and in the image he had of him and the way he looks at him. God is no longer only the powerful organizer of the Paradise of Eden, the benevolent witness of the happiness of man and woman among the trees and with the animals. Now he appears as a competitor, a rival, as one who would take away with one hand what he gave with the other. Who is he really and what is to be the first word of man as he finally emerges from his silence: an invocation or a blasphemy?

If he loses his original simplicity and childhood, man does not, by temptation alone, leave his innocence. The consent to temptation should not be projected onto the temptation itself; man is not already a sinner. There is no *fatum* in the account of Genesis. To be sure, tragedy is there in all its magnitude, but the drama is not over before it has begun: everything is located at the level of the *responsibility of the word*. The intervention of the tempter was "necessary" to promote human innocence to a fully reflective level and to endow a possible future invocation of God with all its density. Now it is up to man to take a stand on the identity of God: a jealous God, whose benefits are henceforth to be ignored in order to appropriate his power, or a God who is ever good, to whom one submits even when he forbids, because nothing justifies doubting his word and expecting from oneself rather than from him the eventual fulfillment of the capacities that his word has revealed. This judgment regarding God is in the power of man: once he has agreed to utter a word, God can only await the response that he will receive. This response itself proceeds from desire. God has hastened the loss by man of his original simplicity only to enable him to let himself be transported into authentic invocation: that which would utter the Name of God from the loving heart of human freedom, which would acknowledge without scandal the element of Mystery introduced by precept and renew its loyalty to God instead of exacerbating a desire at once turned in on self ("you will be like gods") and, by the same token, deicidal.

Such are truly the stakes of the Precept that temptation brings into the limelight. If it is no longer merely a matter of a "set of instructions" or a "rule of play" for life in the garden, it is because something else is really in question. The acts of God relative to the garden or to the animals—even to woman—were in some sense explicable in a context of human environment. On the other hand, by formulating the Precept, God has gone beyond the language of beings and of the world; the attempt of the serpent is aimed precisely at reducing the Precept to this language, by suggesting to man that since he is capable of doing what he has been forbidden to do, the Precept is fallacious and its author a liar. In reality, however, the Precept is not only nor primarily a word directed toward just any object of the world: it is there to hint at the Mystery of God and to invite mankind to acknowledge this mystery. At the heart of the demand for obedience there is a personal offer of Truth, in what it has that is incommensurate with any human perception, an invitation from God in Person to a renewed invocation and, to employ finally the fundamental scriptural term, a Covenant offer. It is only through Precept that God really addresses man as the God that He is. By provoking man to go beyond the merely human measure of what is accessible to him, he invites him to another "knowledge"; in the Commandment we receive the first glimpse of a Revelation.

The place of the knowledge of self

Temptation cannot manifest the Precept and, through the Precept, God himself as Mystery and as Word, without at the same time revealing man to himself as a free subject confronting God. Indeed, this new light results necessarily from the prospect of transgression opened by the serpent. Even before either one of them has taken sides, the mere fact of having been confronted clearly with the divine Precept, of understanding concretely the possibility of ignoring it and of having to take a clear stand, creates for the couple and for each of them individually a moment of self-awareness before God. If God reveals himself as Mystery and if this manifestation calls for a response, man vaguely perceives himself in tune with this Mystery; he discerns, but in negative image, a dimension that his response will bring to reality. It is in the act of responding to the word of God that man discovers himself; it is in the non-response that he loses himself and at the same time loses God. In other words, when God reveals himself to man as mysterious Word by way of the interdict, man perceives that he too is Word and he understands himself in the response that he chooses to make. Thus temptation, that has revealed God in himself, also discloses man to himself, not only as power over the world and as person before woman, but as liberty called to posit itself as Word before God.

The world as symbol of the Mystery

Temptation is for man a summons to declare himself, an inescapable invitation to Word. At the same time, it enables man to arrive at a perception of his own mystery, whether in his wish to set himself up as a counterpart to the Mystery of God or in his attempt to assert himself in independence. But we must add the following as well: if a divine Word prohibits anything at all within the enclosure of the marvelous garden and in this way unveils the Mystery of God and the correlative mystery of man, it also has a significant aftereffect; it affects everything that was already at man's disposal and marks it in a new way: the other trees of the garden, the animals, the woman herself with respect to man and man with respect to woman—all of these appear as given a second time as soon as one becomes aware that a single tree has been refused. At this moment it becomes clear that everything else could have been refused or given in another way. Thus the Gift, experienced and praised at the level of the first creation, seems redoubled, rooted in the same Mystery as the Precept. If a single word becomes a symbol both of the transcendence and of the nearness of God, all other words are illuminated in retrospect; it is the creation as a whole which, in its turn, now appears in the dark light of the Mystery of God addressing himself to man. Conversely, the creation itself begins to point "sacramentally" to this Mystery and to make it known in its own way: remaining a witness of the "blessing" it becomes also a sign of the Mystery.

By presenting in this way what is at stake in the temptation, I hope I have not distorted the orientation inherent in the narrative form of the story of Eden, even if the literary genre of commentary and of interpretation leads to explanations for which the most one can expect is that they do not betray what the narration says in a way that is both less obvious and more real. To come back now to the point of departure, to the intention of the Yahwist author to grasp in its nascent state the blueprint of human history that will acquire new coloration in each of its successive stages, it is interesting to observe that this author, in his attempt to understand history and to give the reasons for his hope, brings to light in the form of a narrative, an extremely profound vision of the Word of God. This Word establishes a space, within the realm of a good creation—a space designed to arouse love and obedience and to set man in a position of responsibility before God. A positive exercise of this responsibility should have the effect, but only at the price of the necessarily onerous respect for a Precept, of transforming the view of God, the understanding of creation and the very knowledge that man has of himself.

2. The trial of Job

In my concern to illuminate the signification of the Precept as revelation of the Mystery offered to man and invitation to a discernment of which only rectified desire or love is capable, I have laid little emphasis on the content of the Precept, the interdiction regarding the knowledge of good and evil or, as a recent translation puts it, "of happiness and misfortune." The reason for this is that the narrative of Genesis does not enlarge on the exact meaning of the expression; at the dawn of humanity to which the text would transport us, it is hardly possible for this expression to have a very precise sense. It seems that God is forbidding man a certain autonomy in the directing of his own life, that he is barring him from the path of a certain wisdom, since the Covenant relationship established on the basis of the Precept is in a sense to furnish man with another light by which to conduct his existence.

Whatever the case may be, as we have seen in the Book of Job, this knowledge is acquired both through secular human experience and through the progress of the Word of God. But the same problem as in the original case of the story of Eden is once again about to be posed, redoubled by the very knowledge that man has acquired and received: God is going to behave other than foreseen, allowing misfortune to fall on an innocent man. Here it is no longer just a matter of a symbolic interdict, intervening as before to permit the establishment of a new relationship with God; here it is a matter of the actual behavior of God himself who appears to be breaking the relationship.

The dialectic of the Book of Job

Before continuing with this presentation of the "problem" of Job, we must say a few words about the book itself such as it lies before us today. It is well known that a prose narrative forms the framework for a long ensemble of speeches in which Job discusses his suffering with his "friends" and wrestles with it himself. Now the prose gives us, in narrative form that perhaps masks its depth, the solution to the debate, a solution at which the Job of the speeches does not arrive until very late, through a powerful experience to which I will return. How is this difference of levels to be understood? The distinction of redactional layers does not help us here, because the question is not that of the distinctions within the book but rather its unity: how is the Book of Job to be read *today*, in the unity of its composition? I propose here a particular point of view: the prose narratives actually give us the "solution" to the problem of suffering, that the author wished to bring to light, while the speeches of Job *expand on* the price paid to arrive at this solution. They express the work within a human being and the powerful action of God necessary to reach the apparently very simple attitude of Job in the prose narrative: "If we take happiness from God's hand, must we not take sorrow too?" (2:10).

As I remarked above, we find in this prose narrative the same protagonists as in Genesis: God, the Adversary, the man and the woman. Once again we find the innocent subjected to trial and to temptation, first by the Adversary, then by his wife. But this time the innocent is victorious. The question is the same as that raised in Genesis, but here it is more clearly spelled out: under temptation, will Job persevere in doxology or not? This theme of doxology, scans the entire account.

From the time of his good fortune, Job shows his great concern that God not be cursed, even unconsciously or under the influence of intoxication, by his children, and "just in case," he offers sacrifices, "for Job said, 'It may be that my children have sinned, and cursed God in their hearts' " (1:5). The twofold temptation of Job likewise focuses on doxology: Job will not persevere, "he will curse you to your face" (1:11 and 2:5). As in Genesis, where the woman was persuaded to see God as lying and jealous and induced her husband to do the same through that word in act that was the eating of the fruit, so the wife of Job tries to induce her husband to curse God and die. But here the concerted efforts of the Adversary and the woman do not succeed in overcoming the integrity of Job; he does not allow himself to resort to words against God (1:22 and 2:10). In both cases, for man doxology consists in humbling himself (rending his garments, shaving his head, falling to the ground in worship) and in confessing God, regardless of whether God gives or takes away, of whether he sends happiness or misfortune: God beyond his conduct vis a vis man. But how does one arrive at such an attitude and, above all, how does one justify it? This is what the prose narrative fails to say; in contrast, the struggle of Job with these questions runs through the entire body of the work.

In fact, the prose narrative could lead us astray. In heaven, surrounded by his court, God appears benevolent and imperturbable. He remains the same from beginning to end and seems to be playing with the Adversary, making Job the unfortunate object of a wager he is sure to win. The enormity of subjecting a just man to a heavy barrage of trials does not appear at all in the narrative, and even less in that God wins his wager, that seems to justify the whole adventure *a posteriori*, without drawing particular attention to the God who allowed it. But viewed from below by a man who is subjected to suffering and has no access to the deliberations of the heavenly court, "God" becomes problematic; the story raises a question: who is this God who allows misfortune to overwhelm a man of integrity and righteousness, faithful to the Law and to Wisdom? Who is he that he can play with a human existence? Such is the painful question that plagues Job to the point of obsession in his speeches: he turns it over and over, from every angle, without finding a response.

Who is God?

The misfortune that assails Job is incomprehensible: it opens a profound crevice in a spiritual, moral and cosmic edifice whose origin Job rightly recognizes in the Wisdom of God and in the decrees of his Law. We are not dealing here with merely speculative problems: Job enters at a single stroke into the world of anguish. Stripped of his goods, of his economic rootedness in the world of things, deprived of his children, of his familial rootedness in human time, he is prey in his own person to painful and incurable decay: his body, he himself, is falling apart. Little by little he approaches a point of no return: every prospect for the future, every constructive idea or enterprise is henceforth denied him because of his ailing body and his social isolation, so that his life on parole is already beleaguered by death. And in this anguish that results from the disappearance of all human stability in his person and in his environment, no one can come to the help of Job: first of all, because no human aid can really do anything to still the panic of a man who is on the way out and knows it, then because such anguish is insupportable to Job's entourage, because it is a reminder of the forgotten and always impalatable reality of suffering—people prefer to escape from it. Accordingly, it is Job in his very person who heads toward collapse; nothing, from the earth, from the flesh, from friends or relatives, can supply him any longer with solid landmarks that would enable him to understand himself anew, and hence to survive— or if he must die, to find some meaning for his death.

At a certain point the misfortune of Job is total. It results from a series of distortions that have overwhelmed him and piled up on him to the point of becoming unbearable. Nothing has escaped this progressive and slow experience of destruction: goods, family, the flesh, the possibility of communicating with others, finally the psyche—everything is affected, destroyed, ravished. Now this total misfortune—economic, social, personal—is redoubled because it has no foundation whatever, no reason; it is downright excessive, disproportionate, there is no context within which it can be meaningfully viewed, nothing to help make it understandable. Nothing in the world view according to which Job lived his life would authorize his misfortune to come on, because in this world view misfortune was linked with fault and happiness with righteousness. His misfortune is incomprehensible—this is the most painful point around which all the rest revolves—because God himself was the origin and the guarantor of a harmony between righteousness and felicity, provided that man obey the Law and live according to Wisdom. If it should suddenly happen that misfortune follows righteousness and happiness follows fault, what does one think and believe, especially under the destructive hold of this misfortune? Who is God, after all, if a life whose aim was to be faithful to his Word and to his commandment falls through at this point?

The tormented flesh of Job ultimately cries out the question of the Wisdom of God, of God himself. Job's behavior absolutely demanded a response—a response which, in the last analysis, was the fidelity of God to his faithful creature and which expressed itself in the only world in which, concretely, Job lived: that of nature, of life, of interpersonal relationships. The God of Job is a God who *should have* responded, in the name of his very fidelity, by sustaining the well-being of the faithful man. It is a God who *did* habitually respond in this way, as traditional experience could verify. Doubtless, some sages of Israel made the mistake of failing to focus on the person of God who responds, emphasizing instead only the recurrent laws of response: hence a certain danger of rigidity in their evaluation of people and of events. But this was not the case with Job, whose whole sorrowful reaction maintains the character of a word forcefully addressed to God himself. It is God who ought to respond, because it is he who was at the origin of all. Job cannot nor does he wish to call into question his earlier convictions, precisely because they were grounded in God, in his Wisdom, in his Commandments and at a radical level, in his creation itself of which Job grasped the values of distance and of presence, without which a relationship of co-respondence would not have been possible. Presence, in that the evolution and the rhythmic pattern of the world, of the "laws" that regulate it at various levels, have their origin in creative Wisdom. Distance, in that this Wisdom always retains a certain initiative. It constantly presents the aspect of a *gift*. It is precisely because he has experienced this solicitude for such a long time that Job is stunned with the "maliciousness" of God, who no longer responds to the fidelity of his faithful creature. If he is "good," why does he show himself "malicious"? Such is the question that gnaws at Job and leaves him no respite. In the Book of Proverbs, Wisdom appeared in Heaven, radiant with the joyous, creative power of God (cf. Prov. 8); in the Book of Job, no one—and least of all Job himself—knows where this Wisdom is any longer. If one must look somewhere, would it not be rather in the hidden crevices of the earth (cf. Job 28)?

3. The resolution of the trial

Between Adam and Job, there is all the difference between the gratified child, tempted to keep taking to himself even that which has been denied him instead of entering into a relation process, and the mature man who has reflected on and lived this process for a long time but finds himself tempted to blasphemy at a time when his life is toppling into incomprehensible defeat. But the Bible knows that everyone is, in some respects, a spoiled child who refuses to be born to life at the price of a kind of death, and in other respects, that human being who is generous but stands on the brink of total discouragement. Doubtless this is why it sets before us these two men and shows us the divine pedagogy at work in the two cases.

Sin, anger and mercy in the narrative of Eden

It would have been preferable for the spoiled child to have understood what was at stake in the interdict against eating the fruit of the tree in the middle of the garden: God was offering him a relationship of covenant. Having made himself known by the magnificence of his blessing, he wished to go on to reveal himself in the exchange of the word. But if the child did not wish to understand before in his impoverished and suffering condition, he will understand afterwards! Forgetting the fact that everything that he is and everything that he has is received from God, the child wishes to appropriate and to add to his acquisition the very thing that has been denied him instead of waiting for this to be given to him in another way. In a sense, he is to lose everything; in another sense, he is to be made capable, through his very stripping, of becoming the human being before God and others who, in his richness, he had not wished to become.

Of sin in the proper sense of the word there is nothing to say: the final decision of a liberty rests ultimately with itself; one can only take note of it and then spell out the consequences.

Such consequences, if we restrict ourselves initially to considering the behavior of the man and woman before they are confronted with God, could be defined as the loss of identity and the birth of anguish; closed attitudes emerge and the sign of this is the fact that people begin to hide. The irony of the author has frequently been noted, and it has been brought out that when the man and the woman had eaten of the tree of *knowledge*, they really did *know*, but what they knew was the fact that they were naked: they acquire the measure of man by himself. And they immediately come to experience this nakedness as unbearable, with no available remedy that they can bring to it, for it has become a symbol of solitude and of poverty. Then too, these two beings, created to be each other's partner, raise a screen of garments made of leaves to stand between them; the mutuality of their beings is broken and each closes off their body from the other, not by a voluntary decision to clothe themselves, but because such an act is, in what concerns their mutual relationship, the intrinsic result of their rupture with God. This rupture also reveals itself in the temptation to set up a screen to protect themselves from God: the trees of the garden, which had only recently been given to them by God and which, thanks to the word of interdiction, had even become symbols together with all of creation of a relationship at the level of Mystery, become—or at least man wants them to become—a protection against the encounter with God. Thus, through his refusal to obey, man has not only broken with the God of the Word, but he has lost an identity that was supposed to be lived in thanksgiving: with the woman who had been given to him, with God who had formed him and with himself. And the miserable cascade of reproaches that is about to intervene at the moment of the encounter with God, each creature attempting to throw the blame on another, is the sign of the profundity of this rupture of reciprocal relationship.

In a sense, God endorses this rupture, and in the words he utters or the actions he performs, he accentuates and underlines its reality. By driving man out of the place where he could have encountered him "in the cool of the day," he highlights the separation between man and himself. By making garments for the man and the woman and pronouncing a mysterious sentence on the imbalance or inequity of the sexual encounter, he underscores the separation between them. By pronouncing a word on hard labor and ultimate death, he brings out the separation between man and the soil out of which he had been made: the latter will yield its fruit grudgingly and will ultimately get the better of man. In fact, the "wrath" of God consists in not placing any obstacle to the effects, immanent and inevitable, of man's rupture with him—effects that will multiply and intensify every time a human being continues to play the child. We have here a profoundly coherent picture: man who has rejected covenant finds himself outside of it, but this rejection becomes totally inscribed in him and reaches into the place where the truth is impossible to hide: the body. After sin, man is a solitary body who can no longer worship, meet his neighbor face to face, rule the earth—destined to die.

In another more profound sense, God does not endorse the rupture and undertakes to remedy it on the basis of the very situation of sin. This aim of mercy and of renewed involvement is already apparent in the fact that *God speaks*. One might find this surprising since the death sentence was pronounced by anticipation in the very declaration of the Precept, and it was presumably to be executed immediately once the transgression was committed. But nothing of the kind takes place; man does not die immediately. Instead, he is called to hear a word of God. And if this word defines a punishment, it also opens prospects of life. God clothes the man and the woman, making it possible for them to exercise their sexuality as free human beings, to undress and come together after they have exchanged a word of love. God pronounces a word regarding the offspring of the woman, and it is at this precise moment that Adam gives Eve a new name—a rather astonishing name in this context which should have been one of death: he calls her "the Living," for she will be the mother of all the living. Man is driven out of Paradise so that he will not attempt to acquire immortality by himself, which would be even more fatal for him than to unveil the knowledge of good and evil; but this expulsion is also a sending into the boundless wasteland; the borders of the garden expand outward to the entire world, and it is over a very long time, over a History, that man will learn the ways of life.

So it is that the life which is to come—that of man, of woman and of their offspring—is wholly under the word of God: the latter is present in negative image in the whole gamut of sufferings that stem from the fact that this word was not heard and which by the same token echo it in a secret way; it is above all present because of the fact that it makes itself heard once again and thus creates anew a climate of hearing, allowing man to re-enter, though not without pain and sorrow, into the Covenant that he had not wanted. And the wide-ranging scope of this word hints at the fact that it is opening up history, because it speaks of offspring and geography, because it sends man onto the boundless earth.

The creative Word in the Book of Job

Man driven to despair through a defeat as total as it is incomprehensible, at the term of a life of justice and of covenant, is to see himself offered the help of God before he falls into blasphemy. He is at the term of an odyssey that the spoiled child of Genesis had no more than begun, and he has to avoid succumbing to temptation.

That it is indeed a matter of temptation emerges clearly from the story's resolving phase (38–42). When God finally reveals himself and takes the stage, his first words are:

Who is this obscuring my designs
with his empty-headed words? (38:2)

while at the end, Job is led to acknowledge that the one in question is indeed he:

I am the man who obscured your designs
with my empty-headed words (42:3).

If one admits, as I show above, that the questions of Job to God in his agonized speeches were true questions, we must analyze the process that ultimately leads him to silence in order to understand the meaning of this capitulation. At first sight this process is simple; Job hears two long speeches of God in which the latter speaks at length of the creation in its harmonies and in its hostile forces, and poses the question of the power and the wisdom that stand at the origin of all this. Job recognizes that only God is the source of this power and of this wisdom, that he himself has no access to it and consequently, "he retracts all he has said and in dust and ashes he repents" (cf. 42:6).

But this does not work as a solution without itself posing a problem: the fact is that in his earlier speeches, Job had himself recognized, here and there, this transcendence of God's wisdom and had even drawn from this the conclusion that any discussion with God of his own case was impossible (for example, chapter 9); whereupon, he had continued to speak! But here (in chapter 42) he is reduced to silence. Why is this?

I would like to propose a twofold reflection, one on the fact that *God speaks*: these truths on the creation, that Job had himself expressed, he now *hears*; they become word of God and it is at this level that they call forth a response. The second reflection will bear on the fact that, among all the questions that he could have chosen to discuss with Job, God does not choose the *ethical* questions that would constitute, in the eyes of Job, the basis of the debate, but rather the question of creation. We will have to clarify the reason for this particular choice.

1. *God speaks*. There is a saying, and therefore an address and a provocation to a response. The fact that what is said is identical to what Job had already said and that consequently nothing new in content arises, invites us to reflect for a moment on the saying. This saying establishes a doubly unequal dialogue. First of all, God intervenes in a theophanic manner: he speaks "from the heart of the tempest." The whole progressive experience of God's distance that Israel has gone through in the course of its history, whose decisive element may well have been the exile, that is, God's keeping his distance from his people and from his temple, is here present. In the Book of Job, God speaks as God. But the inequality of the dialogue stems also from its interrogative form. God poses questions relative to the *identity* of the one who is the source of the creation; in terms of power, with the recurrent formulas: "Who made . . . ? Where were you when . . . ? Are you able . . . ?"; in terms of wisdom, with formulas like: "Do you know how . . . ? Have you been able to penetrate . . . ?" Man is clearly being invited to acknowledge himself as a stranger to this power and to this wisdom and, powerless as he is, to restore the authority he does not have to the person of God.

Unequal dialogue, but nevertheless dialogue—because there is questioning here, there can also be response, and consequently exchange and covenant, or alternatively, revolt and separation. *The creation speech is, as addressed speech, an offer of covenant*—a burdensome offer and one where we again find the "form of death," that intervened at the heart of a covenant process, as I try to show in the preceding chapter. In order to establish communion with God on the basis offered him through the word that comes "from the heart of the tempest," man must do two things. First he must acknowledge his impotence in founding the creation that surrounds him and that, in a sense, he transcends (the speech of God does not mention the creation of man, but only of the elements and of the animals). Then—and this is infinitely more difficult—Job must accept the consequence, that though implicit has been the goal of the entire process, regarding the case with God on the question of ethics and retribution: if the wisdom and the power of God infinitely surpass man in creation, they surpass him exactly to the same extent in the covenant relationship and one can only fall on one's face without calling for an account. It is clear that the intensity of the death here proposed is incomparably greater than in the case of Eden: to enter into communion with God, man must sacrifice his power, his wisdom and his justice. But then are we still dealing with a covenant?

2. This is where the second aspect of this unequal dialogue between Job and God can be taken into account. In order to bring to light the transcendence that situates him above and beyond all naming, God takes creation and not covenant as his theme. It would have been possible to construct an interrogatory speech following the same format: "Who initiated the covenant? Where were you when I was reflecting on its terms?" Or, in a still more striking way in our context: "Have you penetrated the knowledge of good and evil?" But God does not say this. He launches instead into a very beautiful *description* (the most beautiful perhaps in the whole Bible) of the marvels of creation, whether merely wonderful (the elements and animals) or wonderful and fearful (Leviathan and Behemoth). In other words, he situates himself at an *incontestable* level—incontestable is the mysterious richness of creation, incontestable the power and the wisdom which have "made" and "penetrated" it, incontestable the transcendence of the divine Subject who is behind this power and this wisdom with respect to the power and the wisdom of man. The manifestation of this incontestable is an implicit invitation to apply to the domain of

ethics and of retribution that which is magnificently evident in the domain of creation. The wisdom of God functions at a level to which man does not have access, but if it reveals itself so powerful and positive while transcendent and hidden at the level of creation, does this not supply a real meaning, mysterious and beyond the grasp of man, to the disconcerting conduct of God at the level of morality and of retribution?

If God had chosen to manifest his transcendence on the basis of an immediately ethical discourse, would not his wisdom have appeared arbitrary and tyrannical? "I promised and I'm not keeping my promise; that's all there is to it. I ground morality the way I want to and I overturn it at will. Wisdom is folly and folly is wisdom, but in any case, power is powerful!" The question of Job was that of the wisdom of God at the heart of irrational behavior; a theophany that limits itself to affirming this wisdom, without adopting another approach to make it known or recognized in however tiny a way, would truly have convicted God. Job's wife would have been right: Cursed be God (because he is making sport of you) and morality (because he is stronger than you, and everything is absurd).

Whatever the merits of this theoretical supposition, it remains a fact that God spoke of creation. He did not speak as in Genesis, in terms of *gift* ("You may eat of all the trees of the garden"), but in descriptive and in some sense neutral terms: the elements of the world are witnesses to the transcendence of the wisdom and power of God and, by way of these attributes, they point to the Mystery that is God himself. Basically, God is here employing *analogical discourse* and bringing to light the positive foundations of a doxology.[5] And he expects man, led toward a positive perception of the wisdom of God in the matter of creation, to accept that this same mysterious wisdom is also at work in the matter of covenant. The wisdom of the God who creates the world amounts to a guarantee of the wisdom of the God who makes covenant, even when this God is apparently (with the appearance, for Job, of flesh and blood) unfaithful to his Law and to his promises. In other words, the creation speech delivered by God to Job "from the heart of the tempest" prevents the communion sacrifice, from whose intensity nothing however is subtracted, from being a *sacrificium intellectus*. Analogy comes to the help of the "form of death." And it is the word of God itself that offers this help.

Judgement and restitution

At the end of God's discourse, the self-assurance shown by Job up to this point collapses: he gets the message and he accepts it. At the same time, as in Eden but in the opposite sense, his eyes are opened and he "sees" God. His last words, already cited—"I retract all I have said, and in dust and ashes I repent" (42:6)—say in a negative way, with respect to the whole past struggle, what the prose narrative said in a positive way—"If we take happiness from God's hand, must we not take sorrow too?" (2:10)—but now we understand that in order to pass from the acceptance of happiness to the acceptance of sorrow, we have to be willing to abandon the idea of God that we have constructed for ourselves and to plunge into the Mystery of a God beyond happiness and sorrow.

Ultimately, this is what is at stake in the book. Does not Job receive the challenge, through the trial he passes through, to reinterpret this paradox of a good and wise God who allows misfortune to come, even if he does not exactly cause it? Is he not invited to "hear" this excess of sorrow as a Word, a paradoxical "Revelation"? Or will he understand it instead as the most absurd non-sense, that would condemn God, his Law, and man in his effort of justice and fidelity, and would amount to a kind of desperate nihilism? Will Job be able and will he want to read the excess of sorrow as a question that we could formulate in this way: is there not a good that is above happiness, and an evil that is more horrible than sorrow or misfortune? Is there not a dimension of God that is more profound than that of a Creator and Legislator who responds to the faithfulness of man, and is not a certain undeserved suffering the way to reach God at this level? Is there not a figure of man that is more profound even than obedience "to the decrees of the Most High"? By suppressing happiness, is not God revealing himself as the God of the Good, and would not real evil consist in allowing oneself to be driven by the horror of misfortune to contest the supreme goodness of God? It is no longer possible for Job to remain at the level of sound religious humanism in which he has lived up until now. This stage was not evil in itself, but the excess of misfortune forces Job to go beyond it, either through the discovery or the presentiment of higher or more profound dimensions, for God as well as for man, or through a plunging into absolute despair. This is truly the place of the trial, and the place of a decision that one can well call "faith": at this level, God does not impose himself, he offers himself in an astounding manner, reveals himself, but so mysteriously that only a profoundly spiritual attitude enables one to recognize him. We are here on the threshold of "mysticism" (if we understand by this the proper mode of grasping the Mystery).

Just as the Precept, by introducing tragedy into the garden of Eden, did not cause man to lose his innocence although it made him lose his simplicity, so here the excess of misfortune is not an absolute evil, but rather an almost necessary path toward the personal recognition of the true God, toward the deepening of the innocence of the Just. Cut off from the happiness that no longer necessarily accompanies it, this innocence appears in the stark purity of a relationship with God that excels not only the natural, harmonious balance of health, riches and human esteem, but also that equilibrium which is created by fidelity to the commandments of God, indeed by the fidelity of God to his own promise. The Mystery recedes; it is beyond Wisdom and beyond the Law—and beyond the relations that these define between God and human beings.

In this perspective, the restoration of Job to his former situation, the blessing of his final condition over and above that of the old as they are described in the prose epilogue in strict parallel with the prologue, should not lead us astray. It is not a pure and simple return, even for the better, to the description of 1:1–3. In the meantime Job (and we who read the book) has "seen" God: he knows the one who is the source of the new benefits and the one to whom they are addressed. The restoration is real, but the new condition has a new meaning. Once again there is blessing and the covenant morality remains, but all of this has a more distant starting point: Job can see all of this as a *sacrament* of the Mystery, and he himself receives what is given to him in a different way, he displays the same justice but in a different way. Nothing of what was is lost, but everything is transfigured and is differently related to God and to men.

Reflection on these two great biblical figures, Job and Adam, conducted in the light of the cross of Jesus and destined in return to project more light of spiritual understanding on the cross, ultimately makes two things clear to us. First of all, the path toward knowledge of God is not straight and uniformly progressive. God makes himself known to man and assimilates him to himself through a delicate interplay of presence and retreat, of gift and of interdict, of covenant and of forgetting, an interplay that is really a *pedagogy of communion*. By way of this educative process, God is constantly sending man back to a renewed, more profound quest that will make possible for him an encounter that is honest, situated at the level of the ultimate reality of God and of man, and dynamic, made up of an exchange of liberties through a history of the word. The second lesson dispensed here is that at least at the level of the two figures studied, God has not yet divulged his whole mystery. The covenant that Adam did not want Job accepted; indeed he lived in full fidelity to it. It is just that there is a dimension of God, as well as of man, that is beyond creation and covenant: that which Job begins to feel at the very moment when he worships God who has just revealed himself in a final theophany, but without possessing its secret. *It is Jesus who delivers this secret through the cross by pronouncing the name of Father and by being acknowledged as son.* Nevertheless, even if the two figures studied do not unveil that which they announce, at least they point clearly to the mortifying and transforming concrete process of the divine revelation. It is to this process that I would like to return at the end of this chapter, adopting a far more speculative procedure and one less tied to the letter of the narratives without departing from them altogether.

4. An interplay of death and life between image and symbol

A positive image of God

Whether we are dealing with Adam, Job or Jesus, the adventure always begins with a positive image of God, that we must now try to analyze in its various components. This image is based on a certain experience of the action of God, linked to a word of gift and of promise. God forms man, plants the garden, creates the animals, constructs the woman as partner of man, and gives everything to the first couple: the image of a *good* God, the goodness signifying that which in God founds this gratuitous and unconditional gift. In accordance with the promise he has made in this regard, God does remunerate human beings who obey his just Law and fulfill its precepts: the image of a *faithful* God, fidelity signifying the unbreakable perseverance of God in keeping his covenant. God accomplishes the plan of salvation that he had announced through Moses and the prophets by sending Jesus to establish his Kingdom: the image, that Jesus experiences and publicly proclaims of God as *father* and *king*.

The *names* (placed in italics) that correspond to these images have an ethical connotation and imply an ontological affirmation. To speak of ethical connotation means that God is in some sense evaluated on the basis of a certain experience and idea that man has of happiness: the peaceful, paradisal life, the prosperity of the just, the political preeminence of the chosen people. On the basis of these things the gratuitous initiative, the justice of the law, the positive character of history can be evaluated; judgments are thus made regarding God, whose action meets the desire of man, and a genuine love of complaisance is shown for a God who is thus good, faithful, king, father. One could say that the names of God that come to light in this way have a doxological connotation: while describing him, they also praise him. And implicitly, there is an ontology here: the God so described was before all things, and he remains in the permanence of his blessing. The ontology creates no problem within a positive context; it is neither affirmed, nor denied, nor, consequently, explicitly elaborated; it simply underlies the language employed.

We note, however, that there is a dialectic between these images: in order to arrive at the faithful and just God, the doubt implied by the fact that God forbids will have to have been overcome. To arrive at God as king and father, the repeated incertitudes regarding the fidelity of God, whether relative to the covenant with his people or to the wisdom that characterizes the life of the individual, will have to have been overcome. It is as though the image, peacefully adopted at one stage of experience, had to be won through a difficult struggle at an earlier stage. We were led then to verify the meaning of a negative element that intervened to apparently conceal the positive character of the original image. Nevertheless, it was of capital importance to underline this positive side, and to briefly describe its characteristics because it is always there first.

The image put to test

We must make the effort to distinguish, as much as possible, between trial and temptation. Difficult as this is to admit, trial comes from God, whose behavior breaks with what has gone before and therefore calls into question what one has previously thought of him: one's idea or image of him based on his benevolent action. The good God interdicts, thus revealing to man both the boundlessness of desire (what could be a more boundless knowledge than that of good and evil?) and the limits that he is invited to impose on it. The faithful God allows a situation of misfortune to arrive that amounts to a breach of contract, with the result that man, objectively speaking, does not receive his due and at a personal level no longer recognizes his God, the God who is king and father abandons the Messiah whom he has charged with the establishment of the kingdom and seems in this way to definitively break with his commitment to his plan of salvation for mankind and human history. In contrast, temptation does not come from God (this is the minimal sense one could give to the presence of an adversary in the three cases that concern us). It consists in proposing and inciting to a negative ethical judgment on God that would rigorously contradict what was said before: God is jealous, he who was good, unjust, he who was faithful, indifferent, he who was savior. This judgment on God implicitly embodies an ontological negation (if he is not truly good, he does not really exist) and entails a self-affirmation of man, who alone is god on earth, as we see from the word of the serpent in Eden and from the words of the tempter to Jesus in the desert.

In all the cases of the trial figure, God *absents himself* from the image or idea that has *legitimately* been formed of him. Now this absence pertains to the realm of moral judgment, for it displaces the happiness of man: he can no longer demand indefinite enjoyment of the goods placed at his unlimited disposal, because there is a well-placed limit; he can no longer congratulate himself on domestic happiness without hitch, lived in a religious consciousness without reproach, because the disappearance of the former calls the second painfully into question; he can no longer rejoice over having carried out the mission entrusted to him well, because the forces that oppose this mission turn out to be stronger than the mission itself. Happiness is neither in the naive felicity of the child of boundless desire, nor in the sense, even the modest sense, that the faithful man has of his own justice, nor in the success, even the obedient success, of the mission entrusted to the Messiah.

The point I would like to bring out here is that ethical judgment entails at the same time a theological procedure: in the end, the divine names will have taken a turn either in the direction of mystery or in the opposite direction, that of blasphemy—an anthropological decision: the truth of man is in an obedience to God whose ultimate term is not seen, or in a self-divinization—an ontological affirmation or an ontological negation: God, to the very depth of his mystery, is the foundation and the measure of all things, or, ultimately, there is no God.

The resolution of the trial

The resolution of the trial in a positive sense is perseverance in doxology, insight into the truth of man and awaiting the revelation of God. It takes place as symbolic behavior; one can legitimately designate it by the biblical expression "communion sacrifice."

1. By the fact that it overturns a neat equilibrium acquired in the representation of God and man, indeed of the world, the trial presents a certain tragic aspect. But it is not inhuman and does not resolve itself into nonsense. Even if he accomplishes his purposes by deflecting the affirmation from its true sense, the serpent is not wrong when he says to the couple subjected to trial, "you will be like gods": he is deflecting a desire but at the same time revealing it. And the author of the other creation account in Genesis reveals the basis of this desire in positive terms when he says that God created man "in his image and likeness." The only question, left to the power of man, is to know if it is really necessary to kill the very One who placed it in us, in order to fulfill this desire. If not, the resolution of the trial functions as hope and as expectation: if the desire of man is to be "like God," the best way of fulfilling it, "naturally" to the man who does not consent to the disturbance of temptation, is to allow the love of God to go to work in him and to tranquilly attend to his word, for the process of divinization, participation, communion, can only come from the one who took the initiative here—from God. The displacements of happiness to which I allude in the preceding section blaze a trail toward a dynamic perception of true happiness whose real dimensions gradually come to light as one freely follows the path marked out.

The absence of God (which again is not primary, but always comes after the manifestation of a certain presence) can be experienced as a stage toward the full revelation, which can only come about within a freely consented to actual relationship process. Can we not understand that God is implicated for the very reason that he is absenting himself? He had first of all manifested himself as source of blessing and revealed himself as interlocutor, opening by his word a history aimed at a fellowship in mystery. His absence and his silence can then be interpreted as spaces left open to man for a response. Do we not have, even within human exchanges, those moments of presence and of absence, of word and of silence, aimed at a similar fashioning of communion? The same is true here but in a way that is proportionate to the establishment of a dialogue between God and man. The idea of an event that takes place between them presupposes a word that offers and awaits, so that every silence of God can be interpreted as an appeal to vigilance: he will return. And at this point the moral judgment confirms the ontology: if he is good, he is, but he is better Being and more Being than one might have imagined because his goodness and his Being cover the dimensions of interdict and of absence as well as the dimension of gift and of presence. As for man himself, auditor of the word or victim of the silence, he also discovers himself in an ever more profound dimension, called to an ever more radical behavior: that of persevering under the call of the word that will come, of the act that will save, even if one must wait for a long time. The consent to the interdict or to suffering cannot but include what one could call the *memory of the future*. By conforming himself to the word heard, by keeping alive the covenant and the lived images of God and of self that these imply, man holds himself under the call of a new and impending word, that could be an unveiling of meaning and an unforeseeable resolution of the trial. Hearing, faithful for the present, hopes for the future, without expecting anything.

2. The trial introduces a rupture in the happy image of God and of self that one started with; it jumbles a univocal representation, and this is why the resolution of the trial is first of all ethical. But it takes place as symbolic behavior: the woman could have refrained from reaching for the fruit, Job fell to the ground in adoration, Jesus died—so many behaviors that establish communion, beyond a mere representation has become impossible.

To clarify this theme of symbolic behavior as act of communion that goes beyond representation, we propose the following: that an *image* of God should be formed on the basis of his action viewed at a given level, is not only natural but inevitable, and divine names can be employed to make this image explicit at the level of discourse. The representation is not in itself evil and, we really cannot do without it. But when it becomes apparent that the image is partial, and above all that another apparently incompatible image comes to graft itself onto it (God unjust onto God faithful, for example), we have to know how to go beyond the representation in order to maintain communion. This is what one could call *symbolic behavior*, that is directed toward God whom one continues to praise in his inner reality without any longer being able, at least immediately, to express this reality. Paradoxically, this symbolic behavior can then liberate the possibility of new images that are formed on the basis of this renewed behavior, and the process never comes to an end, except perhaps through the invocation of the name of Father in death. Sometimes, however, symbolic behavior is refused. Man's desire becomes closed in on self and then what some of the human sciences call, in a pejorative sense, the *imaginary* begins to go to work: the closed desire produces images and ideas that attempt to satisfy it or at least to justify it in its refusal to go beyond. These productions of creative fancy, that rationalize the refusal of communion, do not have real consistency; if one employs them as landmarks for the conduct of life, one falls into impasses, individual and collective, of which the first part of this book has supplied a large sampling. It will not be necessary to set the merely symbolic in opposition to the imaginary, as though every image or representation were evil in itself. Embodied and limited beings that we are, we need images, and they are capable of serving our path toward God; there is nothing wrong with them, and indeed they are beneficial when they lead to the threshold of symbol or flow from it and if we remain vigilant even as we employ them.

In sum, there is indeed a positive function of the imagination which, even in what pertains to God, gathers together and organizes the data furnished by immediate experience and enables an initial nomination. Confronted in their potential for conflict with the vicissitudes of desire, the images and the names can form the object of a selection and rejection process governed by the desire of immediate possession rather than by love of communion. This process ends with figures of fantasy and with the production of all the ideologies. On the other hand, confirmed even in their conflict through the love that manifests itself in symbolic behavior, images can find a new relevance and the divine nomination can attain to a depth till then unheard of: indeed, neither the imagination nor the mind become blind; in the light of the ethical judgment and of symbolic behavior, they are now in the position to allow the principle of analogy that I mentioned in an earlier chapter to come into play: the symbolic interpretation through which one chooses to persevere in invocation opens the mind to analogy.

Perhaps this is a way of understanding the expression that so caught the attention of Paul Ricoeur: *le symbole donne à penser* (symbol nourishes thought).

3. It is here, in spite of all its ambiguities, that one can introduce the notion of "sacrifice" and say that the declaration of the ethical judgment or the performance of the symbolic behavior takes on for man the force of a *sacrifice of communion with God*.

We have seen at the beginning of this book, that some contemporary thinkers attribute the enormous confusion of our declining civilization, that has no future, to the concealment of a "form of death" that in reality is essential to the process of a true human becoming or progress. It is necessary to invest this concept of "form of death" with considerably greater precision and to define its application as accurately as possible, but everything we have seen in a biblical context confirms the truth of this claim of a "form of death" as an authentic element of human history. The originality of the Bible, if I am not mistaken, is to interpret this "form of death" as an element (at least) of the authentic process of fellowship with God. It is linked to the irruption of the Word of God, whose originality is that it presents itself as a rupture and calls into question a certain equilibrium of the human condition; the Word of God invites to a *displacement*. It creates an event that does not have its own intelligibility within itself because it appears first of all from its negative angle, that determines on the one hand a history of God with human beings and on the other a renewal, to the extent of the symbolic behavior accepted, of the knowledge of God as well as of the self and ultimately of the world. If one interprets the Word of God or his silence and his absence (which amounts to the same thing in the case which concerns us) at once as his involvement in history and the offer of his Mystery, this entails (or presupposes) that one is personally committed and that one is resolving the *conflict of desires* in favor of God or, more exactly, that one is managing in favor and in function of God the only radical desire of our nature—which is certainly the desire to become like God. The whole question is to know if this desire will drive us to take possession immediately from the time that, in one way or another, temptation makes us understand that we have this inherent capacity, or if it will arouse in us the loving attitude of awaiting that is proper to those who have seen that only the patience of love obtains the desired resemblance from the beloved.

This management of desire is found expressly in Scripture and yields itself to an interpretation in terms of *death*. The story of Eden unveils a threat of death, which the word of the serpent tries to downplay: "you will not die," but that it actually succeeds only in displacing: if human beings do not die when they transgress the commandment, it will be God who will die, because all will become "like gods," and if man does not transgress, this will be because he accept death to a too immediate form of a desire which in itself was well-founded. "Death," before any sin, is immediately susceptible of at least three significations: the death with which God threatens man if he should transgress; the death of God, at least in the intention of man, if the transgression takes on the dimensions of a rejection of the autonomy and the transcendence of God; the death of man, at least in that which concerns a fundamental inclination of his desire, if he does not transgress, assuming instead an attitude of awaiting, of expectation. We could say the same thing for the case of Job. When his wife fires at him: "Curse God and die," she is urging him to an assassination followed by a suicide. Since there is nothing that can prevent the path of destruction and of illness from following its course, let it happen, but let God be included in the destruction: let the death of Job bear witness to the perversity and the nonexistence of God. Conversely, Job's perseverence in doxology is the voluntary witness rendered to God in his mystery, from the depths of darkness and of sorrow.

Since these analyses aim at showing that the "form of death" is the place and the means of a communion with God, I believe it is legitimate (and what follows will show that it is also fruitful) to qualify this form of death by the biblical expression *sacrifice of communion*, as distinct from the "sacrifice for sin" that is not involved here. We hereby designate the "death" that man accepts to inflict on himself, when in the midst of trial or temptation he perseveres in doxology and renounces the immediate and selfish satisfaction of his desire. The term *sacrifice* seems to me to be legitimate here, because we actually have a process of "death" in view of a *relationship*, rendered more profound, with God and with oneself. Sacrifice as defined in the framework of the categories of "violence" and of the "sacred," even if it is that which more often appears in the ritual and cultic world of the religions, is not the most essential; there is undoubtedly a more fundamental attitude that the term can refer to, the one that I have attempted to rediscover and to describe in this chapter, an attitude that speaks of "death" and of "God." Consent to this death, whose symbolic value I have indicated, is on the other hand the only alternative to a putting to death of God, at once the effect and the cause of violence and of the sacred, an "original assassination" that would ground history and civilization. Here, on the contrary, it is a matter of preferring the commandment, obeyed in expectation and in hope, to the immediate satisfaction of a desire, however legitimate in itself, as is that of knowing good and evil or that of escaping as soon as possible from painful and unmerited suffering. But this preference for the commandment is dictated by love, that is to say by the ultimate depth of human desire; it aims at creating a relationship with one whose word is received and honored. Sacrifice—but of *communion*: it differentiates more than it destroys, and through this act of differentiation, it allows a covenant space to be defined where God and man can meet in truth. By this sacrifice of communion, man is not expiating anything, not making any kind of reparation, any kind of compensation: he is simply obeying his most profound desire, whose concrete dimension he discovers in the very act of consent, the dimension being his ability to enter into relationship with the living God. But all this cannot take place except through a choice by which man signifies and renders effective this basic desire, in the Pleiades of movements that run through it. By making vigilance and fidelity dominate, he reaches the place where the deepest level of his person begins to see itself "for God" and wishes to be so.

It certainly seems paradoxical to look in the work of René Girard for some support and light to better understand this notion of *sacrifice of communion*. This notion is one that Girard does not take into account, while in the most recent sector of his work, he equates Christianity with the deliverance, finally, from sacrifice defined as *mimesis*, from violence and from the sacred. Without for the moment referring to this part of his work, I would like to bring out a number of emphatic points made in the foundational book *Mensonge romantique et vérité romanesque*.[6] If I am not mistaken, Girard sees "metaphysical desire" as the dynamic element which, in accordance with different techniques and in varied contexts, inspires the vicissitudes of the novel, and constitutes the profound root of the attitudes and behaviors of the protagonists. This desire can be defined as the always deceptive aspiration for a metamorphosis of Being. This metamorphosis is not otherwise defined, precisely because the desire that supports it is never fulfilled.

It is not fulfilled because it lives, without necessarily knowing it, from an unkept promise, that of autonomy; it is imagined that, through procedures to be found, the desire would by itself trigger this metamorphosis. Now these procedures never reach their goal because they keep taking on the form of desire of the Other: not knowing where it is going, the desire views as models or mediators the others that surround it and the objects that these point out to it. These objects harbor disillusion and prove the very relationship with the mediator deceptive. It never reaches equilibrium and it resolves itself either in violence done to the other or in hatred and contempt of self: neither in the one case nor in the other does the expected transfiguration take place, and it turns out that, contrary to the promise, "human beings are not gods for one another"[7] and their imitation does not lead to anything. The novel, however, arrives at a "true" conclusion (*vérité romanesque*) when the hero (but behind him, the author of the novel) renounces the metaphysical desire, the mediation of the other—which amounts to a conversion, often a struggle and sometimes a death. But this death is either told in the hope of a resurrection or is followed by another period of existence of the hero, characterized by a descent into himself, a new relationship with the other, a true balance of solitude and of communion in a rediscovered time, without further recourse to the metaphysical desire, to diverted transcendence, to ontological evil.

The ultimate truth of the novel, its *vérité romanesque* arrives only in the conclusion, for the novel as a literary development is inspired through and through by the metaphysical desire. But what would be a converted, a reconciled existence, or, if one considers it theoretically before the fall into metaphysical desire, an innocent existence? It would be an existence in relationship to the *true* God. Such an existence appears at times in the work of Girard,[8] but he lacks a formal treatment of the question, and I believe this lack has a damaging effect on the rest of the work. In any case, one must oppose a true transcendence to the diverted transcendence, the Blessed Trinity to the trinity of evil, the promise kept by the living God to the promise not kept of human beings who are not gods for each other. If we proceed in this vein, we see first of all that the desire for a metamorphosis is a true desire: it is true that man, created in the image and likeness of God, tends to perfect communion with him, to as full participation as possible in his Being, to full and beatifying knowledge of God, to a form of divinization that would not be self-divinization. But since man is not

God, he does not know by himself the way of this divinization and although he desires it, he does not have it within his power to acquire it. If he had it within his power, he would be God. Man should then place himself in a state of waiting until he receives from God an indication of the way, and should set forth, without allowing another model of behavior to enter in and without trying to win or produce by himself that which can only be given. This consent to waiting and this fidelity to the path pointed out by God transform the general desire for metamorphosis into love of God. But this love includes an element of renunciation—of every other way than that pointed out by God and of every effort to ravish that which can only be received. It is this very basic renunciation that I call *sacrifice of communion*. One can consider this in two ways: either as a renunciation of values or of powers, real or supposed, which can be tempting but which will prove by experience to be disappointing, or as the movement of love itself, that we can express only as detachment from self for the sake of the other and in view of the other, according to the very words of the Gospel.

The recourse to the theme of *sacrifice of communion* is then legitimate, in the perspectives offered here. It presents a double theological advantage. On the one hand, it makes it possible for us, in a human situation of concrete suffering—firstly that of the cross of Jesus Christ—to discern an element of transcendence of self under the impulse of love that drives toward union, as well as a more negative element of the weight of sin, of history, of evil. This distinction will prove to be important when refining the concept of redemption. On the other hand, as the example of Christ invoking his Father in the very act of death has shown us, one must distinguish in the sacrifice of communion itself between the *movement* of transcendence and the *state* or *act* of the gift: in other words, between the entrance into covenant, which presupposes a certain renunciation through which one accedes to the truth of one's desire, and the covenant itself which is a permanent act of giving and of receiving, whose image or icon we are invited to contemplate in the risen Jesus, who hears the paternal invocation and responds by the filial invocation in the reciprocal joy of a mutual gift without reserve.

Interpretation and analogy

All of the above considerations clearly show that interpretation is not a purely intellectual procedure; it comes in by way of a choice that, whatever it might be, is thoroughly saturated by the "form of death" and takes the form of symbolic behavior.

However, sacrificial and symbolic interpretation is not a *sacrificium intellectus*. Here we arrive at a delicate point: is it or is it not appropriate to situate side by side the doxology that one could call "immediate," based on the experience of blessing, and the doxology that one could call "symbolic," based on willingly accepted sacrifice that is response to the word of God and opens history? Is there an absolute leap from one to the other, such that the first immediate one, is abolished totally and without remainder in the other symbolic one? Conversely, does the refusal of the sacrificial interpretation leave intact the knowledge and the doxology of the God who blesses? The answer to this question is heavy with consequences; in the course of the history of theology, posed in a variety of contexts, it has assumed multiple and divergent forms. But perhaps the narrative of Genesis, by virtue of the simplicity of its form, can give us some orientation on this fundamental point of the relationship between the immediate and the symbolic. The most simple interpretation of the narrative is that, in every way, man had to take a stand *with respect to the God whom he experienced*. It was not a question of erasing the positive names and the immediate image, because it was on the basis of these that the word had made itself heard: at the same time and in the same speech, the same God had said a word of universal gift, and then imposed a specific interdict. It was a question of finding out whether man would be willing to juxtapose the positive names and the negative name, thus losing the immediate harmony of meaning. Would it really have been possible to accept this loss without a strong awareness of the God of blessing? As a matter of fact, the serpent had to try to efface this image and to replace it with that of the jealous god before the temptation could get under way. Conversely, in the Book of Job, God had to show himself in his transcendence as creator in order to make it possible for man to consent to persevere in covenant. Is it not true then to describe the attitude of the simple heart as follows: because God is the Lord of blessings, one can rely on him, accept the fact that he is also the God of the interdict, and *expect* from him, not necessarily the resolution of this divergent convergence, but new words which, at the price of sustained (and therefore, in a permanent way, sacrificial) fidelity, would reveal ultimate meaning?

It is easier to admit this relative foundation of interpretation in the antecedent experience of the God of blessing if we note the *doxological* framework, which, as I pointed out, is implicitly present in our text. Doxology is essential to the procedure. And it enables us to understand how the positive divine names, even if they have not arrived at a refined elaboration, play a role in the interpretation of the negative divine name. If the one whom I praise as good on the basis of multiple experience of his gifts says a surprising word that leads to sacrifice, I do not for this reason have to make of him a perverse god. Conversely, I would not simply substitute the non-image of a God who forbids for the image of the good God, the doxology in Mystery for the doxology based on creation, the symbol for the image. Thus the symbolic interpretation does not annihilate the immediate doxology; it remains true that it displaces it. It is henceforth within and as part of the mystery of covenant and of its history, of its memory, of its hope, that the mystery of creation can take on ultimate meaning.

We arrive here at what one could call the biblical place of the principle of analogy, that was enunciated above and to which I will return at length in the third part of this book. If, after having consented to the "form of death," one wishes to continue nevertheless to invoke the God who created the earth and gave it to us, then one must *think* this creator God in such a way that he could also be the one who imposes an interdict and who communicates himself. This amounts to saying that, in the line opened by the experience of blessing, and relying on it for support, we must arrive at a divine Name that does not limit itself to this blessing, a name which, by way of the specific causality of God, suggests an identity that founds this blessing, but at the same time renders possible the interdict and the covenant. Conversely, if one invokes God in the act and the history of covenant, beginning with the word of interdict, one must think of him in such a way that he can also be the God who creates and who blesses. This amounts to saying that in the line opened by the acceptance of the covenant, one must arrive at one or more divine Names which, through the history of this covenant, found it without being limited to it and which respect the type of transcendence defined on the basis of blessing.

It is obviously anachronistic to speak at the level of the narrative of Genesis, of the *analogy of Being* and *the analogy of faith*; we will have to return to these notions and subject them to further critical elaboration. Nevertheless, I find the mention of these theological procedures of divine nomination illuminating in bringing out the ultimate backgrounds of our texts. Striving for the moment to prescind from the controversies on "Being," I use this word as a term that attempts to express the identity of God, in the line of but beyond the experience of creation. I suggest that whatever further signification one could attach to it, this term will have to include what one could call a "symbolic reservation": this "Being" must be able to communicate. Conversely, all the covenant names, in their unity and their diversity, when we are dealing with the divine partner in history, should be employed in such a way that we take into account an "ontological reservation": the legislator, the friend, the spouse, the father is truly God.

Complexity of time

To conclude this extended complex of reflections, one could attempt to return to the question of time, which is our essential concern in this part. One could say that the man of the Bible, at whatever point of his journey one views him, is obliged to take a stand on the question of the identity of God and on his own identity, whether it is a question of himself personally or of human society. This stand is not a simple one and, except in the case of Jesus dying and risen, it is never definitive; above all, it is a personal commitment and the "interval," which is the basic unit of time, is made up of the *passage from one stand to the next* until the day when the name of God and the corresponding name of man will have been fully uttered in what can only be mutual invocation.

Reduced to its essential profile, this stand plays out according to an exclusive alternative: either God is no more than a god, which man can be as well, and all the rest stems from lying and jealousy (but then "god" can involve lying and jealousy? and man, too, is god?). Or God is truly God, in creation and covenant, but also above and beyond these. In this case, man corresponds in difference to this divine identity, but this relationship cannot be recognized and lived without the "form of death" under the call of a word still to come.

Viewed concretely, the figure of time depends primarily on God, because it is he who establishes the interplay of words that continuously call for a displacement (but not a destruction) of images and affirmations, in view of bringing on the perfect interpersonal relationship. But the figure of time depends on man as well, because the temporally engaged responses that he gives to the intervening word become inscribed also in his body and in his world. To the trial that comes from God and ideally defines time are added the darknesses and the densities that come from man's refusals. This is also why, *in the founding narrative* that announces to us in Jesus Christ the perfect figure of time, it is important that the "remission of sins" also be proclaimed, that the *possibility of true time* be restored.

Notes

1. The comparison is made, in any case, by rabbinic exegesis. Cf. the commentary of Marvin H. Pope, *Job*, The Anchor Bible, (Garden City, New York: Doubleday, 1965), p. 22 (on Job 2:9).

2. More than by the commentaries, I have been helped in this investigation on the Job character by the incisive essay of P. Nemo, *Job et l'excès du mal*, (Paris, 1978). Cf. my study "L'excès du malheur et la reconnaissance de Dieu" in *NRT* 111 [1979], 724–739), noted and exploited by E. Lévinas (cf. "Transcendance et mal," in *De Dieu qui vient à l'idée* [Paris, 1982], pp. 188–207).

3. At the present time, the composition as well as the extent of the "Yahwist" author are the subject of renewed investigations. As far as I can tell, these investigations do not invalidate the resumé which I give here, which is naturally of a summary and simplified character. Cf. R. Rendtorff, "Der Jahvist als Theologe? Zum Dilemma der Pentateuchkritik," in *Congress Volume Edinburg, 1974*, SVT 28 (Leiden, 1975), pp. 158–166 and J. Vermeylen, "La formation du Pentateuque à la lumière de l'exégèse historico-critique," in *RTL*, 12 (1981), pp. 324–346.

4. Here the question of reading *method* is posed. Intelligently practiced, historical-critical exegesis manifests the close relationship between the present composition with its various layers and the historical experiences of Israel such as the authors and "revisers" of "J" could interpret them; it thus brings out the relationship creation-history-covenant. Moreover, since it is a question of *origins*, the beginning of Genesis cannot but be read in function also of the questions we raise on this subject. The approaches of moderns in their investigation of these texts are then very varied. A work like that of E. Drewermann, *Strukturen des Bösen*, 3 vol. (Paderborn, 1978), adds some new approaches by going from exegesis to German philosophy (Kant, Hegel, Kierkegaard) and to the existentialism of Sartre, studying works on psychoanalysis written by Germans. Compared to this monumental work, the conference of J. P. Audet, *Admiration religieuse et désir de savoir* (Montréal-Paris, 1962), 70 pages, is miniscule, but it nevertheless develops with extraordinary penetration the *human question* of the Yahwist author. Some pages of X. Thévenot, in *Les Péchés. Que peut-on en dire?* (Mulhouse, 1983), p. 25–50, show

still more the influence of Lacan. Here, in line with what I said above, I shall attempt to favor a *literary* and *symbolic* approach, while bringing into play, though not exclusively, a number of structural techniques.

5. What I want to say here is that the manifestation of creation, linked as it is to the power of God, will bring Job to a point of marveling "to the second power": in fact, it is against the background of his suffering which remains unexplained that the light of God shines forth. In the final act of adoration, Job allows marvel before the Creator to encompass, to devour the case he has brought against God as "unfaithful"; but the passage through the attempt to conduct this case gives a new depth to the perception of creation—one not attained by Adam and Eve walking peacefully in Paradise.

6. *Op. cit. supra*, Part I, chapter 4, note 64.

7. This phrasing becomes the title of chapter 2 of the work.

8. For example pp. 73–75, 96–99, 309ff., 316, etc.

CHAPTER THREE

DIED FOR OUR SINS

Our investigation has led us to highlight two principal points. The first concerns the ultimate meaning of history and its modality. The second refers to the processes of our knowledge—of God first of all, but simultaneously, of man and of the world.

1. History can be described as the *adventure of sonship*. That to which man is called, his destiny, is to become a son of God, not so much in the sense of a substantial or qualitative determination as in the sense of a dynamic invocation: he is a son who, on every occasion and from the depth of his being, says "my Father." Now the cross of Jesus, elucidated by the innocent and tested figures of Adam and Job, shows us that this total and pure invocation is uttered only at the end of a long process, where all the images and all the names, even the authentic names of God, recede and where, correlatively, all the images of man and of the world, even the legitimate ones, are challenged. The Word of God in its historical economy is the ultimate author of these painful displacements, but the pain here is the reverse side of a positive pedagogical process by which God is drawing man to himself as the latter yields to an ever more free attitude, that is ultimately understood as filial, the attitude of a son.

The modality of this adventure is what I have variously described as perseverance in doxology, symbolic behavior, sacrifice of communion—in every case, a process of transcendence of every equilibrium, even one that is right, in the lived evaluation of the relationship God/man/world, until the moment when man will be dynamically installed in sonship, in a genuine, *concrete* hearing of the word of begetting by God the response to which is *total* thanksgiving and invocation. And it is in the light of this reciprocal invocation in action that all the former equilibriums recover their meaning and their reality, though they are now transfigured, after having been apparently disfigured.

2. In the perspective of this adventure of sonship, the *knowledge* of God undergoes a certain number of transformations and, as long as man has not reached the end of his journey (which is the case for all of us), depends on different principles that it is important to distinguish. We must also endeavor to see what is at stake in each of these principles.

First of all there are the *positive* divine names that derive from the consideration of a divine activity that one simply notes: thus, creator God or faithful God. When the content of these names is challenged by divine actions or words which appear to be negative at first sight, it is nevertheless *saved and transposed* by an *ethical* judgment that is implicit in the perseverance in doxology; allowing himself to be guided by the momentum of love, man continues to invoke God with positive names; he does not substitute a moral concept for an indicative concept, but the deviation that the doxology necessitates leads to a subtlety, a reserve and profundity of the indicative concept that one would never have been able to reach without the intervention of the word that has challenged a too immediate or superficial naming. In other words, the ethical judgment expressing itself in the form of doxology does not substitute one divine name for another: it frees the mind for a more profound knowledge. One could say that doxology *goes with* analogy.

On the other hand, there are divine names that correspond to the successive irruptions of the word. Even if these take a negative turn, they lead to another way of coming to know God: God who speaks, who calls, who risks, who commits himself and therefore compromises himself. These names are also accompanied by doxology, for it is by the latter that the purified mind can discern the involvement of God at a point where an attitude of refusal sees only mortifying contents. If we do not want these "historical" divine names (since the time of Jesus we know that they culminate in the name of Father) to fall rapidly into immediacy in the evaluation of the relationship God/men, they too must be supported by analogy, for only in this way can they remain truly *divine* names.

Sacrifice for sin

Now we must take another step forward: up to this point, in the analysis of the Paschal Mystery of Jesus and of the figures of the innocent that herald it, we have remained outside of the question of sin. The latter was merely indirectly evoked to the extent that it enabled us to better understand, by contrast, the exact place of this history that I call the adventure of sonship. For there is history and adventure before any sin and, from man's point of view solicited by the word of God, the driving force of this history is that consent that can be called sacrifice of communion. One could also say, using the language of Saint

Paul (Rom 12), "spiritual sacrifice." When Saint Paul speaks of "offering oneself as a living sacrifice, holy and acceptable to God," he is describing the modeling of existence according to the Word of God and in response to it, and not the offering after the event of an existence already wholly defined before the irruption of this word. Spiritual worship is not cheap worship that is defined only in terms of life and lacking the element of (sacrificial) death; on the contrary, it includes this aspect of death to self for God (and also, in dependence on God, for others) that makes man a son permanently. In such a sacrifice, "the body, soul and mind" (to use a trilogy used elsewhere by Saint Paul) are equally implicated, and this applies first of all to Jesus.

Nevertheless, this analysis of spiritual or communion sacrifice as field of sonship has left out of consideration to some extent an extremely important point on which Scripture lays great emphasis: the death of Jesus as filial gift *to* his Father was also a death *for* us, for us men. If the tested innocence of Jesus receives some clarification thanks to reflection on the innocent and tempted figures of Adam and of Job, it should also be evaluated in reference to another, likewise innocent figure, that of the Servant, whose suffering is not primarily explained on the basis of relationship to God, but rather on the basis of relationship to human beings for whose sake this suffering is undergone. Moreover, this "for us men" is also expressed immediately in terms of *sin*: "for our sins." How are we to understand this passage from a relationship *to* God to an action *for* men, and (a second question that does not completely coincide with the preceding one) how are we to understand this passage from a spiritual sacrifice as integral part of sonship, to a sacrifice that would redeem, reconcile, reestablish peace, expiate sin, etc.?

These questions emerge with even greater force when we observe that the New Testament actually does not really "pass" from a spiritual sacrifice to a sacrifice for sin in the case of Jesus: each time that scripture speaks theologically of the death of Christ, it does so precisely in connection with sin, particularly though not exclusively, when the authors are employing liturgical vocabulary. Is our presentation valid?

To answer this question, we will begin by investigating the world of sin: how does the refusal of the word of God become inscribed in the body, in the earth and in human society? Jesus came into a world profoundly marked by sin; how was he able to make his life and death become the time of redemption? This is our second question, to which we will respond by showing that Jesus' sacrifice of communion took on concrete and painful forms and characteristics precisely because it was offered in this world of sin. It will then remain for us to say a few words about the relationship between Jesus and *all* human beings; how did it happen that this apparently individual adventure of Jesus of Nazareth was and remains a universal redemption?

1. The world of sin

The world in which Jesus turns toward God is marked by sin. If a doxological, symbolic behavior accomplishes the entrance into covenant and thus opens the ways of the knowledge of God, the refusal to believe in the hope of becoming "like gods," or the revolt in the face of suffering that puts God on trial, have the opposite effect: man becomes closed in on himself and falls back into the paths of forgetfulness. A brief analysis of these paths is necessary in order for us to see how Jesus travelled them and liberated us from them. Although necessary, this analysis is not easy for the paths of forgetfulness are many and twisting, and one cannot recognize them merely by negative deductions on the basis of what would have been if man had not sinned. The Bible, however, gives us some constant features, of which the figure of Adam the sinner is a vivid illustration. As for philosophical reflection, it has never been able to dispense with reflection on the reality and origins of evil and, even if this reflection most often takes a gnostic turn, it is worthy of consideration and evaluation.

The desire to be "like gods" does not disappear with the failure of any attempt to accomplish it by oneself; it lives on, above all if it is a perverted form of the desire for God, without which man cannot exist. On the other hand, condemnation does not suppress or annul man's destiny to covenant and to divine knowledge, and consequently, man always tries to adjust life, its spaces and the thoughts that it provokes, in order to foster hope for his basic desire. I would like to suggest four directions of thought or action according to which we could try to understand the vicissitudes of human existence in rupture with doxology and covenant: (1) a process of theological occultation: the true God is forgotten; and thus, (2) the parallel process of various attempts to replace him at the levels of knowledge and relationship; correlatively, (3) forgetfulness is also at work at the level of the true reality of man:

work and sexuality, gifts perpetuated by God at the very moment when he separates himself from man, will be lived under the sign of violence—the "like gods" are actually in search of power and they prove to be liars and full of jealousy; finally, (4) historical memory, instead of being primarily orientated toward the future of the divine word about to come, turns back with obsessive earnestness to the past in order to try to understand—but without success, because the origin is always already hidden.

Disappearance of invocation

What disappears with sin is the invocative and doxological function: God, having been rejected, withdraws, and man can no longer praise a God whom he has not believed. Between God and man the word is no longer addressed, with the result that a forgetting becomes progressively installed: where there is no longer word, there can be neither name nor image. Where words no longer support a communication, they vanish, they become *obsolete*. Analogy functions only within a covenant behavior, and the God of covenant is known only through the effective act of fellowship, that should have been obedience and awaiting. The mystery, so difficult to conceive, of a God who is both creator and who involves himself in history, is lost to knowledge when the living relationship is broken. Thought, when its object is God, is at the limit of its possibilities; the concepts and the judgments that it forms hold up only on the basis of a faithful covenant experience, and in their very ductility they help to maintain the latter in truth. But if the covenant is broken, one can only go from recognition to lack of recognition, and the primary form of the latter is forgetting. And if some faint memory persists, it would be remote and without effective bearing: *Deus otiosus*.[1]

Anxiety and cult

I have stressed the fact that the divine precept gives us an insight not only into the divine dimension of the Mystery, but also into the real depth of man, made for communication with God. The fact that he refuses this does not change anything of what he is in reality: the desire and the capacity for covenant remain, but henceforth in a state of impotence. Is this not perhaps the ultimate root of *anxiety*? In any case, history shows that man cannot bear the rupture of covenant, even if he has profoundly forgotten the origin of his evil. And he attempts to fill the gap. This search for substitutes is at work perhaps in two areas, that of "cult" and that of "wisdom."

Eden knew a space that one can call "cultic," for the symbolic communion sacrifice of the covenant, a space in reciprocal relationship with the rest of the garden for the life and the work of man. Driven out of this space, man is constantly attempting to rebuild others; having failed to offer the sacrifice of communion at the opportune moment, he does his utmost to invent other sacrifices, less to reintroduce into his life the "form of death" than to conjure away the other death to which he has been sentenced and which threatens him all through his life, to claim victory over it in the end. Having forgotten the true God and no longer in touch with him through an exchange of word, he will seek to appease the beings that he imagines are capable of keeping him alive or of giving some meaning to his death: the heavens, from whence come the rains, the sun that gives warmth, the heavenly bodies that rule the elements, and his ancestors (those who, wherever they are, have in some sense conquered death) with whom it is important to maintain contact, to whose tradition he must remain faithful—both to conciliate them and to be able to join them one day. All of this helps to explain the necessity of initiation, a ritual that naturalizes man into these worlds of the beyond, the worlds of those who have gone before us.

In cultic places, at sacred times (defined by cosmic time and the legends of the dead), one offers sacrifices: one "experiments" with everything that might be capable of pleasing or appeasing the gods and the ancestors: every conceivable offering, from human beings to plants. In this way, a tradition of rites is formed, while at the same time fantastic stories are told whose purpose is to explain to people how things began: the origin of the human race as well as that of the "fall" or of evil. Finally, what characterizes these places is their separation from the world and from history: sacred ambients, where the actions are repetitive, the initiatives rash, and where a determination is made, through unbreakable traditions or oracles, regarding what is to be done in the outside world. The theme of the Law comes in here—no longer viewed from the point of view of a Precept coming from God as an offer of covenant to which corresponds a symbolic behavior of obedience, but rather Law as a sacred ordinance, whose origin is imprecise and immemorial and whose observance is believed to keep man in a reliable way on the path of a guaranteed salvation.

Naturally, I do not pretend, with these summary remarks, to exhaust what a phenomenology of the forms of cult or a history of religious ideas could offer. I have only been trying to bring out the coherence between the development of a cult and the loss of the "form of death" and of the sacrificial interpretation of the word of God. Formally, the process consists in filling in as much as possible the spaces left empty by the rupture of covenant and the subsequent forgetting— of God as well as of the ultimate identity of man. This great filling in effort aims at establishing a situation from which man senses he has fallen: it is a quest for salvation. The forms that this effort has taken throughout the whole course of history are obviously innumerable. And need we add that one may, unfortunately, find them in certain cultic or legalistic behaviors or practices of the Christian community?

Too-short wisdom, too-long wisdom

There is, however, another way of salvation, more marked by reflection and meditation: the way of "wisdom," along whose path man once again seeks to understand God, himself, the world and evil. Here too, I limit myself to a few summary observations and offer the suggestion that man in covenant rupture oscillates continuously between what one could call a "too-short wisdom" and a "too-long wisdom."

The "too-short wisdom" brings God into an excessively close relationship with man, with his world, with his history. It characterizes those modes of thinking in which God is viewed as "part of the system" with the rest, even if he is acknowledged a specific place, a certain "transcendence." To employ an expression of Lévinas that says succinctly what is at stake here (although Lévinas himself does not apply it to God), the God of the "too-short wisdom" is not "absolved of the relation" which exists between the world and himself; he is involved in it in a way which is ultimately univocal, as creative cause, as God of history, etc. It would be interesting to trace in biblical history the progressive purification of the elements of a "too-short wisdom" that are undoubtedly found there. A fortiori, one could undertake a process of evaluation, on the basis of this hypothesis of a "too-short wisdom," among the philosophical thinkers and wisdoms of various cultures. In this perspective, on the other hand, the impact of evil tends to be reduced to a bare minimum. Evil is assimilated to finitude, or to "non-being," or to the inevitable mistakes of history. The jolts that evil transmits to the course of the world or to human life are not "tragic" and one seeks to account for them in such a way that they do not break the harmony between God, man, the world and time. The breaches that it attempts cannot break this well-balanced totality in a lasting way or, if they do, one has only to think of ways of putting things back in place in order to erect a new and enduring universe. Certainly, the onto-theology that Heidegger describes for us (but not only this) would belong to this "too-short wisdom."

The opposite of this "too-short wisdom," according to which God is inserted into this world a little too well, and in which the concept of God tends toward univocity, is a "too-long wisdom," the wisdom which keeps stressing a *God beyond* in such a way that there can be absolutely no concept or language for him. In this type of wisdom, God is very much talked about but always by stressing the fact that in reality nothing at all can be said of him. To use terminology taken from the Eden story, we could say that this perspective pushes to the extreme the theme of the God who forbids, the God of interdict, whom the human mind can in no way fathom. But the interdict here is one that does not create covenant. This God can be sought indefinitely, but never found. There is nothing in common between the world and him and at the same time, in sharp contrast to the preceding tendency, finitude itself takes on the color of evil: *omne corpus fugiendum*, and the anxious soul, not knowing itself, will always go looking in the most profound regions of self for an unutterable source in which it would ultimately annihilate itself. In other words, theological language would be totally equivocal, which means that there is no such language at all. We are at the extreme opposite pole from onto-theology, and one could speak here of a "meontological perspective" whose influence would extend to all fields of language.

Without wishing for the moment to press these terms rigorously, one could say that the "too-short wisdom" is continuously haunted by the *temptation of the enclosed imagination*, where the latter term would designate all the productions of the human mind in its tendency to fill the voids of knowledge, to stop up the crevices of history, personal or universal, to reduce the tragic, to assure the full and immediate significance of language, etc. Conversely, the "too-long wisdom" would be tempted by the *exclusivism of metaphor*, retaining for the term metaphor its essentially transitive etymological meaning: man can do no more than effect transfers, but ones which start from nowhere and do not really lead anywhere. The "too-short wisdom" transposes a radiant vision of space to all planes, in the nostalgia for a center from which it would be possible to see clearly the entire outline of the enclosure; the "too-long wisdom" is that of an itinerant perception, but of a journey of which it is not known where or when it began, nor if it will ever come to an end.

The body, envy and violence

On the basis of the Genesis text alone, the analysis of the coming of violence into the interplay of human relationships is difficult because nothing is told us regarding these relationships before sin. We simply observe that the rupture with respect to God immediately entails a mutual fear between the man and the woman, as well as the establishment of a hierarchy whose immediate locus is sexuality. But perhaps we could go deeper in our reflection on this matter.

One could suggest that the very first experience which the man and the woman have after sin is that *they have a body*. Until then, there was no perception properly speaking of a body: naked man had a correct relationship, in his integrity, with the soil, with woman, with God; man called to duty by the interdict discovered himself in his entirety in reference to this new word and eventually knew himself to be in a state of awaiting for a next word which would fully reveal to him what he was, according to that dimension which is at once *other* and *more intimate* to himself than the first word of God allowed him to glimpse. The refusal of covenant is a revelation of the body, in its *separated* individuality, in its weakness (nakedness becomes stripping, spoliation), in his mortality. This body is no longer under the word; it is no longer caught up in the dynamic of reciprocal naming: from God to man, from man to God, from man to woman and from woman to man. The perception will quickly arise that the body is the first "having" that must be safeguarded. This body is no longer organically linked to its other self which only the offer of covenant revealed; it becomes a value in itself and assumes an oppositional stance toward every other body. Its desire to survive takes on autonomy and gives birth to mechanisms of defense and of aggressivity, rooted in the radical fear of dying. The love of the other, of his "vis-a-vis resemblance" becomes concupiscence, rabid desire of pleasure for its own sake: what we have here, ultimately, are animal behaviors, except for the fact that man lacks the regulatory controls of animal life because he has been endowed with another regulatory system, wholly governed by covenant. The discovery of body as an objective, fragile, exposed entity is perhaps at the root of mutual fear which engenders all the "defense mechanisms" against the other, against nature, even against God—which take the form of lust for power, violence in relationships (and especially in sexual relationships), non-exchange of possessions, etc. Man, deprived of his profound identity, of his *other self* whose revelation was outlined in the word of God, no longer knows how to find his bearings with respect *to others*. Work and sexuality are in no way the "flowers of evil"; but the painful character of work, the part played by concupiscence and violence in sexuality (and consequently, the establishment of power relationships of oppressive character) certainly are. And what will man need in order to be able to rediscover work and sexuality in their truth if not a new offer of covenant which will allow him the sacrifice of communion now become impossible?

Alongside this painful experience of the body separated and defensive, one could introduce here, to explain violence among human beings, the theme of the indefiniteness of desire which René Girard sees as the origin of mimetic behaviors and subsequently, of rivalries that culminate in violence, at least if they are not channeled by the "sacred." I do not think that human desire is in itself essentially indefinite, or indeterminate: radically it is a desire for God and an openness to receive from God, by way of the renunciation of self-sufficiency, that communion with him which is man's true fulfillment. But the forgetting of the living God which characterizes the cultural world marked by sin is also a forgetting of human desire in its truth and a loss of the guide marks which would enable man to discern and organize the more particular desires. No longer aware that he is "in the image and likeness" of God and having determined on his own to become "like gods," he has lost the essential reference point to guide him in organizing his life, with the result that the way is open to an endless and fruitless process of *mimesis*. Taken at this level, the explanation of René Girard is suggestive and offers abundant resources for the analysis of behaviors, both religious and cultural. Unfortunately, as I have already observed, Girard does not bring out in his most recent works the crucial fact that *mimesis* first of all came into play against the true God and his Word, and against the communion behavior to which this Word was inviting humanity. This is why I am convinced that his conclusions on violence and the sacred, but also on the interpretation of the Christian event, have to be corrected and refined by being inserted into the *theocentric* ambient of faith.[2]

Lost history

Finally, it is clear that the memory of lost humanity turns toward the past in a twofold way. Superficially, this "historical research" has an etiological character: how did we get where we are? The explanations of the myth always aim at answering the great question: where does evil come from? And in a certain sense, the narrative of Genesis is also an etiological explanation of evil. But more profoundly, memory is a hope or longing for the past before the fall; its language expresses a desire to trace back the thread of evil to a point before the initial drama, however one conceives of this. The only future for which one has an image and a desire is the "paradise lost," although its conceptualization is difficult and this movement of return impossible, except perhaps in the enclosed and sacred space of cult or, for some who enjoy a special wisdom, in an ineffable and incommunicable experience with an unnamed beyond.

If we combine this compulsive and essentially repetitive movement toward a lost past with the fear and envy triggered by the mere sight of any other human being whose body is perceived as a screen and a threat, instead of being a means of proximity and mediation, it is easy to understand why no *history* would be possible, why no *risk of the future* can be taken, why the formation of various groups should be based essentially on *shared fears* and on the *defense of interests* against every potential aggressor. To forget God, to lose time, to produce divisions among human beings—these are three movements of one and the same attitude.[3]

2. The Time of the Redemption[4]

The world of sin, as I have just attempted to describe it, does not exist and has never existed as such. I only wish to bring to light a number of constants that flow from every refusal of God and become profoundly inscribed not only in the human heart, but also in the body and in the earth of man. According to the different periods of history and the areas of civilization, this or that aspect can be more pronounced; the outline I have given can, however, generally serve to locate the places where the rupture of faith and of doxology are more pronounced and become inscribed in the real world. Nevertheless, as I emphasize in commenting on the narrative of Eden, the world of sin is always permeated with the gestures of redemption; and this is so true that sin itself and its consequences can be located only by way of the revelation of Pardon. From the time of Genesis, the modalities of redemption are there to be discerned: God *speaks again*, keeps the communication channels open and thus does not leave man to his ruin. He does, however, take note of the situation created by sin and does not erase its asperities; he turns this situation into a springboard for life. The framework thus begins to appear—one of sorrow and pain, and at the same time one open to hope—within which we will begin to see new words of God aimed at realizing the communion intended from the beginning. The figure of Job, among many others of the Old Testament, is there to show us that the resumption of the word, fruit of God's forgiveness, continues to challenge man to rise above, to go beyond. Whether the starting point is a situation of happiness or one of desolation, God is always leading beyond, and the dilemma of the "form of death" never disappears—either the "form of death" which can be identified with the risk of faith, of a people or of an individual, or perdition: "if you will not believe, surely you shall not be established" (Is 7:9). And what is at stake in this process of transcendence is a *new and more profound knowledge of God*.

The ultimate sin

After the prophets and the sages, Jesus is sent as the final messenger of God, the Son after the servants, as the parable puts it (Mt 21:33–46). He announces the imminent Kingdom and reveals the Father's name. Now it is important to see clearly that his Messianic word, like every other word of God in the preceding history, offered a dilemma of attraction and repulsion: however radiant may have been the figure of Jesus or his power as a wonder worker, which accredited his message, the latter was nonetheless extremely onerous, and at the limit of the tolerable. The fact is that Jesus took a position with respect to the Mosaic Law that was at the same time one of liberty and one of respect. It was hardly evident how this position should be interpreted. One would have to have understood that the *fulfillment* of the Law of Moses in the Kingdom passed through a transformation whose authority was guaranteed by the word of Jesus alone. Like their fathers in Israel (and like all human beings after Easter), Jesus' hearers were invited to run the risk of symbolic behavior. This meant running the risk that their *image of God* and concrete behavior, right and holy as they may have been until then, be modified, henceforth interpreted not only through the Law and the Temple but through the teaching of the Galilean who walked their streets. This also meant running the risk of *another political allegiance* for a people strongly united on the basis of the Law. It was anything but evident that this risk could be taken, and in fact it was probable that any modification in the direction indicated by Jesus would have weakened the situation of Israel as a people confronting the powers of the day, particularly the Romans. However, a look at the past of Israel, whether to the time of the patriarchs, the tribes or the royal regime, makes it abundantly clear that the image of God and a certain political organization were connected, and that in order to progress in the first one would have to risk the other, and vice versa. What was true at the level of the people was also true at that of the individual—the message conveyed by the adventure of Job. Everything is always risked together: the image of God, the image of self, the image of one's prized possessions.

Accordingly, what the hearers of Jesus should have allowed to come into play, in their judgment on the Galilean, is that which was most precious in the prophetic proclamation of Israel and in its wisdom: ultimately, the Spirit of God at work since the beginning. Then they would have been able to run the risk of the "destruction of the Temple," knowing for sure that it would be rebuilt and confident that they would understand the depth of the revelation of the Name of Father disclosing a God more than good in his creation and more than faithful in his covenant. But we see also the enormity of the risk: no longer to defend the acquired knowledge of a religion, even a holy one; no longer to nourish the hope of a political restoration, even a legitimate one; instead, to await the Kingdom, reinterpreting the Law in all of its detail in the light of the first two commandments alone.

The sacrifice of communion demanded by the message of Jesus was refused, and this refusal, in its opposition to the ultimate and full manifestation of the word of God, recapitulates all the other tragic categorical refusals, those of the Gentiles as well as those of the Jews, of people who came before Jesus and of those who came after him, in the way that a global refusal of a definitive offer can encompass all partial denials. The refusal of the Name of Father, as well as of the messenger who came to announce it, is a totality: it is the "sin of the world" that stands in opposition to the sacrifice of communion. It is repeated even today, every time a bypassing or transcending of any kind of the image of God, of self and of our prized possessions is refused, every time the breath of the Spirit is cut off; and in a sense this repetition adds nothing to the crucifixion of Jesus. It confirms and ratifies it, but everything was played out back then.

The pardon of Jesus

Jesus suffered this refusal in his body; the "no" that was the response of human beings to the word of God is the Cross, a tragic writing that spells out human violence in its ultimate foundation. If violence is done to Jesus, it is because in him God is rejected. But Jesus intercedes, asking for pardon even for this ultimate offense; as far as he is concerned, he forgives. Although, through the violence of which he is the victim, human beings have in a sense definitively closed the adventure of sonship, Jesus suspends this tragic conclusion by invoking God's pardon on all: a new Moses, he asks that grace remain open even where there should no longer be any possibility of grace. Jesus begs his Father not to look at the Cross for what it is, the bloody inscription of a rejection, and by the same token he invites Him to see it for what it was not and for what he has made it become: the symbol of love for his brothers. The Cross is, from the side of human beings, a symbol of fundamental hatred of God, of the rejection of his name of Father, but by interceding for those who crucify him and by forgiving them, Jesus transforms this symbol of hatred into a symbol of love; the Cross will henceforth signify that all human beings are at every moment forgiven by God, because he who became sin in his body has chosen "pardon" (etymologically, the superabundance of gift).

In order for it to be correctly understood, the behavior of Christ should be linked to his whole teaching on forgiveness and mercy, as acts in and through which man is able to become perfect as the heavenly Father is perfect, to bring to perfection in himself the image of God and to render him glory in the fullest possible way. By asking for pardon at the very moment when he is dying, Jesus pushes to the extreme limit the second commandment that is like the first and thus offers to God the spiritual sacrifice of absolute fidelity to the essence of the Law. The forgiveness demanded and granted by Jesus is the transcending of all violence, of all love of self; it is the effective accomplishment of peace. "He is our peace . . . in his flesh, he has brought hostility to an end"; these two expressions of Saint Paul (Eph 2:14 and 16) apply to the reconciliation of Jews and Gentiles with one another and with God, but it is permissible to understand them, in a general way, in the universal reconciliation that exists thanks to the transformation of the Cross from an instrument of hatred into a symbol of love.

The silence of God

We could summarize what we have said on the subject of pardon by saying that if the Cross is a "sacrifice for sin," it is only because and to the extent that the fullness of the fraternal love of Jesus for human beings has completely reversed its meaning: it is Christ's superabundant intention to establish communion that opens a way where there was no longer a way. This perspective is not, however, exclusive. When one brings to the fore the theme of pardon, one situates Jesus in a position of mediator, which, after all, he is. As suffering Messiah he stands between God and human beings; as just man, never separated from God, he intervenes to enable sinners to be reunited with Him ever anew. Scripture, however, goes still further. It does not describe the relationship of Jesus to sinners, who by killing him make one final attempt to kill God, only in terms of mediation and of intercession. It does not situate Jesus only vis-a-vis human beings. When it says that Jesus died "for us" or "for our sins," the term *for* can also mean "substitution" value: in some sense Jesus died in our place. We are saved because he took our sins upon himself, or again, as Saint Paul says in strong terms: "God made him sin for our sake, so that we might become through him the justice of God." A transfer, a commutation has taken place—and this is sometimes expressed in ritual terms like "expiation," "propitiation," etc. How are we to understand this?

If the place of pardon in the Passion narrative according to Saint Luke has helped us to situate the theological meaning of this pardon, it is the theme of abandonment in the narrative of the Passion according to Saint Mark, which we will now make our guide. Right up to the last moment, God does not intervene to come to the aid of the one who finally has revealed himself as Christ and Son, and who, all through his life, has testified to the nearness of the Kingdom and revealed the Name of the Father. If, viewed with reference to the human beings who inflicted it on him, the death of Jesus is the fruit of absolute violence with reference to God who remains silent, it is a *trial within a framework of sin*. In analyzing the world of sin, I noted the place God's forgetting, of which bodily death is the symbol; in pointing out the attitude of God in the story of Eden, I noted that God does not simply cancel the consequences of man's sin, but while allowing them to follow their course, he transforms these consequences into new possibilities. We have here the dialectic of what Scripture calls the *Wrath*, the effective inscription in the world of signs of the absence of a rejected God, and of what it calls *Mercy*, the appeal addressed ever anew to the lost. By not coming to the aid of Jesus, even at the very last moment, God allowed the external signs of the Wrath to play themselves out—bodily death and the silence of God—but even this was no more than the framework of what was fundamentally, the *trial* of the perseverance of Jesus. Though he was the revealer of the Father's Name and prophet of the imminent Kingdom, Jesus was nonetheless treated as if he belonged to the family of those who chose the most fundamental forgetting; no assurance was given to him regarding the future, or if he had any, it was taken away from him—from the very one who had never been anything but the living memory of the Father. But what was required of him through this act of abandonment was precisely what is required of every human being: to persevere in doxology, to believe in the promise of God, which is capable of opening history even beyond death, to consider one's own death as a mysterious path of universal salvation. Thus, the death of Jesus, considered in his personal relationship to God, realizes the *sacrifice of communion* with an immeasurable intensity: not only because of the perfection of the charity which pardons, but because of the perfection of the charity which obeys. It is from the depths of the silence of God, a kind of immanent response to the forgetting of man, that Jesus, in the very act of dying, acknowledged the Name of Father, and by the same token, became its living Memory for all men.

It is the convergence of the death on the Cross and the silence of God who neither speaks nor acts to come to his aid, which makes of Jesus an embodiment of sin and not only the mediator between God and sinners. It is not that God is "dead set against" Jesus: the abandonment of which the crucified complains is the absence of God who does not allow himself to be seen, who allows death to follow its course, who allows sin to have its total effect on Jesus. It is then against all hope that Christ on the cross is to hope for this "hearing" of which the Letter to the Hebrews speaks, in response to his cry of bewilderment. It was not before but after the death of Jesus, not as salvation from death at the last minute but as resurrection, that Jesus was heard; before this, the crucified had to endure death in its dimension that could be called "a-theologal": the suffering in the human body, of separation from God. But Jesus persevered in the filial attitude: he transformed the second death into a sacrifice of communion, so that sin disappeared, and with it, all of God's wrath.

In sum, Jesus on the Cross lived the separation *from human beings* and surmounted it through forgiveness; he lived the separation *from God* and surmounted it through invocation. These two separations, experienced to their absolute limit *in death*, constituted the context of his sacrifice of communion, and this is why the latter is "sacrifice for sin."

When we reflect on it, there is something wonderful here: the hearers of Jesus, here representing all of humanity, had been invited to the ultimate *sacrifice of communion*, which would have fully purified and refined their image of God and their human hope. They would have done so by listening to Jesus who was bringing them the word of God. But they did not do this. Jesus then turns towards God, not only interceding for them but persevering himself from within his fate, more devastating as he was more noble and great in doxology and invocation. Paradoxically, the word which God was awaiting from humanity from the very beginning is finally addressed to him and it transforms an ultimate rejection into definitive invocation.

The Lamb without blemish

If Jesus died for our sins, it was as one who was himself *without sin*. If he was offered, it was as a Lamb *without blemish*. The theme of innocence put to the test, subjected to the "form of death," is fully applicable to him. One dimension of his relationship to God is indeed that of the innocent subjected to a painful lot, who, by refusing to the very end to put God on trial, lives up to his condition as son. If there is something in Jesus which achieves redemption, it is and can only be his attitude of obedience to God even to death, the perfection of the sacrifice of communion of which his death is the symbol. As painful as they may also have been, the events of the passion have no meaning except as a trial of obedience, of doxology, of communion, and it is precisely here that Jesus was found faithful. Entering resolutely into the "death" through which all sonship is fulfilled, he was the first to render perfect glory to God. He understood God's design, and this is why he was able to open a path of salvation for all.

The theme of innocence put to the test and emerging victorious, in a framework of sin, should be able to serve as a hermeneutical principle for evaluating and putting into perspective the images and concepts which convey the theme of redemption in Scripture and in the patristic and medieval tradition. One could distribute these images and concepts in three basic directions: *victory*—over the devil, sin, death; *cult*—expiation, propitiation, sacrifice for sin; and *right* or *law*— merit, satisfaction, redemption. This list is not exhaustive, nor is this distribution into three orientations; at least these themes exist, and I think that they can be reinterpreted in the perspective proposed. I would like to take an example in the domain of cult and of cultic terminology. This is often theologically unacceptable because it has been taken literally and conceptually; the attempt has been made to verify in the passion and death of Christ definitions taken from the Old Testament or from the common stock of religions and applied in a univocal way to the Christian mystery, while this should have been taken in a perspective of objective fulfillment and of spiritual exegesis. In fact, this is the perspective of the biblical authors. There was much discussion some time ago, for example, over the chronology of the passion of Jesus and on the date of the Last Supper.[5] However interesting these discussions may have been, I ask myself whether they did not tend to lose sight of what really seems to be the common intention of the Synoptic Gospels and John. Since they do not agree in the manner in which they present the Last Supper of Jesus, we can conclude that the question whether or not this Last Supper was actually and literally a Jewish paschal meal is not a major concern of theirs. On the other hand, what they are trying to tell us and what each in his own way says very clearly is that the death of Jesus, celebrated in the Church's Eucharist, is the *true Passover*. It is on the basis of this insight that we should understand the use of *Passover* terminology to describe the redemption. We should allow a mutual interplay between type and antitype: if the Jewish theology of the Passover at the time of Jesus, can clarify the meaning of the passion and death of the Lord, conversely, it is this passion and death that fulfill the meaning of the ancient Passover, so that the total meaning of the latter cannot be understood except by reflecting on the former. And if it is proper for us to speak, for example, of "paschal sacrifice" with reference to Jesus, we do not do so by reducing his passion and death to a "variant" of the paschal theme, but by reading them as a transformation and a fulfillment of this theme. We could say the same for everything that has to do with *expiation*.[6] In a Jewish context, the word designates the high point of the Temple cult. After the death and resurrection of Jesus, the disciples quickly had to take a stand with respect to the cultic life of the Temple, and their decision was to renounce it. If they describe the death of Jesus in terms of the sacrifice of expiation, it only means that everything the Jewish religion sought through the liturgy of expiation has been given in the death and resurrection of Christ; one should not reduce or compare the passion and death of Jesus to the sacrifices of cattle practiced on the Feast of Atonement. Rather, the theme of expiation should be seen as transfigured and perfected on the basis of the passion and the death of Jesus; the ritually expiatory aspect is abolished and disappears altogether, absorbed into the communion aspect, signified and accomplished by the cross.

One could also say that the Bible contains a progressive "sacramentalization" of sacrifices and of Law, which effects a gradual transformation in them from ritual sacrifice and positive Law to sacrifice of communion and Law of love. Jesus accomplishes the ultimate step and signifies the ultimate truth of this sacramentalization. The cultic terms expiation, propitiation, ransom and others are thus to be understood in the light of a comprehensive symbolic system: that of access to the dimension of filial communion, which is the proper vocation of man, and which requires a "death." This death itself is not, on the part of God, an absurd and cruel demand: it is the call of love to love, and the response becomes symbolically inscribed on the body of the human being who responds. If such a call is inscribed in a framework marked by death, violence, the forgetting of God, then the "death" will be profoundly marked by this framework and if victorious, will blot out the other death, the violence, etc. It is in this sense that one can reinterpret the cultic categories.

If one does not give special emphasis in the evaluation of the passion and death of Jesus, to the primacy of the sacrifice of communion and to its necessary presence on the path that leads to the fulfillment of sonship or, in other words, if one views sacrifice only in its alleged modality of expiation, it becomes impossible to absolve God of the charge of cruelty. However one looks at the question, this god is demanding a "bloody" sacrifice as a condition for receiving his pardon! And then the Cross of Christ is interpreted by way of recourse to cultic categories proper to religions in general, whereas it is exactly the opposite that is called for: to understand these categories and these practices as receiving their ultimate meaning from the Cross of Christ and as being abolished in the very act of their receiving this signification.[7]

To conclude this series of reflections on the time of the redemption, it could be suggestive to simply mention here the old and ever new question of the "motive of the Incarnation": would the Word have become flesh if man had not sinned? If one answers in the affirmative, one must indeed maintain that the incarnate Word in a world of innocence would still have had to perform, in his humanity, a filial gesture belonging to the level of the "sacrifice of communion." And all the other acts of this type, posited in innocent humanity, would have found their ultimate meaning in the sacrifice of communion offered by Christ. Since in fact he has come into a world of sin, Christ offers the same and fundamental sacrifice of communion, but within the framework of a profoundly disturbed situation: in this case, his perseverance takes on an aspect not only of recapitulation, but also of reconciliation.

3. Living for men and dying for their sins

The preceding remarks are an attempt to respond to one of the questions posed at the beginning of this chapter: how are we to "pass," with respect to the history of Jesus, from a sacrifice of communion to a sacrifice for sin? The response is that there is no passage properly speaking—that for Jesus too, what is essential is the symbolic behavior by which he lives up to his condition as son, while the tragic aspects of the passion and of the cross are the modality through which communion necessarily reaches perfection when it is a world of sin that is the point of departure. In offering this solution, I also touch extensively on the other question posed: how do we pass from a sacrifice of communion, from a relationship *to* God, to a life and a death *for* human beings? What right have we to say that what Jesus did, he did "in our name," or "for us," or again that it is "in him" that we are saved? It is possible to say more on this subject.

Jesus, the man for others

Could it be, after all, that this question of the passage from a relationship *to* God to a relationship *to* human beings is really a false question? The fact is that Jesus' journey toward his Father is inseparable from his mission for human beings: these are the two facets of a single reality. It is for men that Jesus is a prophet of the Kingdom of God; it is to them that he has come to reveal the name of the Father. From this point of view, the spiritual sacrifice of Jesus becomes identified with fidelity to his mission. And if a paroxysm of suffering was necessary in order for the intensity of Jesus' sonship to be manifested, this paroxysm itself, without requiring that anything be added to it, would also reveal his universal brotherhood. Never was Jesus' life a life for himself—this is obvious—but it is also true that it was never a life for "God alone," in the sense that it would have left human beings outside of its effective aim and of its concrete unfolding. Jesus lived only to prepare his contemporaries, through his word and action, for the imminent irruption of the Kingdom. His manner of living was from the very beginning essentially selfless and at the service of others.

This life "for" men was lived "to" God, simply because it was obedience to a mission received from God, animated by the conviction Jesus had in speaking the words of God and not his own. Whatever concrete hesitations Jesus may have experienced at certain moments regarding the manner of conducting his mission, however great the bewilderment and suffering he may have felt at its failures, these things changed neither his conviction that he had been sent nor his decision to obey. One could say that before *dying for* us, Jesus *lived for* us in his effort to prepare the coming of the Kingdom among men. These simple remarks tie in with a traditional theme of the theology of the redemption: Jesus saves through his office of prophet and teacher: he speaks the words of God in order to effect the conversion of human beings.

The death of Jesus does not change anything in the orientation of his life "for" men; it is but its natural sequence. Jesus dies rather than renounce that which he had come to proclaim: no longer able to do anything for his message of salvation, he dies, and by his death he witnesses once again to this message. One could say that by dying rather than compromising on the message which was to save them, he continued to love human beings in spite of themselves; by this very fact, he continued to love God, because he died rather than change anything in the word that had been entrusted to him. In this sense Jesus died for the truth of God (sacrifice *to*), and for men whose well-being he was serving by being unshakably faithful to this word of salvation (sacrifice *for*). Moreover, the pardon which Jesus, from his cross, demands for human beings or himself extends to them can be viewed as an ultimate affirmation of this solidarity; even in death, Jesus does not separate himself from those to whom he has been sent. The martyr does not reject those who are putting him to death, and he hopes beyond death in the strength of his witness.

If these observations are correct, the question of a "passage" in Jesus from a relationship *to* God to an action *for* men hardly arises: the mission received from God, to which Jesus remains faithful even at the moment of apparent abandonment by God, is entirely for men. Jesus is never more brother than at the very moment when he reveals himself perfectly as son: the cross is just as much a fraternal moment as it is a filial one. The one cannot go without the other, and in this way one can also understand what was said above about the pardon that Jesus demands from his Father for human beings.

Jesus the "representative"[8]

All the above observations also indicate in what sense Jesus can be called our "representative." To the extent that an individual's life becomes *totally* identified with his mission, a fact attested to by the very name Jesus, whose salvific significance the evangelist himself brings out (Mt 1:21), it becomes almost evident that when this individual posits any act, he does so *in the name of* those for whom he posits it. If Jesus is the man *for* others, then others can find themselves in him.

One can attempt to deepen the theme by taking into account the distinction made by Dorothée Sölle between "representation" and "substitution"; I will make use of this distinction here, giving it a slightly different interpretation. What is it that authorizes a human being to speak or to act in the name of others, and what is it that gives this word a value that goes beyond the person of its bearer? We emphasize first of all that whatever foundation might be given to the fact of representation, the representative does not take the place of, or substitute for, those whom he represents, because personal subjects are irreplaceable: they too have to bear the word and posit responsible acts. One could conclude from this remark that a representative fully acquits himself of his task when he specifically liberates others for their word and task. But the fact that every human being is irreplaceable, individually or with respect to the communities to which he belongs, does not exclude the possibility of his having to be represented. Outside of the question of sin, which is not my precise concern at the moment, this is explained on the one hand by the finitude of the human subject and on the other by his existence-in-relation. Being finite, man cannot by himself immediately cope with all the words and all the acts which could be posited in a given set of circumstances. His insertion in space and time alone makes this impossible. It is inevitable that there be substitutes and proxies, but ones in which absent man recognizes himself, to the point of knowing that he is bound by the words or the acts which will have been posited "in his name" to the terms of the contract by representation. More profoundly, representation is grounded in the relational existence of man: his individuality is not separated and aloof from the relational ties through which he is recognized and situated within a variety of human spaces. In this sense, beings in relation can speak for one another within the proper perspective which unifies their communities, and the communities themselves need spokespersons who embody this unity and, accordingly commit it in one direction or another—so that here too each member may be bound by the commitment made or beneficiary to the advantage obtained.

On the basis of these elementary observations, which I hope have shown that representation is a necessary organ of human existence, and without destroying the irreplaceability of the individual, one can go on to specify what is to serve concretely as the foundation for representation. Broadly speaking, there are three bases to be considered here: the genetic one, that of primogeniture; the contractual one, that of election; the moral one, that of quality.

It is readily acknowledged that a first-born can speak in the name of all those who come after him; being the first to have made parents of a given man and woman, he will speak, indeed he will act, in the name of those who, after him, have caused these parents to repeat the process of generation. He does not replace them, he represents them, and they accept recognition of themselves in the words he utters and the deeds he posits. He also represents but does not replace, who by his fidelity to a community, his understanding of its needs or of its capacities, can speak with the consent of all or act in its name: here again, all agree to implicate themselves freely in whatever their representative says or does. Finally, one could conceive of a situation where, in a given group, there would be an individual so integral, so unique, that he would be able to recapitulate, without destroying them, the persons in the group who have the capacity to express themselves or to act: representation by the best. Such a person is to be found in all groups, even if all do not have the generosity to recognize him and to allow him to speak or to act in their name. But if he is acknowledged as such, then in his word or action, every member of the group recognizes himself, even if he knows that he is surpassed in this individual by a quality that is beyond his range of achievement. Primogeniture, excellent sense of the community, personal perfection, such would be the titles or grounds of representation.

To Christian faith it is clear that Christ can lay claim to these various titles of representation, indeed that his being and his mission would have no meaning at all if he could not make this claim. In a sense the whole development of the theology of the redemption in the New Testament consists in an ever more comprehensive discovery of the *titles* or the *names* of Christ which ground the reality of salvation in an ever more ample fashion: First-born before every creature, First-born from among the dead, Head of the Body which is the Church, Son of God in power, but also powerful Word and Word turned toward the Father—all these "Christic" names ground the "Christic representation" and reveal ever more clearly what was already there in the filial and messianic mission of Jesus before Easter.

However, these titles do not turn the people Jesus represents into individuals without personal substance of their own: Jesus represents, he does not replace. Even if it is posited in our name, the redemptive act can be, for the community of Jesus, only the principle of words and of actions through which this act is personally ratified. We could say, in the terms we are employing here, that if Jesus posits for us a sacrifice for sin, he is restoring to us by this very act the possibility of positing our own sacrifice of communion; this "possibility" has a proper name, and it is the same for Jesus and for us: the Holy Spirit.

Conversely, if we were to analyze the redemptive act of Christ with no reference whatever to its spiritual fruit in us, we would be making Christ a substitute rather than a representative.

Finitude and suffering

In the perspective opened by these reflections on representation, it is possible to begin to discern the principle of a solution to the basic problem which we have seen in the first part to underlie all gnosis: finitude and/or culpability.

On the one hand, our analysis of the figures of Adam and of Job has clearly shown that the finitude of man had been called to transcend itself in order to respond to the word of God inviting to communion, a transcending that cannot take place without the renunciation of one's own autonomy and consent to a symbolic behavior which has the "form of death" and thus implies some suffering. On the other hand, in the beginning of this chapter we were able to analyze the elements marked by culpability of a world and of a society which obstinately refuse this symbolic dynamism: in a culpable way, one dies of not wishing to die in a loving way. But if Jesus, from the depths of a world profoundly marked by culpability, lived and died in a perfectly symbolic manner, and hence even to the marks inscribed by evil on the body, in the psychism, in the social fears and in the destructions of the land, then the sacrifice of communion becomes possible once again: there is no longer anything that is formally culpable and everything, under the impulse of the Spirit, can serve to reestablish peace: with God, within the self, with others, with the world. We have here the principle of a renewal and of an up-grading of the moral order to which I hope to return succinctly in the conclusion of this book: between deceptive revolutions and expectations of the unnameable perhaps there is a history to construct, at least on condition that we *hear the founding narrative* in its two phases of resurrection and of death, and that we conform to the norm for behavior that this narrative gives us.

Notes

1. Cf. M. Eliade, *Patterns in Comparative Religion*, trans. Rosemary Sheed, (London, New York: Sheed & Ward, 1958), p. 46, section 14 : "Deus otiosus" and M. Augé, *Génie du paganisme*, (Paris, 1982), p. 133.

2. R. Schwager, who wrote on Girard before *Des choses cachées dupuis le commencement du monde*, and attempted a systematic application of *La Violence et le Sacré* to the biblical texts, does not mention the story of Eden as primal type of culpable *mimesis*, but also begins with Cain and Abel. He had however noted, following Westermann, that the story of Cain and Abel is presented in the Bible as a consequence and a reproduction, at the level of human relationships, of what had taken place between man and God, cf. *Brauchen wir einen Sündenbock* (Munich, 1978), pp. 78–81. On p. 57 one finds an excellent description in five points of the theses of Girard and of how they relate to each other.

3. Cf. J. Moingt, *op. cit.*, pp. 136–137.

4. In general, I refer to the two works of Hengel and Schürmann, cited in Chapter 1, note 9. It seems to me that these authors supply the theologian with the necessary exegetical reference not only through the quality of their documentation but also through the methodological principles which they articulate and follow.

5. Cf. e.g. A. Jaubert, *The Date of the Last Supper: the Biblical Calender and Christian Liturgy* (New York, 1965). J. Jeremias, *La Date de la Cène. Les paroles de Jésus*, French translation (Paris, 1972).

6. Cf. Hengel, *op. cit.*, pp. 168–171.

7. Allow me to remark here that I am not the first to give a *spiritual* and *sacramental* value to the cultic formulas imported from the Old Testament into the New. This has been done since the earliest ages of the Church, from the New Testament era itself; the great scholastic era, on this point as on many others, simply continued in the trajectory of the Fathers. The theology of the Mysteries of Christ, in the *Summa* of Saint Thomas, is free of all "sacrificial" stench (in the sense of Girard); very recently, B. Sesboué cited texts of Anselm which caution to greater nuance in the negative judgment habitually made on his works. I think that Father Moingt is right on target when he lays the blame on the scholasticism of the Baroque period and the unlikely theories of Eucharistic sacrifice developed in the seventeenth and eighteenth centuries. All of this does not truly form part of the tradition of the church, but rather gave rise to a certain mentality, indeed to a certain spirituality which lasted well into the 19th century and which it will still take several generations to uproot. (Moingt, *op. cit.*, p. 169 and B. Sesboué, "Esquisse critique d'une théologie de la Rédemption," in *Nouvelle Revue théologique*, 106 [1984], pp. 801–816).

8. Cf. D. Solle, *La Représentation*, French trans. (Paris, 1969), especially pp. 17ff.

EPILOGUE

THE PATERNAL INVOCATION

The name of Son

At the beginning of this second part, I showed why it was appropriate to take up the question of a *founding narrative* by way of the resurrection, since it is here that we find the conditions for a *total hearing*, receiving as we do the testimony at once of the fact and of its interpretation. I also brought out the fact that the resurrection appeared as a *total act* of God, opening up a history for all men in the footsteps of and in dependence on Jesus Christ, a history released from past sin and capable of releasing a path for the future. Finally, the resurrection revealed a fundamental *name* of God: "He who raised Jesus from the dead."

Projected onto the *death of Jesus* and onto the figures which announced it, the light received from the resurrection revealed in Jesus the *fundamental modality* and the *meaning* of *history*. It is a question of a *total pedagogy of sonship*. From the side of God, it is a question of an ever more marked *withdrawal*, of a paradoxical rupture of images, which we are mysteriously given to understand as an invitation to a *new* relationship of communion, a rupture between the one who creates and blesses in the Garden of Eden and the one who then issues a prohibition against the knowledge of good and evil, a rupture between the faithful God who rewards in the land of Hus and the same God who then shows himself indifferent if not downright cruel in turning away from the just man; a rupture, finally, between the one who sends his son as the final and definitive prophet of a kingdom of grace, and the one who then allows this son to die, a victim of his very mission, without seeming to make the slightest saving gesture on his behalf.

But if God withdraws in this way, it is to insure that humankind enters freely into the ever-expanding depths of its *relationship with him*, beyond all the gifts that he might have received, so that by persevering in invocation and in obedience, he might arrive at the pure relationship of son, within which one can finally "know" God and discover his own real self. Here is the place to complement the picture by reflecting on the *Holy Spirit* as light for discernment and strength for risk, as *love* through which the sacrifice of communion appears not only as possible, but also as desirable—a love that makes us enter with faithful endurance into God's very withdrawal.

In an effort to reach a minimal understanding of this pedagogy and to avoid experiencing it as a scandal, we must once again remark that sonship with respect to God is not a static quality of a human being, an extra endowment, on a par with numerous others even if superior to them. Sonship is rather an endless and dynamic process: it is the bringing together of the entire being into the invocation of the name "Father." It would not have been possible for God to have revealed this Name except actively, by *making* man his son and, since it is a question of a relationship which is interpersonal to the highest degree on the side of man, this installment in filial relationship could only be the work of the Spirit and of human freedom. So it is that the mysterious withdrawals of God with respect to his words of blessing were already the Revelation of the name of Father, an invitation to name him Father in virtue of a total nomination which would resume, recover and recapitulate the whole of man in the act of invocation. This is what God was anxiously awaiting when he risked speaking to man, and the response to this awaiting could only take place as symbolic behavior, sacrifice of communion, "form of death."

But now that the work of paternal solicitation and of filial response has reached its perfection in the very moment of the death of Jesus, the painful ruptures are no longer justified. Their meaning had been to send man into the orbit of sonship; once this is accomplished, everything in man can and should be recreated and transfigured. It is impossible that the one who revealed himself in his death as son in the fullest possible sense could live now otherwise than for his Father; if he recovered what he had previously left behind by way of "symbolic exchange," this can only be in order to incorporate it into this perfect and definitive invocation in a new way. But it is also impossible that the Father should not now *fully* utter to him whom he has conducted to the perfection of invocation the word which had never left his lips, even when he was allowing so much suffering: "my Son." This invocation directed to Jesus by God, the text of which was provided in advance by Psalm 2 (cf. Acts 13:33), also perseveres beyond the time of the trial. To invoke Jesus as Son is to give him, in this process of begetting, the transformed riches of creation, the glorious plenitude of the human essence finally arrived at its true stature. It is to "exalt" Christ, to "raise" him, not by a single and soon forgotten action, but by a permanent act, because it, too, is invocation. God no longer holds back anything of what his goodness as creator and his fidelity as a covenant partner had given and then withheld, in order to open the field of the filial relationship: the transformation amounts to the manifestation, in the body and in the earth, of that relationship offered from the beginning, henceforth permanently established and forever alive. On the basis of the reciprocal invocation and from within it, Jesus can be constituted Lord, can now be the New Temple and the first fruits of a transfigured cosmos. In him, all the powers of Being, now reconciled, unite to receive the Father's call and to respond to it in endless "symbolic exchange."

This is why one can say that just as the cross appeared as the space of sonship, so the resurrection reveals itself as the *field of fatherhood*, or to put it another way, if the cross is the place where the name of "Father" is revealed, the resurrection gives access to an understanding of the name of "Son," for Jesus first of all, but after him and in him, for every human being.

In order to advance a little further in our reflection on this theme of the *paternal invocation*, it is important to make a methodological observation regarding the texts of the New Testament. Through what is perhaps an error of perspective and certainly an anachronism, the attempt has sometimes been made to interpret these texts according to a chronologically and intellectually rigorous progression going from what would have been a Christology "from below"—a Christology of the "Servant" to a Christology "from above"—a Christology of "the Word with God." In reality there is no reason to believe that things happened so neatly. Even at the time when the disciples were first coming to understand, through the gift of the Spirit, how the resurrection overcame the unspeakable scandal of the cross, they were not so unequipped that they were unable to express the Messianic character and the sonship of Jesus and to render account theologically of his crucifixion. Indeed, it should not be forgotten that by their orientation, the late Jewish and rabbinic theology which guided the reading and the understanding of Scripture at the time were not unfamiliar with conceptions such as that of a heavenly Messiah, of a divine Word tending toward hypostatic existence, of a creative Wisdom of God, of a Son of Man participating in transcendence: these conceptions were there ready made to interpret the figure of the risen Jesus of Nazareth. And in return, this figure endowed them with the reality, with the flesh and blood which they still lacked.[1] The work of reinterpretation, in the New Testament, and later, seems to have consisted above all in establishing the total supremacy of Christ, thus identified with these Old Testament figures, with respect to every angelic being and to all those creatures who in any way functioned as intermediaries between earth and heaven, and to express in every possible way, the divine level of the sonship of Jesus. In fact, if we look at the first centuries of Christianity, it would seem that more time was required to arrive at an expression of the full humanity of Jesus (e.g. the Monothelite controversy was still going on at the end of the seventh century) than to recognize and confess his full divinity.

This methodological observation seems to me to liberate exegetical research so as to enable a weighing of the scriptural witnesses which would be free both from an overly simplistic evolutionary prejudice and from the opposite concern to find in every passage of Scripture an immediate support for the Council of Nicea. Perhaps one could say that on the basis of the resurrection experience and by reflecting on the death, life and words of Jesus in the light of the scriptural figures, the authors of the New Testament were impelled to *push beyond the level of metaphor* the meaning of the expressions they had at their disposal. This was done more or less rigorously depending on the individual case; perhaps certain expressions were more apt than others to engender meanings which stretched linguistic capacity to its limits. But the general aim of the reinterpretation process is to be sought on this side.

Taking into account this remark regarding method, one could propose reducing to three major categories the language types employed in the attempt to express the *paternity of God* with respect to Jesus which was manifested in the resurrection: the historical, the typological, the theological. By *historical* language should be understood that which employs the registration of enthronement/generation/nomination/mission at various levels of signification. We have here a whole messianic and royal vocabulary, which can supply a metaphorical interpretation of the resurrection such as we find in certain passages of Peter's speeches as presented by Luke in the Acts of the Apostles. Conversely, the resurrection can appear as the *live metaphor* through which the heavenly realities designated by these terms arrive at our understanding. I believe this is the meaning of the "retroactive principle," whose validity is sometimes contested, according to which the infancy narratives, for example, would have been constructed in the light of and on the model of the resurrection narratives; it is not a question of subtle logical deductions or of pure creative imaginings but rather of the principle that *what God had done for Jesus at the resurrection he had already done for him at the beginning; and what God was for Jesus after the resurrection he was for him also as it were before the beginning.* It is only through such a principle that the traditions on the infancy of Jesus, whatever exact form they may have had, can be properly illuminated and correctly explained.[2]

The second available language form was the *typological*: what is meant here are the human figures, already endowed with a certain theological perception, such as Adam, the Servant, the Son of Man, etc. Here it is a question of bringing these back to the beginning and of showing that what became evident in the Risen One existed in a certain way before all the ages: "First-born before every creature," "First-born from among the dead. . . . "[3]

Finally, I call *theological* the language which designates heavenly "hypostases," such as the Word or Wisdom: proceeding from God or created by him or even uttered by him—identified, in one way or another, with the Risen One who, once again at this level, is spoken of as having known a relationship to God in preexistence.[4]

This is not the place to develop these considerations nor to enter into the detailed exegesis of each and every one of the pertinent passages. My intention here is to bring out what is at stake in the matter: if language does not transcend metaphor, then the name "Father" is also metaphorical, *God is established as Father through the agency of human language*—which amounts to saying that he is not truly so—or again, that God sets himself up as Father *in response* to the death gesture through which a human being willed to become son. Both of these interpretations bring us back to a primacy of the production of meaning over hearing, which is what we have viewed from the start as the danger which must be avoided at all costs.

If the linguistic expressions of the New Testament that describe the origin of the Risen One did not transcend metaphor, they would fail to explain why Jesus of Nazareth gave the name of "Father" to God even before his death with great insistence. The fact is that he addressed

God in this way, not as by a name expressing a hope, which God would later acquire through an unprecedented action in favor of the one who was ready to give his all: no, he addressed him in this way as by his *proper name*. In other words, if Jesus manifested sonship in his death, it is not in order to *constitute* God as Father, in spite of everything that was happening, but rather because God *was* indeed Father and he, Jesus, Son from the very beginning. At the time of his death, Jesus lives up to the name that he bears and thus renders testimony to God the Father; at the time of the resurrection, God likewise lives up to his own name and thus renders testimony to God the Son.

If the preceding observations are correct, we are obliged to conclude that the *founding narrative* also gives us the *names* of the protagonists whom it portrays, such that the metaphorical terms refer ultimately to a proper name, truly involved and revealed in the narrative, while the proper name, thanks to the metaphors as well as the episodes of the story told, acquires a wealth of colorful dimensions which suggest its unutterable signification. In the beginning was the "symbolic exchange" of the *Father* and of the *Son* in the *Spirit*; through the *name* and the *paschal mystery* of *Jesus*, this "admirable exchange" (*O admirabile commercium!*) was offered to our earth. And each new time this earth accepts and reflects upon the name and the mystery of Jesus, it is sent back to the divine exchange which is the ultimate ground of all.

This perspective gives us an insight into what one could call the theology "games": theology sometimes takes its starting point, as I have tried to do here, from historical man longing for heteronomy, that is, in search of salvation. Sometimes its starting point is man, situated within the creation, and longing for fulfillment; sometimes, in virtue of its faith and of its tradition, it takes God himself as its starting point—God from whom it has received the trinitarian revelation. The plurality of these "games" is inevitable, and the figures they provoke are constantly being renewed: they are linked to the very economy of revelation and to the complexity of human history. The important thing here is to be careful that the figures or patterns developed within one perspective do not mix with but also do not forget those developed within another and that there always be communication of theologies just as in Christology there is communication of idioms.

* * *

This second part is entitled "Time Rediscovered in Jesus Christ." Does the material presented justify such a title? This is a question I would like to answer in conclusion.

The hearing of the community

One thing is certain: if one takes an overall view of what has been proposed here, one sees immediately how ridiculous, given the complexity of reality, would be an idea and a practice of time as pure presence to itself in the transparency of consciousness. In reality, the figure of time reveals itself only to the *hearing of a founding narrative*, and consequently by way of an abdication on the part of the consciousness with respect to any founding pretension. And the hearing itself should not be conceived abstractly as a form or a duty of this very consciousness: it presupposes necessarily a *human place* where *testimony* is borne and where it is effectively responded to. The hearing is in fact completed only by the response which seals the consent to the testimony received. This human place is a *community* where the founding testimony is heard, celebrated, responded to and where the figure of human time to be lived is defined and given direction. This figure, whatever it might be in the concrete reality of circumstances, cannot be perceived except on the basis of what I have called the *superimposition of times* to the components of which we must now return.

Figure, disfiguration, transfiguration/ Creation, withdrawal, fatherhood

The double subtitle of this section points to what is involved here, according to whether one contemplates it on the face of Jesus Christ or deduces it from the behavior of God with respect to his Christ. The testimony received and responded to in the community is in fact rendered to God and to Jesus Christ. To the temporal path followed by the latter corresponds a certain "path" of God, and this path of God accounts for that of Jesus Christ. The figure of Jesus is *concrete*: what we have here is a human being in a time and in a space to which we are naturally linked. In itself, this insertion validates our own human dimensions: if Jesus belongs to them, or belonged to them, they are not lost, or at least they are capable of being saved, and if this is the case,

God should be able to express himself or to be expressed in relation to them in some way.

Nevertheless, the mission of Jesus *displaces* him from these human coordinates and allows us to glimpse a *transfigured* dimension of existence and hence of the entire time/space complex, provided that his *word* has been acknowledged in a vital way; whether it be for Jesus, called to another mode of life, the prophetic, the messianic, or whether it be for those to whom his word is addressed, called to a new and paradoxical relationship to God, this displacement does not take place without risk. The path from figure to transfiguration is not uniform: it passes through the trial of a *disfiguration*. This term is to be understood with reference to the figure, which can no longer develop according to its time/space coordinates alone, and with reference to the awaited transfiguration, which is not the crowning point of a homogeneous development but rather the response of God to the risk run by man. Or in other terms, at the level of man the disfiguration is the name of what we could describe as *withdrawal* at the level of God. The withdrawal/disfiguration defines the space where a *symbolic exchange* becomes possible: by withdrawing, God is offering himself, by renouncing himself, man is giving himself. The adventure of Jesus finally reveals to us the ultimate sense of the entire process: that the relationship between God and his transfigured creation might be a relationship of *Father* to *Son*.

A sterile disfiguration?

The above observations show that the *created* figure of time (it should now be clear why I prefer "created" rather than "*vulgaire*" as does Derrida) is inscribed in a figure which one could call *symbolic*, which is that of a reciprocal path between God and man, of which our time/space is as it were the ground.

But in the evaluation of time, it is also necessary to reckon with the disfigurations that one could consider purely negative, and which stem from the rejection, inscribed on the humiliated Face of Christ, of the symbolic dimension, of the necessary disfiguration, of the "form of death." Christ also reveals to us that man dies of not having been willing to die. This "second" death is the turning in on self, the obsession with pure presence, self-divinization, that leads to the dissolution of human communities and to the methodical exploitation of created time/space. Both the fruit and the cause of all these things is the *forgetting* of God, to which should be attributed perhaps not only the destruction of time, but also the forgetting of *true being*. Nevertheless—and this is precisely what we call Redemption—the way of Christ transforms this negative situation itself into a possible point of departure for symbolic exchange: if it is not materially abolished, the accelerated and negative aspect of disfiguration becomes once again a path of transfiguration and of sonship. So it is that a rediscovery of time and of being, even in their created dimension, can begin to appear on the horizon. *Abandonment by* God can become *abandonment to* God.

The super-imposition of times and the trinitarian key

We can say that each moment of time results, in its inner structure, from five different levels: what we call time/space, dimensions which, in a way, are identified with us and with our world and which we take as constitutive before any free act on our part; secondly, time governed by the *history of God's words*, which creates successive "intervals" of active response through which each individual and humanity as a whole progressively take on the covenant figure; then the time of the *fall*, of human refusals in the form of opposition to the word—refusals which become inscribed in the human body and pervert the entire complex of man's relationships with God, with himself, with others (we should note however that, since the coming of Jesus, it is possible for this time to subsist as no more than a stigma of a truly bygone past); the time of *Jesus of Nazareth*, marked by the perfection of the word offered by God and of the response rendered by man: whence the *transfiguration* which gives rise to this time, for Jesus and for every human being to whom Jesus has been sent; and finally, the time of *God*, if we can use the expression, which is that of *symbolic exchange in its fullness*, consisting of the mutual relationship between the Father and the Son giving rise to the Spirit, of whom I venture to suggest that he was sent, together with the word, to prepare the transfiguration of man.

Moreover, the order here really should be reversed, but this can only be done after the entire scheme has been elaborated: in the Beginning, there is the Trinity of God in a relationality that exists only in the state of perfect gift, in a ceaseless exchange of the fullness of being; there is the time of Jesus, which is at once space/time, mission,

THE PATERNAL INVOCATION 251

word and response; there is the time of man, figure/disfiguration/transfiguration. This is what I call the "trinitarian key": the end is present in the beginning, the end being that man, even in his finitude, be transported,to the extent that this is possible for him, into the symbolic exchange that is the Blessed Trinity.

Salvation of time and truth of being

Doubtless, the reader will have noted that throughout the whole course of this second part, we have been impelled to function on at least three levels of divine nomination and three corresponding levels of the human condition. Jesus revealed to us the name of *Father*, but this name could take on its full significance only when linked to the names *God the Creator* and *God of Covenant*, which function in a reciprocal way, although not in the same direction, to help us understand the figures of Adam and of Job. In man, likewise, there is a filial dimension, a covenant dimension, a creation dimension.

Now in order for time and history, defined by the mutual interplay of these divine and human names, to become fully intelligible, is it not necessary that each of these names, even if they are destined to enter into creative communication with one another, be able to give evidence of a certain consistency? Under various influences, where we might see a convergence of a certain reading of Hegel, Saussure's principle of the difference, the structuralist principle of opposition and numerous other factors, it frequently happens, even in Catholic theology, that the primacy of the relations over the terms and the total unknowability of the terms outside of their relations is accepted absolutely. Perhaps this is true for God, or at least it is legitimate to consider God from this point of view. But strictly speaking, the assertion is true only of God; if there is anteriority of relations over terms, how are we to understand *time* and *history* precisely as *passages* and *intervals* offered to human liberty with the aim that this liberty accept a *modification of relations*? And if in reality the terms *are* only in relation, how are we to conceive of *God himself*, inasmuch as he is precisely "absolved of relation" (and did we not see that this is an absolute requirement of the principle of heteronomy, as we began to perceive it at the end of our first part?). Finally, still in this hypothetical perspective of the anteriority of relation over the terms, what would the *resurrection* itself mean? For even if, as I have said, the Risen One lives *for* the Father, he has quite definitely received from the Father a trans-*figure*-ation, both of his body and of the world, and the term "figure" does not in itself denote a relation. Now we cannot challenge the resurrection or devaluate it in any way since it stands at the heart of a *founding narrative* that, according to our working hypothesis, one must *hear* before engaging in any production of meaning whatever.

The whole approach offered in this book is that of a dynamic articulation of divine and human names, which is the key of the *salvation of time*. But, in the manner in which it has been established, this articulation requires a certain consistency of each of the moments, a value of *images* (and not only of symbols), a truth of *words*. At least in part, this remains to be said; the salvation of time goes hand in hand with the *truth of being*. This applies to the divinity of God, but also to the humanity of man, not only in order to make possible a history of salvation, but also, perhaps more fundamentally, in order to ground a *morality* which would correspond as much as possible to all the dimensions of man: if communication is the supreme rule of ethics, it is nevertheless communication of man with God, with his neighbor and with himself, and finally with the world. If neither God, nor man, nor the world can be the object of rational reflection or understanding, can we be sure of being able to establish an authentic communication?

The very movement of this book, as well as the motifs which I have just briefly enumerated, calls then for those "ancient and new revelations of Being," without which the authenticity of the entire procedure would be significantly truncated.

Notes

1. Cf. M. Hengel, *Jesus, Fils de Dieu*, French trans. (Paris, 1977). The Jewish and Rabbinic background is particularly well verified for the hymn cited from Phil 2:6–8, the study of which begins Hengel's investigations. Cf. also F. Manns, "Un hymne judéo-chrétien: Phil. 2. 6–11," in *Essais sur le judéo-christianisme* (Jerusalem, 1977), pp. 11–42.

2. Regarding this type of "historical" language (I do not press here the meaning of the term), the bibliography is immense. But the necessary material may all be found in Raymond Brown, *The Birth of the Messiah*, (Garden City, N.Y.: Doubleday, 1977), especially in the sections concerning the pre-gospel traditions of the Infancy Narratives.

3. This typological language would be rather that of Saint Paul: especially when he speaks of Christ in antithesis with Adam: I Cor 15:21–22; Rom 5:12–21, or in the hymns of the Captivity Epistles, especially Col 1:18–20.

4. I am thinking here of the prologues of the Letter to the Hebrews and of the Gospel of Saint John, but also of the Pauline texts where Christ is portrayed as Wisdom, as in I Cor 1:17—2:16 and 8:6.

PART III

Ancient and New Revelations of Being

INTRODUCTION

At the beginning of the second part of this book, I propose that the *principle of heteronomy*, called for by the investigation conducted in the first part, proves to be a principle of *analogy* and a principle of *narrativity*. These two valences are not external to each other; the implementation of the theme of narrativity calls for analogy and already gives something of a hint as to where and how this analogy would have to function. The founding narrative did not in fact turn out to be homogeneous in all of its parts, and the divine names to which it gave rise are not only not synonymous, but correspond to different levels and different valences of time for which we must make an effort to account.

For example, if one speaks of the Trinity of God in narrative terms, as is readily done today, such as by describing it as "event,"[1] one has to engage in a minimum of criticism of this theological language to avoid being duped by the apparent conceptual clarity (what exactly is an "event" after all?) or falling victim to a certain naiveté in the attribution of this new "divine name." It is on the basis of a chain of events, whose tradition faith organizes in the light of the Paschal Mystery of Jesus and in which this faith recognizes the progressive manifestation of God to human beings, that we come to recognize an internal process within God himself that we likewise designate as (the trinitarian) "event." But what are the nuances that the term should take on when we apply it successively or simultaneously: to a set of circumstances situated in time, like the accession of David to the throne or the death of Jesus of Nazareth; to others that seem to be both in time and outside of time, like the passage through the Red Sea and the resurrection of Jesus; to the action of "God" properly so-called who intervenes (how and in what different ways?) to make these events come about; and finally, to the very life of God, if it is possible to speak of the transcendent subject of the acts of salvation in and for himself?

As one reads through these questions, as inevitable as they are simple, it becomes apparent that the word "event" is an *analogical* word. The chain of events that we label the "history of salvation" is continuous in its orientation, but discontinuous in the density of each of its moments, diverse in the modalities of God's action, which give rise to divine names which are not synonymous. Even if one leaves behind these divine names as turned toward salvation, by a temporary and methodical abstraction, and endeavors to direct them toward God in himself and to employ the same "event" terminology to cover the new designations thus obtained, then "event" takes on a new value, and it should be possible to say what this value is. If when employing event terminology, we neglect to recognize the *analogy* of the term, do we not thereby create confusions which *endanger the narrative process itself*? Such is in any case the hypothesis according to which I would like to continue this work: *taking analogy into account is necessary to the truth of narration.*

Of Being in theology

From where could an objection to this hypothesis come? Perhaps from the fact that in order to clarify the analogy of event, we will find ourselves immediately sent back to the question of the analogy of *Being*. Indeed, if it is a matter of attempting to distinguish between event *levels* which, although all open to each other, do not stand in a totally homogeneous continuity with one another, it is not very clear what term could be employed to establish these distinctions, if not precisely the term Being (*être*) utilized not in a simple and univocal way, but *according to analogy*. In this way, the term *Being* could serve as a hermeneutical category to interpret the history of salvation and its unfolding, taking into account the various levels that it would have helped to distinguish and their connecting links. Nevertheless, even if this would appear to be an interesting approach, it must be acknowledged that the attempt to introduce the question of Being into theology today is a delicate, suspect, almost hopeless enterprise. Our culture, as we have seen clearly in the first part, no longer stands under the banner of metaphysics. Scientific discourse, which has an almost total hold on it and derives its justification from experimentation and from practical successes, axiomatically rules out any speculation that would overstep its proper level of discourse; the thinkers who reflect on the "death of God" in the contemporary world are eager to emphasize that this dead God is precisely that of metaphysics. If God were to "come back to life," it would certainly not be within the framework of ontology. As for the theologians, they have developed a profound mistrust of Being, to the extent that it appears as the symbol of those "compact ideas" of which I speak in the first part: Being, it is thought, is a concept that supports the systems. It generates a well-defined, all-encompassing totality, and is consequently incapable of expressing the unutterable and unpredictable otherness of God; again, it is an exclusively positive concept, that ignores ruptures and distances and is consequently incapable of remembering or supporting the scandal of the cross and the irruption of history, in themselves and for what they tell us about God. Being is also viewed as a static concept, unsuitable for explaining exchange, mutuality, and relations, which are regarded as more important in reality than the terms; it would foster a tendency to express the dynamic reality of salvation and of the Kingdom by way of fixed, speculative constructions. Moreover, these characteristics and others like them are viewed as being far from innocent in their effects. They contribute to the maintenance, whether in political society or in the Church, of a total, if not a totalitarian "order," organizing possession, knowledge and power, unaware of deficiencies, of sexuality, of death, more concerned to preserve the sterile lessons of orthodoxy than to follow Christ in promoting human and spiritual liberations. Sterile at the level of history, the thinking associated with Being, linked as it is to seeing and knowing more than to loving and to ecstatic experience, is also thought to discourage the mystical life, and by its ponderousness, to suppress the upward surge of the Spirit.

If a thinking centered on being were only what I have just briefly described, it is clear that the proper response is to drop it altogether and strive instead to repair the damages for which it has effectively proven itself liable. Nevertheless, it is possible that the description given here does not really exhaust what can be said on the subject of Being; perhaps it even misses what *truly* needs to be said on the subject. One hint of the possibility of an entirely different approach can be derived from the very problem which is ours here: I pose the question of *Being* in order to account for the *event* with greater veracity. In other words, I am inquiring whether one can speak of the *Being of the event*, as if even at the level of *history*, one has to speak of *ontological differences* (in the sense that Heidegger speaks of these). In this hypothesis, on the basis of the ontological difference of the event and of its Being, it is possible to discern and coordinate event *levels*—which would respond to the question posed at the beginning of this chapter. Naturally, the term *Being* would then no longer have the same characteristics as those given above; it would have another *meaning*.

To find this new meaning of Being, it will be useful to return to Heidegger's critique of ontotheology, to his investigation of "forgotten Being," and to his effort to reach the "unthought of metaphysics." We will find invaluable suggestions here. However, ultimately we will not find a way to analogy here—and we will have to try to see why not. And in order better to elucidate this Heideggerian way of thinking which profoundly marks recent theological style, whether or not one is aware of it, we will find it useful to study two contrasting works, very different in origin, in their concerns, their solutions, both of which reject analogy in favor either of parable and narrative, or of the most profound internal experience. We will then be in a better position to see if a way still remains open for our hypothesis.

Notes

1. Thus, J. Moltmann, *The Crucified God: the Cross of Christ as the Foundation and Criticism of Christian Theology* (New York: Harper & Row, 1974), pp. 244-247; E. Jüngel, *God as the Mystery of the World*, op. cit., infra note 13, English translation, pp. 324 and 367; B. Forte, *Trinità come Storia* (Turin, 1985), pp. 139-144 (the term employed is "storia").

CHAPTER ONE

GOD WITHOUT ANALOGY

1. Back to Heidegger[1]

If, in the present cultural situation, it is scarcely possible to raise the "question of Being" without encountering Heidegger, it is necessary nevertheless that this encounter be as complete as possible and that it take into account both sides of his thought: first of all the theme of the ontotheological constitution of metaphysics and its repudiation, and also that of the "unthought of metaphysics" with its provisional designation by way of the triad Being/Time/*Ereignis*, which is perhaps less innovative than Heidegger himself seems to believe.

The ontotheological constitution of metaphysics and its scope

It will be recalled from the first part of this work[2] that Heidegger has a certain view of history and of Western civilization (in which Christianity appears nowhere as a decisive factor): this history is that of the *forgetting of Being* (être) in favor of the being (l'étant), a forgetting which has triggered a kind of continuous decomposition or breakdown of which technological totalitarianism appears to be the ultimate stage—catastrophic in the etymological sense of the term.

The important point to retain from this theme of the history of the forgetting of Being, from Plato on down to our own day, is that the "*on*" (particular being) of ancient philosophy, Cartesian consciousness, Hegelian spirit, Nietzschean will to power and modern technology are so many *metamorphoses* of particular being which has forgotten Being. It is this one and only form of being which will go on trans*form*ing itself, holding to a fatal trajectory whose direction never changes, sustained as it is by particular being.

Throughout this history, thinkers stumbled on the question of God and conceived of him in such a way that "God" was part and parcel of the universe of being as they perceived it—hence the expression "the ontotheological constitution of metaphysics" which could also be applied to the history of the forgetting of Being as well as to each of its stages.[3] This "God" can be defined as Supreme Being (*Étant-*, not *Etre suprême*) *causa sui* and rational foundation of particular being. He is the personification of the "principle of reason"; one could say that he is worth no more than the human mind, engulfed in the universe of being, which posits his existence—that is, he is worth very little indeed. But it is important to point out that this "God" actually experiences metamorphoses which follow those of particular being. He is just as much the god of Greek philosophy, under all its forms, as that of Descartes or of Hegel, and one could without too much trouble seek to identify him with the "non-god" that is part of the language of a modern atheism linked to the self-sufficiency of technology. Theoretical concepts and practical attitudes may well come together in very diverse patterns in the course of the ages, but these will never be anything but variants of the *enduring ontotheological constitution of metaphysics*, in which the pair being/god move forward together through ever-new historical transformations.

It is important, it seems to me, to keep in mind this broad scope of the "ontotheological constitution of metaphysics" when one wishes to use it as support for the condemnation of certain themes or certain forms of Christian theology. In his essay *Identity and Difference*, it is not apropos of ancient or medieval philosophy/theology, based on Hellenistic thought, but apropos of Hegel that Heidegger makes the case against the ontotheological constitution of metaphysics and objects to the god *causa sui*: apropos then of a philosophy where the pair Being/being is treated in a dialectical manner and where the Christian figure of the *cross* is assumed into a speculative process. One cannot, for example, invoke Heidegger in the effort to challenge a theology of creation by way of promoting a theology of the *cross*. To be sure, Heidegger regards the latter with approval, but only when, with Luther, it is folly for language and transcends the securities of being, and not when, with Hegel, it belongs to the dialectic of Being and consciousness as part of a complete system: in the latter case, one remains within the forgetting of true Being and within the ontotheological constitution of metaphysics. Again, Heidegger raises serious objections regarding creation, but this is because he sees no possible way of taking up this theme while keeping Being as "question" for thought; for him, the theology of creation belongs necessarily to the forgetting of Being. But if one could demonstrate that this is not in fact so, would not his objection fall?

In other words, when one reflects on the ontotheological constitution of metaphysics, the fruit of the forgetting of Being, one must distinguish between what one could call the *model* and the *matrices*. The *model* is that faultless speculative construct, animated by the principle of reason,[4] that seeks the "compact," "full presence"; the *matrices* are the individual notions that are organized according to this model (but could actually be organized according to others' models): not only the "Being" of the Greeks but all the "values" that have subsequently been retained in the course of the history of philosophy. Thus, in the term "ontotheology," the component *onto-* would divide into various matrices. This amounts to saying that it is not sufficient, in theology properly so-called, to reject words and concepts taken from Hellenistic thought in order to escape "ontotheology": one must also, and perhaps above all, maintain reserve with respect to the speculative *model*. If one is not careful here, for example, the matrix "cross" could give way to *staurotheology*, the matrix "suffering" to *pathotheology*, and the same for "history," "love," etc. On the contrary, whatever matrix one wishes to employ, it is important, in order to escape from ontotheology, to treat it within a style of thinking which would always retain an element of spontaneity, of surprise, of sudden insight, a way of thinking whose "logic" (to the extent that this would be possible) would unfold only within the dynamic of an always *open receptivity*.

This distinction between model and matrices is obviously not a rigorous one, in the sense that any given mould or matrix could have more affinity than another with the model. However, it remains illuminating: one can strive to exit from ontotheology by repudiating model and matrices alike. This would be the most radical solution—the most difficult too, when it comes to finding an alternate solution. But it is also possible to repudiate the model alone, and to ask oneself if this or that matrix could not function in another way: this is what I suggest above when I distinguish between the theology of the cross according to Luther and the theology of the cross according to Hegel.

Toward the unthought of metaphysics

To keep oneself "in the open" is not an easy thing to do in every case and, to adhere to our proposed terminology, I would say that

Heidegger attempts to do so by repudiating model *and* matrices alike. On the one hand, he attacks the "principle of reason" as responsible for the compact structure; on the other, he awaits a manifestation of *forgotten Being* apart from and outside of all reference to any variant whatever of the matrix "being" (étant)—it is a question for him of a return to the unthought. Now in order "to think Being without regard to grounding Being in terms of beings," Heidegger turns to a very simple formula which he takes literally, so to speak: "*es gibt Sein*, there is (or better: *It gives*) Being."[5] The German idiom here is revealing, for it situates Being within a context of *gift*. What is Being? The question is not appropriate because true Being is precisely that which is not on hand,[6] within reach, but which one receives as donation by remaining attentive to precisely this modality. This attention will then perceive *time*, not at the superficial level of the past/present/future sequence, but as the milieu where *Being* arrives or rather as the force which deploys its presence, so that man can be called "the one who perceives Being by persevering in the midst of true time."[7] Meditation can open up into even broader vistas, to the mysterious point from which time and Being, which go hand in hand, spring up together. This "point" or "instance" (how are we to describe it?) where time and Being become intertwined, given that they are for one another, is called by Heidegger *Ereignis*, a term not only untranslatable but without proper contents because it names the gift only with respect to its terms, without in any way specifying *who* it is that gives.

To the false security of one who believes he possesses what he thinks, Heidegger opposes the blissful fragility of one who remains in the realm of the gift without appropriating anything to himself: without facile wordplay, one could say that the true philosopher "lives in surrender," from whence comes the economy and the tentativeness of his speculative utterances, and his careful recourse to symbols.

It is difficult, in the desperate context of our civilization which is sick with its own successes, to elude the attraction of a "thinking of Being," such as Heidegger proposes and according to which the unexpected and the novel character of Being are always preserved, a thinking based on a gift-giving which invites us always to remain open, possibly even to a manifestation of God. We have greater empathy with an attitude of this kind than for a "system of being" where everything, God included, is subjected to the empire of reason and of representation.[8]

Before yielding to this attraction, however, the Christian theologian should ask himself how far such a thinking of Being can illuminate his purpose—here, for example, how much light can it throw on the reciprocal and autonomous interplay of the *salvation events*. It is difficult at this point, not to be aware of certain weaknesses in the orientation proposed by Heidegger: the first concerns the truth of a presentation of the history of philosophy from the point of view of the forgetting of Being; the second has to do with what we could call the malediction of particular being.

Apropos of the history of Being

In fact, there is something surprising in Heidegger's way of presenting things: one gets the impression that the unfolding of cultural history was permeated with nothing but the successive vicissitudes of the systems of particular being, while only today has the dawning of the era arrived that could be called the "*kairos of the Ereignis,*" of which Heidegger himself is presumably the prophet, inviting to a conversion from rationality to expectation or awaiting. It must, however, be acknowledged that this is not really the way things happened; there has actually been a continuous opposition throughout history between the ideas of the compact and of full presence, on the one hand, and ideas of the unknowable, the search, more spiritual than intellectual, for pure Being or for unity without mixture, on the other. Alongside the tradition regarded by Heidegger as harmful, there is another tradition which has always been there, striving to compensate for the limitations of the first.

In "theology," from the beginning, the "cosmic god" has had to compete with an "unknown god"; the dilemmas of Plato's Parmenides became in Neoplatonic thinking the degrees of an adventure of unknowing of which Proclus was the most articulate and conscientious guide. Christian thinking appropriated this orientation without difficulty which, after all, was not without biblical support: with innumerable variants and continual revivals, a line can be reconstructed which would go from pseudo-Dionysius, a Christian disciple of Proclus, to Kierkegaard, passing through Scotus Erigenus, Meister Eckhart, Luther, the "abstruse" sides of the mystical doctrine of the age of Louis XIV, and perhaps also certain aspects of the thinking of Fichte and Schelling. This list is certainly not exhaustive; it suffices at least to highlight the reality (and we should add the effective influence on cultural and human reality) of a current of thinking which is certainly not ontotheological. The *Ereignis* finds its place in this lineage as a (for the time being) final and secularized variant of an insight which has offered itself from of old to human thought under the guise of terms like One, Being, Cross, Faith, etc.

It is strange that Heidegger, who was obviously familiar with the authors just mentioned and others, did not take their endeavors into account in his interpretation of the history of culture. After all, is not culture made up precisely of the constant *struggle* between two conflicting tendencies? And could one not say that the cultural and human situation in which we find ourselves today is traceable to the fact that these opposite ways of thinking have alternately claimed supremacy, with concrete effects that ultimately resemble each other very closely? Does this not place us in the dilemma of what I call in an earlier chapter the "too-short wisdom" (compact ideas and variants of a god *causa sui*) and the "too-long wisdom" (meditations on the unthought, and the unknown god)?[9] And if this is indeed the case, would not the appropriate response be to seek to escape the dilemma by restoring a balance between concept and representation on the one hand, and a sense of Being and of mystery, on the other? At the very least, this urgent "escape" could be attempted.[10]

A return toward particular being?

Another question (not unrelated to the preceding one) can be formulated, even by one who accepts the basic intuition of Heidegger and agrees to participate in the proposed course of a return to the very foundation of metaphysics, to its "unthought." The question is: what becomes of particular being if one undertakes to "think Being without particular being"[11] and if "one abandons Being as foundation of particular being in favor of the giving which plays in retreat in the liberation from retreat, that is to say, in favor of the "It gives" of "*es gibt Sein*"? One does not have the impression that Heidegger was really very concerned with this question; his approach to "Being" has something nihilistic about it. The human failure of a thinking centered on particular being in neglect of Being opens for Heidegger the "question of Being," but it apparently does so in forgetting particular being. The term and the reality of the being never return, purified and transfigured as they would be in the light of Being and the gift of the *Ereignis*. Paradoxically, however, it never seems possible to be rid of them entirely: right up into the last works of Heidegger, the being keeps turning up, like a bad penny, as that which must be left behind, so that it is at once that which is absolutely left behind and at the same time that which one never really seems totally able to shake.

This situation of the being as that which never really definitively disappears while also never really being allowed to fully return, never being accepted or welcome, is neither healthy nor satisfying. It prevents any positive description of beings, whether as subjects of Being, or as almost infinite diversity of everything which has name and reality on this earth (and not merely as poetic urging of what is to come), or as elements which undergo a transformation in the course of history. Perhaps this inability to think particular being anew, in the new light of Being and of the *Ereignis*, stems from what I called in the first part of this book the "gnostic attitude," which turns away from all finitude because it cannot get itself to distinguish between limit and evil. The truth is that one must probably accept the founding narrative and confess God the creator in order to have the wherewithal to make and to live this distinction.

The two questions thus posed mark the limits of allegiance to Heidegger in theology. From his enormous effort of reflection, we must retain the strict reserve with respect to a "thinking of the compact," one without death and without fault (while keeping in mind that the "compact" can take on numerous guises), and the rediscovery of a mysterious and ever-present giving at the heart of the universe; but the questions which remain invite us to think the one whose name is "Being" otherwise than in a never ending conflict between ontotheology and the pure "un-thought." Perhaps the solution to this dilemma (a solution which is indispensable if we want to think about God in connection with a salvation history) is an attempt at the philosophical level *to rehabilitate particular being in a qualified way*: the figures (matrices) rejected by Heidegger may be deformed and corrupt figures, but could they not recover some authenticity, which would enable a certain return of "values," of their corporeity, of their history and, consequently, a less pessimistic or less futuristic outlook than that of Heidegger? It is here that an *analogical*, not an ontotheological model would come in handy, in as much as it would allow a mutual reconciliation between Being and the being. Theologically, such a perspective would also be of great assistance to help us establish this analogy of the event which we are seeking here.

Nevertheless, before presenting an effort in this direction, it is useful to consider two theological proposals which both discard recourse to analogy, although they do so for opposite reasons: in the case of E. Jüngel, we will see an effort to bring out the history of God in itself and in the word it utters to the world; in the case of Henri Le Saux, everything is reduced to the unutterable unity of a spiritual experience, which would be shattered by any analogical word. A careful and respectful confrontation with these authors will help us to situate our own theological approach.

2. To tell God without analogy. E. Jüngel: God the Mystery of the World[12]

The problematic of Jüngel does not seem to be very far from that of Heidegger.[13] If Jüngel, in the theological wake of Bonhoeffer, qualifies the cultural moment in which we live as that of the "death of God," the interpretation of this moment appeals to an overall view of the history of culture in which we find once again the recurrent elements noted by Heidegger. This history can be accounted for on the one hand by underscoring the context of human autonomy which gives rise to the theme of the "death of God," and on the other by establishing a link between this experience of autonomy and the history of metaphysics.

A context of autonomy

The experience of modernity is that of a "human ego which is giving ever increasing weight to the world and which on the other hand is becoming more and more incapable of finding a meaning for it."[14] The reference here is to the increasingly impressive technological competence which enables humanity to pass "from the mere continuous *exploitation* of the created world to a kind of *production* of a world." Such a humanity, which is feeling its autonomy to a greater and greater extent, obviously has no place for a necessary God, foundation and guarantor of the order of the world and of the correspondence between thought and Being. Moreover, it well understands how laughable it would be to resort to a provident God, who would appear on the scene solely to ward off just in time the disastrous consequences of this production which is less and less under his control. In this sense it is not easy to imagine *where* a god might be.[15] Having been driven out, or having simply vanished from the space which was traditionally his, and hence being impossible to conceive, God is, in this sense, dead.

The death of the God of metaphysics

For Jüngel, this "death of God" is linked to a history of metaphysics whose stages are transparently those identified by Heidegger: the stage of classical metaphysics is defined by the question of *truth*, to which corresponds a necessary and absolute god, while with Descartes and thereafter, the question is that of *certitude*,[16] to which corresponds a god defined as guarantor of this certitude; like Heidegger too, and even if the authors discussed are not all the same, Jüngel shows how this god-guarantee disappears, in particular thanks to German philosophy, from Fichte to Nietzsche. We will briefly follow Jüngel in his personal reinterpretation of the Heideggerian history of metaphysics, before seeing, in a second stage of this presentation, how, within a situation evaluated in the same way, Jüngel adopts a theological attitude almost diametrically opposite to that of Heidegger.

1. The God of classical metaphysics is characterized as necessary Being,[17] in whose absence the contingent order of reality would have no raison d'être. He is absolute, and because he ceaselessly grounds the ordered multiplicity of beings, omnipresent: the categories of absence or of retreat have no meaning applied to him; if one speaks of him according to spacial metaphor, one will say that he is "above" the world and man, the global figure of reality being viewed according to the figure of the upper and the lower or the above and the below. There is no contradiction in saying that this radically necessary Being is also unknowable and inexpressible: if he is "above" or "on high," those who are "below" cannot equal him intellectually. Thus, just as truth in general takes place by way of a correspondence between signs and things (*signa* and *res*,)[18] so too God will be "signaled," but never comprehended, as long as the language capable of uttering him, classical analogy, will ceaselessly emphasize "the even greater unlikeness" within any possible likeness.

The twofold recognition of the necessity and the absolute character of God, on the one hand, and of his inexpressibility[19] and incomprehensibility on the other, entails the position, inevitable in our view, of a distinction between his existence (required by his necessity) and his essence (inaccessible to comprehension). The classical metaphysician, however, attributes this distinction to the weakness of human reason discoursing on God: what we have is a "distinction of reason," but not a real distinction in God.[20]

2. A turning point of modernity is reached when man no longer feels the need of a necessary being to ground his cosmos, but grounds himself and the world with him through the evidence of his own thinking: this is the Cartesian approach. However, God does not disappear from the figure, at least not immediately, to the extent that he is called on, if not to ground the validity, at least to guarantee the permanence of the *Cogito*, which experiences itself in a punctual manner and not in duration. God will be the more perfect Being whose superior essence guarantees the grounding effected in the *Cogito*.[21]

The point to underscore here is that this type of approach introduces a rupture between the essence of God, which is superior to that of man because it guarantees his founding experience, and his existence, whose affirmation is entirely dependent on the existence of man grounded in the *Cogito*: there is in fact no perception of existence outside of this, so that the *Cogito* takes on the charge (too heavy for it to support) of the very existence of God: it is situated "between God and God."[22] The essence of God, on the other hand, far from being incomprehensible as it was in the old metaphysics, tends to be thought of as fully penetrable by man, because it can be defined on the basis of the guarantee function which is attributed to it.

That this "theological" position is really untenable becomes clear if one studies Descartes' posterity: Jüngel wisely selects Fichte, who returns to an affirmation of the incomprehensibility of God; Feuerbach, who totally humanizes God; and Nietzsche, who forcefully and with reason, proclaims the death of God. God as guarantor of human certitude disintegrates "naturally."[23]

One could conclude these reflections by saying that contemporary atheism results from a double and irreversible failure of theism: the "necessary" Being is not really so if man is the autonomous producer of a world; as for a "divine" Being which would be no more than a guarantee of permanence for this autonomy, he has no real substance and disintegrates on his own. The effort to revive this kind of theism therefore will not overcome atheism; quite the contrary, "one can eliminate atheism only by overcoming its presupposition, modern metaphysics, and calling it radically into question."[24] This freedom respecting the procedures of metaphysics leaves open, however, the possibility of "making critical use of the metaphysical traditions."[25]

The Being of God in coming

If up to this point one has been able to discern a real affinity of thought between Jüngel and Heidegger, the same will no longer hold true when it comes to interpreting the present and the future of our modernity.[26] To put it briefly, one could say that the philosophical attitude of waiting and of patience outlined by Heidegger is replaced with *faith in the Word of God* by the theologian Jüngel. The latter is, however, presented, as with Heidegger, in opposition to the epistemologies of truth and of certitude. There is an epistemological displacement: to knowledge defined by the theme *res/signa*, where the word comes in only as external expression of an autonomous idea, he opposes the *primacy of the word*, with its relational aspect of summons, or appeal.[27] It is within the word heard and understood, within the relationship thus created between the one who speaks and the one who hears, that thought can unfold. This fact which is intended to define a general epistemology is true in a very special way with respect to God: God is "the one who speaks on his own," the one who takes the initiative of a word, and man is the one who receives this word, abandons himself to it and allows himself to be carried away to wherever it calls him.[28]

It is clear how this theme of the primacy of the word modifies the understanding of both man and God. Far from being one who grounds his own being by himself or one whose thinking is based on himself— and *a fortiori* far from being the one who bears the charge of the existence of God whose essence is to guarantee his self-grounding, man is one who abandons himself. Far from being "above," inaccessible, unknowable and unutterable, God is the One who comes, and his Being is in the coming, the One who takes place in the word here and now. This word has the particular effect of "breaking the guarantee" which Cartesian man sought in God: God no longer guarantees anything.[29] He addresses a word that requires faith, and it is in this relationship word/faith, deprived of any guarantee whatsoever, that the knowledge of God and the humanity of man are played out.

This primacy of the word which alone is compatible with the very idea of a revelation, modifies the *spacial metaphor*: if God takes the initiative in speaking to man, he is not "above," but "among, with"; it belongs to his Being to make himself one with the perishable, the ephemeral, and, ultimately, sin.[30] This is what the identification of God with Jesus crucified makes unmistakably clear. God exists (eksists) to the extent that he comes into nothingness; he is, but only in the overflowing of his Being toward that which is not, in his victory over nothingness, obtained not by a work of power over nothingness, but by a coming on his own initiative into this very nothingness.[31]

Ultimately, what is being said here in speculative terms is the very core of the Gospel, that is, the justification of sinful man through the identification of God with the crucified—an identification whose effective character Hegel brought out more than anyone else (even if it was developed as part of a comprehensive philosophical system from which one might wish to keep some distance).[32]

On this basis, one can see why the language proper to theology will be one which insists not on the ever-greater distance, but rather on the ever-greater resemblance (within a difference which no one wishes to deny). This will not be the language of analogy, but that of *parable*, which suggests similarities by way of image games.[33] This will also be the language of narrative: since the Being of God is in his coming, it is *by telling*[34] this coming that one will respond to the perennial questions who is God, and above all, where is he?

God as event of love

The preceding observations remain on a relatively formal plane; they clarify the theoretical condition of a God-language that would be relevant. In the last analysis, they create the possibility of making the concrete confession: God is love. They opened the only possible way of thinking the theological core of the Christian faith: God reveals himself in the act of identifying himself with the crucified.[35]

This identification of God with the crucified, attested by the resurrection of Jesus, is the only way we have access to a *concrete* idea about God. It gives us an insight into the Being of God as taking place, as *existing* in this coming toward "nothingness" of which the death of Jesus is the symbol in the strong sense of the term. After this, if it wishes to express God, theological language must situate itself somewhere between the categories of the "necessary" (God "above" foundation of the world) and the "arbitrary" (God as pure indetermination and inviolate darkness).[36] The notion retained will be that of *auto-determination*[37] expressed in a proposition of the type "God comes from God" and not from any necessity or anything arbitrary. Narrative theology is the account of this divine self-determination: it recounts the event of *liberty* through which God sets his own course (determines himself) at once toward himself and toward humanity. Toward himself—this is the trinitarian moment of auto-determination; toward human beings—this is the christological moment. Or again, God is he who comes (and who speaks) on his own inititiative, freely (the Father), he to whom he comes (the crucified Son), he who comes as God even into death itself (the Spirit). This divine dynamic takes place *for us*, that is to say that it is impossible to think God without an "overflowing" of his Being toward nothingness and sin.[38] But in all of this, it is the *same* self-determination, the same *liberty* which is at work; this is why the same narrative can serve for both.[39] By means of this theme of the liberty which acts in self-determination, one avoids the double reef of a god dependent on man and a god necessary to man. God is not dependent on man (nor is man the completion of God), because God freely determines himself toward man. God is not necessary to man; having freely posited created man, he awaits an equally free response. If the relation God/man is not marked by liberty, there is no such relationship. The non-necessity of God for man or of man for God does not stem from the fact that God could have "come toward himself" without coming toward man and the world or, in more classical terms, that the Trinity could be thought in itself, without it being necessary to take into account its movement toward the world: such a proposal would be "impious" to the extent that it would give God the arbitrary and self-sufficient character we denounced above.[40] The non-necessity stems from the fact that the relationship of God, both to himself and to man and the world is free. And if the word of the cross *says* this coming of God to man, one cannot claim "to 'think God' in his divine Being without 'thinking him' at the same time as crucified." Now it is indeed this word of the cross which "says" the coming of God to humanity; indeed it expresses the *excess of love*, because it tells of a God who unites himself to the perishable, a God who sacrifices himself, a God who does not hold on jealously to his relationship with himself, but rather loses himself for humankind, a God who does not wish to find his Being in anything but victory over nothingness.[41]

The essence of God: Mystery of the world

While noting the failure of theism, Jüngel had been no less insistent on its need *to think* God; the question did indeed remain that of the essence of God:[42] who is God (and where is he?) if he is neither the *ens necessarium* above us, nor the permanent guarantee of our sufficient certitude? The response lies in the dialectic between the coming of God, who has manifested himself in his identification with the crucified, revealing himself as Trinity of love, and the invisibility of this same God, God is *presence in retreat*, within the world: presence, because he comes, retreat, because he always leaves free the space for recognition.

God is Mystery, not in the sense of a plenitude at once inaccessible and omnipresent, or an insoluble puzzle. He comes to the heart of the world, acting in it, identifying himself continuously with the crucified and bringing about a history which is always open to the faith of man who lives in the world. And man perceives God as Mystery of the world and responds to this God, not when he seeks Him as the remedy for his limitations or the fulfillment of his desires, but on the contrary, when he opens himself up to a true autonomy and remains turned toward the future by stripping himself of self through an attitude of faith, charity and hope.

Is God dead? No: he is hidden at the core of the world, identifying himself with it in a "coming more than necessary" through which the nothingness of this world is surmounted and that of man the sinner justified. The loving *Word* which tells this "coming" of God grounds both theology and anthropology: love, the only movement that enables someone to address a word to another (above all if this other is steeped in nothingness), is to reveal itself as the *ultimate essence of God*, who bears this love at once toward himself and toward that which is not, a constitutive tension which appears and actually takes place in the crucified. And *man*, banishing all pride and all self-sufficiency as well as all pretension to divinization,[43] recognizes himself in the movement of faith in which he abandons himself to the *Word* of liberty which justifies him: thus, without wishing to restore a god necessary to his logic or guarantor of his self-affirmation, man rejoins the hidden God who never ceases to utter in the crucified, the ultimate Word of appeal. The dead god of metaphysics and of subjectivism does not resuscitate, but the *living God who always comes* allows himself unceasingly to be recognized by the man of faith.

For a critical reflection

With respect and honesty, Jüngel strives throughout his work to bring out the *particula veritatis* present in the points of view which he ultimately rejects. Following his example, I would like first of all to emphasize the fecundity, regarding both the knowledge of God and of man, of the *word/faith* pair and of the developments that are devoted to it, especially in terms of *love*. We have here considerably more than a "particle of truth"! The whole second part of this book is built on the theme of the anteriority of the *founding narrative*, on the opposition between *hearing* and *production of meaning*, in favor of the first (at least in an initial moment), on concrete faith in the word as *sacrifice of communion*, all of these categories enabling an *intellectus fidei* of the Paschal Mystery of Jesus and of its trinitarian basis. Therefore, it seems to me that with different terms and within the context of a different problematic, the theological concern is the same here as with Jüngel. It is not at this level that critical reflection can be brought to bear.

Criticism bears rather on the fact that, in keeping his distance respecting God as "necessary Being" and seeking to conceive him in the conceptual framework of the "more than necessary," and on the other hand in rejecting God as "guarantee of the *Cogito*" and seeking to set him beyond all guarantee, in the mutual risk of the word addressed and the faith consented to, Jüngel does not seem to have at his disposal the intellectual tools necessary to ground theologically the *distance* that he nevertheless confesses between God and the world and is absolutely required to enable the words *love* and *liberty*, that are fundamental to his working model, to have an *intelligible* sense and not just to function as opposites, posited but not truly thought, of that which one wishes to exclude. This remark applies to the numerous texts in which Jüngel employs the *same* vocabulary of decision and liberty for the coming of God toward himself and his coming to the perishable. Moreover, not only is the vocabulary identical, but the conjunction between the two moments of the coming of God is "untraceable," so that "thinking" God always implies this double and, in a sense, one only coming. Likewise, if Jüngel expresses himself in terms of "overflow," it seems that he does not conceive the Being of God without this overflow. But then the question is: does not this *decision* of double and single bearing, this simultaneously inward directed and overflowing Being, amount in terms of event and cross, to an *exact counterpart* of that which is, in terms of particular being and Being, the god *causa sui et nostri* rejected by Heidegger?

In other words, are we not precisely in what I refer to above as "staurotheology"? Ontotheology, which unfolds in the metaphysical register, attempts to find the ultimate foundation of Being in a god *causa sui*: we have here a god who, in the same movement, posits himself and the world and does not therefore show the *distance* which would enable us to recognize him as God. "Staurotheology" would be the discourse, which, unfolding in the register of narrative, seeks to recount God in his determination *at the same time* to be in himself and for us: its narrative, whatever nuances one strives to impose on it, is *fundamentally of a single block*, and from this point of view falls under the same criticisms to which ontotheology is liable.[44]

Indeed, when one speaks of the "coming of God toward himself *and* toward man," how is one to understand this *and*? And if "one cannot 'think' God in his divine being *without* thinking him at the same time as crucified," how are we to understand this *without*? One can interpret these conjunctions either as implying a distinction (even if only a "distinction of reason") between two *levels* of divine liberty, or as indicating a distinction of moments in the very existence of God. In the first case, the liberty of God coming toward himself concerns his *identity* and the liberty of God coming toward human beings, his *identification*; the elaboration of this relationship identity/identification, with all that this entails in speculative analyses, is not undertaken by Jüngel. His way of viewing the problem actually seems to be that of the second case, according to which there is no place for elaborating a distinction, because everything takes place in a single movement of existence; but in this case the *identity* of God *is* just as much his *identification*, so that one no longer sees what the conjunction *and* could mean. This effacement of *meaning* is confirmed by the fact that one can simply reverse the proposition and say: the *identification* of God with man *is* his *identity* and *vice-versa*.[45] Whatever one might intend here, does not this kind of discourse show a "monistic" tendency, that is to say, does it not treat the *matrices* "coming," "cross," etc, according to a *model* of discourse that is uniform and uniformly positivistic?[46] The fact of championing the cause of "liberty" cannot then in any way alter the reality of *narrative necessity*, which is scarcely less oppressive than *metaphysical necessity*.

To this critical remark, which is aimed more directly at the way of conceiving God, one could add a related observation which would bear on history and event. Jüngel nowhere supplies the principles which would enable us to elaborate the differences of terminology, but also of reality between the objects of the coming of God; *nothingness*, the *perishable*, *man*, the *sinner*, the *crucified*. These terms are not synonyms and the modalities which they designate are not all identical, either in themselves, or in their relationship to God and among each other.[47] That which distinguishes them from one another should have been stated and justified, and it should have been shown how their interplay (and hence their mutual distance which at the same time both remains and is surmounted) constitutes precisely event, events, history. On the basis of these analyses, painfully lacking in Jüngel, one would also have had a better basis for speaking of God himself as "coming" and as "event." In order to speak sensibly both about the "God who comes" and about man toward whom God comes and who is himself on his way to God, we would have to undertake very refined analyses which the "definition" of God as self-determining at once with respect to himself and to the perishable, as well as the absence of precision in the word game describing the human side of the coming of God do not, unfortunately, seem to allow.

We will doubtless have occasion to clarify this basic criticism a little later, when we touch on themes such as that of the "necessary God" or that of the "interruption of guarantee." But what has already been said should suffice to reveal what this chapter is about: ontotheology is in reality a *form of discourse* which can keep its basic character even when it changes "matrix": as it functions with the matrix *Being*, it can also function with the matrices *history*, *cross*, *love*. The passage to the historical realm does not suffice to avert the danger of missing (at the level of theological elaboration) the true God, that is to say a God, as we put it above, relatively "absolved" of the very thing which he created and with which he mysteriously involves himself.

3. Experience and discourse: the orientations of Henri Le Saux in "Intériorité et Révélation"[48]

Must we return to the "unthought of metaphysics," the *Ereignis* and the attitude of meditative awaiting to seek in this direction a word, reserved but true, about God and man such as faith confesses them to be?

I would like to study this question with the help of a new example. I do not know if Henri Le Saux, a Benedictine monk who became an Indian swami and undertook a search for possible points of contact between his spiritual experience in India and his Catholic faith, ever knew Heidegger. However, at the beginning of the collection of essays which forms the second and more significant part of his posthumously published book *Intériorité et Révélation*, there is a passage which I would like to cite here, which coincides with Heidegger's critique of ontotheology.

> Being is essentially PAROUSIA, with the twofold meaning of the term: presence and advent, arrival; a twofold and reciprocal meaning which the *maturing* character of the created order accentuates still more, for the creature, "germ of Being," attains its identity only in its developing process. The divine monad, the monad of Being was never anything but the invention or speculation of the philosophers who, going back from the creature to the Creator, from contingent Being to Being in itself imagined this monad on the basis of what their senses perceived and their mind conceived; whether we like it or not they were able to apply to it only the *measure*, the norm of their intellect and they had before them no other standard but their own. By the very fact that it was conceived, thought, Being had fled before them.[49]

We find here, with the approach to Being as "parousia" (which is also Heidegger's term), the observation of a "flight" of Being, chased away by the effort of metaphysical speculation, which looks identical to the "forgetting" linked to the ontotheological constitution of metaphysics. The criticism mounts in the following pages where Le Saux strongly calls into question the notion of *analogy* and *participation* which are, in fact, the pillars, logical and metaphysical, of a certain type of occidental theology.[50] What then is the basic direction of his thought and what are his own theological proposals?

A primacy of experience as awakening

The reflection of Le Saux is expressly and closely linked to the basic *experience* called in Hinduism *advaita*—an experience that is actually beyond the power of words to describe or characterize, but which is somewhat, if poorly, expressed by the term "awakening":[51] at the level of the senses and of the intellect, our life can be compared to a dream, which is neither without symbolic value (sense) nor without signification (intellect), but from which one is nevertheless expected to "wake up," precisely in order to discover in the depth of the heart what the dream was pointing to with the means that are its own: *unity, in the depths of the self, with God in his ineffable "I am."* This experience is in no way sensible, but it is for this very reason unexceptionable; it is the true *salvation*[52] for which humankind is in search, and the gift of this "awakening" (illustrated by an allusion to the Platonic myth of the cave)[53] is the "saving act." The interior man, who is born of this salvation, who wakes up to this experience of self, is at the same time in communion with God (and the theological theme of *divinization* is mentioned here) and with the universe.

This transforming awakening is "given": man does not wake up on his own, but by the sound of the clock or the light of the sun: thus the essential illumination of the *advaita* is not in logical or practical continuity with whatever might precede or prepare it, while, conversely, no word, no form, no idea can render it adequately.[54] So it is that the inevitable attempts of *objectification*, which no cultural or religious tradition can escape (not even the Hindu traditions themselves),[55] need to be continuously corrected: in fact, they almost always more or less end up placing man and God "face to face" and thus establishing a *dualism* which is absolutely inadequate to the *advaita* experience which is par excellence *non-duality*. The practices and formulations will always maintain a provisional and inadequate character; they lead to the threshold of the experience and are judged by it. One scarcely departs from the thinking of Le Saux if one says that these practices and formulas have more a pedagogical value than a truth value.[56]

Practices and formulas

The approaches according to which Le Saux strives to situate the pedagogical preparations of the experience are not systematic; various registers become mixed, without full assurance that they are mutually consistent. The presentation that follows is inadequate, but perhaps this is not so important if it is true that everything should be evaluated in function of the ineffable experience of self in God and of God in self.

A particular framework, treated in a synchronic and diachronic fashion recurs rather frequently: symbols (*archetypes*, *myths*)/concepts (*eidos*, *logos*)/spirit (*experience*, *unity*).[57] Synchronically, this enables us to define succinctly the *ways* of access to the experience: knowledge, the more logical and conceptual path, which effects a certain purification but is powerless in itself to produce the experience; devotion, at the level of symbols and of rites, but also of fidelity to laws; and finally, disinterested activity, that is to say the service of neighbor. These *ways*[58] have this in common that they turn man outward and/or inward (it all depends on what level of man is under consideration), and conduct him to the threshold of an experience which they can at most signal, but not produce. The *guru* is there to direct man according to these various ways; he steps back into the shadow as soon as there is no more "way" to go and man has finally awakened in his heart to the "One who has no second."

Diachronically, this framework defines a kind of trilogy of ages of the world: a *mythical* age, dominated by archetypes and symbols, a *logical* age, pregnant with concepts and syllogisms, and finally, an age which one could call *spiritual*, where the fundamental experience itself would reside. If symbols and rational discourse are still needed at this moment, these would proceed, we know not how, from the primordial experience of unity.[59]

Concretely, the mythical age or stage is represented by the *primitive religions*, which, perhaps without being aware of it, tend toward the central experience through their symbols, their rites and their laws; then come the great *monotheistic religions*, Judaism, Christianity, Islam, whose sense of God was awakened by prophets who were careful to combat the danger of idolatry, always present in cultic ritual, and to decipher the profound signification of the symbols; historically, this stage or this age corresponds to that of the Greco-Roman expansion and to its continuing influence on subsequent history; the time of the *Spirit* and perhaps of the spiritual religions would now be approaching, paradoxically prepared by two contrary emerging factors; that of the *purity of the experience of the self in unity*, as found in the purest elements supplied by far-Eastern spiritualities, and that of *humanism*, whose attachment to temporal values and religious skepticism witness in their own way to the beyond of an experience which the most correct expressions of symbol and of logos are unable to express.[60]

Of Christ and the Trinity

To situate Christianity and to confess oneself a Christian in this perspective of the fundamental spiritual experience to which all religion and all spirituality tend, one must begin neither with words, nor with dogmas, nor with *theologoumena*, but with the *perfection of the spiritual experience of Jesus*.[61] Of him, indeed, one can say that he had in perfection, without preliminary purification or preparation, the experience of the *advaita*, so that he is the model of this kind of experience: all human interiorization is patterned after Jesus'. Conversely, one can say that the closer a human being comes to the experience of the *advaita*, the better able he is to comprehend the mystery of Jesus. And it is on the basis of this identification or participation in the experience of Jesus that the *words* which have traditionally expressed his Mystery can be understood. Le Saux is very attentive here to the plurality of languages: in the Judeo-Christian milieu, the experience of Jesus communicated through the apostolic preaching was expressed by way of the *names* given to Christ within the framework of the history and the expectation of Israel—thus "Son of man" or "Messiah"; from the time of the New Testament, the encounter with Hellenism gave rise to the use of *names* more closely linked to Greek culture, such as "Logos" and "Kyrios". One should not attach exclusive value to these names and to the distinct modes of language or expression that they tended to generate, and one should not become overly wedded to them as though other names and other propositions could not legitimately be introduced.[62] Hinduism could, in its turn, enable a reinterpretation of the experience of Jesus, but only on condition that one's point of reference is indeed this experience itself, and that one is not content to find Hindu equivalents, on the level of categories, to the Greek or Jewish terms.[63] Any renewal can come about only by reference to the experience of Jesus and to that which, under its guidance, we have or hope to have ourselves.[64]

The *theologoumena*, indeed the "dogmas" of the Christian faith must also be understood in the line of this experience. For example, we cannot confess and express the *resurrection* of Jesus if we separate it from the experience of life that it signifies for us. It is this experience, already inchoatively present in the core of our consciousness, that enables us to perceive the meaning of the resurrection archetype that expresses its perfection and fullness.[65] Here as elsewhere, the formulas should help us to "cross over to the other shore of the heart,"[66] that of spiritual experience, in the absence of which formulas would obstruct precisely what they should serve. In a discrete and interrogative eschatological allusion, reminiscent of a line of reflection marked by Origen and Evagrius Ponticus, Le Saux asks what might be the significance of the returning of the Kingdom by Christ to his Father at the end time: at this moment, God will be All in all, the experience of unity will have attained its perfection for all. In what sense could one continue to speak of the mediation of Christ? Le Saux leaves the question open, but at least it is clear why he raises it.[67]

On the subject of the Holy Trinity, the orientation of the author's reflection is the same: before "thinking" it with words, one must grasp its reality and grasp our own reality in it, already in our inchoative experience of God, then in the experience of Jesus which the apostolic preaching transmits to us. The most abstract terms, which are the least capable of signifying, as Augustine and Gregory of Nyssa remark regarding Greek terms necessitated by dogmatic exposition, are not the place where we should stop. It is important that we hold as closely as possible to the biblical revelation, where the term God (*ho theos*) designates the Father (in whom the fullness of the divinity is found), God in himself, while the same term *God* (*theos*—without the article), which qualifies the Son and the Spirit, refers rather to God in his twofold manifestation, in the complementary fields of *Logos* and *Pneuma*. There is a sense in which we attribute to God the characteristics of the unifying experience which we have of Him, so that, at a certain eschatological level, one could raise the question of the possibility of a pure experience of God, the Father-in-himself, *ho Theos*, pure Deity, beyond the mediations of Word and Spirit. This interrogation is not a "doubt" nor an intellectual problem; it is rather the work of an awakened attention that leaves open the field whose infinite horizon will not be discovered until Hindu spirituality shall have borne its final fruits of spiritual experience.[68]

From his birth, man is endowed with a kind of spiritual intuition of self, at the level of the greatest interior depth, where he is in unity with

God and with the universe. But real as it may be, this intuition is hidden in the consciousness and must be awakened: one could say that everything that has value in life is linked to a capacity of awakening and should be taken, not in itself, but within the dynamic of awakening. The language types (myths, symbols, concepts, etc.), the ways of purification (cultic practices, laws, service, etc.), the stages of civilization and doctrinal formulations, all take on meaning in the light of the *awakening* which brings the primitive intuition to its perfection of total experience—the latter defying all nomination, except perhaps the "I am" where the religious traditions, especially the biblical traditions and Hinduism, meet again at their common core. The *guru* is the indispensable guide who, having had the experience of the *advaita*, is capable of awakening and conducting his disciple to it. In virtue of the immediacy and the perfection of his experience, Jesus is the Incarnation of the "I am," and it is at this profound level that he is reached by faith which, unfolding within the *yoga* of love, is set on its way toward the experience. It is on the basis of this dynamic, at once spiritual and cosmic, that one must understand and interpret the words and the forms (*namarupa*) of doctrine. These latter find their true meaning in the very act of going beyond them, until the moment when GOD (the pure deity of the One whom we call Father, in a "limit" designation which cannot be directly thought but which reveals itself to the heart) will be "all in all."

For a critical reflection

Naturally, it is not a question here of contesting the authenticity of the spiritual experience of Henri Le Saux, nor the note of *absolute simplicity* of this experience, which consists of such a full entrance into the "I am" of God that it becomes very difficult to feel or to express a *distance* between God and self. We have enough witnesses of this type of experience in the history of Christian mysticism, and in this respect we have here more a matter for thanksgiving and for marvel than for theological criticism.

The problem comes from the fact that the experience to which Le Saux witnesses, true of similar experiences in other religions, was *prepared* by *ways* which are not only those of asceticism but also of teaching, and these have also been followed by *expression*. Even if one were to maintain absolute silence in the meditation that surrounds and follows the experience, it is nevertheless impossible not to interpret it, even for oneself and for the exclusive purpose of remaining faithful to it, with the help of *terms* which the *guru*, himself nourished by a tradition of words, employed when striving to awaken his disciple. The fact is that there is no total solution of continuity between the terms and the experience. Even if the terms appear inadequate, they are nevertheless there, chosen with care; whether one takes them in a symbolic or in a speculative key, they orientate the disciple in a certain interior direction, so that when the experience takes place, it will be received and then interpreted in the line traced out not only by the ascetical practices recommended, *but by the terms employed*. Thus, the outcome of a spiritual path guided into an unutterable experience with the "One which has no second" will not be lived in the same manner, will probably not even be the same as a path marked out with the help of a mystical tradition stemming from the Song of Songs, formulated in Bridegroom terminology focused on the Word, indeed on the Word incarnate.[69] There is, therefore, a *theoretical problem of the relation between the terms and the experience*, a problem that one can raise in both directions: to what extent are the terms suitable for expressing the experience? To what extent does the experience itself engender terms to express it?

Now Le Saux does not really deal with this problem. He knows of course that the fundamental experience is expressed with words; he insists, as I put it above, on the plurality of the cultural keys employed, and in particular on the possibilities that will be opened up thanks to the encounter between the profound thinking of India and Christianity. Nevertheless, his assertion, constantly repeated without ever being *philosophically qualified*, bears on the absolute inadequacy of terms to the experience, in virtue of the latter's pure simplicity. This affirmation thus causes him to keep going back beyond linguistic expression to rediscover the experience in its native spontaneity or to hope for a new and better efflorescence of language, which amounts to the same thing.[70] Now it must be emphasized here that such an affirmation does not, in spite of appearances, convey *evidence* but rather represents a *theoretical stance* external to the experience itself and linked to an interpretive tradition of the "apophatic" type which can legitimately be subjected to discussion, because it is not the only possible option with regard to the relationship of experience to its linguistic expression.

Such a tradition offers the advantage of bringing out strongly the transcendence of the spiritual experience over the human word and of God over what we can say about him; in this sense, it constitutes an invaluable antidote to theological rationalism, wherever this is found. Its weakness lies in the fact that it is incapable of justifying the terms that it nevertheless employs; it devaluates and finally destroys them somewhat in the way one might throw down a ladder once one has reached the platform.

As I recall at the beginning of this chapter, regarding the *Ereignis*, Christian mystical theology contains a very strong current that very much resembles this tradition. Le Saux does not fail to allude to this current where the NeoPlatonic influence is fundamental.[71] The other side of the coin is the dilemma with which every apophatic tradition must deal: if the "divine names" do not *truly* express God, either the Gospel revelation is provisional, together with that to which it gives expression (such that trinitarian theology and Christology will be abolished in the eschaton), or they are not, but it is then extremely difficult to coordinate the mystical non-language, the language of the *itinerarium mentis* and that of the christological and trinitarian foundation both of the experience and of the journey.[72] The Christian authors which belong to this apophatic tradition have always been forced, with more or less success, to avoid these snags: the task was imperative if one wished to avoid divorcing the theologal experience from the history of salvation and from a human ethics.

Whatever his hesitations and his backtracking, the full importance of which I remarked at the beginning, Le Saux seems to be taking a direction toward an eschatological effacement of everything which could resemble any form of duality, distinction or distance. He posits from the start the *essential non-alterity*[73] of God with respect to man and to the cosmos, to which corresponds the non-alterity of *human beings with respect to each other*, if one grasps the evangelical *koinonia*[74] at its true level. *Salvation* is the awakening to this Presence which is not alterity; *creation* is "ordered to the awakening of the human heart to God and to itself,"[75] an awakening not to be understood, for example, as "indwelling of the Trinity in the soul,"[76] a formulation which allows a dualism to persist, but as a reawakening of the self in God. The *Incarnation* is the perfect and immediate awakening of Christ to the "inner mystery, which is without external and internal" and, as I suggested above, one can say the same for the *redemption* and the *resurrection*. Le Saux insists less on the actual reality in Christ of everything each of these words designates, than on the essential experience which, *symbolically*, they suggest and, in their place, arouse. At the very least, the experience of Christ can take place without the confession of these symbols. Conversely, precisely because it is a question of archetypes, indeed of conceptual organizations which evoke a unified and total experience, it makes no sense to speak of Christ without reference to the human beings whom he awakens, of the Trinity "in itself," independently of us or again of God outside of the creation: *the experience of awakening shows us that, at the essential level, outside and inside have no meaning*. Thus, according to a paradoxical but comprehensible logic, the archetypes, the *theologoumena* and that which they superficially distinguish, can disappear, while there is no sense in thinking the divine "I am" which they designate apart from and outside of them.

Can we legitimately conclude that E. Jüngel on the one hand, and Henri Le Saux on the other offer us as it were two extreme positions of the theological *spectrum*? With Jüngel, the *ek-sistence of God* is like the unfurling of a liberty which gushes forth from the paternal spring and expands to the ultimate limit of nothingness, man abandoning himself to this liberty when it reaches him in the word and *recounting* its marvels in faith. Analogy, to the extent that it emphasizes an "ever greater distance"[77] between God and man, thus accentuating at the extreme limit the spacial scheme above/below, breaks the movement of Love and the address of the Word, while it scarcely provokes, on man's side, that abandonment which we call faith; it follows that it has no place in Christian theology. With Le Saux, the divine "I am" mysteriously invests everything that is "creation" without really being alterity, until the "awakening" to this "I am," of which Christ can be viewed as the supreme paradigm, brings everything back to God. Human words, even those that are most true, have only precursory or initiating value. Their content matters less than their paradigmatic value; so, to the extent that it would speculatively institutionalize a "distance" between God and man, analogy would be an obstacle on the path of unity with God which man is travelling. And this is indeed why it can have no place.

Thus in both cases, analogy is rejected in theology, but for opposite reasons: in the case of Le Saux, it is a concrete obstacle on the spiritual path through which *man is entering into God*; in the case of

Jüngel, it would prevent us from telling of the *God who comes towards man*. It would perhaps be an oversimplification to say that these reasons reinforce one another in view of a resolute rejection of analogy, or conversely, that they cancel each other out and therefore leave the path open to this same analogy. I simply note here that, with these two theologians, the distinction between God and the world, between the Trinity and history, is difficult to *say*, the "reason" for history difficult to explain, the impact of "sin" difficult to determine:[78] it is because of these uncertainties that I believe it is possible to review the whole question of analogy.

Notes

1. It is not possible here to treat the important question of "Heidegger and theology" in depth. For a general treatment, I refer the reader to a collective work *Heidegger et la question de Dieu* (Paris, 1980), to my own study "Écouter Heidegger en théologien" in *Rev. Sc. phil. theol.* 67 (1983) pp. 371-398, and to the article devoted to Heidegger by P. Coda in a series of works on "Jesus Crucified and the Trinity": "Dono e abbandono: sulle tracce dell'essere heideggeriano," in *Nuova Umanità*, nn. 34-35 (1984), pp. 17-57 (with an abundant bibliography).

2. *Supra*, part I, chapter 3, part. 1.

3. One could refer here to *Identity and Difference*, (New York, 1969), pp. 55-76. I refer to this text because it is often cited. Actually it is a difficult passage, and I have not found a satisfactory commentary on it. I attempted an interpretation in "Écouter Heidegger . . . ," *art. cit.*, p. 376ff. See also in D. Janicaud and J.-F. Mattei, *La Métaphysique à la limite*, (Paris, 1983), pp. 28-32 (Janicaud) and 74-76 (Mattei).

4. Besides the references given in Part I to the texts of Heidegger on the "principle of reason," see also the discussion of Jüngel, *God as the Mystery of the World*, p. 29ff and that of E. Gilson, in *Constantes philosophiques de l'être* (Paris, 1983), pp. 74ff. All these authors agree in questioning the validity of this principle which was strongly affirmed, if not introduced, by Leibniz.

5. The theme "es gibt" is already present in *Sein und Zeit* (1927) in particular in section 44 where it is essentially a question of *truth*, but I would refer most especially here to the last conference, "Zeit und Sein," in *Zur Sache des Denkens* (Tübingen, 1976), published in English as a book: *On Time and Being*, trans. Joan Stambaugh (New York: Harper & Row, 1972).

6. *Vorhanden*. On this term and its importance in Heidegger, particularly in his confrontation with Greek thought, cf. Rémi Brague, "La

phénoménologie comme voie d'accès au monde grec," in *Phénoménologie et Métaphysique* (Paris, 1984), pp. 247-273.

7. *On Time and Being*, p. 23.

8. If the origin of the category of *gift* in Heidegger is more Christian than it seems at a simple reading of the texts, the way in which it is developed philosophically can in turn spark theological reflection in a very vivid manner. The theologian of the *Gift* of God, revealed in the Paschal mystery of Jesus Christ, would do well, for his faith understanding, to keep in mind the way of "donation" to which Heidegger has been able to lead him. The dialectic of appropriation and disappropriation (*Ereignis/Enteignis*), which appears as one of the last words of the philosopher, can be regarded by the theologian as an opening toward the understanding of the Gift which was at the beginning and which reveals itself without dissolving itself in the cross and the resurrection of Jesus Christ. Sometimes one asks oneself what Augustine, who was always so eager to experiment with the trinitarian significance of available triads in his cultural environment, would have done with this one: *Ereignis/Time/Being*. These remarks and others like them which could be made may help to explain why theologians are so favorable to Heidegger. Cf. in particular on the *Ereignis* and *Gelassenheit* the observations of P. Coda, *art. cit.*, pp. 29-46. One should not however lose sight of two things: the non-theological character of the thinking of Heidegger in itself, which comes out especially in the finitude of the *Ereignis* (well restated by J. Greisch in his remarkable study "La contrée de la sérénité et l'horizon de l'espérance" in *Heidegger et la question de Dieu, op. cit.*, p. 168-193) and on the other hand, as I will soon bring out, the failure of Heidegger with regard to an idea of *Being*, in the proper sense of the term, which could somehow be serviceable for theology.

9. Cf. Part II, chapter 3, n. 1.

10. Perhaps the entire history of philosophy should be viewed as a history of the variations on these two "enemy" tendencies, as well as of a possible mediating tendency, and of their presuppositions. And if this is the case, it would be impossible to escape the primacy of Plato and of the first positions taken with respect to Plato, by Aristotle and in Hellenistic philosophy. Drawing on Pierre Aubenque, "Plotin et le dépassement de l'ontologie grecque classique," in *Le Néoplatonisme* (Paris, 1971), pp. 101-108, I briefly analyzed these models, such as they appear in Greek thought ("Le 'Parménide' de Platon et saint Thomas d'Aquin" in *Analogie et dialectique* (Geneva, 1982), pp. 57-62). The opposition between the "cosmic God" and the "unknown God" on which A. J. Festugière constructed his great work *La Révélation d'Hermès Trismégiste* (Paris, 1942-1949), is instructive here. The knowable cosmic God, "father" of this world, belongs perhaps to what Heidegger calls ontotheology, while the supercosmic God, beyond all being

and all knowledge, would belong to what one could call "meontology" (a favorite term of Stanislas Breton); between the two, however, would there not be room for a God at once beyond the world and capable nevertheless of being reached, even by the mind, in that "mediating" perspective which one could call "metaphysical"? I do not think, in any case, that Heidegger himself escapes this framework: if he rejects ontotheology, his "manner" of inviting us to remain in the unthought of (ontotheogical) metaphysics amounts to "meontology," a fact that can be verified, for example, by analyzing the neo-Platonic turn of the final triad he left us: Being/time/Ereignis. The profound relationship between the quest of Heidegger and some aspects of the thinking of Plato is forcefully brought out by the studies of J. F. Mattei, *L'Étranger et le Simulacre* (Paris, 1983), and above all "Le chiasme heideggérien" in *La Métaphysique à la limite, op. cit.*, pp. 49-162. New as they may be in the cultural moment in which they were formulated, the suggestions of Heidegger could not have gone completely beyond the major moments of Greek philosophy: who, after all, has ever been able to do so?

11. *On Time and Being*, p. 2.

12. *Gott als Geheimnis der Welt* (Tübingen, 1977). The references here will be to the English translation: *God as the Mystery of the World: On the Foundation of the Theology of the Crucified One in the Dispute between Theism and Atheism*, trans. Darrel L. Guder (Grand Rapids, Mich.: Eerdmans, 1983). Because I introduce the examination of this book in the context of a discussion on the *different types* of ontotheology, I run the risk of not doing full justice to the many profound and penetrating insights which the book contains. I hope to have escaped this pitfall by being as honest as possible in the presentation of this work that is written with a modesty that equals its mastery of the material. In my defense, I believe that certain of the book's options, both as to methodology and as to substance, justify my bringing it in for discussion at precisely this point.

13. "The reader will observe that the line of my argument is rather close to the thinking of Martin Heidegger" (from the "Préface à l'édition française," *Dieu Mystère du monde* [Paris 1983], I, p. X).

14. P. 52. Cf. Introduction, p. 14f. The autonomy of man is likewise what is at issue in the section on Bonhoeffer, pp. 57ff.

15. Cf. Chapter II, Section 6: "Where is God?" This spacial metaphor recurs constantly in this book. Cf. the subject index: GOD—Over us, me (*supra nos*).

16. Pp. 112-113.

17. On the *necessary* God, cf. the presentation of the Introduction, Section 2 (p. 14) and the subject index: GOD—*ens necessarium*, Necessity of God and Worldly Nonnecessity of God. Cf. *infra*, note 85.

18. See p. 3ff.

19. On the ineffability of God, cf. chapter IV, p. 232, Section 15: "The Classical Thesis 'The Deity, therefore, is Ineffable and Incomprehensible' "; the presentation and rejection of analogy in Section 17 in the same chapter: "The Problem of Analogous Talk about God" (p. 261).

20. See pp. 122-126.

21. On the theodicy of Descartes, cf. pp. 132-141.

22. See pp. 123-4 and 150.

23. "We could emphasize that, in this process of *guaranteeing the ego cogito* ('I think; therefore I am') *through the being of God*, which is fundamental for the modern age, we recognize the precondition for the possibility of a completely new and quite radical disputation of the necessity of God for man. This proof of the necessity of God is the midwife of modern atheism" (p. 19). On the ensuing "disintegration," cf. chap. III, Section 9b (p. 122): "The Securing of God as the Disintegration of the Certainty of God."

24. P. 43.

25. Pp. 48-9.

26. It is the *Hegelian* influence which is to come in here. Cf. Chapter II, Section 7b: "Hegel's Mediation between the Atheistic Modern Feeling and the Christian Truth of the Death of God" (pp. 63-100). See the general evaluation given on p. 94: "Regardless of any theological criticism which must be rendered, we are dealing here with a grand theological accomplishment, namely, a philosophically conceived theology of the Crucified One *as* the doctrine of the Triune God." This critical recourse to Hegel is fully justified, since, in Christian theology, we cannot be content with apophatic procedures or attitudes: if God communicates himself, one should be able to *think* him. From this point of view, Jüngel is reserved in his attitude to the theme of a *Deus absconditus*, even if he does find it in Luther (cf. among other places, pp. 344-345). This reserve would not have much sense with Heidegger, for whom "Christianity" and the "cross" are, as I have tried to show in "Écouter Heidegger . . . ," *art. cit.*, pp. 372-374, close to the "unthought."

27. Pp. 11-13 and the very important Section 11 of Chapter III: "The Word as the Place of the Conceivability of God" (pp. 152ff.).

28. "If man is the being who is addressed by God, and thus can be addressed about God and therefore ontologically constituted by language, then the presumption that one should become involved with the word of God is a presumption which accords with the very nature of man" (p. 162); "to be human means to be able to depend, to trust" (p. 179); which, however, does not take place without self-denial, indeed, without "annihilation" (cf. p. 175).

29. Cf. chapter III, 12: "The Certainty of Faith as the Deprivation of Security." There is a paradox here: the pair Word of God/faith deprives man of the security he looked for in God for his *ego cogito*, but this faith

establishes the truth of man in a relationship of commitment with respect to God who also goes out of himself in the word. One is in a different theological world.

30. Cf. chapter III, 13: "God's Unity with Perishability as the Basis for Thinking God."

31. Thus, in contrast both to the existence of necessary being not really distinct from his essence and to the existence of the being which guarantees, demanded by the *Cogito*, the existence of God who speaks is the movement by which he conquers nothingness by coming to it; cf. 223. This existence is "overflow" (*ibid.* and p. 369), which one may compare with the theme frequently evoked by Jüngel of God "more than necessary."

32. Cf. *supra* note 26.

33. Cf. chapter IV, 18: "The Gospel as Analogous Talk about God."

34. Cf. chapter V, 19: "The Humanity of God as a Story to be Told; Hermeneutical Preface."

35. "God has defined his deity in that event which we have understood as God's identification with the dead Jesus. . . . Thus, the actual meaning of theological talk about the death of God is revealed as the most original self-determination of God for *love*, whereby this self-determination of God itself already belongs to love. God defined himself as love on the cross of Jesus. God *is* love" (pp. 219-220). Cf. the numerous texts which say the same thing, Index of Subjects: Identification—of God with Jesus (the Crucified One).

36. Pp. 35-36.

37. Words like *self-determination*, *liberty*, *decision* are used continuously by Jüngel. For example: "God is an event which *determines* itself. God determines himself. In this twofold sense, God is the event of self-determination, God is self-determination taking place. The theological category for this ontological matter is called *freedom*," (p. 36); "On the divine way of life, God makes himself into that which he is. The formulation of this content is this: God's being is in coming . . . " (p. 159).

38. I am summarizing here what is "recounted," from various points of view, in Sections 23-25 of chapter V (p. 368ff.).

39. A few formulations, among many others: "God's coming to himself must be understood as an act of freedom, in which God gives himself a future in such a way that he disposes over his future and thus over himself. That God does not desire to come to himself without man is to be understood in such a way that God has definitively decided about his future" (p. 38); "God's being must be thought as a being which allows that it be participated in, that is, a being which turns *outward* what it is *inwardly*" (p. 176); "The being of God so understood is then already comprehended out of its unity with perishability" (p. 209). "God has defined his deity in that event which we have understood as God's identification with the dead Jesus . . . " (p. 219).

Conversely; "the history of European Christianity . . . has considered itself capable of thinking of God in his being as God without thinking of him simultaneously as the Crucified" (p. 39), etc.

40. Cf. p. 37, the important note 6 to which I will return below.

41. On God's unity with perishability, and on the victory over nothingness, cf. chapter III, section 13. On the opposition relation to self versus loss of self and on God who *is* sacrifice, cf. p. 369.

42. Cf. chapter II, 7, c: "The Significance of Talk about the Death of God: The Problem of the Essence of God," p. 100ff.

43. Jüngel is strongly opposed to the theme of divinization. Cf. pp. 95, 97, 190. One might question however whether it is not a matter of terminology, because when writing on the subject of eschatological hope, he speaks of the "*transformation* of that earthly existence," of a "life in unsurpassable fellowship with God" (p. 394-395).

44. Is not *self-determination*, as decision and liberty, precisely the same thing as *causa sui*? And do we not have an effacement of distance precisely in the fact that this self-determination is oriented toward the coming of God both toward himself and toward us? I do not think that the fact that the *causa* is here called "love" changes anything at all as to the ontotheological *form* of the discourse.

45. We find here what I think is the weakness of the famous axiom of Karl Rahner on the *mutual* identity of the immanent Trinity and the economic Trinity. I am unable to withdraw the criticism I made of this mutuality, in the direction of immanence to economy, in my book *Peut-on connaître Dieu en Jésus Christ?* Cogitatio Fidei 44 (Paris, 1970), pp. 213-225, and which would apply to Jüngel's resumption of the axiom, here pp. 369-370. Would not the transcendental theology of Rahner likewise fall into the category of the theologies of the ontotheological model?

46. It should be quite evident that I am here somewhat critical of the *theology* of Jüngel, though not of his *faith confession*, in particular as to the distinction between the generation of the Son and the *creation* of the world (cf. pp. 384-5). Nevertheless, the attempts made at the end of the book (pp. 380-389) to clarify this distinction, besides being rather difficult to follow, do not appear to me to be fully coherent with the central theme of the book on self-determination toward the self *and* toward the perishable.

47. "Nothing" and "the perishable" are not terms formally identical with "sinner" and "crucified." The note on sin (p. 225, note 73), though relatively lengthy, is inadequate given the scope of this book.

48. Henri Le Saux, O.S.B. (Swami Abhishiktananda), *Intériorité et Révélation: Essais théologiques* (Sisteron, 1982). The work is preceded by a very important introduction of P. J. Dupuis, S.J. I will limit myself here to a critical presentation of the second part, which contains certain late writings of the

author—fragmentary studies, sometimes incomplete, in need of very delicate evaluation if one looks at them from the point of view of traditional dogmatics. Since I am here trying to grasp some of the main lines of his thinking and to present them in a coherent manner, I could incur the reproach of "hardening" what was only preliminary research, investigation, overture. But, on the other side, it must be recognized that Le Saux was dramatically aware of the problems raised by the existential confrontation of his interior experience and his Christian faith. I do not think that he would ever have arrived at a "harmonious synthesis," which he well knew was impossible, at least at the level of speech. It is not being unjust or insensitive in his regard to bring to light the elements in his writings which stand in conflict. This approach, limited as it is by the very problematic of the present book, leaves open, however, the possibility of other comparisons, in particular at the level of the meeting and the mutual inspiration of monastic experiences, but also with other currents of Christian thought, which would perhaps be more congenial to a project like that of Le Saux than that which I am here attempting to define.

49. Pp. 139-140. Cf. also the following passage, which reminds one of Heidegger's critique of God *causa sui*: "The existence of creatures—of that than which God is other—is a mystery which no philosophy has ever been able to penetrate. Or else, one settles for a *super-man* god to explain the world, for a god who possesses in an eminent way all the powers and the perfections which man can discover, or even deduce in himself and in nature: this god by this very fact is in the image and measure of man. This conception of God which man makes for himself was found ultimately empty of God. Empty of the very thing which makes God God—and man did not find God" (p. 148).

50. P. 141. The grievance against analogy is that it leads to viewing God on one side and the creature on the other; in other words, it allows duality in principle, which is contrary to the essence of the experience of the *advaita*, which is that of "the One which has no second."

51. The image of *awakening* is employed throughout the work. It is however most especially developed in the essays "Appels à l'intériorité." pp. 153-175 and "Expérience spirituelle (*anubhava*) et dogmes," pp. 209-216.

52. Pp. 212-213, e.g.: "The saving act is necessarily beyond any particular form. What I call the saving act is the act by which man arrives at his full stature, or rather at his center." See also on pp. 275-280 the discussion on the *theologoumenon* of the Redemption, e.g.: "Nevertheless, the fundamental process of salvation or of conversion takes place at the level of the human heart, that is to say at the deepest center of the being which we reach—both in ourselves and in others—only at the most profound level of self in the revelation of the Self, of the *atman*. And here it is absolutely impossible to view God as a partner, and still less, to view oneself as a partner of God."

53. Allusion to the myth of the cave, p. 211.

54. Pp. 163-164 and 212.

55. On the inadequacy of the Indian speculations themselves, see pp. 164, 169 (with the important note 33 on the inadequacy of language to the experience), 218, etc. Even the "*advaita* formulas" are not *advaita*!

56. "All of this is merely a stepping-stone . . . " (p. 169).

57. Cf. especially the three first sections of the study "Archétypes religieux, expérience du soi et théologie chrétienne", pp. 178-183. See also pp. 213: "For a way of thinking which has gone beyond the mythical stage and which moreover has reached the stage of self-criticism with respect to the very notion of concept and to the process of reasoning, it is clear. . . . "

58. On these *ways*, which *are not* the experience itself, cf. pp. 169-170 and 288-289. On the *guru*, pp. 171-172, 240-241, etc.

59. On these three stages, cf. the last paragraph of the study cited in note 58: "IX. Mythe, Logos, Esprit," pp. 203-207.

60. Cf. the references given in the preceding notes and in the study "Révélation cosmique et révélation chrétienne," section II, "La convergence chrétienne," pp. 260-263. The three great monotheistic religions and the far-Eastern religions (which I call here "spiritual" but which it would be better to call with Le Saux "cosmic") constitute the "two opposite poles in which the interior experience has expressed itself: 1. the Abrahamic pole and its three descendants; 2. the Vedantic pole with its complement in Buddhism" (p. 302). And the author adds: "One then becomes aware of the essentially *namarupa* value of all expressions/structures, whether Upanishadic, Buddhist, Islamic or Christian" (*namarupa* designates the entire complex of names and of forms which attempt to translate the primordial experience and/or to structure it).

61. Cf. the study "Archétypes religieux . . . " (*supra*, note 58), section V: "Le message et l'expérience de Jésus" (pp. 188-191). There are very strong expressions in the "Notes de théologie trinitaire" (pp. 235-247); e.g.: "Christian theology is essentially based on the experience which Jesus had of himself, such as this was shared by the Apostles. . . . Fundamentaly, Christianity is the transmission through the ages and to all human beings reached by the apostolic preaching of this primordial experience which Jesus had in the Spirit of himself, of the Father and of human beings who are his brothers" (pp. 238-239).

62. Cf. in the study "Archétypes religieux . . . " section IV, "Théologie chrétienne" in which, in a way more or less parallel with the theme of the various stages or ages of thought, Le Saux distinguishes between Judeo-Christian theology, then Hellenistic-Christian theology, while he sees a new theology dawning, a truly "catholic one . . . liberated from all subjection to

time and place" (cf. pp. 182-187). The same reflections are found on pp. 245-246.

63. On the inadequacy of an Indo-Christian theology based exclusively on analyses and comparisons of notions, cf. pp. 236-238 and 299-300. A theology of this type would remain at an excessively inadequate level of *namarupa*.

64. The demand is precise. What exactly would it amount to if we had to *say* what the Mystery of Christ is? It is not very easy to determine this from the text of Le Saux. Reflecting on the last three texts of the book, one could say that Jesus, having himself performed to perfection the experience of the *advaita*, to the point of saying *Ego eimi*, that is to say, to the point of allowing the pure consciousness of God to be awakened in himself, is for us an awakening to this same experience, to which his *yoga*, his *way* of charity and of communion leads us. And every human being who allows himself to be lead to the experience by Jesus (who can for this reason be called the Word or the Presence of God) becomes in turn an agent of awakening for his brothers.

65. P. 182: the different values, present in the different archetypes, their complementarity, their mutual openness are based on an "original and fundamental intuition, pre-archetypal, from which each archetype or symbol receives its proper value." On the resurrection and its archetypal value of awakening to the life in self, cf. pp. 212, 219, 224, etc.

66. An expression of the Upanishads, cited on p. 182.

67. Cf. pp. 227 and 231.

68. This section on the Trinity summarizes more particularly the study *Theologoumenon Upasana: méditation sur la Trinité*, op. cit., pp. 217-233. I am aware that this resumé hardens somewhat an exposition which is actually full of nuances, reservations, etc., and not necessarily consistent in all of its affirmations. To present this exposition without reference to its hesitancies and reservations is to some degree to betray it. The reader will restore the nuances which I have resigned myself to omitting in order to bring out what I believe is a fundamental line of the exposition.

69. Saint John of the Cross speaks of "the divine conjunction and union of the soul with the divine substance" (*The Collected Works of St. John of the Cross*, trans. Kieran Kavanaugh O.C.D. and Otilio Rodriguez O.C.D. [Washington, D.C.: ICS Publications, 1973], p. 190), but he also speaks (in the "The Spiritual Canticle," stanza 37, *The Collected Works*, p. 550) of the entrance into "the high caverns of the rock" which are "the sublime, exalted, and deep mysteries of God's wisdom in Christ, in the hypostatic union of the human nature with the divine Word, and in the corresponding union of men with God. . . . " It seems that these truths, expressed here in their scholastic dryness, are the object of spiritual understanding when one has reached the

highest levels of mystical union. Saint Teresa of Avila writes that "the soul is so much out of itself that it no longer sees the distance which separates it from God" (*Autobiography*, chap. 34), which does not prevent Christ from being and remaining at the center of her spiritual journey. One could give a volume of citations which testify to the presence, *within* the most exalted spiritual experiences, of the essential realities of the Christian faith, whose true reality is revealed by the grace of mysticism.

70. Beyond the text cited *supra* note 66, cf. other expressions on the primacy of the "initial awakening" of "direct", "supramental" revelation, pp. 151, 230, 254, 268, 280, etc.

71. P. 154.

72. M. Corbin has very recently emphasized the necessity of bringing to light the Christological foundation of the mystical way in Pseudo-Dionysius, without which one would interpret him within the framework of a philosophical and cosmic mysticism rather than a truly Christian one. Cf. "Negation et transcendance dans l'oeuvre de Denys", in *Rev. Sc. phil. théol.* 69 (1985), p. 65-66. I do not know if the attempt is really convincing, but it is one that had to be made.

73. Cf. pp. 141, 228. I do not know if Le Saux correctly sees that non-alterity of God with respect to man and non-alterity of man with respect to God are not interchangeable expressions. Quite frequently, I might add in passing, Le Saux utilizes or criticizes a popularized, neo-Thomistic theology, which is neither *the* Western theology, nor even necessarily the thinking of Saint Thomas.

74. On the *koinonia*, cf. especially the essay "Jésus le Sauveur," pp. 275-293 and particularly pp. 279-281 and 288ff.

75. P. 254.

76. See the critique of this expression on p. 243.

77. Cf. the discussion of the principle stated by the fourth Lateran Council on the *major dissimilitudo* in Jüngel, *God as the Mystery of the World*, p. 283ff.

78. See the evaluation of sin and the critique of the classical theory of the Redemption, in Le Saux, pp. 275-280, to be compared with the single note in which Jüngel speaks of sin, *op. cit.*, p. 225, note 73.

CHAPTER TWO

GOD
BEING AND CREATION

The task which we have before us can be clearly delineated on the basis of a comparison between the authors we have just discussed. It is a question of finding the *right distance*, that would enable us to talk about God in himself not only without cutting him off from human history, but also without assigning him exclusively to it, respecting the fullness of his Being but without tending to nullify, even eschatologically, the reality of human Being and human history, a Being and a history whose significance and value are attested by the Risen Christ.

The path toward this point of proper distance passes through what could be called *reunion, or reconciliation with particular being*. This is necessary: from a philosophical point of view, first of all, if the remarks I make above apropos of Heidegger are correct, the effort must be made to exit from the dubious situation in which particular being is left. Then, from a theological point of view, because we have to think and to talk about the event of God in himself and with human beings, without discontinuity but in a way that respects "thresholds" which narrative theology on its own is unable to locate and that maintains on the other hand the enduring value, even into the eschaton, of the Christian mediation: the Risen Christ dies no more, but neither does he disappear into the divinity, so that he indeed belongs in a way (and we with him) to the realm of what can generally be called *particular being*.

Paradoxically, the return toward particular being releases a *notion of Being*, on the basis of which it becomes possible to attempt a *divine nomination*, which avoids the pitfall of the Supreme Being (Etant) *causa sui*, the "Necessary Being," and the "I am" which would ultimately not allow anything to subsist outside of Itself. We will see that this ontological divine Name can serve as a "hermeneutical key" for evaluating and uttering the complex relationship God in himself/God toward us, to which corresponds on the side of particular being, the relationship creation/history of salvation.

1. Reconciliation with particular being

But what is particular being anyway? We do not have to look very far: it is the flowers on my table, that loud noise in the street, the tense and suffering face I encountered a few moments ago, the thought I have in my mind, everything and anything—things, people, encounters, *events*, but understood very precisely *as beings, as things that are*. The difficulty involved in thinking of particular being may be reduced solely to that of achieving this grasp of reality as that which *is*. No demonstration can compel the mind to it, no argument inevitably yields it, and all the talking we can do about particular being cannot achieve anything except to provoke this type of "regard," this "encounter," this "judgment of existence." The fact that a definitive accord among philosophers has never been reached on particular being and the Being of the being is evidence enough not only of our human weakness but also of the introductory or "initiation" character of all discourse on this subject. One can hardly do more than point out its proper route, indicate the term toward which this leads and invite the willing individual to take the first step by himself.

The grasp of particular being, whatever it is and wherever it is, *as that which is* can be recognized by its effect, which is wonder, in the sense that Socrates spoke of this to Theatetis (155d): "This state which consists in marveling is the proper state of the philosopher." Wonder, marvel are our first reflexes when we encounter the Being of beings: not the question "why is there something rather than nothing," nor a comparison which brings out limits—"how does it happen that some things are and others are not?"—but marvel before a "there is," which is *not yet* an "It gives" (*es gibt*). The why and the how will come, but if one posits them before marveling at the Being of the being, one will quickly forget the being to launch out into the quest for the "It" which gives or into an analysis of the gift: one is then "beyond metaphysics" without having ever been within it, in "meontology" without ever having marveled at the ontological. In reality, there is nothing that provokes true *wonder* except precisely the fact that a being (a flower, a face or myself) is; reason and desire will eventually break down all other wonders, but not this one.

Of terminology, for the being and for Being

The question of terminology is of capital importance here. If the experience of the being as being is so fundamental, then it is undoubtedly this experience itself which engenders the terminology and not the opposite. All words or terms presuppose *Being*, for everything capable of being communicated and exchanged in the word *is*; Being is the undefinable term which underlies every definition as well as every judgment, and the attempted equivalents remain approximate. But for this very reason they are important, for certain images or certain notions can lead into error. From this point of view, even if it is not always perfectly clear from one work to another, the Heideggerian critique of Being as "presence" is pertinent.[1] Besides the fact that what is intended by this term is not always clear (the Being of the being in the ontological difference, Being beyond the being, or even the being?) this word itself has spatial-temporal connotations which are not the best for expressing the being as that which is or the Being of the being. The spacial connotation sets the being there, without leaving any opening for what could be a withdrawal, a retreat, or a reference to an elsewhere, while it circumscribes Being to the individual being which harbors it. The temporal connotation devaluates that which is not pure presence and scarcely allows a perspective on the possible complexity of the levels of history. But above all, neither the spacial nor the temporal dimension really defines Being as Being.

Language itself puts us on guard against the primacy of presence: would a composite term be likely to explain its root? Would not rather the opposite be the case? *Parousia* points back to *ousia*, *An-wesen* to *Wesen*. If one accepts this verdict of language it is clear that presence cannot claim to reveal the foundation either of the being which supports it or of the Being which makes it happen. We must look elsewhere—not at the level of *prepositions*, which find their meaning only on the basis of what is "posited," but at that of the dialectic between the *nouns* (*ousia*, *Wesen*) and the *verbs* (*einai*, *sein*) which preserve their mutual autonomy and their originality even in their interrelation. It is the right appreciation of this dialectic which enables us to understand the ontological difference while maintaining for the being and for Being their identity which is at once proper and reciprocal. Attentive as he was to etymologies, Heidegger had reflected long and hard on the relationship between Indo-European words which designate Being and breath: Being as absolutely originating *spiraculum*, as primary upsurge.[2] It is here that one must return to *re-experience* the primacy of the *verbal* sense of "Being" without depreciating the *nominal* sense of (a) "being." The most suitable linguistic equivalent would perhaps here be the Aristotelian terminolgy of *act*. Heidegger interprets this as "energy" and "entelechy" of "presence"; this does not seem to me to be well-founded at the level of the texts of Aristotle, nor illuminating at that of the idea itself.[3] The *act* terminology, with its twofold connotation of *actual* and *action*, is differently situated than *presence*: *action* energizes what can perhaps be too static about the term *actual* (precisely when taken as connoting merely presence here and now), while *actual* avoids dissipating Being too quickly into action and thus facilitates a focus on the *act of Being*.

The expression *act of Being* refers then to that stupefying reality which is spontaneously at the core of everything and anything and causes us to marvel *that there should be*. But it is clear that it is *in the particular being itself* that the mind perceives that which transcends every definition of essence, every measurement of quality, every material evaluation and even every historical insertion in time, grasping *the pure actuality of the Being through which the particular truly is*. Heidegger was doubtless right in thinking that, in many if not all cases, metaphysics has swallowed up Being in the being to allow reason the pleasure of reducing everything to the concept. However, when it has yielded to this temptation, metaphysics has missed not only Being but the being as well; conversely, when it has succeeded in reading Being as pure actuality of the being, not only has it salvaged the status of the being, but it has also overcome the forgetting of Being.

Multiplicity, analogy, donation

At this point comes to light what one can very truly call the *mystery of Being*. Indeed, when the mind's eye acquires the capacity of reading *Being as act* in the being, it finds it at once exactly measured by the being, which without this measure *would not be* and would not be *what* it is, and "open" to every other being which also *is*, but according to another, distinctive measure. Very probably (but this would open a whole field of investigation which the present study need not include), this perception of a communication of Being and of a diversity in the measure of Being is linked to the perception of *my* own act of Being, in itself and in its relationship, precisely a multiple relationship, with so many other beings; it is possible here to take up again the whole tradition of the Ego, stripping it of its transcendental idealism. Whatever the process employed, *Being* appears as at once totally appropriated to each individual being and in a certain way common to all, because it is the fact of Being which makes possible the multiple communications, connections, relationships between different beings. Being at once grounds multiplicity, because it is the proper act of every particular being, beginning with myself, and it is the source of unity because every being, without exception, *is*.

Analogy is nothing other than the *statute* of the language of Being, when one considers the latter as the act of a particular being, at once belonging to this being and overflowing it on all sides. The term Being (and with it, the term being) says at once property and diversity on the one hand, universality and unity on the other. This is why it is such a delicate term to handle: its immediate sense arises spontaneously from the evidence of the particular being, but it points at the same time in the direction of everything which is or can be called Being or a being, so that it is not evident that the particular being on the basis of which and in which Being is grasped is that which most fully verifies the reality of this term.

One will better understand this preciseness of the measure of Being, perfectly appropriated to each particular being, and the immeasurable aspect, the excess which links together these multiple appropriations if one reflects on the fact that, paradoxically and by the very fact that it is, particular being *both is and is not*. It is in fact a focal point which assembles and unifies everything that constitutes it, including the act of Being. It is not, to the extent that it does not exist on its own, the act of Being which one speaks of here is anterior to all liberty, life, finality which one can attribute to oneself or to which one might give one's consent. From where then does the particular being get this "beyond the self," this transcendent something without which nothing would be and through which alone the being is?

It is now apparent that one can say of the Being of and in particular being what Heidegger said of Being apart from particular being: "It gives (*Es gibt*)—Being." If, while being of and in particular being, Being is not the being and is not derived from it but rather causes it to arise as a being, then "It gives—Being"; but, consequently and concomitantly, "It also gives—being." The relative exteriority of Being is indeed a summons to carry our reflection further in the direction indicated by Heidegger, that of *donation*, *gift*, and to raise also with him the question of the "it" which gives. But—and here we part company with Heidegger—there is no good reason why we should not pursue this reflection without abandoning particular being.

It is now clear that however primary it may be, the notion of particular being is extremely delicate to grasp. In itself, it escapes every material determination (it is not "reified" in any particular direction) or temporal determination (even presence does not enter into its definition). It says no more than *that which is* and precisely under the formality that it *is*: and this recognition of Being is itself paradoxical, by reason of the totally appropriated, entirely open and absolutely given character of Being. One could say that, like Being, the being is also an object of patient reflection or meditation which must constantly be resumed. One must not believe too quickly that one has it down, that one has fully grasped or understood it and may therefore dismiss it in order to devote oneself to more subtle abstractions. This is a case where one is always a beginner.[4]

2. "I am," the proper name of God

But how is one to conceive the donation when one situates oneself, as I have done here, at the level of Being as *act* rather than as presence? The donation of Being as act cannot be referred to Time; this level of donation, which had some raison d'être at the level of presence, is no longer immediately intelligible here and we are forced onto another track than that indicated in the triad Being/Time/Ereignis, even if the preoccupation with truth is ultimately the same: indeed we are attempting, in the hypothesis, not to abandon particular being and to contemplate Being in the being. We must then reflect on *the appropriation of the gift to the being without its ceasing to be donation* and attempt a *nomination of the "It" which gives*.

"It" must be thought and named at the same time as *author of the donation* and as *outside of, beyond* it. On the other hand, "It" cannot be named except as author of the donation: we have no access to it other than through reflection on the donation. If we are able to think of it, it is only by reflecting on the gift as never ceasing gesture through which the Being of the being is there: it is only by returning to the secret essence of what the philosophical tradition calls "cause." This term has become ambivalent.[5] It has been down-played and criticized to the extent that it was thought to represent little more than an ingenious scheme to express connections between very down-to-earth and concrete realities. To the extent that it was identified with a rational principle of sufficient reason, it has aroused mistrust. It is, however, not unlikely that the devaluation of *cause* is linked to the *forgetting* both of Being and of particular being. Indeed, when one makes the effort to leave forgetting in order to rediscover the being and Being in their truth, one is led, as we have seen, to the recognition of a *gift* through which Being comes to the being: it seems likely that this theme of the gift, with its two connotations of *gratuitousness* and *real efficiency*, would be able to restore its full density to the term "cause": "cause" is here nothing other than the gift through which Being comes to a being while, conversely, at the level of Being, causality can only be donation. One could say then that "It" is the *cause* of Being in the being and, consequently of the being itself, if it is true that nothing in the being has any reality except through its Being. On the other hand, however, it is not sufficient to say that "It" is "cause" to truly *name* it: "cause" remains a functional designation, as was also, for that matter, *Ereignis*: neither the one nor the other of these terms expresses what "It" is *in its own right*, thus naming it truly, for, when it comes to naming a thing, there is no place for variation of degree. If one wishes to name "It" (and this is moreover exactly what Heidegger was trying to do), one must arrive at a term which would express not only external *activity*, but immanent *actuality* as well: it is in this sense that "It" must be named "outside of the act of donation."

Now the term "Being" comes in handy here. On the one hand, it comes to us from reflection on the being in its most internal or intimate principle, the fruit of donation. With it, we do not leave behind the reality in which we are anchored to focus on an unnameable beyond. On the other hand, "Being" designates precisely the ultimate act and nothing more: not presence, nor even donation, and *a fortiori* not any specific and limiting determination. Nevertheless, it does not designate a void but a fullness, because it is from it that the being has Being, and hence the ability to be what it is. Taken absolutely, the term "Being" can serve to designate "that which gives" without implying the donation immediately, but also without excluding it. As "pure act of Being," "It" (which we habitually call God) is unbound to any necessary relation to particular being, but it is also capable of donation, and what it gives is that by which both the being and the Being of the being actually are.

The pure act of Being, the necessary and the absolute

To try to clarify the significance of the name "Being" as a designation for the "It which gives" and which, in theology, we call God, it is useful to compare the theme of the *pure act of Being* with those which Jüngel confronted and criticized, those of the *necessary* and the *absolute*.[6] These two substantive adjectives are contradictory ways of qualifying God and the world in their relationship. *Necessary* links the world to God. To produce this term, one reverses an experience, vague but incontestable, of contingency. From whatever angle we choose to view the world around us, it cannot lay claim to anything more than a *possible* coherency. Here there is something spontaneously felt as inadequate, indeed intolerable which one neutralizes by the affirmation of a "Necessary Being" thanks to which the contingent acquires a certain right to exist. The term *Absolute*, on the contrary, underscores the independence of God with respect to the world. It distances God from contingency, which the contingent subject can interpret in two ways: either taking away from it any right to existence here and now, which would lead to a never-ending journey aimed at rejoining the One who is very far away, "on high," beyond all finitude, corporeity, culpability; or conferring on it a certain affinity, but one whose fulfillment can come only from this "on high" itself, with this *absolute* itself. This second interpretation requires that the negative term *ab-solute* (*ab-solve*) be understood as a positive infinity, an idea which in itself borders on contradiction, at least if one does not link it to another perception, hitherto neglected in the present perspective: that precisely of *Being*.[7]

As we consider the usage of these notions, it is striking that they are ultimately satisfactory neither with respect to God nor with respect to man. Taken in itself, the category *necessary* subordinates God to humanity and to the world. He is the one through whom the contingent is assured of his reality: if one worships him, it will be in order to *guarantee* the assurance, not to express a loving adoration. Conversely, the category *absolute*, likewise taken in itself, distances God from humankind and from the world to the point that the contingent being finds himself deprived of any value whatever. We can understand why Jüngel stressed the unsuitability of these categories for thinking and talking about God.

What, then, can we say? Jüngel attempts to escape the dilemma by proposing a category which enables the determinism of the necessary to run off the top, and he suggests that God is "more than necessary," while in order to avoid the category of the "arbitrary," he interprets this "more than necessary" as "liberty." Likewise, he proposes reversing the classical priorities concerning man and the world, and affirms the ontological primacy of the potential over the actual, the possible over the real. By doing this, however, Jüngel *is not shifting into a new epistemological key*: he is playing *in a new way* with *the same categories. To a more static use of the categories of the possible and of the necessary, he is opposing another usage, which seems more dynamic and open, and which highlights ek-sistence.* I indicate above how the idea of God which results from this new game with old categories seems to me to be deficient, but perhaps it is only now that we are able to grasp the root of the problem. Whether it is a question of God, of the world or of man, *Being* is never grasped and expressed in Jüngel's treatment except by way of certain qualifications with which it is endowed. However sensible and useful they may be at a certain level of reflection, these *adjectives* really conceal the pure signification of the Name which one is seeking. In Jüngel, the mind approaches realities not so much under the formality that they *are*, but rather inasmuch as they are *of such a kind*. My own view is that in spite of anything one might say, one remains under the spell of *forgetting*, both of Being and of the being. It is from this forgetting that we must escape. The particular being vivified from within by the act of Being, God as pure act of Being are radically liberated from every adjective, and it is at both a verbal and nominal level that we must confront them.

If one arrives at a divine nomination at the level of *Being*, then, but only then, it becomes possible once again to speak of the *necessary* and of the *absolute*, as descriptive attributes of Being and not as primary terms, which perceptibly alters the meaning of these adjectives. The primary terms are (the) *being*, imbued with the *act of Being* which it measures but also which it receives from the *donation* which the *pure Being*, God, constantly makes to it of this Being. God is then necessary because it is impossible for Being not to be.[8] The being, although it really is, is not necessary, because it is born unceasingly of a donation-cause. Gracious as it may be, this donation has really been made to it, so that the being finds itself bound to God who gives to it and who is necessary for it; one need not then speak of a "nonnecessary" God, but at the same time the level of *Being* and of *donation* which defines our perspective avoids any kind of determinism.[9] On this basis, there will be *another* level of liberty and of possibility, with which we will concern ourselves further, that of the Word, addressed and heard.

Pure act of Being and experience of unity

In a sense, the direction followed by Henri Le Saux, as we summarize it above, because it points toward a perfectly unified experience of the divine "I am," helps us to admit the possibility of speaking of God in terms of "pure act of Being" and gives us the measure of these very terms which in reality are without measure and at the extreme limit of our human languages. However, we must be careful here: the term *Being* does not have the same meaning within the two perspectives. For Le Saux, the divine "I am" is essentially the unutterable term of an experience, itself prepared for by a pedagogy of awaiting. In ontological terms, this experience is expressed by the verb *Being*, but it can also be expressed by means of reflexive vocabulary (pure awareness of *Self*) or in the terminology of the *One* (which has no second).[10] And, in both cases, on the one hand the vocabulary is far from doing justice to the experience, and on the other, the experience ultimately annuls everything that is not itself—realities, mediations, words, etc. The same is not true in our perspective where the perception of the *being* imbued with its *act of Being* remains fundamental, so that one does not arrive at the "I am" of God except through reflection on the donation-cause, which itself enables a nomination of God as Being, *by analogy*. Naturally, such a speculative approach does not constitute a rejection of the spiritual experience. It does not imply either the *a priori* rejection of the transcendence of the experience with respect to the language which strives to interpret it. It simply says that if there is an interpretation of the experience, the latter, in order to be truly in conformity with the very thing which is experienced, should be conducted in such a way that, on the one hand, it respects mediations and analogy, and on the other, it does not make it extremely difficult, if not impossible, to talk about a possible Word of God, the

The act of Being as hermeneutical key

The comparisons we have just made make it possible perhaps to better situate the procedure followed here. Initially leaving aside the adjectives of the being, but, conversely, taking some distance with respect to the immediate mystical quest, it consists in focusing the attention first on the being, precisely as a being, as something that is, then on the donation-cause which at once posits the being in its proper Being and holds it open to every being and to all Being, and finally on God, the author of this donation, whom one can legitimately name Being, "pure act of Being" or again, without further qualification, "I am."[11] This procedure offers the advantage of positively acknowledging the reality and the value of every being and of all beings, and of arriving at a divine nomination which at once indicates a real communication between beings and God (because the word employed, *Being*, is the same) and signifies God in his difference, "absolved" of beings (because the term *Being* does not express, in itself, the donation-cause, but only its author in his proper reality).

It should be added that the significance and importance of this procedure, as well as the confidence one can have in it, also derive from the *moment* in which it appears on a comprehensive theological trajectory. It comes in here as a necessary element of *interpretation* of salvation and of history, as well as of the divine names which they reveal. In the investigation of the way of God with human beings, one gives oneself the means of *thinking God in God*, of evaluating the divine names at the level which is their own, that of Being in its total actuality and its absolute purity. But it should be quite clear that such an evaluation in no way annuls the historicity of the divine names or weakens the reality of "God with us." On the contrary, it grounds them *in truth*.

Two remarks are useful here for clarification:

1. In an effort to bring out the involvement of God in history as it emerges from the whole Bible, there has been a widespread tendency in recent theological literature to call into question the *immutability* of God, considered "Greek" or "metaphysical," in order to better emphasize the passibility, the suffering, the humility, even the temporality

of God, in a word, in order to counter this speculative immutability with a revealed *mutability* which alone is believed to be ultimately authentic. What are we to think of this orientation, in the perspective which occupies us here?

a) It is hardly possible to contest that in Greek and Hellenistic philosophy, the immutability of the Prime Mover, of the Good above all else, etc., implies a radical separation from the world of movement and of time and leaves no room therefore for a "wonderful commerce" (*admirabile commercium*) between God and human beings.

b) It is doubtless true that the first Christian theologians, especially after the Council of Nicea, adopted this theme of immutability and interpreted the theology of the Incarnation and of the Redemption in such as way as to respect it. They were certainly not drawn, for example, to see in the cross of Christ the place of a revelation of God, not only in his benevolence and compassion, but in his reality itself.

c) It is, however, perilous to be satisfied with more or less reversing the terms and to posit God as Mutable or as supreme Suffering in full continuity with the mutable and suffering beings that we are. Besides the fact that such a "pathotheology" does not respect the specificity of God, it is not at all clear how this helps to resolve for us the "problem of evil and of suffering."[12]

d) It is here that reflection on the name of God as pure Act of Being reveals its value. To speak of immutability means to deny God the movement which affects the being as limited to a form, to a species, to a time, these limitations having no meaning at the level of pure act of Being. But if in various ways, Revelation (and in certain domains, even the human mind) speaks to us of the movements of God toward human beings, or of the internal movement of the divine life itself, theology will be able to employ terms implying mobility, being aware quite simply that they must be *interpreted* taking into account the simplicity and the perfection of God, "I am." It is here that *the principle of analogy cannot but come into play* (the analogy of Being and/or of faith). By employing analogy, one confesses by this very act that our words see their sense verified in fullness when they *aim at* that in God which they cannot say in a univocal way, since the terms themselves have been formed by beings (ourselves) to express beings (these flowers on my desk, that noise in the street, that suffering on my brother's face). To be honest with respect to our precursors in theolgy, must we not acknowledge that, on this question of the divine nomination, they have amassed treasures of reflection of which it would be very wrong to deprive ourselves, even if we wish to carry them further and transpose them into new conceptual contexts?[13]

2. A certain reticence with respect to analogical procedures also derives perhaps from the fact that they are more or less historically linked to a theory of *theology as science* ("subordinated" to the divine knowledge). Within this framework of "science," the theme of God as pure act of Being comes in as a "primary truth," in the double sense, chronological and logical, of the term *primary*. One affirms first of all of God that he *is* (and one examines all the ins and outs of this affirmation) and it is on the basis of this *de Deo uno*, the first object of a theological science, that one procedes, for better of for worse, to lay out the rest of the material to be treated. Analogical procedures play a considerable role in this type of "science"; it follows from this that if one rejects the idea of theology as science, it is easy to reject also the intellectual instrument which made it possible. It would no longer have a place in a *theology as history*.

To this we must reply, as did Father Chenu recently with regard to Saint Thomas Aquinas, that the logical rigor of a science is softened by the intervention of biblical categories and themes, so that entire panels of the construction of such a "theological science" are tributary not only to the revealed data, but to the biblical mode of expression as well.[14] It is only at the level of the manuals that the supple articulation of vocabularies and perspectives can become transformed into a rigid scholastic edifice. I would say that *theology as science*, for its very authenticity, *absolutely* requires recourse to the *vocabulary of history*, which plays a *hermeneutical role* in this case: it orientates, indeed corrects an interpretation of the datum of faith in which intellectual terms and constructions play a formative role. But the opposite seems to me to be just as true and just as prerequisite: *theology as history* demands the *vocabulary of Being* for the correct interpretation of a presentation in which the text and the narrative have the primacy.

Being and liberty in creative action

These remarks can be illustrated by an example: how are we to conceive of the *creative action* of God with respect to the *pure actuality of his Being*? We should return here to the genesis of the trinitarian faith which emerges from the Paschal Mystery, as we tried to understand it at the end of the second part of this book. On the one side, the death of Jesus appeared to us as the way by which man can accede to a movement of total gift, to a filial attitude, to the pure invocation of God, while the resurrection establishes him permanently in this dynamic which will never cease and which sanctions the perfect extraversion of man toward and in God. On the other, the resurrection of Jesus, taken from the side of God who raises, was shown to be the paternal invocation through which the Father, in his turn, communicates himself totally. The Paschal Mystery thus reveals itself in its ultimate reality of *vital communion*, absolutely free of all egoism. If, as we likewise observed, this vital communion is an *icon of the proper reality of God*, then the trinity is that "Admirable Exchange" where the fullness of God is ceaselessly and entirely communicated between Father, Son and Spirit in that dynamic movement of communion which has traditionly been called "circumincession." The recognition of God as pure Act allows us to conceptualize and to express, according to analogy, the properly divine level of the trinitarian Exchange while, conversely, evangelical contemplation of this Exchange allows us to comprehend that the pure unicity of God and the total perfection of his Being do not imply any divine "egoism," because the Gift/Response interplay is here as eternal as is the Being himself.

In other words, but words which the preceding ones illustrate, "God *is* LOVE": he does not decide to Love, he *is* it. But the intuition of faith senses, without being able to fully explain it, that this Love which is total and free of all egoism can *decide* to "overflow," that the intra-trinitarian divine "processions" wish to be a vital source of divine "missions" toward that which is not, and that the purity of the divine Being, ceaselessly exchanged between the Father, the Son and the Holy Spirit, offers itself as "Goodness" for a creation which it will conceive, produce and direct toward its end of transfiguration and of communion.

Do we then fall into impiety when we thus distinguish in God between the Love that *is* and the Love that *decides*? I think not: God is still acknowledged as Gift and Communion even as we acknowledge Him as Being, and because this distinction seems to me on the contrary to make possible an *adoration* of God in the transcendent Mystery of the Love which he *is* even as we worship Him in the benevolent Mystery of the Love which *communicates itself*.[15]

I will not pursue here the investigation of the divine names, trinitarian and essential, their articulation within a theology of the Incarnation, nor will I go into the technical aspects of the procedure of analogy. It is essential to make the point that the properly *theo*logical interpretation of the data which come to us from the history of salvation, and most especially from the Paschal Mystery, entails the usage of the *ontological key*. Once this has been admitted, it is clear that careful analyses of the divine names with which we are endlessly supplied by the ancient and the medieval tradition of the Church, retain all their value for a correct vision of the great "mysteries": Trinity, Incarnation, Creation. On the other hand, they provide us with a method, when, in order to talk about God, we wish to introduce other notions than those of the Fathers, holding closer to what comes to us from the history of salvation.[16] This is the moment to return to the point of departure of this chapter, which is itself linked to the analysis of the "superimposition of times" which we conducted at the end of the second part. It appears more clearly now that the *event* is an analogical notion which responds to various inflexions of time and to various levels of Being. If we use this term to talk about the intimate life of God, which we would more classically express in terms of generation, procession, spiration, or in terms closer to the Paschal reality like love, gift of self, sacrifice, resurrection, in any case we are speaking according to the analogy of faith, which is itself linked to the analogy of Being. Everything we say about God in these terms is true, on condition that we understand them *at the level of pure act of Being* whose hidden reality they reveal. Undoubtedly the interior event of the divine life is closely linked to God's involvement with respect to the perishable, in creation, the incarnation, the cross, but here too there are thresholds of Being and of intelligibility, both between what God *is* and what he *decides on*, and between the various modalities of the decision of God, which objectively distinguish between creation, incarnation and redemption. It is with a few remarks regarding these levels of God's decision, creation and salvation, that I would like to close this chapter.

3. Creation and salvation: a proper focus

If the discernment, in the *being*, of an act of *Being* fully appropriated and at the same time dependent on a *donation-cause* enables us to go back ultimately to God, the *pure Act of Being*, and thus gives a key for a critical evaluation of the divine names, it will also enable us to situate more acurately the notion and the reality of *creation*, in itself and in its relation to salvation.

Liturgy, prophecy and wisdom in the announcement of creation

It has often been stated that, in the genealogy of biblical themes, *creation* is not primary. The precedence goes to the experience of the *events of salvation* of which Israel, in its beginnings as a people and in the course of its history has been beneficiary, and of *the divine offer of covenant* which these events signified.[17] The theme of creation, as also that of the end of this world which is connected with it, is thought to derive from a procedure which traced back to the origin what was actually experienced in the course of the history of Israel. What God did *in* this history, he must have done likewise "in the beginning." Thus, creation is the "time one" of history; it corresponds to the beginning of "prophecy"; it is also an object of *narrative*. One may conclude from these observations that the history of salvation is the appropriate interpretative key for the creation narrative and not the other way around, and one can take this occasion to express doubts on the pertinence of a theoretical, let us say a metaphysical speculation on creation.

There is to be sure no reason to contest the link between the biblical presentation of the creation and reflection on the events of salvation. Indeed this observation should be given its full scope. The atmosphere of the first creation narrative, at the beginning of Genesis, is eminently liturgical: in the perspective of the priestly author, there is a correspondence between the description of the Tent and of the cultic objects, as well as of the narrative of Aaron's consecration, and the progressive creation of heaven and earth which reaches its climax in that of humankind, "created man and woman." This correspondence gives a liturgical character to creation. Conversely, it gives a cosmic significance to the worship of Israel; it anticipates the meaning of the Temple cult and points far ahead to the fulfillment of the World and of the Temple in the Body of Christ. In the second narrative, the perspective is no longer liturgical, but historical-messianic: it situates at the very beginning a game of creation, of word, of sin and of mercy which can serve as an interpretative code to the things with which the destiny of Israel's royalty was concerned, while, conversely, it underscores the ethical and historical finality of the creation of man and woman. In the texts of Second Isaiah, a correspondence is established and developed between various stages of salvation. The return from exile harks back to the passage through the Red Sea, and both of these echo the initial victory of God over the primeval chaos. Here too, if the power of salvation experienced in the deliverance of Israel is brought back to the creation to make it appear as an extraordinary work of this power, the creation, conversely, gives cosmic and universal significance to the salvation experienced. It guarantees its perennial nature, the historical covenant taking on the security attached to the stability of the earth and to the regular return of the cosmic rhythms. It anticipates, for eschatology, the convergence of creation and salvation. In the book of Proverbs, the creation of the world by the Wisdom of God is brought in to testify on behalf of this wisdom, when it is man who receives its precepts in the course of his life experience; conversely, it is this engagement in a lived wisdom which helps man to discern the face of God as wisdom.

These brief remarks bring out a plurality of approaches to creation at the level of the Bible itself in a prophetic perspective, but also in a messianic, liturgical, sapiential perspective. They also suggest that hermeneutics is "reciprocal": if the insertion of a reflection on creation into a field of thought which does not immediately call for it can lead to thinking about creation in the line opened by this field, conversely, this insertion gives to this field a cosmic dimension, a temporal extension and a human universality which it would not have without it. If then it is fruitful to interpret creation in a prophetic, liturgical, etc., key, it is no less so to interpret prophecy, liturgy, etc., in a creation key.

Thus, the problem of the *original contribution* of this creation theme remains: what does this "time one" of history, of liturgy, of wisdom, of salvation represent if one has felt the need to resort to it?[18] What is its specific character? How could one express it? These questions still have to be answered even when one has shown that the "genealogy" of the theme of the creation passes through the multiform experience which Israel has of its relationship with God.[19]

Level of liberty and level of word

On the basis of these reflections, one can discern a double movement in the liberty of God which exteriorizes itself toward that which is not: a movement of *creation* through which God creates the heavens, the earth and everything in them, and a movement of *salvation* through which God addresses himself to those of his creatures who are capable of hearing and responding to a word. That the first of these movements is ordered to the second is incontestable, but this should not make us miss its specificity. One could likewise, and with good reason, distinguish between the *word of creation* and the *word of covenant*. The first is *not* addressed, it *constitutes*: an efficacious word which *makes* both the world and man, outside of any other liberty but that of God the creator himself; a word which is always actual, for if it were to cease, from that moment on neither world nor man would be there at all for a salvation; a word which sustains a "natural history" (in the sense of Buffon) to the extent that things and bodies pass through processes of development or of regression, to which moreover the activity of man is not unrelated.

Conversely, the word of covenent presupposes a world already constituted as well as a human being standing erect in this world and acting in it in virtue of a liberty and of a body that have been given to him by the creative word. To this human being, God can then *address* himself face to face, in an interplay of election and covenant in which man is partner; created by God, his liberty can confront God and choose the sacrifice of communion or the rejection of covenant. In its turn, the choice thus made becomes inscribed in his body and on his earth so that "natural history" will be penetrated through and through, without being annihilated, by the "history of grace and of sin."

A distinction would then exist, one with a biblical foundation, between two fields of the divine liberty, specifically diverse but intimately coordinated, or between two modalities of the word of God, distinct but such that the first is ordered to the second. To this distinction, made on the side of God, would correspond, in man, the field of his *created* Being (body and liberty) received from God and that of his *invoked* Being, his Being (in body and liberty) as solicited or invoked by God. Far from annihilating the history of salvation, these distinctions make a balanced view of it possible.

It is here that metaphysical reflection can be helpful. The rehabilitation of particular being under the light of Being as act and in the perspective of the donation-cause actually gives us a mode of expression for creation and for the creature. On the one hand, the word "creature" expresses in theological terms the paradox in the being of a gift fully appropriated and of an act of donation which never ceases. It expresses a being which can be thought of in the light of Being, without any suspicion of obscuring the latter. On the other hand, as soon as the being is no longer that which one must leave behind because, by being held back by its weight, one would necessarily fall into the forgetting of true Being, it becomes possible to reflect on it calmly under all its aspects: not only the ontological difference between the being and Being as well as its true signification, but the differences between various beings, measured as they are by different forms and potencies, and also the difference, within each particular being, of the various qualitative levels can be taken into consideration. In a word, we have here what the Christian tradition calls the *opus distinctionis* as opposed to the *opus conditionis* which focuses more exclusively on the absolute positing in Being.

In this perspective, the *creative* word of God constitutes the particular being in its act of Being, its specificity, its particular dynamism, but also, in the case of the free being, in its infinite openness. The *addressed* word of God would proposes a *symbolic rupture* in the dynamic linked to creation, with the sole purpose of allowing this openness to expand to the point of divine communion and eventually to the transfiguration of a world.

This presentation seems to me to be capable of according to *sin* (but also and even primarily to the *sacrifice of communion*, of consenting to the trial, which as we have seen is what is ultimately at stake in human existence, from Jesus to Adam) an organic locus and signification which more monolithic perspectives seem unable to accord it. Sin is the refusal to accept the symbolic rupture, the willfull deafness of man as solicited, as invoked, to the Word which addresses itself to him. This refusal becomes inscribed in his flesh, his world, his liberty. But for it to have been possible at all, is it not necessary that man and woman already *were*, as each other's partner and in a world, with a certain project before them? Within the context of such a *created* milieu, the *addressed* Word can then introduce its spearhead: a disfiguration leading to a transfiguration. What will man do? And what will be the impact of his behaviour on himself, body and spirit, on his partner and his next of kin, on things and on the world?

But if one blocks the perspectives by so unifying the Word as to make it immediately and with a single movement directed toward God himself, toward the nothing or the non-being, toward the perishable and toward sin, where is one to find room for a trial and for a salvation? Or if the Word is already in the depths of the heart, such that it need only be allowed to awaken, is there really a history of salvation or merely a repeated succession of more or less fruitful attempts aimed at this awakening, until the moment when man will find himself "such as he is after all in himself," absolved "in God" of his creation, of his body and of his liberty?

If the observations presented here are correct and the questions posed not without a certain foundation, the implications of our original hypothesis become more apparent: the principle of narrativity cannot go without a principle of analogy, for the history of salvation presupposes both an *ontology* of creation and the *adventure* of a clash of liberties under the impulse of the Word. It appears that the second element is not be possible without the first. To conclude this chapter, let us attempt a final confirmation at the epistemological level.

History, interruption of truth?

Every critique of ontology aimed at substituting a historical mode of thinking, a poetic approach or a mystical experience, implies or entails a critique of epistemology. At the philosophical level, one notes that the forgetting of Being is just as much a forgetting of truth: if metaphysical thinking focuses on particular being and thus loses sight of the ontological difference, it will look for a "faultless" ("compact") correspondence between its concepts and the beings: *adaequatio rei et intellectus*. This "Greek" definition of truth thus always comes up for attack or criticism by the philosophers who seek truth, whatever this may be, beyond a rupture with particular being. In theology, the motto of Augustinian epistemology, *res et signa*, is subjected to the crossfire of a critique very close to that issued by the philosophers, to the extent that this motto also implies the search for static correspondences ultimately devoid of meaning, while the correct procedure is that of engaging the mind on a path of history, of the cross and of experience.[20]

An initial observation should perhaps be made here: the criticism of the ancient epistemologies sometimes seems to me to be quite superficial in its approach. It is too simple to reduce to a Latin scholastic formula, which concerns only speculative knowledge, the immense work of the Greeks in their effort to respond in an nuanced way to the question, what is truth, without paying attention, for example, to the whole discussion related to the question of the pair *aletheia/doxa* in the framework of the polemic against the sophists, or again, ignoring the distinction between speculative truth and practical truth which corresponds to the two distinct functions of knowledge and action, etc. The Greeks and their Arab successors, and subsequently the Latins, were very advanced in their investigation of how knowledge functions and of how truth is structured. To reduce all of this to a simple formula, immediately to be rejected, is to lose the benefit of an extended effort of a structuring of truth which we should instead be rectifying and building on. Thus, at the level of philosophy alone, one would be justified in having strong reservations with respect to the critique of "Greek" truth, and one is tempted at times to regret that theologians are so quick to latch onto a critique that is really so superficial.

Whatever one thinks of this observation regarding philosophical epistemology, the restitution in theology of a specific reflection on *creation*, supported by a rehabilitation of *particular being* in the light of Being should allow one to reconcile an epistemology governed by the motto *res et signa* with a type of theological knowledge marked by the audition of the Word of the cross and of the resurrection and by abandonment to this word. Indeed, if what we said above is correct, the Word of creation, ordered to be sure to the Word of salvation but distinct from it, *constitutes* a world and a humanity *before* any decision of created liberty; now it should be possible for created man to *recognize and to talk about* both this world in which he has been placed and this man-in-relation that he is. There would then be a certain level of truth where everything would be there "to be received" and nothing "to be done," at least in a first moment. To establish this level, the resources of Greek philosophy or of any other epistemological investigation would be invaluable.

But if the Word of salvation makes itself heard, it cannot but provoke an *interruption*, not of certitude but of *truth*. It introduces, in the form of *invocation* and of *law*, that to which man was open, to be sure, but which, once expressly stated, requires a reconsideration and a recasting of the criteria of truth. Here the free abandonment to the truth of the Word of salvation is decisive and it puts into new perspective the datum already recognized thanks to the Word of creation. If the commentaries offered in the second part of this book, regarding the trial of the "innocent," of Jesus and of Adam, are correct, it is only now that the epistemological foundation is more clearly revealed: this resides wholly in a delicate interplay, continuously resumed, between the data which are accessible to man through a view of the created world and of created humanity as they come from the creative hand of God, and an obedient hearing of the Word of salvation which comes forth from the mouth of God. This interplay is a ceaseless back and forth movement: in the case of Adam, it is the truth of a certain state of the creation which is "interrupted" in view of the hearing of the Precept, while, in that of Job, it is the truth of a true but limited conception of Covenant which is "interrupted," to prophetically announce a filiation, which the Creator in all his majesty comes on stage to confirm. To be sure, the connections between the truth of creation and the truth of salvation are such that a whole network of relations and analogies becomes established, so that the motto *res et signa*, for example, will eventually cover a whole gamut of symbols and figures which only the history of salvation could have made possible. I do not claim to have resolved the question of theological truth by the sole means of the distinction between the two distinct and coordinated domains of creation and salvation, but I think that this elementary and necessary distinction enables one both to keep one's bearings in the process of theological analysis and to give reality to a *history* of salvation where the invocation, at once gracious and onerous, of God, and the faithful or sinful response of man play out against the background of a world and transform it.

It is then a question of the *interruption of truth*, and not only of *certitude*. As Jüngel noted, in studying Descartes, the certitude which the latter demanded for the affirmation of God as ultimate *guarantee* of the *Cogito* is illusory, and it is necessary to interrupt this pseudo-guarantee by abandonment to the Word of salvation. But this abandonment is not merely renouncement of an *appearance*, the self-styled guarantee; it is the abandonment *of* a legitimate acquired level of *truth*, in order to have access, through faith, *to* the Word of salvation, to *more truth*.

An additional note on love

Regarding *truth*, I have just distinguished two levels or two fields: that which corresponds to the dimension of *creation*, and which can be expressed in catch phrases of the type *res et signa*, and that which corresponds to the dimension of *historicity*, where the decision of liberty confronted with the word and the spaces of interpretation come into play in the elaboration of the true. In the process of decision, the *created* truth is "interrupted" in order to allow the formation of *historical* truth, through which moreover the created level will eventually be transfigured.

These distinctions are likewise pertinent for putting into proper perspective the problem of image versus symbol, to which I refer above.[21] The *image* corresponds to a created level of perception and of organization of the real; the *symbol* introduces this real into exchange, which does not happen without a certain mortification of the image, which will ultimately recover its radiance. The *imaginary*, in the pejorative sense of the term, is the work of fabrication of images, not merely as distinct from symbol, but as opposed to it, as a way of refusing to follow the symbolic course. The imaginary is the imaginative function which refuses to be "interrupted"; in contrast, image and symbol are in the dialectical interplay of value, of interruption, of transfiguration.

But this holds true perhaps for *love* as well. In a brief work which was profoundly penetrating and which is still thought provoking today, Fr. Rousselot noted some time ago the duality, in the Middle Ages, of the ideas of love.[22] One could say a harmonious, "reasonable" conception of love as "intelligible appetite for the good" stood in tension with a conception of love that one could call "foolish," whose essence would lie in the loss of self for others, in "death." Is it not possible to suggest that these two conceptions correspond respectively to a *creation* way of thinking, where natures go toward their natural ends, faculties toward their objects, virtues toward their rewards, and to a *history* way of thinking, history as *response* to a *Word* where the unexpected causes a kind of death and where the correspondence with the order of creation is understood only *after the fact*, in the filial transformation of the love of the good?

It is not my purpose to develop this hypothesis here in depth. I only wish to mention it because it seems to me to supply a principle of reconciliation between two orientations. If after closer examination, this hypothesis proves true, it would become clear that the pair creation/salvation, truth/interpretation, analogy/narrative (or any other way you want to name it) is truly decisive for the equilibrium of any theological pursuit.

Conclusion

The salvation for which we hope will not come to us without the acceptance of a principle of heteronomy, which will furnish us with the norms and ways of a truly human mode of acting in our world. This principle of heteronomy comes to us in concretely, first of all, in the founding narrative which is announced to us, to which we listen, to which we come with faith because it tells us what no human being could know by himself and without which he cannot live: where we are headed, where we come from.

The Christian faith recognizes this founding narrative in the narration and celebration of the Paschal Mystery of Jesus of Nazareth, illumined by the figures and the history of the Old Testament and tirelessly reflected on by the Tradition of the Church. In this unique adventure of Jesus, it discovers at once the blueprint of all human existence and the very meaning of history and of creation: access, offered by God and freely accepted by man, to filial life in the Spirit, that is to say to the "admirable exchange" where everything that has been given in joy is given back in thanksgiving. This access takes the form of death and of resurrection, because it is a path of freedom, but still more profoundly, death and resurrection are the "icon" of the "admirable exchange" in its definitive realization which is fellowship in the intimate circularity of the life of God.

Thus, if we look at it from the point of view of knowledge, there is a true reciprocity: the Paschal history of Jesus introduces us to the intimate mystery of God, but conversely the Mystery of God is the interpretative key of the history of Jesus (and of our own history in him). This is why the principle of heteronomy is not only a principle of narrativity, but also a principle of analogy, to the point that the one cannot exist without the other.

In fact, in whatever direction we look, the correspondence between the Paschal history of Jesus and the Mystery of God requires that there be a *distance* between them: if the history of Jesus (and ours in him) is *access* to and then *communion* in the Mystery of God, then it will never be possible, even eschatologically, to *reach an identity* with him: both history and communion presuppose a *tension*, without which they would have neither existence nor meaning, between the uncreated level and the created level of Exchange. Conversely, in order to offer his communion, his fellowship to a humanity living in a world,

God must *posit* this world, distinct from himself, and then *open himself* to it. These gestures take for granted that God retains his incommunicable originality at the very moment when he communicates himself. We have no problem saying the same thing when it is a question of interhuman relations which, in order to be authentic, must absolutely respect incommunicability and distance. Why should we not say the same thing of God? But if we do say this, does it not follow that our language is capable of saying it and that it can speak about God without immediately involving the human beings that we are and the world in which we live? Analogy would then be the instrument of this "God talk," and that is why we have tried in this chapter to establish the authenticity of this procedure, however limited may be its results, however delicate its use must remain in order not to fall under the suspicion of idolatry. The present chapter is not then in any way an optional "excursus" within a process of theology of more narrative origin which could in theory hold up without it. On the contrary, I think that the narrative development loses all solid internal coherence if a word is not said to point out the transcendent ontological level of God in himself.

We must, however, acknowledge that there is a kind of circularity in the procedure which leads us to speak of God in himself and to acknowledge him as creator. This procedure rests on a recognition and on a positive appreciation of *particular being*, that which we see around us (e.g., these flowers on my bureau) and which allows itself finally to be perceived at the level of its *act of Being*. Now such a recognition and such an appreciation are perhaps *actually* possible only for one who *already* inhabits the world of *God's salvation*, which includes the redemption of particular being. Indeed, faith in the salvation already granted to this world is perhaps the necessary (if not sufficient) condition for being liberated from the gnostic attitude to which I have alluded on several occasions. This faith implies that there is a line of demarcation, if not visible at least real, between finitude and its legitimate constraints which result from the very status of a being as a being, and culpability with its sequels which spread out over history. Practically speaking, one would not be in a position to *rediscover analogy* until one has *heard and understood the founding narrative*. If this observation is correct, we return here to what I had occasion to say earlier: *doxology frees analogy*. The faithful praise of God who saves us places us in a state of *intellectus fidei*. Doxology and analogy are not opposed to one another, do not need to replace one another. The first frees the second, and the work of wisdom of the second gives new life to the first. This observation also ties in with what we said with regard to *theology as history* and *theology as science*. It is in reality the first that governs the whole thrust of the theological movement, for the narrative of salvation comes first, with faith in God who saves. The second furnishes the key of ontological interpretation without which the first risks on the one hand not establishing the correct *distance* between God and the world, and on the other, not knowing how to handle, in history itself, the *thresholds* and the *levels* that are indispensable to the understanding of the *events* of salvation. The principle of heteronomy is twofold: narrativity and analogy, but the order of these two terms is not indifferent.

Notes

1. The interpretation and sometimes the criticism of *Being* as *presence* is constant in Heidegger and is also fundamental in Derrida.
2. *Einfürung, op. cit., p. 54ff., 80ff.*
3. For example in *Nietzsche*, (Pfüllingen, 1961), vol. II, pp. 404ff.
4. It is obvious that the perspective on the being and Being offered here owes much, if not everything, to the renewed interpretation of St. Thomas for which É. Gilson, C. Fabro, L. Geiger and others in their school are responsible. I was struck to observe how in his posthumous book *Constantes philosophiques de l'être* (Paris, 1978), É. Gilson considers only M. Heidegger to be a worthy partner in dialogue (pp. 126, 141, 150, 179, 200, etc.), and Jean Beaufret refers frequently to Gilson in his contribution to the colloquium *Heidegger et la question de Die* (Paris, 1980) (see "Heidegger et la théologie, pp. 20-36). Cf. also P. Coda *art. cit*, pp. 51-56.
5. This is why I habitually speak of "donation-cause," hoping that by this apposition, the two terms will strengthen each other.
6. E. Jüngel, *op cit*, pp. 14-20 and 39-41. Cf. also the subject index under "Necessity": of God, Worldly Nonnecessity of God.
7. As I said above, when speaking of Derrida, the critique of the theme of "positive infinity" is conducted by J. Derrida a propos of E. Lévinas, in "Violence and Metaphysics," in *Writing and Difference* (Chicago, 1978), pp. 79-153. In this essay there are extremely illuminating insights on *Being*, which point more towards Saint Thomas than Heidegger, in particular the first pages of the section "Of Ontological Violence" (pp. 134-144). On p. 143, Derrida writes: "By means of more than one mediation we thus are referred

to the Scholastic problem of the analogy. We do not intend to enter into it here.'' It is too bad, though understandable, considering Derrida's own orientation, that he did not discuss the question of analogy. See also the long note 84 that goes with this section (p. 319). On the substance of the question, I think that if one takes the view of Being as act, "infinite" becomes an *adjective* which expresses negatively the unutterable positivity of God. One can then, in a limited way, speak of "positive infinity," which would not be the case if "infinite" were a substantive.

8. "Dieu existe, non parce qu'il est *parfait*, mais parce qu'il *est* parfait. L'être nécessaire est Dieu, non parce qui'il est *nécessaire*, mais parce qui'il *est* nécessaire" (X. Tilliette, "Sur la preuve ontologique," dans *Rech. Sc. Rel.* 50, 1962, p. 213).

9. E. Jüngel, *op cit.*, pp. 23 and 30.

10. Here I think the terminiology of Le Saux is equivalent in meaning to that of Porphyry, in his effort to express the neo-platonic One with the verb *to be*, in the infinitive, to the exclusion of any substantive use. See the references (in particular to the investigations of P. Hadot) and the discussion in my article "Le 'Parménide' de Platon et saint Thomas d'Aquin," in *Analogie et Dialectique* (Geneva, 1982), p. 60ff.

11. Cf. *PCDJ*, pp. 263-265: "Nom et Verbe. Affirmation et négation en 'Théologie.' "

12. On this question, see my reflections on the work of Y. Labbé, *Le Sens et le Mal* (Paris, 1980) in *Rev. théol. de Louvain* 14 (1983), pp. 369-371.

13. Cf. *PCDJ passim*, especially pp. 89-91 (Saint Augustine), 126-139 (Saint Thomas) and for today, 184-187 (Rahner) and 271-286 (my suggestions). All of this needs to be taken up again, added to, critically evaluated within a general theory of theological language, which cannot be done here.

14. *Introduction à l'étude de saint Thomas d'Aquin*, (Paris, 1950), p. 217.

15. Here I attempt a response to the accusation of *impiety* launched by Jüngel against the position according to which "God would also come toward himself without coming toward man"; the reason given is that if this were the cause, "the liberty of God is here being thought of as simple possession of self"; I do not think so: in a trinitarian perspective intimately bound up with the Paschal Mystery, it is apparent that God does not "possess" himself, but rather "exchanges himself." And if one thinks "God" at the level of the unity of his essence, then one should follow Saint Thomas who considers the Goodness or Bounty of God as mysteriously forming part of his Perfection, without, however, making creation in itself necessary for this Perfection (cf. my book *Structures et Méthode dans la Somme théologique de saint Thomas d'Aquin* (Paris, 1961), pp. 46-55 and *PCDJ*, pp. 292-296. Cf. *supra* p. 290, note 41.

16. In this regard, the complex game of "nominations," "attributions," "appropriations," when it is a question of speaking of God in himself or in the trinitarian missions, appears to be an attempt, continuously taken up again and refined, to express the living and true God such as he *is* and such as he *has revealed himself, while avoiding any form of idolatry*. Such procedures will always be necessary, not only to enable to us *think God* but also to enable us to *become involved* responsibly in the *history of salvation* which is proposed to us.

17. References and discussion in P. Gisel, *La Création* (Geneva, 1980) pp. 19-25.

18. On questioning some Tanzanian Christians about their faith, J. Treivel received this spontaneous answer: "I believe that God created me, that he takes care of me, that he guides me and leads me." And he comments: "These replies belong exclusively to the domain of the first article of faith. Faith in God the creator has a peculiar significance in a milieu where the ancient tribal religion is still present, and its value should not be minimized as though it were without significance" ("Strukturen des Bekennens," in *Kirche und Dogma*, 1980, p. 323 and note 41.

19. In an important note, P. Gisel, after having noted "the irreducible link, in biblical and Christian theology between Being and time, origin and human drama, the real and act," remarks: "What is at stake in a theology of creation may be summarized by the double necessity of understanding Being against the background of active affirmation *and* even so, of not directly or without remainder identifying it with salvation, with history, etc." (*op. cit*, p. 153, note 38). One must also avoid the opposite danger of reducing history, salvation, etc., to mere accidental episodes of creation. This is why I think that a theology of history should recognize a language of creation that is not totally homogeneous with it, and vice versa. This is what I am trying to do in this chapter, especially in this section. Acknowledging the fact that Scripture knows a creation *ex nihilo*, E. Jüngel writes: "We are not to expound the word of the cross on the basis of the biblical statements about the imperishability of God which are directed toward God the Creator. Rather, conversely, we learn how to understand who God the Creator is on the basis of the biblical statements directed toward the Crucified One" (*op cit.*, p. 218). For my part, I think that the *two* procedures are *both* absolutely necessary.

20. On this point with Jüngel, cf. *supra* note 28. More generally, cf. my study "La pertinence théologique de l'histoire," *art. cit.* p. 189ff.

21. Cf. *supra* Part II, chapter II.

22. *Pour l'histoire du problème de l'amour au Moyen Age* (Münster, 1933).

CONCLUSION

OPENING TOWARD ETHICS AND ESCHATOLOGY

One of the principal criticisms that I formulated regarding the cultural field whose traits I briefly describe in Part I bears on the impossibility of crediting this culture with the presence of the moral foundations necessary for the concrete management of our time and of our history. Returning to this cultural field in the light of our subsequent discussions, one could refine this criticism and specify its exact place, without substantially subtracting from it. Indeed, there is a sense in which, whether directly or by the strength of contrast, the tendencies examined taken together bring to light the poles of evangelical morality: GOD and the POOR, but they do not seem to have the resources to go beyond this point into an effective praxis.

The concern that inspires the practices and the ideologies of revolution is in the final analysis betrayed by them, because experience has repeatedly and tragically shown them to be incapable of effectively establishing the socio-political conditions that favor the access of the poor to the very status of justice and dignity that one presumably wishes to achieve, with them and for them, by promoting insurrection.[1] However, if revolution is not the solution, the concern reflected here remains fundamental for ethics. One could say that it must be conducted *in another way* and that this *other way* is precisely that which the Gospel proposes. And one might be tempted to think that the theologies of the cross are just the place to look for the perfect solution. I personally am not convinced that they are adequate to the task: if we say that it is of the essence of God to be "toward the poor" or "toward that which is not," does this automatically give us *the means to correctly discern* what, in a given situation, actually responds to the evangelical exigency? To cite here but two uncontested figures, Mother Teresa's way of acting and speaking is not identical in all points to that of Dom Helder Camara for reasons that are surely related to the diversity of the places in which they first worked, India and Brazil respectively, but perhaps also to theoretical differences of approach. Alongside of these one could cite other figures or other tendencies that are more contestable, a fact that suggests that *analytical criteria* are necessary in order to specify concretely the "toward the poor" of the God of the Gospel in different contexts. But where are these to be found? And how, when one identifies "God toward himself" and "God toward others," can one avoid absolutizing *a particular* form of this orientation that has been surreptitiously charged with the uncontestable authority attached to "God"?

Similar observations can be made regarding the other pole of Christian ethics. GOD is indicated "negatively" by a great number of cultural currents. The "awaiting," vague and in itself not at all theist, to which approaches like that of Heidegger and Derrida arrive in different ways, acquires such an intense appeal from the depth of the analyses that have led up to it, that the Christian theologian, following his distant predecessors who were seduced by Neoplatonism, might be tempted to take over and try to transform this awaiting into negative theology—with a few indispensable correctives. The failure of neopagan rituality as well as that of the mimetic desire operative in literature leads in its own way to a presentiment of God. However, the question remains: how are we to go from a "negative affirmation" or from a "presentiment of reality" to an actual system of behavior? If God is absolutely beyond any word, one practically has no choice at all except that between the "cosmic dis-insertion" of those monks of whom Leroi-Gourhan spoke, i.e., moral anarchy, and the authority, totalitarianism in disguise, of the charismatic leader over his disciples or of the priest over his faithful, where the weight of a word without human foundation or criterion replaces an ethical analysis that has become impossible.

In this book, I offer a theological perspective that attempts, by carefully articulating narrative and analogy, to surmount the apories of theological discourse that in my opinion are insoluble when one focuses on the extremes (that appear to be opposite but that really meet) of *kenosis* and *apophasis*. An ultimate proof of the validity of this perspective should be furnished by its capacity to ground an ethics: is it able to furnish elements of discernment for an analysis and a commitment that is *of* and *in* our time, a time not repudiated nor on the contrary over-valued, and in view of an *eschatology* whose idea would be admissible? Part of our task would be to indicate an ethical space where the Beatitude of poverty remains what it is: the first (and hence the last) word of the teaching of Jesus, where monks would keep their title to a withdrawal that, in its own way, would be communion, but also where, for all the problems of bioethics, of economy, of power and of peace, one would have access to certain *landmarks* that would make possible an *action* or a convergence of actions that, taken as a whole, for all of their inadequacy and weakness, would nevertheless be faithful to God and construct the truth of man and of history.

In reality, I do not have the means to supply such an ethical verification in any detail, and I can only wait for theologians who study the problems of man and of society to say if this presentation of the Mystery of God, salvation of time and truth of Being is of any help or use to them. I will limit myself here to what is within my power: to point out or to propose a number of very general categories, even if I will be unable to verify, in the detail of the human domains mentioned above, if and how they actually function.

1. Toward some basic ethical categories

An atmosphere of hearing and of doxology

Let me first of all state emphatically that, in this ethical domain as well, the primacy goes to hearing and to doxology. Is it not a question of carrying over into the area of human behavior what the *founding narrative* reveals to us? Very concretely, here would be the place where one could articulate a *theology of the Church*, continuously being constituted by the two great *gifts* of the Lord: the Eucharistic memorial of his Paschal Mystery, through which the founding narrative is communicated and celebrated ever anew, and the Spirit, who inspires human behavior in conformity with this Mystery. This continuous repetition and re-audition, this steadfast remaining in obedient listening to the Spirit are by no means irrelevant to *ethics*: they supply not only its fundamental norms (that may be reduced to the two commandments of the Lord) but also its *vital source*. It is these attitudes that oppose the "Pelagian" principle against which Heidegger rightly protested: "everything depends on us."[2] No: everything depends on Christ and on the Spirit, without whom the most correct norms remain a dead letter. Hearing, liturgical and spiritual, and the doxology that corresponds to it remain the first principles of a concrete ethics in accordance with the ways of God.

But we must insist here on the fact that it is a question of a hearing and a doxology *kept alive*. This hearing of the founding narrative and giving thanks for it is not a once-and-for-all matter: we must be careful not to allow the mind to be diverted to *contents* that are no longer under the present, actual *impulse* of spiritual *attention*. Detached from hearing and from doxology, categories or analyses, even if good at the start, become transformed little by little into assorted *rigid and integrist repetitions* of logical deductions. Whether it be Catholic, Moslem, Marxist or other, the integrist attitude is the ruin of all living ethics. Conversely, where there is attention and listening, dialogue can take place among people of various religious and human traditions—people who differ from one another, but are equally concerned for the ultimate well-being, the "salvation" of human beings and for the progress of history. Do we not have the assurance of Saint Paul that the Law is inscribed in the *hearts* of men, even if they do not know its letter (Rom 2:14-16)? One who is careful to *remain* in hearing and in doxology will be able to hear God speaking to him in the word of other people, if necessary to work out a common, if limited, "production of meaning," and discern when dialogue is no longer possible, because a hearing of God, as we believe we hear him, does not allow us to go beyond the limits of a word which does not originate with us.

Invocatus, creatus, vulneratus

In an atmosphere of hearing, according to narrative and according to analogy, of the word of salvation and of creation, it is possible to define categories of *fundamental anthropology* that can serve as criteria for an ethics that avoids the confusion between finitude and culpability that I bring out in Part One. What alternative should we offer to an outlook of the tragic but necessary violent breaks that involves a backward movement, a return to an earlier condition, even if this portrayed as utopia? To that kind of fatality in evolution, as Leroi-Gourhan described it, where love and aggressiveness lead to alienation from man and from matter? To that kind of negative coefficient, brought by the ideologies of evolution to human activity, whether of production or of consumption, where every intervention that *differentiates* is immediately confused with the exploitation of man by man and translated in terms of class struggle? To that sort of "fall" that is supposed to be immediately linked to the evaluation of the real in terms of Being?

One could propose a vision of man in which, according to patterns that continuously evolve in accordance with history and human liberty, the three characteristics that figure in the title of this section converge. Interpreting the present state of the documentation, scientists distinguish today between *homo erectus*, *homo habilis*, *homo sapiens*, *homo sapiens sapiens*, but without being able to determine at which of these stages there was, plainly and simply, *man*.[3] Where and when did the reality appear that *we* designate by this term today? Where and when did *man* attain his unique signification, where the modifying adjectives distinguish *states* and no longer *species*? Might one not suggest that man came to be at the moment when the development, both of the physiological forms and of the environment, had gone far enough to make *man* capable of *hearing a word of God*?[4] This does not require an intensive cultural development, but only a *threshold of symbolic capacity* that allows the hearing and the discernment of a Word coming from elsewhere than the horizontality of relationships among likes and of a primary governance of nature. Moreover, whatever one may say about humanity's accession to the dignity of *invocatus*, the fact remains, in terms of general ethics, that every human being *today* is under the call of the Word (in whatever symbolic way this might make itself heard)—every human being is invited to a transcending that simultaneously mortifies and transfigures his condition until the covenant relationship reaches perfection.

Man under the call is also *created* man, in accordance with what I attempt to express above by making the distinction between the creative word and the addressed word: situated in the world of things and of human beings, he is capable of technological development and of social organization, all of which are activities to be developed either in expectation of or under the impulse of the Word to which his creation opens him. The ordered and dynamic management of these three registers man/nature, man/man, man/God defines an ethical program in which activity and retreat are the object of an ever renewed harmonization.

One could attempt to express the relationship vocation/creation by hazarding a few cautious remarks on another difficult relationship: nature/culture. These two terms do not stand in opposition to each other either essentially or chronologically, but it is difficult to express their vital articulation. "Nature" corresponds to the "creation" dimension. It encompasses all human reality in its "hearing intention": from the animal needs of his body, his capacity to work, his aspiration to social existence, to the very essence of his radical desire, that the scholastics describe as the urge "to love God more than himself." "Culture" corresponds to the "vocation" dimension. It includes the whole register of symbols that enable the created capacities to interrelate for the benefit of life, but at the price of the "rule" and of the "interdict." In this perspective, the primary and ultimate symbolic moment would be that provoked by the irruption of the Word of God and the response made to it. The religious intention of culture is fundamental and it is this that explains how it is that, where this is lost, the other levels of human life, even if they can develop according to a dynamic of their own, do not reach their right measure and are more or less lived out in the form of culpability.

The same things could be expressed by an appeal to the subtle but profound distinctions of scholasticism between what is "of nature" (*a natura*), "against nature" (*contra naturam*), and "according to nature" (*secundum naturam*).[5] Both the ways in which man relates to the world of things and to his likes and his waiting or yearning for God are "of nature." In an initial moment, culture, that comes in to "regulate" what is "of nature" by an ever-changing process of prohibitions and permissions, can appear to be "against nature," because it imposes limits on development. But to one who submits to these rules, it is immediately evident that, without them, apparent development is anarchic in reality, and hence the interdicts or the taboos of culture, in virture of what they make possible, are in reality fully "according to nature." But such a discernment presupposes the consent of freedom that is not always given. And this is then the place for the third dimension considered: *hurt, homo vulneratus.*

What we mean by this is that the refusals with which man has responded to the Word of God and, in consequence, to the words of his brothers, have actually become inscribed in his body and in his psyche, as well as in the very fabric of the world, so that the interplay of interdict and death from which life proceeds is joined by an "evil," inscribed in history, whose traits I attempted to portray above when I spoke of the "world of sin." This permanent wound, that is not suppressed, but whose meaning has been transformed by the Mystery of Christ, will have to be taken into account in the process of ethical discernment.

What I present here as a hypothesis (that conforms, the reader will have noted, to the analysis offered above of the Paschal narrative) is that these categories of *call*, *nature*, and *wound* can serve as a grid, effective because true, in the analysis of a collective as well as individual situation, and in the discernment of the decisions that must be made. The correct decision is that which, in every circumstance, endeavors to respond to a call, but while taking into account the structures and the desires of a nature, as well as the limits that a wound can impose. And if these categories of general ethics remain formal, they can become filled with content by a careful hearing of the Word of God and by an analysis of human nature. In any case, it is essential to maintain all of them in a well-articulated harmony: deprived of a reference to *nature*, human activity risks becoming inscribed in the pure contradiction of a state of congenital *wound*, to which one would have to substitute an exchange also viewed as pure: the subversive exchange of Baudrillard, a matriarchal society, fusional and totalitarian, that urged by Engels, but also, if one is not careful, a disincarnated practice of "charity" that would avoid any institutional reform. Conversely, deprived of its attention to the *call* of the Word that comes and of the difficult "work of bereavement" or sacrifice that it imposes, human activity can become transformed into a wild expansion of native potentialities, into a disordered exploitation of the body and of the earth, into contempt for the divine Other as well as for other human beings, under the pretext of letting *nature* and creativity have rights that nothing from outside can limit or channel. In reality, the concrete management of a life of sacrifice without being one of suicide, that would not only be "of nature," but "according to nature" because it accepts the prohibitions of faith and of culture, that would be decisive involvement in time and in the world, but with an awareness of limits that stem from human woundedness—such life management is not easy, nor is it something that can be prescribed in advance. Rather, it must be continuously improvised as circumstances arise, in the game of encounters and of oppositions. But through its "patience," this way of living actually moves history forward by means of the cross.

2. For what can we hope?

If the Christian Mystery, treated according to narrative and analogy, can help us to perceive this "ethical triangle" that can serve as a key for making decisions in a realistic and creative way at the present juncture of history, then it also opens up for us the region of hope. Interpreted "upstream" in terms of *creation*, it aims "downstream" at an *eschatology*. We saw this in our brief analysis of the significance of the resurrection narratives. The two articles of the Creed: "he has risen from the dead" and "I believe in the resurrection of the body and life everlasting" are of a piece. It is to the second of these that I would like to devote the last pages of this book, in continuity with the reflections that have marked its course on God, on Christ and on man.

Given the peculiar character of that which is here in question and of that for which, as I said when speaking of the founding narrative situated at the extreme border of the word, we have no proper language, we will procede first of all with an accumulation of metaphors, not exactly the same as those found in Scripture, but analogous. In the light of these, it will be possible to establish some theological conclusions that we hope will be convincing.[6]

Of mountain-climbing as an anthropological metaphor

Telling of his climb in the Himalaya range, Maurice Herzog informs the reader of his inmost thoughts as he reaches its highest peak of eight thousand meters, never yet reached by man:

> I felt as though I were plunging into something new and quite abnormal. I had the strongest and most vivid impressions, such as I have never before known in the mountains.
> There was something unnatural in the way I saw Lachenal and everything around us. I smiled to myself at the paltriness of our efforts, for I could stand apart and watch myself making these efforts. But all sense of exertion was gone, as though there were no longer any gravity. This diaphanous landscape, this quintessence of purity—these were not the mountains I knew: they were the mountains of my dreams. . . .
> An astonishing happiness welled up in me, but I could not define it. Everything was so new and so utterly unprecedented. It was not in the least like anything I had known in the Alps, where one feels buoyed up by the presence of others—by people of whom one is vaguely aware, or even by the dwellings one can see in the far distance.
> This was quite different. An enormous gulf was between me and the world. This was a different universe—withered, desert, lifeless; a fan-

tastic universe where the presence of man was not foreseen, perhaps not desired. We were braving an interdict, overstepping a boundary, and yet we had no fear as we continued upward. I thought of the famous ladder of St. Teresa of Avila. Something clutched at my heart. . . . [7]

Then, after a few lines, when Herzog arrives back with his companions, a few hundred meters below:

> Terray, who was speechless with delight, wrung my hands. Then the smile vanished from his face: "Maurice—your hands!" There was an uneasy silence. I had forgotten that I had lost my gloves: my fingers were violet and white and hard as wood. The other two stared at them in dismay—they realized the full seriousness of the injury.

And further on, this commentary:

> For our comrades it was a tragic moment: Annapurna was conquered, and the first eight-thousander had been climbed. Every one of us had been ready to sacrifice everything for this. Yet, as they looked at our feet and hands, what can Terray and Rébuffat have felt?[8]

Although the place where he finds himself is no less real, material, than the soil he tread two hundred meters below, Herzog experiences it in a totally different way; he describes it with the vocabulary of novelty ("neuf," "nouveau"), but with this newness taking the form of the unusual, the strange ("étrange," "extraordinaire") and, finally, of the dreamlike: the mountain he finds himself on is no longer the mountain he knew; it is "unreal," "fantastic," it is the mountain of his "dreams," not—let us observe—that the mountain of his dreams has come true, but rather that the real mountain has entered into the unreal, to the domain of the dream, that is ultimately more true than the real world itself. At the summit of the mountain never before scaled, reality changes in significance and in meaning.

This more true unreality affects not only the mountain but the very being of the climber who experiences the feeling of a split personality: if, in actual fact, he continues to climb with the same upward gestures, the effort is somehow "abolished," gravity has somehow disappeared, a kind of interior level is reached from which man can maintain a distance from his ordinary self. To the dreamlike character of the mountain corresponds a kind of ecstatic, outside-of-self existence, another level of body experience.

Now this access to the dreamlike and to the ecstatic that are more real that the real takes place by way of a "break," of a rupture. Significantly, it is perceived as a kind of transgression: an entrance into a "forbidden," "barred" domain, into which, however, one enters with "joy," all fear being banished.

Finally, it seems that this transgression of the interdict, this passage beyond the break, beyond the established threshold. was made possible because, from the beginning of the climb, "everyone was prepared to give his all" in order to reach the summit: all known, objective, palpable reality, all avenues of access to it, all complicity with it had been denied, if necessary, from the outset. Permission for access to the forbidden had thus been granted with the renunciation on principle of everything else: having taken his distance from everything else, the climber was assimilated in advance to this forbidden domain. Though revealed only at the end, the break had nevertheless taken place at the beginning; however, when the climb is completed and when the climber has returned to a reality that is concrete and nevertheless less real than the other, a stigma on his flesh attests to the fact that he has acceded, beyond the interdict, to the reality of the dream: something terrestrial in him is definitively dead—a permanent mark in his flesh, a sign of the impossible altitude to which he was permitted to climb.

This brief, "literal" commentary on the text of Maurice Herzog can orientate our reflection in the following direction: what is experienced in the act of acceding to the summit of the mountain calls into play a kind of dialectic between the state of the body, such as one experiences it in ordinary life and *another* state, felt only for a very short time, but that one somehow knows is the ultimate state, that to which all our human activities are directed, without necessarily being aware of it. On the other hand, the passage between the ordinary state and the state that, so as not to prejudice the matter, I will simply call "other," is described as a break and seems to require a renunciation in principle: we have here a paradox, a certain discontinuity, if not an opposition between the ordinary body and the "other" body, without a real substitution of one for the other being implied: it is the same human being who experiences at successive moments the two distinct body states.

The paradox is more striking in that in order to reach the experience of the "other" body, singular attention had to be given to *this* body. Indeed, what the body was put through in the course of this climb was extremely onerous. The arrival at the summit is not simply the result of a physical mastery beyond all comparison with what is required by a "normal" usage of the body at the level of its customary operations of movement and of productivity. It actually provoked, moment by moment, the discovery and the construction of this body, as musculature and as respiration, as attention and intelligence incarnated in the specific space of the mountain whose reality must be felt constantly, whether as friend or as foe. Real-life experience of bodily transformation, because the body has had to go so far in exploring its resources and the means of engaging them in a forward movement that is always difficult; an experience of wear, of unfathomable fatigue, of constant powerlessness that must be consented to without bitterness and without tension; finally, and perhaps above all, an experience of concrete human relationship and of vital solidarity, by means of the body, with the climbing companions.[9]

Now all of this only took place—and perhaps could only take place—in a perspective of *gratuitousness*. The work of the body and its mobilization are not ordered to any useful movement, to any object production. From the start, they have as their aim the conquest of the summit: that amounts to saying that their finality is *man himself*. Climbing to a height never before reached signifies the will to move back the limits of man's power over his own body, that is made to yield its maximum. At a profound level, was not the climb actually a search for the response to the question: *what is man*?

By undertaking the climb, the man knew that the response to this implicit and decisive question could not be merely verbal, that it must result from a new and laborious construction of the body in the process of which one *would risk* all the true dimensions of man, putting into the balance and so to speak losing in advance the very body whose ultimate truth one was after. But the climber never suspected that the truth of a body thus mastered and at the same time risked would turn out to be *other*.

The term of this ascetic climb can in fact only be described by the climber on an *other* level of word and of experience. It is indeed of his body, of himself, that he continues to speak, and nevertheless, he cannot as before. The prose of his narrative gives way to evocation, to images, to suggestion, as if words failed him for describing the novel experience, as if they were suitable for talking about the climb, but not for describing man as he arrives at the summit and begins to experience that for which he was looking but which, until the precise moment of the arrival, he did not really know. The term *transfiguration* is perhaps suitable enough here: a new figure appears, that the climber was searching for all along, but that he could perceive in himself only at the term of the ascent. And when he has come back down from the top of the mountain, his companions see only dead hands.

Set in the context of our study, the adventure of Maurice Herzog takes on a powerful metaphorical signification: man in search of his ultimate identity *transcends* himself, but in the exact line that his body of flesh traces for him. He is ready to *sacrifice* everything, but only to find himself. And it is then that this discovery of himself takes place as *revelation* of an "other," more truly "self." If the ascension of the climber, in which he risks his whole being, himself and his team, to the point of losing his hands and feet in the process, is the metaphor of this search that man makes for himself and of the sacrifice that it involves, would not the dream-like experience of the mountain and of the "other" body then be the metaphor of the *gift* of this ultimate identity that we cannot produce on our own but that we confess as resurrection beyond "death"?

The Kyrie of the Mass in B

In the experience of Maurice Herzog, it is at the end of a long preparatory endeavor that the "other body," one might almost say the "body in the spirit," at once in total rupture and in genuine continuity with the real-life that went before, is revealed. Sometimes, however, the irruption of the other body and the experience of the totally new seem to break in without any preparation whatever. I would quote here a text from Julien Green:

> I did not know Bach, but one day while Fickenscher was talking to us about the *Mass in B*, he played with one hand the theme of the *Kyrie*, and when I heard these simple notes (there are exactly nineteen of them), it seemed to me that heaven opened up. It was one of the most powerful religious experiences I have received from music. In this phrase which a child could have retained and sung, what magnificent and sovereign faith!

Everything mediocre that there had ever been in my life God swept away with his great hand. I experienced such happiness that, if I had dared, I would have shared it with the people who were there, I would have proclaimed it in the streets. What Bach believed, I too believed with love and with violence. It found it difficult to keep still. . . . I felt compelled to take this phrase and all of its richness to my room and to keep singing it to myself, aloud and in a low voice, like a mad man: Kyrie eleison! Kyrie eleison!

I was not abandoned. Together with the whole of humanity, it seemed to me, I was walking forward toward a luminous world where neither the flesh nor sin would come to darken the soul. For the first time in my life I felt united to the world, joined to everyone perhaps in a common salvation.[10]

This text of Julien Green contains more distinctly Christian turns of phrase than does that of Herzog. The melody of the Kyrie of the *Mass in B* is an "opening up of heaven," here characterized as a "luminous" world that here is opposed not to a real world, but to a sinful world: "flesh" and "sin" are banished from it, and the "shadow" that they throw on the soul is swept away by the light that the music reveals. The "passage" here is not from the real to the dreamlike, but from evil to good: the "mediocre" is swept away.

Moreover, the entire text is marked by "trance": faith, love and violence bring the author to the point of being "like a mad man," but paradoxically he would like to communicate his experience and his state of being: *expressing* them, *proclaiming* them, but this is because the experience was already a revelation of a universal harmony. Admitted to a heavenly and luminous dimension through the grace of the music, Green no longer feels alone: "with all of humanity . . . , united to the world . . . , with everyone else." The salvation that this possession through music involves is not individual, but total, and this explains the urgency that it be announced.

It would be interesting to investigate the question of the extent to which every spiritual experience involves a feeling of liberation from sin or evil. I would like to leave this question aside and emphasize rather the two final points: the bodily modification, that one can rightly call trance and the sentiment of universal human harmony. To be sure, in our text, the trance is limited in its manifestations; it is however not without significance that we find the expression "like a mad man": man is no longer in possession of himself and he is tempted to behave in a way that in no way resembles his ordinary behavior. Each of us in his own way may have experienced something similar to what Green experienced. "Trance" can be induced not only by music, but also through an insight that has struck us very strongly as the truth. A propos of the *Essai sur le don* of Marcel Mauss, Lévi-Strauss recalls the trance experienced by Malebranche when he discovered Descartes:

> Few have been able to read the "Essai sur le don" without feeling the whole gamut of emotions so well described by Malebranche as he recalls his first reading of Descartes: the heart throbing, the head teeming with ideas and the mind invaded by a still undefinable, but compelling certitude that it is assisting at a decisive event of scientific evolution.[11]

The point which I would like to underscore here is that a certain intensity at the level of an experience of beauty or of truth which one perceives as fundamental puts the body into an "other" state, throws into turmoil the essential functions in which the rhythm of the human body is revealed: respiration, heartbeat, as though the body, in its present state were not made for the fullness toward which it tends, and as though the least touch of this fullness would launch one toward a "madness" of the body, which is the shadow of its ultimate reason for being. I would like to cite here a text from Saint John of the Cross, who speaks of the effect on the body of the mystical union when it has reached its highest level. There is a continuity between the elementary trance produced by perceptions of beauty and truth, which the mystic would describe as crude, and the experience of quasi-transfiguration of which the text of the Carmelite speaks:

> Sometimes the unction of the Holy Spirit overflows into the body and all the sensory substance, all the members and bones and marrow rejoice, not in so slight a fashion as is customary, but with the feeling of great delight and glory, even in the outermost joints of the hands and feet. The body experiences so much glory in that of the soul that in its own way it magnifies God, feeling in its bones something similar to what David declares: All my bones shall say: God, who is like to you?[12]

I read in this text the revelation of the ultimate meaning of the trance. The disorder that this inscribes in our body is at once a negation and a hope: a negation of the order of this present body that, even if it has a right to existence at the level of certain types of activity and behavior, does not exhaust the desire and the profound resources of bodily reality—hope, to the extent that the trance anticipates the new order of the body or, in the terminology employed above, the "other" body. Now this anticipation reaches its supreme degree when the spiritual experience is itself supreme: the new order of the body is inscribed in the body and in the bones, granting them access to what they desired as their ultimate truth or, at least, to a state that comes as close as possible to signifying this ultimate truth, that the Christian confesses will be realized at the resurrection.

Thus, just as the long training period of which we found an image in the exercise of mountain climbing was able to conduct man to a spiritual experience through a transformation of a bodily experience, so here, conversely, an experience that one would be tempted to call immediately spiritual does not take place without its manifestation in the body and the presentiment vitally experienced in the body of a transfiguration of one's whole being.

Universality, the reconciliation of human beings in a kind of thanksgiving for beauty, is also an element of the experience described by Julien Green: the *word*, not the calm and measured word, but the urgent, cried out, proclaimed word finds here its raison d'etre that is exchange: to tell everyone so that everyone may share, but also, perhaps, to thank every human being for what one experiences, as though every human being were a giver of the happiness that one feels. Jean-Louis Barrault expresses this aspect perfectly, in the way in which he tells of his first encounter with Paul Claudel:

> A memorable interview for me, in the course of which, to employ his terminology, we made each other's acquaintance (nous fimes co-naissance) or rather recognition (gratitude, re-connaissance): yes, we recognized each other (nous nous re-connumes).
>
> A propos of *Numance*, we were in full agreement on the power of gesture, on the resources of the body, on the plastic quality of speech, on the importance of consonants, on the mistrust of vowels which are always too drawn out, on the prosody of spoken language, on the longs and the shorts, on the iambic and the anapaest, on the art of respiration. . . .
>
> As I left him I was exultant. . . . He must have been sixty-nine years old, and I twenty-seven. This immediate rapport between the two of us astonished me and made me long to say thank you to everything: to God, to life, to the first person I met in the street.[13]

Exultation, marvel, longing to thank everything and everybody, in other words, the yearning for a humanity finally brought together in the grace of the truth, a truth for which gratitude is extended from every human being to every other human being, but also from every human being to the earth, and from all mankind to God.

The butcher of Tchouang-Tseu and the Anagrams of Sausure

The preceding paragraphs can help us to understand now the enigmatic words mentioned above,[14] with which Jean Baudrillard perceived, a propos of the apologue of the butcher of Tchouang-Tseu a "body under the body,"[15] and a propos of the *Anagrams* of Fernand de Saussure "something, a name, a formula, whose absence haunts the text."[16] The true butcher is the one who not only does not damage his knife by striking into the bones of the animal on the table, but doesn't even use it when he cuts up the meat: to cut the animal to pieces, he aims at the "interstices" of the joints, the "empty spaces" that hold the whole together; he does not work on heavy matter that is subject to touch and manipulation, he goes to the very "structure of the void where the body is naturally articulated." It is in this intangible structure that the parts of the body converge; it is the *corpus princeps* that runs under the other body; the knife that explores it not only does not get nicked, but its cutting edge does not even blunt, as though there were a *symbolic exchange* between the body grasped in its "other" and the fine knife.

The same is true for the anagram, where the poet deconstructs the syllables, indeed the very phonemes of the word and, ignoring the signified, "sacrificing" the signifying, reaches subtly, beyond all substance of sense and all structure of form, into a "void" that is revealed, without the slightest semantic residue, only in the pronounced of the poet. As though the truth of a word were not in the meaning that it expresses and the various ways in which one can use it, but in the intangible "other word" that the anagram "recognizes." Body and word are, moreover, exactly analogous here: just as it is the interstices, the voids of bone and flesh, that articulate the body and are recognized by the knife of the refined butcher, so it is the nameless that runs through the anagram that constitutes the profoundity of the word, recognized by the poet who bypasses the heaviness of meaning and of structure.

The cutting of the steak, the deconstruction of the word are without return. The steak as such is not of interest to the master butcher; his sole concern is the mysterious exchange with the "other" intersticing body. The poet likewise does not re-compose the word; instead he takes delight precisely in that which reveals the rupture. In neither case is there a "retotalization after alienation, a resurrection of an identity," for then there would no longer be this "intense circulation" without anything other than itself, truth stripped of bodies and of words—a truth that anihilates the latter when it manifests itself.

The myth of the butcher of Tchouang-Tseu and the anagrams of the poets, that bring out the body under the body, the word under the word, point in the same direction as the Annapurna of Herzog and the Kyrie of Green; they add a dimension of subtlety that refines the theme of the "other body," that is at play under *this* body *here* and mysteriously reveals itself only by putting it to death, not only in its defects but even in its truth. The difference between Herzog and Green on the one hand and Baudrillard on the other is that, for the first, there is a kind, if not of "resurrection," at least of "transfiguration" of *this* body. In one moment, Herzog perceives himself other and the same, while Green experiences a moment of personal liberation and of universal communion. As if, for a time, *this* body had acceded to a "symbolic exchange" that would make him "other" without ceasing however to be himself.

Spiritual body and new name

It would doubtless not be very difficult to pass all the literary genres in review, discovering texts that would be analogous to those cited or referred to above. But I would like to rest content with these and to take seriously the message of the *other body* and of the *hidden name* that they communicate. I discern here the presentiment of a triple relationship: of the future to the present, of life and death, of offer and gift. And perhaps it is this relationship that presents itself for reflection when we speak of "resurrection of the body" and of "eternal life."

1. These metaphors are *not regressive*. They do not seek the salvation of the body in the area of a return to the native or pre-native state, before the body ever became diversified or provided with organs. If salvation can be somehow perceived through a "metaphorical"

practice, in which this body in its entirety, or the musical ear, or again the poetic art invest in actions whose end is not useful, this practice leads to an experience that, at once, gives and promises meaning. It promises it in the sense that it causes to flower, even for a fleeting moment, that which reveals itself as ultimate truth, redemption, purification, symbolic exchange: if it points in any direction, it points in that of a further revelation that would confirm and establish what has already allowed itself to be perceived; it gives this also here and now, if it is true that it is in *this* body and on the basis of *our* words that the "other" body and the "hidden" name are experienced. In this way, and without our being able to say why, what is other and hidden are perceived, without confusion or separation, as the *truth to come and already at work* of our bodies and our expressions. The metaphorical practices have thus a "liturgical" character: they signify, but already realize meaning, that in any case does not lie behind us, in the past.

2. In the text of Julien Green, the relationship of life to death and vice versa does not perhaps appear in its ultimate essence, to the extent that the experience is primarily one of purification: what is put to death is that which should die anyway, since it is already intrinsically dead with the second death, marked by fault (one would not say the same of the other texts introduced a propos of that of Green). With Baudrillard too, the relationship is distorted, to the extent that concrete bodies (the steak) and unintelligible words (the anagramed name) are radically transcended and are no longer of any interest: *this* side, whether body or language, is characterized as "remainder": it is the insane weight or density of that which cannot accede to (or that has fallen from) symbolic exchange: the climate remains gnostic. The experience of Herzog, on the contrary, perhaps because it is at a radically human and earthly point of departure, seems perfectly *right*, although it is almost impossible to organize its elements rigorously: we find here in fact, as I observed, a very exacting work of this body taken in its physical truth and its psychic exigencies, a renouncing, a break, a "sacrifice" that orientates this work to something other than itself, and finally a perception of otherness, that reveals itself at the end of the race, but reveals by the same token that it was at work from the beginning. There is a very subtle interplay of life and death, these two terms being exchanged throughout the whole course of the climb.

3. What we have just said can serve to bring out the *theologal truth* of our metaphors, namely, that "eternal life" is the interplay of this

process of word and of gift that we have seen take place in fulness in the Paschal Event of Christ, that was at work from the beginning, will continue now and forever, and that our metaphors suggest and evoke by their constant use of life and death imagery. One can perfectly well say that this theologal truth is "symbolic exchange," but on condition that one does not establish this on the negation of a "rest," because it effects the transfiguration of everything. "It is permitted" to hope that the the Word of God never cease to provoke man to transcend himself, inscribing this transcending process painfully into his body and into his language but inscribing there at the same time his filial condition in love; and it is permitted to hope that the Word that provokes will lead every son to the transfiguration of his body and of his language, so that the "admirable exchange" can go on, without end and without remainder, beyond what we refer to as "death" and "life": brought to their ultimate truth, in fact, these two terms say the same thing or, more exactly, they are both together necessary to point from afar to that which we confess when we speak of "eternal life." The "spiritual body" is *this* body, but transfigured by love, the fully blossomed fruit of that which we know only as seed. The "new name" is our name of origin, but come to its fullness of reciprocal invocation, body and name at once ceaselessly received and ever given.

4. This way of presenting the resurrection, the new body and name, seems to me not to bypass a conviction to which the modern culture, since Freud above all, is sensitive, namely that *the truth of man passes through the acceptance of his own death*. The fear is often felt, and not without reason, that the theme of "resurrection of the body" and still more of "immortality" are actually the expression, speculatively disguised and conceptually adorned, of a rejection of death, an escape, consequently, from the humanity of man such as he is.

But must we not introduce here what one could call *the analogy of death*? If by "death," we express by its negative facet (because our words can do no better) the *gift, loss of self, mad love* side of symbolic exchange, then this death is in reality the object of a profound *desire* that drives man toward the *infinite* of this exchange. If a "resurrection" was necessary to enable *everything*, without remainder, to enter into exchange, then this resurrection would be, purely and simply, the object of the same desire and thus acceptance of "death." If by "death" we intend the continuous steps of transcendence of self, that I called "trial," "sacrifice of communion," etc., above, then our attitude is ambivalent, and is made up at once of attraction, for our truth and that of the other is there, and of repulsion, for all "sacrifice" of this sort stands in opposition to one or another manifestation of "life"; let us say that experience proves to us that these "deaths" are principles of "life" and effect, if not resurrections, at least partial transfigurations: man discovers that he is that which he gives and that which he receives, not that which he strives to accumulate. However, to the extent that these "sacrifices" take place within a framework of temporality and finitude, necessary choices can perhaps make it difficult for every possible value to enter into exchange: once again, if a resurrection is necessary so that exchange can be without remainder, one can only desire this resurrection. And finally, if by "death," we understand the stigma in us of the history of all the refusals of humanity, mysteriously inscribed in all human flesh and of which corporal, animal death, to which we are destined is perhaps the sign, there is at once repulsion, if it is true that our desire carries us toward exchange and not toward annihilation, and acceptance if, through the cross of Christ, this death itself takes on the colors of the ultimate sacrifice of communion.

In all of this, the essential is that our desire of the infinite does not carry us toward the *appropriation* of God as our Supreme Good, nor toward the *reappropriation* of our bodies, as well as of our inalienable particular good: it carries us toward the perfection of *exchange*, in which nothing will ever be appropriated, because we ceaselessly receive it from God, in communion with all men, and because we give it back immediately with all the love with which we will be endowed. And, by doing this, we will not look back with any contempt to our life here below, for, through the right management of the "ethical triangle" of call, of creation and of wound, this life will *already* have been exchange and happiness, and it will have scanned a history that flows naturally into eschatology.

> GLORY TO YOU, JESUS CHRIST
> WHO LAID DOWN YOUR LIFE
> TO TAKE IT UP AGAIN
> SO IN YOU AND THROUGH YOU EVERY HUMAN BEING
> WHO LOSES HIS LIFE GAINS IT
> AND LEARNS THAT THERE IS NO GREATER LOVE
> THAN TO GIVE HIS LIFE FOR HIS FRIENDS

Notes

1. This is the poignant conclusion of a recent book of John Ziegler, *Contre l'ordre du monde. Les rebelles* (Paris, 1983). Whatever legitimacy there may be in the insurrections recounted and analyzed and the generosity of the combatants, military victory never seems to be followed by a political establishment capable of effecting the ends of which the struggle had been undertaken in the first place, and the situation of the populations is not—and this is the least that one can say—amelioreated. Even if one makes generous allowances for extermal influences and pressures, this consistent failure (largely confirmed by the examination of the earlier Marxist revolutions) allows us to cast doubt on the validity of the ideology. It invites us as well, and with urgency, to seek to implement another vision and other procedures.

2. Cf. Part I, Chapter III, note 10.

3. Cf. *Les Processus de l'hominisation* (Paris, 1981), especially the second part: "Les stades evolutifs du genre *homo* et l'apparition de l'*homo sapiens sapiens*."

4. This suggestion is obviously not susceptible to scientific verification. It is in line with the conviction of Lévi-Strauss according to which the ability to symbolize can only have appeared all at once (cf. Part I, Chapter I., Note 11). It adds that this ability, this faculty of symbolizing must, from the beginning, have been able to direct itself to the threefold relationship man/world, man/man, man/God. Even if one leaves aside here the whole question of "original sin" which I do not want to enter into here, what is in question is the value or meaning of the very concept *man*: if one admits "progress" in the appearance of the symbolizing faculty, how is one to picture this? When can one say that there has been "man" and ultimately in what does "man" consist? If one reads the presentation of René Girard, for example, it is difficult to avoid the impression that the social configuration defined about the theme of the "scapegoat" is a quasi- "natural" extension of the behavior of animal societies; in this sense, the first man to merit the name would be Christ (cf. *Des choses cachées depuis le commencement du monde*, [Paris, 1978], pp. 93-113) since it is he who first breaks out of this configuration.

5. On the usage of these categories of Saint Thomas in the problem of nature and the supernatural, see *Structures et méthode, op cit.*, p. 272. I don't think that a reference to Scholasticism is out of place here, because if I am not mistaken, the issue is in fact the same here: what is a "nature" and how can a non-natural element (one therefore deriving from an external liberty) encounter it without destroying it?

6. I am borrowing here, with slight modifications, some extracts from my study "L'esperienza spirituale e il corpo," published in *Problemi e prospettive di Spiritualità* (Brescia, 1983), pp. 11-30.

7. Maurice Herzog, *Annapurna: First Conquest of an 8000-Meter Peak* [26,493 feet], translated by Nea Morin and Janet Adam Smith (New York, 1953), pp. 206-207.

8. *Ibid.*, pp. 213 and 215. It may be noted here that the return to the companions marks a return into the familiar universe, "this side" of the experience related above: "The sight of familiar faces dispelled the strange feeling that I had experienced since morning, and I became, once more, just a mountaineer" (p. 213). As if reaching the crest of the mountain, the term of the entire course, had removed Herzog from this mountaineer status, apart from which, however, it never would have been climbed!

9. It is clear from a reading of a book on climbing technique like that of Gaston Rébufat, *Glace, Niege et Roc* (Paris, 1970), that mountain climbing is a form of humanism, which practically brings into play the real life of the body and the mental attraction to experience.

10. Julien Green, *Terre lointaine* (Paris, 1966), p. 171.

11. Claude Lévi-Strauss, "Introduction a l'œuvre de Marcel Mauss," in Marcel Mauss, *Sociologie et Anthropologie* (Paris, 1950), p. xxxiii. The story of Malebranche, reported by various contemporary writers, may be found in vol. xix of the *Œvres complètes de Malebranche* (Paris, 1961), pp. 46-50.

12. Saint John of the Cross, *The Living Flame of Love*.

13. Jean-Louis Barrault, *Souvenirs pour demain* (Paris, 1972), p. 122. Recalling his conversation with his companions on the way down from the summit of the Annapurna, Herzog notes a remark made by one of these named Terray: "What I did was for the expedition, my dear Maurice, and anyway, you've got up, and that's a victory for the whole lot of us." And Herzog comments: "I nearly burst with happiness. . . . The rapture I had felt on the summit, which might have seemed a purely personal, egotistical emotion, had been transformed by his words into a complete and perfect joy with no shadow upon it. His answer proved that this victory was not just one man's achievement, a matter for personal pride; no—and Terray was the first to understand this—it was a victory for us all, a victory for mankind itself" (*op cit.* p. 213-214).

14. Cf. *supra* Part I, Chapter 2, note 45.

15. *L'Échange symbolique et la Mort, op cit.*, pp. 187-191.

16. *Ibid.*, and pp. 285-303.

INDEX OF PROPER NAMES

Abelès, M., 44 (n. 28)
Aeschylus, 82
Aristotle, 61, 74, (n. 30), 288 (n. 10), 300
Artaud, Antonin, 80–89, 115 (n. 74), 100
Aubenque, Pierre, 288 (n. 10)
Augé, Marc, 114 (n. 55 and 60), 91, 240 (n. 1)
Audet, J.-P., 214 (n. 4)
Augustine of Hippo, 70, 117 (n. 83), 288 (n. 10), 282, 323 (n. 13)

Bachofen, Johann J., 42, (n. 5)
Barrault, Jean-Louis, 111 (n. 21), 339
Bataille, G., 36
Baudrillard, Jean, 30–41, 78 (n. 81), 80, 89, 95, 99ff., 104, 117 (n. 82), 167, 331, 340ff.
Beaufret, Jean, 322 (n. 4)
Benveniste, E., 17 (n. 11), 61, 76 (n. 61), 78 (n. 81)
Betz, H. D., 171 (n. 5)
Bonhoeffer, Dietrich, 289 (n. 14)
Bovon, F., 172 (n. 11)
Brague, Rémi, 387 (n. 6)
Breton, Stanislaus, 289 (n. 10)
Brown, Raymond, 252 (n. 2)
Buffon, Georges-Louis, 314
Burkill, T. A., 172, (n. 10)

Chabrol, Claude, 131–132 (n. 1)
Chenu, Marie-Dominique, 309
Claudel, Paul, 339
Coda, P., 287 (n. 1), 288 (n. 8), 322 (n. 4)
Corbin, Henry, 74 (n. 26)
Corbin, M., 296 (n. 72)

Darwin, Charles, 42 (n. 5)
Deleuze, G., 113 (n. 47)

Derrida, Jacques, 32, 57–68, 96, 101, 109 (n. 3), 112 (n. 32), 114 (n. 56), 136, 249, 322 (n. 1 and 7), 326
Descartes, Rene, 50–51, 59, 75 (n. 30), 262, 269ff., 318, 338
Dodd, C. H., 171 (n. 7)
Dostoevski, Fyodor, 93, 114 (n. 69)
Dournes, Jacques, 109 (n. 3), 117 (n. 83)
Drewermann, E., 214 (n. 4)
Dupuis, P. J., 292 (n. 48)
Durozoi, Gérard, 109 (n. 3), 114 (n. 53)

Eckhart, Meister, 265
Eliade, M., 86ff., 109 (n. 3), 117 (n. 83), 240 (n. 1)
Engels, Friedrich, 20–29, 30, 45 (n. 62), 114 (n. 77), 98ff., 331
Evagrius Ponticus, 282

Fabro, C., 322 (n. 4)
Festugière, A. J., 288 (n. 10)
Feuerbach, Ludwig A., 270
Fichte, Johann G., 265, 269, 270
Forte, B., 260 (n. 1)
Freud, Sigmund, 59, 68, 75 (n. 49), 77 (n. 63), 114 (n. 64), 343
Fuller, R. H., 171 (n. 8)

Gadamer, H., 140
Geiger, L., 322 (n. 4)
Giblin, C. H., 171 (n. 8)
Gide, André, 111 (n. 12)
Gilson, Etienne, 287 (n. 4), 322 (n. 4)
Girard, Renee, 90ff., 93, 208ff., 225, 241 (n. 7), 345 (n. 4)
Gisel, Pierre, 171 (n. 6), 324 (n. 17 and 19)
Gouhier, Henri, 109 (n. 3)
Gregory of Nyssa, 282
Green, Julien, 336–340, 341ff.

ANALYTICAL INDEX

Greisch, Jean, 75 (n. 45), 288 (n. 8)
Guattari, F., 113 (n. 47)

Haar, Michel, 73 (n. 22)
Hadot, P., 323 (n. 10)
Haenchen, E., 171 (n. 7)
Hegel, G. H. W., 50ff., 70, 74 (n. 30), 116 (n. 80), 214 (n. 4), 251, 262ff., 272, 290 (n. 26)
Heidegger, Martin, 32, 47–57, 59, 665, 68ff., 72, 99ff., 105, 108, 142, 223, 259–268, 276, 278ff., 290 (n. 26), 297, 322 (n. 1), 299–300, 301, 302, 326, 327
Hengel, M., 172 (n. 9), 241 (n. 4 and 6), 252 (n. 1)
Herzog, Maurice, 332–336, 341, 342
Hésiode, 115 (n. 77)
Hölderlin, Johann C. F., 47, 54
Husserl, Edmund, 59, 64

Irenaeus, 170 (n. 2)

Jüngel, E., 131 (n. 1), 260 (n. 1), 268–278, 287 (n. 4), 286–287, 304ff., 324 (n. 19), 318
Janicaud, D., 287 (n. 3)
Jaubert, A., 241 (n. 5)
Jeremias, J., 172 (n. 9), 241 (n. 5)
John of the Cross, 295 (n. 69), 338
Juel, D., 172 (n. 10)
Jullien de Pommerol, P., 171 (n. 8)

Kant, Emmanuel, 51, 72, 74 (n. 30), 142, 214 (n. 4)
Kierkegaard, Søren, 214 (n. 4), 265
Kristeva, Julia, 17 (n. 11)
Kümmel, W. G., 172 (n. 9)

Labbé, Y., 323 (n. 12)
Lacan, Jacques, 32, 116 (n. 80), 122
Lacarrière, J., 116 (n. 80), 117 (n. 81)
Lafont, B. & M.-O., 132 (n. 6 and 19)
Leibniz, Gottfried W. von, 51, 287 (n. 4)
Léon-Dufour, X., 171 (n. 8)

Leroi-Gourhan, André, 7–17, 20, 39, 41, 99, 132 (n. 4), 326, 328
Le Saux, Henri, 26
Lévêque, J.-M & A.-M., 132 (n. 6)
Lévi-Straus, Claude, 17 (n. 11), 32, 46 (n. 62), 68, 104, 114 (n. 60), 132 (n. 2), 338, 345 (n. 4), 346 (n. 11)
Lévinas, Emmanuel, 59, 66ff., 68, 75 (n. 47), 77, (n. 74), 214, 222, 322 (n. 7)
Luther, Martin, 262f., 265

Malebranche, Nicolas, 346 (n. 11)
Manns, F., 252, (n. 1)
Marin, Louis, 131 (n. 1)
Martin-Achard, R., 132 (n. 5)
Marx, Karl, 15, 20f., 24, 26, 29, 30, 32ff., 44, 74 (n. 28), 50, 74 (n. 30), 99, 100
Mattei, J.-F., 287 (n. 3), 289 (n. 10)
Mauss, Marcel, 17 (n. 11), 40, 45 (n. 40), 338
Metz, J.-B., 40, 131 (n. 1)
Meynet, R., 172 (n. 11)
Moingt, J., 170 (n. 1 and 3), 241 (n. 3 and 7)
Moltmann, J., 260 (n. 1)
Mongis, H., 117 (n. 82)
Morgan, Louis H., 42 (n. 3 and 5), 43 (n. 14)
Mounier, Emmanuel, 150

Nemo, P., 214 (n. 2)
Nietzsche, F., 50ff., 59, 68, 70ff., 74 (n. 30), 75 (n. 49), 77 (n. 63), 269, 270

Origen, 282

Paulhan, J., 111 (n. 12)
Perrin, Norman, 171 (n. 5)
Plato, 49, 51ff., 70, 74 (n. 30), 99ff., 261, 265
Plotinus, 288 (n. 10)
Pope, Marvin H., 214 (n. 10)
Porphyry, 323 (n. 10)

INDEX OF PROPER NAMES

Poulat, E., 170
Préau, André, 73 (n. 15)
Proclus, 265
Pseudo-Dionysius, 265, 296 (n. 72)

Racine, Jean Baptiste, 82
Rahner, Karl, 292 (n. 45), 323 (n. 13)
Ramphft, C. & C., 132 (n. 6)
Rébufat, Gaston, 346 (n. 9)
Reeves, H., 132, (n. 4)
Rendtorff, R., 214 (n. 3)
Ricoeur, Paul, 104, 109 (n. 3), 131 (n. 1), 206
Robert, Marthe, 90-94, 114 (n. 64)
Rousseau, Jean-Jacques, 76 (n. 61)
Rousselot, P., 319

Sartre, Jean-Paul, 214 (n. 4)
Saussure, F. de, 32, 35, 45 (n. 40), 61ff.
Schelling, Friedrich W. von, 265
Schmitt, J., 171 (n. 7)
Schneider, G., 171 (n. 7)
Schürmann, H., 172, (n. 9), 241 (n. 4)
Schürmann, Reiner, 73 (n. 13), 74 (n. 33), 75 (n. 46)
Schwager, R., 241 (n. 2)
Scotus Erigenus, 265
Sesboué, B., 241 (n. 7)
Shakespeare, William, 112 (n. 25)

Simonis, Y., 46 (n. 62)
Socrates, 53, 298
Sölle, Dorothée, 237, 241 (n. 8)
Sontag, Susan, 109 (n. 3)

Tacitus, 144
Teresa of Avila, 296 (n. 69)
Thévenot, X., 214 (n. 4)
Thomas Aquinas, 76 (n. 52), 296 (n. 73), 322 (n. 4 and 7), 323 (n. 13)
Thucydides, 144
Tilliette, X., 323 (n. 8)
Tinland, F., 19 (n. 42), 46 (n. 62)
Treibel, J., 324 (n. 18)

Valadier, P., 46 (n. 63)
Van Der Leeuw, J., 109 (n. 3)
Van Goudoever, J., 109 (n. 5)
Van Tilborg, S., 171 (n. 8)
Vasse, D., 132 (n. 6)
Vermeylen, J., 214 (n. 3)
Virmaux, Alain and Odette, 109 (n. 3), 112 (n. 25), 113 (n. 47), 114 (n. 56 and 58)
Vögtle, A., 172 (n. 9)

Westerman, Claus, 241 (n. 2)

Ziegler, John 345 (n. 1)

ANALYTICAL INDEX

Analogy: vii, 105ff, 132, 197, 205, 211ff, 217, 257f, 261ff, 278, 287, 301, 308, 322, 323
  Cf. also Narrativity, Doxology

Being: viff., 4, 47ff., 54–57, 61ff., 85, 97, 103, 105, 109, 132, 212–13, 252, and all of Part III
  existence and act, 298ff, 303, 311
  forgetfulness of being, 52, 54ff., 74, 80, 99, 250, 260, 261ff, 278, 303, 305
  history of being, 105, 265ff, 285
  particular being (*etant*), 51–2, 58, 97, 101, 103, 105–107, 261, 266ff, 297ff, 315
  presence, 58–59, 64, 65, 69, 70ff., 96ff, 102, 299
  question of being, 49, 105, 261ff
Birth: 29, 68, 80, 85, 87ff., 91ff, 115, 121, 122ff, 129ff
Body: 4, 8ff., 13, 31, 35, 45 n. 45, 85ff., 88, 113, 122ff, 130, 140, 192–93, 224ff, 335ff, 339
  Cf. also the section "Spiritual Body and the New Name," 341.

Celebration/Feast: 125, 127ff, 130, 141ff
Eucharistic, 136, 139ff, 146, 170, 233
Church: 136, 139, 142, 143, 170, 171, 248, 328
Cogito: 50–51, 59, 64, 69, 122, 128, 270, 275, 291, 318
Covenant: vii, 88, 127, 176, 184, 191, 193ff, 200, 208, 210, 314, 329
Creation: vii, 82, 84, 88, 91, 110, 135, 174–75, 177, 186, 195–97, 248–49, and all of Part III

Death: viff., 17, 31, 35ff., 55ff., 64–65, 67, 69–70, 93, 103, 115, 207, 231

analogy of death, 207, 244–5
form of death, 35ff., 70–1, 96, 97, 104, 107, 167ff, 196–97, 206ff, 211–13, 221–22, 227, 240, 249
  Cf. also Symbolic (exchange); Sacrifice, of communion
second death, 36, 168, 193, 232, 249
Desire: v, 80, 90ff., 114, 184
  of God, 203ff, 209, 219, 225
  mimesis, 91, 208ff., 225, 241
Doxology: 139–40, 164, 188ff, 197, 201, 207, 211, 212, 216–17, 219ff, 231–32, 322, 327
  Cf. also Narrative, Analogy

Eschatology: 21, 32, 80, 88, 100, 106, 153–54, 172, 332ff
  Cf. also History, Time
Ethic: 4, 49, 72, 97, 144, 252, 285, 325ff
Evil: 4, 26–27, 70, 88, 91, 96, 103ff., 107, 113, 121, 124, 129–30, 189ff, 198, 226

Filiation/Sonship: vii, 24, 91, 115, 161–62, 164, 165ff, 172, 173, 216ff, 237, 242

Gift/Cause: 34–5, 57, 127, 169, 174ff, 186, 190, 197, 264ff, 288, 302–3, 305–6, 311
Gnostic (Attitude): 5, 84, 95, 100ff., 112, 123, 148, 170, 240, 267, 321
God: 41, 86, 95, 117, 189ff
  commandment (precept, interdict), 177, 181ff, 201, 211–12, 223
  death, vi, 131, 207, 258, 268ff
  distance (difference, withdrawal, retreat), vi, 67, 108–9, 174, 188, 195, 199, 202, 206, 242–43, 249, 274, 276ff, 283, 297, 322

350

Divine names, v–vi, 67, 109, 148–49, 155, 156, 169, 201–2, 212, 217, 282, 285, 297, 302ff
Father, 156, 167, 169, 216–17, 228–29, 243ff
forgetfulness of God, 219, 225, 250
images of God, 183, 198, 200ff, 212, 228–29
immutability, 304–6, 307–8
love, 272ff, 310, 319
necessity/absolute, 268ff, 273ff, 289, 304ff
silence, 161, 166, 203, 206, 230ff
Supreme Being, *Causa sui*, 53, 67, 70, 108, 261–62, 276, 292, 293
Trinity, 41, 209, 250–51, 257, 273, 282ff
unknowableness, v, 108, 190, 197ff
word of God, vii, 141, 174, 176, 180f, 182ff, 192–93, 194ff, 206, 211, 227, 271f, 275f, 314ff, 329
wrath, 193, 231

Hearing: 93, 97–98, 106–07, 121ff, 129, 131, 134–36, 139, 142ff, 152, 170, 171, 204, 216, 240, 248, 252, 275, 327
Cf. also Production of meaning
Heteronomy (Principle of): 95ff, 105–6, 131, 132, 135, 154, 251, 257, 320
History: viii, 4, 14, 20ff., 29, 37ff., 50, 66, 69, 71, 88, 96, 100ff, 121ff, 176–77, 193, 216ff, 226, 251
event, 75, 257ff, 268, 272, 277, 311, 322
failure/impossibility of, 98ff
Cf. also Interpretation, Narrative, Narrativity

Image: 115
and symbol, 154, 204ff, 212, 252, 319
imaginary, 29, 71, 80, 87ff., 92, 102, 154, 205, 223, 319
Cf. also Symbol/Symbolic

Interpretation: 106, 136ff, 173, 211ff, 284ff
and Being, 307, 309
inspired, 138, 143
reinterpretation, 136ff, 141ff, 146, 170, 171, 245

Literature: 4, 80, 90, 144, 215
Love: 13, 16, 184, 186, 203ff, 229–30, 234, 272ff, 319

Memory:
of future, 88, 204
of past, 94, 97, 226
Memorial, 141, 169, 173
Metaphor: 223–24, 245ff, 272, 332
Cf. also Image, Symbol
Mission: 136, 137, 151ff, 171, 236–37
Myth: 28, 40, 81ff., 85, 86ff., 100, 107, 109, 113, 115, 124, 130, 153, 280ff

Name: 67, 122, 125ff, 224, 252
Cf. also the section "Spiritual Body and the New Name," 341
Narrative: vii, 87–89, 92, 103, 106, 113, 131–32, 146, 152–55, 272, 309
founding, 92, 93, 98, 106–7, 121ff, 129ff, 132, 134ff, 140, 141ff, 168, 169–70, 171, 173, 214, 240, 248, 252, 257, 267, 275, 322
"limit," 154
Narrativity: 105ff., 121ff, 132, 134, 257, 273, 316
Cf. also History, Narrative
Nature: 101
and culture, 88, 104ff, 329ff
natural selection, 21, 23–25, 28–9, 46

Ontological difference: 52, 58–9, 223, 259
Ontotheology: 53, 60, 66ff., 106, 117, 131, 149, 260, 261ff, 276–77, 278, 289

compact thinking, 68ff., 96, 106, 108, 167, 258, 263, 267
Origins: 15, 24, 63, 87–89, 106–7, 115, 121
   denial of origins, 62ff., 90ff
   return to origins, 21, 40, 84, 87, 92, 126ff
   the "original Fall," 27–9, 99, 101ff
   to speak of origins, 121ff, 137, 154, 176
   Cf. also Gnostic (Attitude)

Poverty: vff., 23, 25, 140, 192, 325ff
Primordial conflict: 82ff, 89, 111, 113, 116, 117, 121
   Cf. also Gnostic (Attitude)
Production of meaning: 105–6, 121ff, 125, 134ff, 142, 144, 246, 275

Responsibility: 38, 105, 127, 136, 138, 181, 184, 186
Rite: 4, 80, 81–2, 86ff., 109, 111, 115, 130, 169, 221ff

Sacrifice: 35–6, 41
   for sin, cf. Sin
   of communion, 140, 197, 203, 206ff, 216ff, 228–29, 231ff, 275, 315
Sin: 29, 139, 191ff, 229, 272, 287, 292
   original sin, 129, 346
   remission of sins, 138, 147ff, 155, 169, 173, 214
   sacrifice for sin, 207, 217ff, 230, 232, 233, 235
   ultimate sin, 227ff
Spirit: 137, 138–89, 141, 142–43, 148, 169, 171, 228, 239, 243, 280
Symbol/Symbolic: 4, 8ff., 20, 89, 186, 192, 280ff, 329
   behavior, 9ff, 84, 128, 140, 203ff, 211, 216, 228, 240, 243

sacramentality, 138–39, 186, 199, 234
symbolic exchange, 30, 33ff., 37, 39–41, 46, 78–9, 89, 97, 99, 101, 104, 167ff, 243, 249ff
   Cf. also Death (form of death); Sacrifice, of communion

Temptation: 182ff, 202–3
Time: viii, 15, 29, 40–41, 47–8, 53, 57, 100, 106, 109, 123–24, 130, 146, 168, 226ff, 251–52, 264
   linear/created, 32ff., 37, 40, 46, 64ff., 141, 249
   "middle"/milieu, 137, 148, 153, 155, 168, 173
   myth, 31, 37ff, 87, 130
   of Jesus, 137, 141, 155, 157, 167, 173, 250
   presence 57–8, 61, 69, 96–7, 146, 153, 248
   superimposition, 128, 141, 213ff, 248, 250, 311
Trial: 174, 176, 191ff, 198, 201ff, 231ff
   Cf. also God, commandment/word; Temptation
Truth: 103, 112, 122, 128–29, 140, 143ff, 152
   adaequatio intellectus et rei, 69, 73, 316
   interruption of truth, 316ff
   res et signa, 269, 271, 316–17

Witness/Testimony: 121ff, 130, 131, 135ff, 142, 146, 147ff, 149, 152ff, 173, 248
Word: vii, 46, 97, 104–5, 81–2, 106–7, 122, 126, 127, 129, 136ff, 140, 183ff, 200, 252
   Cf. also Responsibility

www.ingramcontent.com/pod-product-compliance
Lightning Source LLC
Chambersburg PA
CBHW031231290426
44109CB00012B/244